SALAD OF THE DAY

GEORGEANNE BRENNAN

PHOTOGRAPHY BY ERIN KUNKEL

weldonowen

CONTENTS

A SALAD FOR EVERY DAY

Tossed, chopped, shredded, composed—salads are versatile in both form and flavor. They're also an inviting and healthy way to showcase favorite seasonal produce. From light starters to protein-rich main-course salads to palate-cleansing accompaniments, these much-loved and adaptable dishes can play a delicious role in virtually every lunch or dinner, every day of the year.

This revised edition of the original calendar-style cookbook offers a fresh mix of 365 enticing salads suited for any meal, occasion, or mood. Guided by the seasons, and drawing on fresh ingredients in their prime, you'll find plenty of ideas in the pages that follow. In the cool months of the year, hearty salads fit the bill: bowls brimming with sturdy greens, grains, and roasted meats. In warm weather, light fare is apropos: try refreshing fruit salads or just-picked lettuces tossed with herbs and grilled seafood. Or, choose from a wealth of modern and tantalizing recipes suitable for a full meal, such as zesty strip steak salad with creamy wasabi dressing, smoky chicken salad with green apples and jasmine rice, grilled calamari salad with padrón peppers and harissa, garlicky pasta salad with crab and shrimp, and more. All the classics, like iceberg wedges with blue cheese dressing and classic Caesar, are here, as well as contemporary riffs on old standards—such as a Niçoise-style salad with seared wild salmon—to bring new life to your old favorites.

Each recipe includes a complementary dressing or vinaigrette, and helpful notes offer serving and substitution ideas. You'll learn how easy it is to vary salads by swapping in ingredients that you have on hand; varying herbs and spices; alternating dressings; and adding a protein element like seafood, poultry, or beans—even a scattering of crumbled cheese or a handful of nuts.

With this abundance of recipes as your guide, and the garden's yield as your inspiration, you're sure to find an appealing salad that fits the occasion, no matter what the day brings.

Start the new year right with healthy, hearty salads. Sturdy greens such as kale and escarole provide a perfect canvas for proteins—creamy cheeses, eggs, meats, or beans. Warming main-course salads help to take the chill away. Wilted winter greens with poached eggs and pancetta make for pure comfort food, while roasted chicken partners with whole grains, and bright citrus with fennel and nuts.

january

1

FENNEL SALAD WITH BLOOD ORANGES & ARUGULA

serves 6–8

2 fennel bulbs, trimmed

2 Tbsp red wine vinegar

Salt and freshly ground pepper

6 Tbsp (3 fl oz/90 ml) extra-virgin olive oil

4 cups (4 oz/125 g) loosely packed arugula leaves

4 blood or navel oranges, peeled with a knife and sliced crosswise into thin slices

To make this crisp salad even more refreshing, slice the fennel just before serving rather than in advance, and keep the bulbs cold until just before slicing. Unless it is dressed, fennel will discolor if allowed to sit more than 20 minutes after slicing.

Halve the fennel bulbs lengthwise and, using a mandoline or a very sharp knife, cut the halves crosswise into paper-thin slices.

In a large bowl, whisk together the vinegar, ¼ tsp salt, and ¼ tsp pepper. Add the oil in a thin stream, whisking constantly until the dressing is smooth. Add the arugula and fennel and toss to coat evenly with the vinaigrette. Mound the mixture on a platter, distribute the orange slices over and around the salad, and serve.

2

WARM ESCAROLE, EGG & PANCETTA SALAD

serves 4

4 slices thick-cut pancetta or bacon, chopped

¼ cup (2 fl oz/60 ml) extra-virgin olive oil

1 clove garlic, bruised

1 Tbsp whole-grain mustard

2 Tbsp red wine vinegar, plus 1 tsp

4 large eggs

2 heads escarole, tough outer leaves removed, torn into bite-sized pieces

Salt and freshly ground pepper

Use the freshest eggs possible for poaching, as they have a more solid white. If the white starts to spread, use a spoon to nudge it near the yolk. Before placing the eggs on the salads, rest the base of the slotted spoon on a kitchen towel to blot away excess moisture.

If using bacon, bring a small saucepan of water to a boil. Add the bacon and simmer for 5 minutes to tame its smoky, salty flavor. Drain, transfer to paper towels, and blot dry. Wipe out the saucepan, place over medium-low heat, and add the oil, garlic, and pancetta or bacon. Cook, stirring occasionally, until the garlic is golden and the pancetta is crisp, about 3 minutes. Be careful not to let the garlic burn. Remove from the heat and discard the garlic. Stir in the mustard and the 2 Tbsp vinegar. Set aside.

Choose a large, wide pan with a tight-fitting lid. Fill with a generous amount of water, add the 1 tsp vinegar, place over high heat, and bring to a rolling boil. Reduce the heat to a very gentle simmer. Working quickly, crack the eggs one at a time into a small bowl and then slide the eggs into the simmering water. Poach the eggs until the whites are set and the yolks are still soft, 3–4 minutes.

Meanwhile, bring the vinegar mixture to a boil. Put the escarole in a large bowl. Pour the vinegar mixture over the escarole and immediately toss to wilt the leaves slightly. Season with salt and pepper. Toss again and arrange on individual plates. Remove each poached egg with a slotted spoon, blot the bottom dry, and slide onto the salads. Season the eggs with salt and pepper and serve.

JANUARY 3

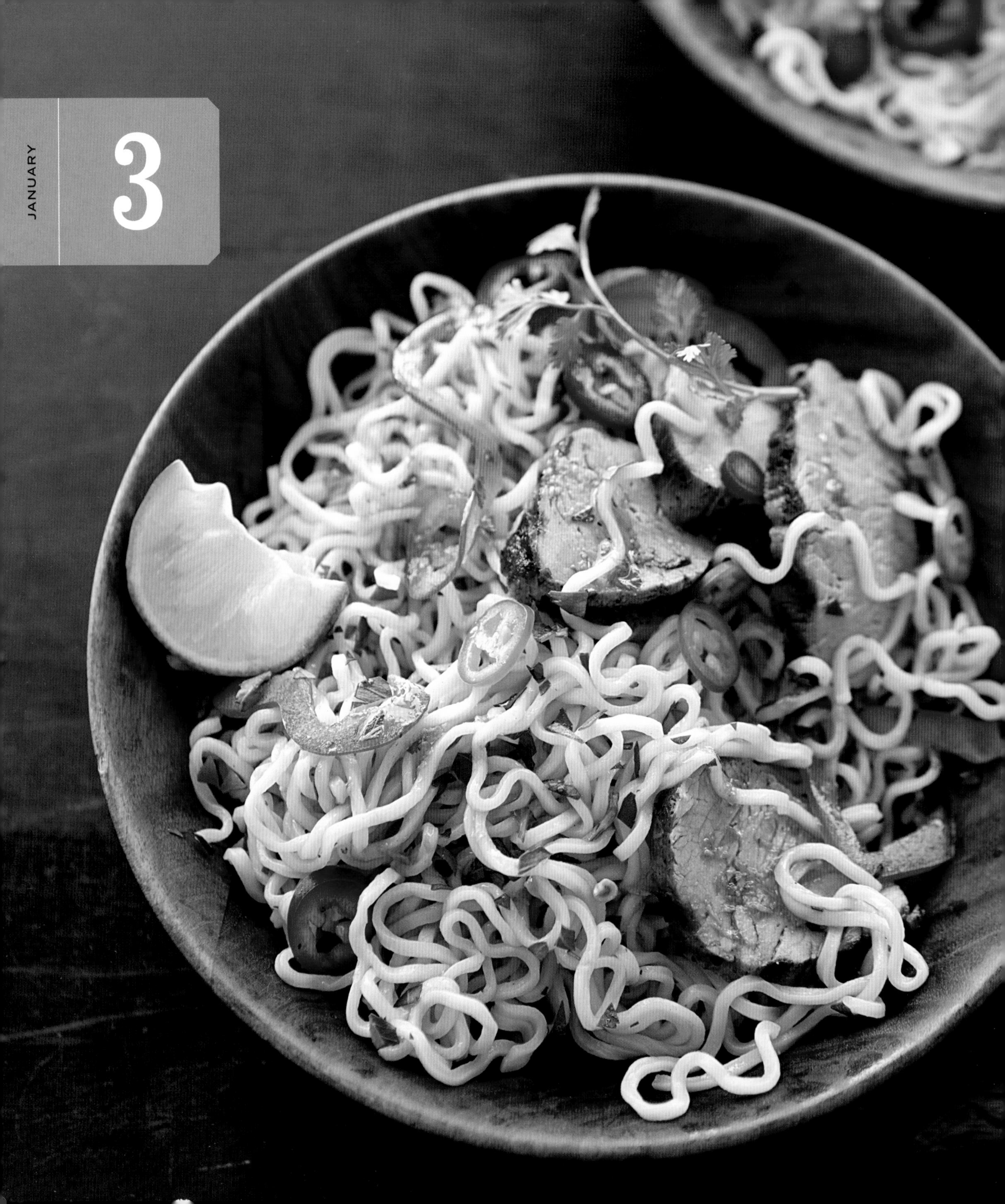

3

NOODLE SALAD WITH PORK & ASIAN LIME VINAIGRETTE

serves 6

Chinese egg noodles are a versatile ingredient for soaking up flavor and making a salad into a heartier main-course dish. Regular vermicelli pasta may be substituted.

2 pork tenderloins, about ¾ lb (375 g) each, trimmed

1 Tbsp peanut oil

Salt and freshly ground pepper

FOR THE ASIAN LIME VINAIGRETTE

2 Tbsp peanut oil

1 Tbsp soy sauce

Juice of 1 lime

2 tsp sherry vinegar

1 tsp peeled and minced fresh ginger

⅛ tsp sugar

2 or 3 drops Sriracha or other hot sauce

1 lb (500 g) fresh Chinese egg noodles

1 red bell pepper, seeded and thinly sliced

1 small red serrano chile, seeded and thinly sliced crosswise (optional)

¼ cup (⅓ oz/10 g) *each* chopped fresh flat-leaf parsley and cilantro leaves

Prepare a charcoal or gas grill for direct-heat cooking over high heat, or preheat the broiler. Brush the pork tenderloins with the 1 Tbsp oil and season with salt and pepper. Place on the grill rack or on a broiler pan 4 inches (10 cm) from the heat source and cook, turning occasionally, until an instant-read thermometer inserted into the thickest part registers 150°F (65°C) or the pork is pale pink when cut in the thickest portion, about 12 minutes. Transfer to a cutting board and let rest for 2–3 minutes before carving. Cut crosswise into slices ¼ inch (6 mm) thick.

Meanwhile, to make the vinaigrette, in a blender, combine the 2 Tbsp oil, soy sauce, lime juice, vinegar, ginger, sugar, and Sriracha to taste. Purée until smooth.

Bring a pot three-fourths full of salted water to a boil. Add the noodles, stir, and cook until just tender, according to package directions. Drain well and transfer to a large bowl. Add the bell pepper, chile (if using), vinaigrette to taste, and half each of the parsley and cilantro, and toss to mix well.

Transfer the noodles to bowls and arrange the pork and remaining herbs over the top. Serve warm or at room temperature.

4

GRAPEFRUIT, CHICKEN & PISTACHIO SALAD

serves 4

This salad takes advantage of the winter citrus season for a new twist on a classic chicken salad, spiked with lime juice and cilantro for extra zing. You can serve the salad in small butter lettuce leaves for appetizer portions, or mound on toasted peasant bread for sandwiches.

2 cups (16 fl oz/500 ml) dry white wine

2 Tbsp white wine vinegar

Salt and freshly ground pepper

1 tsp whole peppercorns

2 skinless, boneless chicken breast halves

½ cup (2 oz/60 g) pistachios

2 grapefruits, peeled and segmented with a knife

¼ cup (2 fl oz/60 ml) mayonnaise

1 tsp Dijon mustard

2 Tbsp minced fresh cilantro

Juice of 1 lime

Combine the wine, 2 cups (16 fl oz/500 ml) water, the vinegar, 1 tsp salt, and the peppercorns in a shallow pan. Bring to a boil over medium-high heat. Reduce the heat to low and simmer for 5 minutes. Add the chicken, cover, and poach until just opaque, 6–8 minutes, occasionally skimming off any foam on the surface. Remove the chicken from the liquid and let cool for 5 minutes, then cut into cubes.

Meanwhile, in a dry frying pan, toast the pistachios over medium-low heat, stirring, until fragrant and starting to brown, about 5 minutes. Pour onto a plate to cool.

Cut the grapefruit segments in half crosswise and put them in a bowl with the chicken and half of the pistachios. Add the mayonnaise, mustard, cilantro, lime juice, ½ tsp salt, and ¼ tsp pepper and mix well. Garnish the salad with the remaining pistachios and serve.

5

Bottled Caesar dressings abound, but none will ever taste as good as the one you've whisked up fresh at home. Use a high-quality olive oil, and choose one with a character you enjoy. Oils from Greece tend to be rich, yet mellow; Tuscan and Californian oils are distinctly peppery; Sicilian oils are "big" and earthy; and those from the south coast of France are buttery.

CLASSIC CAESAR SALAD

serves 4

2 cups (4 oz/125 g) cubed sourdough or other country-style bread (1-inch/2.5-cm cubes)

3 Tbsp extra-virgin olive oil, plus ⅓ cup (3 fl oz/80 ml)

Salt and freshly ground pepper

6 cloves garlic

4 anchovy fillets, plus extra for garnish (optional)

1 tsp Worcestershire sauce

2 tsp red wine vinegar

2 hearts romaine lettuce, separated into individual leaves

1 large egg (optional; see Note)

Parmesan cheese for shaving

Preheat the oven to 350°F (180°C). Spread the bread cubes on a baking sheet and sprinkle them with the 3 Tbsp oil, ½ tsp salt, and ½ tsp pepper. Bake, turning once or twice, until golden, about 15 minutes. Remove the cubes from the sheet, let cool, and rub one or two sides of each cube with the garlic, using 3 of the cloves. Set aside.

In the bottom of a serving bowl, using a fork, crush the remaining 3 garlic cloves with ½ tsp salt to make a paste. Crush the 4 anchovy fillets into the paste. Whisk in the Worcestershire sauce, vinegar, and ½ tsp pepper. Add the ⅓ cup oil in a thin stream, whisking constantly until the dressing is smooth.

Add the lettuce leaves and three-fourths of the croutons to the bowl with the dressing and mix gently but well. Break the egg, if using, into the bowl and mix again. Top with the remaining croutons. Shave the cheese over the salad, and serve, garnished with anchovy fillets, if desired.

Note: Raw egg can carry salmonella. The risks involved in salmonella poisoning are greatest for children, the elderly, pregnant women, and anyone with a compromised immune system.

6

Citrus salads are a refreshing treat in the middle of winter. Here, the orange slices are grilled so that the outsides become slightly charred for a bittersweet taste that pairs well with escarole. Valencia oranges are ideal for this recipe because they are so sweet, but any orange variety will do.

CHARRED ORANGE & ESCAROLE SALAD WITH ALMONDS

serves 4

4 large Valencia oranges, peeled with a knife and sliced crosswise into thin slices

¼ cup (2 fl oz/60 ml) extra-virgin olive oil, plus more for drizzling

1 head escarole

¼ cup (⅓ oz/10 g) coarsely chopped fresh flat-leaf parsley

1 Tbsp sherry vinegar

Salt and freshly ground pepper

½ cup (2 oz/60 g) Marcona almonds, coarsely chopped

Prepare a charcoal or gas grill for direct-heat cooking over high heat. Alternatively, preheat a stove-top grill pan over high heat.

Drizzle the orange slices with oil. Grill, turning once, until well charred on both sides, 2–4 minutes total. Set aside.

Remove the tough outer leaves of the escarole and tear the inner leaves into bite-sized pieces. In a bowl, combine the escarole, parsley, the ¼ cup oil, and the vinegar and toss to coat. Season with salt and pepper. Add the oranges and almonds and toss well. Divide the salad among individual plates and serve.

7

CRAB SALAD WITH GREEN APPLES & GRAPEFRUIT COULIS

serves 8

1 grapefruit, peeled and segmented with a knife

2 tsp sugar

Juice of 1 lemon

2 Granny Smith apples

1 lb (500 g) cooked crabmeat, picked over for shell fragments

3 Tbsp extra-virgin olive oil

1½ Tbsp white wine vinegar or champagne vinegar

3 Tbsp minced fresh chives

Salt and freshly ground black pepper

Pinch of cayenne pepper

Here, the apples are cut into matchsticks with a mandoline, but a sharp knife will also work well. The syruplike grapefruit coulis, slightly sweetened, is drizzled on top and around the salads for an artistic presentation.

Set 2 grapefruit segments aside and coarsely chop the rest. In a saucepan, combine the chopped grapefruit with ¼ cup (2 fl oz/60 ml) water. Bring to a boil over medium-high heat, reduce the heat to low, and simmer, stirring, until soft, about 5 minutes. Transfer the mixture to a blender and purée it. Strain the purée through a fine-mesh sieve into a clean pan. Add the sugar and bring to a boil over medium-high heat, stirring. Continue to cook, stirring often, until the liquid is reduced by about half and is syrupy, 3–4 minutes. Remove from the heat and let cool.

Fill a bowl with water and add the lemon juice. Quarter and core the apples, placing them in the lemon water. Using the julienne attachment on a mandoline or a very sharp knife, julienne the apples and return them to the lemon water.

In a bowl, combine the crabmeat, oil, vinegar, 2 Tbsp of the chives, ½ tsp salt, ½ tsp black pepper, and the cayenne. Pat dry half of the apples and add them to the bowl. Squeeze 2 tsp juice from the reserved grapefruit segments into the bowl. Turn gently to mix, being careful not to shred the crab.

To serve, divide the crab salad among salad plates, mounding it on each plate. Pat dry the remaining apples and divide them among the salads. Drizzle about 2 tsp of the grapefruit coulis over and around each salad. Sprinkle the remaining 1 Tbsp chives evenly over the salads and serve.

8

COUSCOUS SALAD WITH ROASTED CHICKEN & DRIED CRANBERRIES

serves 4

Salt and freshly ground pepper

1 cup (6 oz/185 g) instant couscous

2 carrots, peeled and chopped

2 green onions, including green parts, chopped

⅓ cup (2 oz/60 g) dried cranberries

2 Tbsp sherry vinegar

½ cup (4 fl oz/125 ml) extra-virgin olive oil

2 cups (¾ lb/375 g) sliced roasted chicken meat

1 Tbsp thinly sliced fresh mint

Couscous, a granular pasta made with durum wheat flour, can be treated like a grain in salads. It works best when mixed with finely chopped ingredients, like the carrots and green onions used here. In this salad, the classic combination of poultry and cranberries is enhanced with fresh mint and a bracing sherry vinegar dressing.

In a small saucepan, combine 1½ cups (12 fl oz/375 ml) water and ⅛ tsp salt and bring to a boil. Stir in the couscous and return to a boil. Remove from the heat, cover, and let stand for 5 minutes. Transfer to a bowl and fluff with a fork to separate the grains. Add the carrots, green onions, and dried cranberries.

In a small bowl, whisk together the vinegar and salt and pepper to taste. Add the oil in a thin stream, whisking constantly until the dressing is smooth. Pour over the couscous mixture and stir to mix well.

Transfer the couscous to a serving dish and arrange the sliced chicken on top. Sprinkle with the mint and serve.

9

SEARED TUNA
WITH ASIAN SLAW

serves 4–6

Crisp in texture and mild in flavor, napa cabbage is a common ingredient in Asian cooking and works well with tropical fruits as well as vegetables: try adding a little diced mango to this slaw.

FOR THE DRESSING

1 tsp peeled and grated fresh ginger

1 Tbsp mayonnaise

2 tsp honey Dijon mustard

1 Tbsp soy sauce

¼ cup (2 fl oz/60 ml) rice vinegar

5 Tbsp (3 fl oz/80 ml) peanut oil

2 Tbsp toasted sesame oil

1½ lb (750 g) sushi-grade ahi tuna steaks, patted dry

2 Tbsp peanut oil

Salt and freshly ground pepper

1 large head napa cabbage, halved, cored, and thinly sliced crosswise

6 green onions, including tender green parts, thinly sliced

2 red bell peppers, seeded and thinly sliced

To make the dressing, in a large bowl, whisk together the ginger, mayonnaise, mustard, soy sauce, and vinegar. Add the 5 Tbsp peanut oil and the sesame oil in a thin stream, whisking constantly until the dressing is smooth.

Prepare a gas or charcoal grill for direct-heat cooking over high heat. Alternatively, preheat a stove-top grill pan over high heat. Brush both sides of the tuna steaks with the 2 Tbsp peanut oil and season generously with salt and pepper. Place the tuna on the grill rack or in the grill pan and sear without moving the steaks for 1½ minutes. Turn and sear for 1½ minutes longer, again without moving the steaks. Transfer to a cutting board and let stand for 5 minutes.

Meanwhile, whisk the dressing to recombine, then add the cabbage, green onions, and bell peppers to the bowl and toss to coat evenly. Arrange the cabbage mixture on plates. Slice the tuna steaks across the grain, arrange on top of the salads, and serve.

10

ITALIAN CHOPPED SALAD
WITH SALAMI, PROSCIUTTO
& FONTINA

serves 4

In this hearty dish, the flavors of a typical Italian antipasto platter are transformed into a main-course salad anchored by radicchio and escarole. Because both greens have firm leaves that maintain their character when chopped, they can support the substantial toppings called for here.

1 head radicchio

1 large head escarole

¼ cup (2 fl oz/60 ml) extra-virgin olive oil

2 Tbsp red wine vinegar

1 tsp dried oregano

Salt and freshly ground pepper

3 oz (90 g) thinly sliced prosciutto, cut into ¼-inch (6-mm) slivers

½ lb (250 g) sliced cotto salami, cut into quarters

6 oz (185 g) fontina cheese, cut into ½-inch (12-mm) cubes

¼ lb (125 g) pitted black or green olives

¼ lb (125 g) sliced or chopped pepperoncini, drained

Coarsely chop the radicchio and set aside. Remove the pale green and yellow inner leaves from the escarole. Coarsely chop those, along with the pale stem ends of the larger green leaves. Reserve the green leaves for another use, such as soup or braising.

In a large bowl, whisk together the oil, vinegar, oregano, ½ tsp salt, and ¼ tsp pepper until the vinaigrette is well blended. Add the radicchio and escarole and toss to mix well.

Divide the salad among individual bowls or plates or transfer to a platter. Arrange the prosciutto, salami, cheese, olives, and pepperoncini on top of the salad and serve.

11

Grain salads like this one will last for several days in the refrigerator, and will take on even more flavor as they sit. You can make the salad on a Sunday and pack it for lunch any day of the week.

QUINOA & RADICCHIO SALAD WITH DRIED CHERRIES & PISTACHIOS

serves 4

1 cup (6 oz/185 g) quinoa

½ head radicchio

¼ cup (2 fl oz/60 ml) balsamic vinegar

2 Tbsp extra-virgin olive oil

¼ cup (1½ oz/45 g) dried tart cherries

¼ cup (1 oz/30 g) chopped pistachios

3 Tbsp chopped fresh flat-leaf parsley, plus a few whole leaves for garnish

Salt and freshly ground pepper

In a saucepan, bring 2 cups (16 fl oz/500 ml) of water to a boil. Add the quinoa and reduce the heat to low. Cover and simmer until the grains are tender and the water is absorbed, about 15 minutes. Fluff with a fork and transfer to a large bowl.

Core and thinly slice the radicchio. Stir the radicchio, vinegar, oil, cherries, pistachios, and parsley into the warm quinoa. Season with salt and pepper and garnish with the whole parsley leaves. Serve warm or at room temperature.

12

Think of egg salad as a canvas for your favorite flavor combinations. In this Indian-spiced version, the salad is given some heat with fresh chile and cayenne, while the ginger, cilantro, and tomato add vibrancy. Try whirling up the egg yolks with the spices and filling the whites for a delicious deviled egg hors d'oeuvre.

WARM INDIAN-SPICED EGG SALAD

serves 6

8 large eggs

2 Tbsp unsalted butter

1 yellow onion, finely chopped

1 tsp peeled and chopped fresh ginger

1 serrano chile, thinly sliced

¼ tsp cayenne pepper

⅛ tsp ground turmeric

¼ cup (1½ oz/45 g) finely chopped tomato

Salt

¼ cup (⅓ oz/10 g) chopped fresh cilantro

6 slices bread, toasted just before serving

To hard-cook the eggs, place them in a saucepan just large enough to hold them. Add cold water to cover by 1 inch and bring just to a boil over high heat. Remove the pan from the heat and cover. Let stand for 15 minutes. Drain the eggs, then transfer to a bowl of ice water and let cool. Peel the eggs and chop into ½-inch (12-mm) pieces. Set aside.

In a nonstick frying pan, melt the butter over medium-high heat. Add the onion and cook, stirring occasionally, until golden, about 5 minutes. Stir in the ginger, chile, cayenne, turmeric, and chopped eggs. Mix well and cook, stirring gently, until the eggs are lightly fried, about 3 minutes.

Fold in the tomato and turn off the heat. Add ¼ tsp salt and stir in the cilantro. Serve alongside the hot toast.

13

To make the lemongrass-mint paste, thinly slice the tender pale green inner parts of 2 lemongrass stalks, put in a food processor, and process for 10 seconds. Add ½ cup (½ oz/15 g) mint leaves; 2 Tbsp lime juice; 2 Tbsp grapeseed oil; 1 tsp minced jalapeño; 2 minced garlic cloves; and salt and pepper to taste, and process until a paste forms, about 10 seconds.

GRILLED LAMB & PINEAPPLE SALAD WITH THAI FLAVORS

serves 6

2¼ lb (1.15 kg) boneless butterflied leg of lamb, trimmed

Lemongrass-Mint Paste *(left)*

FOR THE DRESSING

¼ cup (2 fl oz/60 ml) fresh lime juice

1 Tbsp rice vinegar

1½ tsp Asian fish sauce

½ tsp minced jalapeño chile

3 Tbsp firmly packed light brown sugar

3 Tbsp minced fresh mint

Salt and freshly ground pepper

5 Tbsp (3 fl oz/80 ml) peanut oil

1 pineapple, peeled and cut crosswise into rounds about 1/4 inch (6 mm) thick

Peanut oil for brushing

1 cup (5 oz/155 g) unsalted dry-roasted peanuts, chopped

2 heads red-leaf lettuce, leaves torn into bite-sized pieces

8 green onions, thinly sliced

Lay the lamb in a large baking dish and rub the lemongrass-mint paste into both sides of the meat. Cover and refrigerate for at least 6 hours or preferably overnight.

To make the dressing, in a small bowl, whisk together the lime juice, vinegar, fish sauce, chile, sugar, mint, ½ tsp salt, and several grindings of pepper until the sugar dissolves. Add the 5 Tbsp oil in a thin stream, whisking constantly until smooth. Taste and adjust the seasonings. Set aside.

About 1 hour before serving, remove the lamb from the refrigerator. Brush the pineapple with oil and season with salt. Prepare a charcoal or gas grill for direct-heat cooking over medium-high heat.

Grill the pineapple, turning once, until grill marked on both sides, 5–7 minutes total. Transfer to a cutting board. Scrape the paste off the lamb and lightly season all over with salt. Grill the meat, turning once, until an instant-read thermometer inserted into the thickest part registers 130°F (54°C) for medium-rare, 10 minutes total, ⟩⟩

or until done to your liking. Transfer to the cutting board and tent with foil. Cut each pineapple round into quarters.

In a small bowl, mix the peanuts and ½ tsp salt. In a bowl, toss the lettuce with ¼ tsp each salt and pepper. Whisk well, then drizzle half over the lettuce and toss well. Divide the dressed lettuce among individual plates.

Thinly slice the lamb. Arrange the lamb and pineapple on the salads, then drizzle each serving with the remaining dressing. Sprinkle with the peanuts and green onions and serve.

14

The classic Middle Eastern tabbouleh isn't a bulgur salad with parsley; it's a parsley salad with a little bulgur. Toasting the cumin seeds heightens their fragrance. Place the seeds in a small dry frying pan over medium heat and warm, shaking the pan occasionally, until they darken and release their aroma, then let cool and grind in a mortar or a spice grinder.

TABBOULEH WITH CHICKPEAS

serves 4

½ cup (3 oz/90 g) fine bulgur

1½ cups (2 oz/60 g) minced fresh flat-leaf parsley

1 bunch green onions, white part only, minced

1 large tomato, peeled, seeded, and diced

2 Tbsp minced fresh mint

1 can (15 oz/470 g) chickpeas, drained and rinsed

3 Tbsp extra-virgin olive oil

3 Tbsp fresh lemon juice, plus more if needed

½ tsp ground toasted cumin seeds

Salt and freshly ground pepper

1 heart of romaine lettuce, leaves separated

Put the bulgur in a small bowl, add cold water to cover, and let stand for 10 minutes. Drain. Place the bulgur in a kitchen towel and squeeze dry. Transfer to a bowl. Stir in the parsley, green onions, tomato, mint, chickpeas, oil, lemon juice, and cumin. Season with salt and pepper. Taste and add more lemon juice, if needed.

Cover and refrigerate for at least 2 hours or up to 24 hours. Bring to room temperature before serving. Taste and adjust the seasonings. Serve with the lettuce leaves for scooping up the tabbouleh.

15

Dry Jack is a grating cheese that originated in California. During the Second World War, Italian-made Parmesan became scarce, and Californians of Italian descent created a substitute by aging local Monterey Jack cheese. Parmesan may be substituted, of course.

CAESAR-STYLE SALAD WITH POBLANO CHILES & CORNMEAL CROUTONS

serves 4–6

2 Tbsp unsalted butter, at room temperature

2 cups (16 fl oz/500 ml) chicken broth

Salt and freshly ground pepper

1 cup (5 oz/155 g) yellow cornmeal

2 Tbsp extra-virgin olive oil

½ tsp chili powder

2 poblano chiles

½ cup (4 fl oz/125 ml) mayonnaise

1 Tbsp fresh lime juice

1 large clove garlic, minced

1½ tsp honey

½ tsp Dijon mustard

2 heads romaine lettuce, leaves torn into bite-sized pieces

4 oz (125 g) dry Jack cheese

Coat the inside of an 8-inch (20-cm) square baking dish with 1 Tbsp of the butter. In a saucepan over medium-high heat, bring the broth, ½ tsp salt, and the remaining 1 Tbsp butter to a boil. Reduce the heat to medium. Gradually add the cornmeal in a slow, steady stream while whisking constantly. Continue cooking and whisking until the mixture has thickened and pulls away from the sides of the pan, about 6 minutes. Immediately pour the mixture into the prepared baking dish, spreading it evenly. Cover and refrigerate until firm, about 1 hour.

Preheat the oven to 350°F (180°C). Cut the chilled cornmeal mixture into 1½-inch (4-cm) croutons. Transfer the croutons to a rimmed baking sheet, drizzle with the oil, sprinkle with the chili powder and ¼ tsp salt, and toss to coat. Bake until the croutons are dark gold and aromatic, about 30 minutes, shaking the pan after 10 minutes. Let cool to room temperature.

Preheat the broiler. Place the chiles on a broiler pan 4–6 inches (10–15 cm) from the heat source and broil, turning occasionally, until the skins are charred, about 10 minutes. Transfer to a bowl, cover, and let steam for 15 minutes. Remove and discard the skins, stems, and seeds and chop the flesh. ⤳

In a food processor, combine the mayonnaise, 2 Tbsp of the chopped chiles, the lime juice, garlic, honey, mustard, ½ tsp salt, and several grindings of pepper and process until smooth. Taste and adjust the seasonings.

In a large bowl, toss the lettuce with ¼ tsp salt. Drizzle with about two-thirds of the dressing and toss well. Divide the dressed lettuce among individual plates. Top each serving with cornmeal croutons and some of the remaining chopped chiles. Drizzle with additional dressing if desired (you may not need all of it). Using a vegetable peeler, shave the cheese over the salads and serve.

16

You can either cut the Gouda into small squares or use a vegetable peeler to create more delicate shavings. Serve with a rich white wine such as Chardonnay or Viognier or a medium-bodied red like Grenache or Syrah (and use the same red in making the vinaigrette).

RADICCHIO, ENDIVE & AGED GOUDA SALAD WITH RED-WINE VINAIGRETTE

serves 4–6

FOR THE VINAIGRETTE

2 Tbsp balsamic vinegar

¼ cup (2 fl oz/60 ml) dry red wine

Salt and freshly ground pepper

¼ cup (2 fl oz/60 ml) extra-virgin olive oil

4 heads red-tipped Belgian endive

½ head radicchio, torn into bite-sized pieces

½ cup (½ oz/15 g) fresh flat-leaf parsley leaves

Aged Gouda cheese for shaving

To make the vinaigrette, in a small saucepan, combine the vinegar and wine over medium-low heat and bring to a simmer. Cook until reduced by half, about 3 minutes. Set aside to cool. In a large bowl, whisk together the reduced vinegar and wine mixture and ½ tsp salt. Add the oil in a thin stream, whisking constantly until smooth. Set aside.

Cut each endive in half lengthwise and cut away the solid cone-shaped base. Coarsely chop the leaves. Add the radicchio, parsley, and endive to the bowl with the vinaigrette and toss well.

Divide the salad among individual plates. Using a vegetable peeler, shave the cheese over each, sprinkle with pepper, and serve.

17

ROASTED MUSHROOM SALAD WITH BALSAMIC VINAIGRETTE

serves 6

Roasting shallots and mushrooms makes this a hearty and super-flavorful salad, perfect for savoring on a chilly afternoon or evening. Serve alongside roasted salmon or chicken, with a medium-bodied red wine.

1 lb (500 g) mixed mushrooms such as chanterelle and shiitake

8 Tbsp (4 fl oz/125 ml) extra-virgin olive oil, plus 2 tsp

2½ tsp fresh thyme leaves

Salt and freshly ground pepper

4 large shallots

¼ cup (2 fl oz/60 ml) balsamic vinegar

1 tsp fresh lemon juice

½ tsp sugar

1 head Treviso radicchio, thinly sliced

1 small head red leaf lettuce, leaves torn into bite-sized pieces

1 cup (1½ oz/45 g) coarsely chopped fresh flat-leaf parsley

Preheat the oven to 400°F (200°C). Cut off and discard the shiitake stems, if using. Thinly slice the mushroom caps.

On a small rimmed baking sheet, toss the mushrooms with 3 Tbsp of the olive oil, 2 tsp of the thyme, ½ tsp salt, and ¼ tsp pepper. In a small baking dish, toss together the shallots, the 2 tsp olive oil, 2 pinches of salt, and several grindings of pepper. Place both pans in the oven. Roast the mushrooms until golden brown and tender, about 15 minutes, stirring once. Roast the shallots until soft and lightly browned, 25–30 minutes, stirring once. Trim off and discard the root ends of 2 of the shallots and put them in a food processor. Cover the remaining shallots and the mushrooms with foil to keep warm.

Add the remaining 5 Tbsp olive oil, the remaining ½ tsp thyme, the vinegar, lemon juice, sugar, a scant ½ tsp salt, and several grindings of pepper to the food processor and process until a smooth dressing forms. Taste and adjust the seasonings.

Trim and thinly slice the remaining shallots. In a large bowl, toss together the radicchio, lettuce, parsley, 2 pinches of salt, and several grindings of pepper. Drizzle with most of the dressing and toss again. Divide evenly among individual plates. Top each serving with an equal amount of the warm mushrooms and sliced shallots. Drizzle with some of the remaining dressing and serve.

18

ESCAROLE SALAD WITH BLOOD ORANGES, OLIVES & WALNUTS

serves 4–6

The sweetness of the oranges and the sharpness of the brined olives complement each other in this multicolored winter salad. The toasted walnuts add a layer of crisp texture to the escarole. Served with warm goat cheese toasts, this salad becomes a filling main dish.

⅓ cup (1½ oz/45 g) walnuts

3 Tbsp extra-virgin olive oil

1 tsp red wine vinegar

1 tsp sherry vinegar

Salt and freshly ground pepper

1 large escarole head, pale yellow and green inner leaves only, torn into bite-sized pieces

2 cups (2 oz/60 g) baby arugula

2 or 3 blood oranges, peeled and segmented with a knife and seeded

¼ cup (4 oz/125 g) brine-cured black olives, pitted and coarsely chopped

In a small frying pan, toast the walnuts over medium-high heat, shaking the pan occasionally, until the nuts are fragrant, 3–4 minutes. Transfer to a cutting board. When the nuts are cool enough to handle, coarsely chop. Set aside.

In a large bowl, whisk together the oil, vinegars, ¼ tsp salt, and ¼ tsp pepper until the vinaigrette is well blended. Taste and adjust the seasonings. Add the escarole and arugula. If the blood orange segments are small, leave them whole; if not, cut in half. Add the blood oranges, olives, and walnuts and toss well.

Divide the salad among individual plates and serve immediately.

19

CANNELLINI BEAN SALAD WITH TUNA & GRILLED RADICCHIO

serves 4–6

1½ cans (15 oz/470 g each) cannellini or other white beans, rinsed and drained

2 small heads radicchio

2 Tbsp olive oil, plus extra for brushing

Salt and freshly ground pepper

1 cup (5 oz/155 g) chopped celery, including some leaves

½ small red onion, chopped

Pinch of dried oregano

1–2 Tbsp fresh lemon juice

1 can (7 oz/220 g) oil-packed tuna, drained and separated into chunks

Seek out an imported Spanish or Italian canned tuna for this salad. Tuna packed in oil has a much richer, deeper flavor than water-packed, which often has a metallic tang. Tuna found off the coasts of Spain and Sicily is highly regarded for its texture and flavor.

Prepare a charcoal or gas grill for direct-heat cooking over medium-high heat, or preheat the broiler.

Put the beans in a saucepan and cook gently over medium-low heat, stirring occasionally, until warm. Remove from the heat and cover to keep warm.

Meanwhile, cut each radicchio head into 4–6 wedges through the core, so that the wedges will keep their shape. Brush with oil and season with salt and pepper.

To grill, arrange the radicchio wedges over the hottest part of the fire. To broil, arrange the radicchio wedges in a single layer on a broiler pan and slide under the broiler about 6 inches (15 cm) from the heat source. Cook, turning once, until wilted and lightly browned, about 5 minutes total.

Put the beans in a bowl. Add the celery, onion, oregano, the 2 Tbsp oil, and 1 Tbsp of the lemon juice. Season with salt and pepper. Toss well. Taste and adjust the seasoning with more lemon juice, salt, and pepper.

Arrange the radicchio wedges on a platter. Spoon the beans in the center, top with the tuna, and serve.

20

WINTER CRUDITÉS WITH PORCINI & TRUFFLED BAGNA CAUDA

serves 6–8

¼ oz (7 g) dried porcini mushrooms

1 cup (8 fl oz/250 ml) boiling water

2-inch (5-cm) square sushi nori (roasted seaweed)

2 Tbsp extra-virgin olive oil

2 or 3 olive oil–packed anchovy fillets

½ tsp black truffle oil

Salt

8 thin carrot sticks

8 very small radishes with a few greens attached, halved lengthwise if large

8 small cauliflower florets

8 thin rounds small Scarlet or Tokyo turnips

8 thin slices fennel

Bagna cauda, a warm Italian dipping sauce composed of olive oil and anchovies, is given a rich, earthy depth here with the addition of dried porcini mushrooms, black truffle oil, and nori. Laden with umami, this dish will satisfy on even the most wintry day.

In a saucepan, combine the porcini and boiling water. Bring to a simmer over medium-low heat and simmer until the mushrooms are soft and the liquid is reduced to ½–¾ cup (4–6 fl oz/125–180 ml), about 20 minutes. Add the nori and simmer for 1–2 minutes, then remove from the heat.

In a small frying pan, warm the olive oil over medium heat. Add the anchovies and cook, stirring, until they begin to dissolve, about 5 minutes.

In a blender, combine the porcini mixture and anchovy mixture and blend until liquefied. Add the truffle oil and ⅛ tsp salt and blend again.

Transfer the bagna cauda to a serving bowl and serve warm, accompanied by the carrots, radishes, cauliflower, turnips, and fennel.

21

Bright and crunchy, this salad is ideal for a winter menu. It's also quite pretty, adding fresh color to any dinner. Serve it alongside broiled or roasted meats, especially broiled kebabs for a Mediterranean-style meal.

JERUSALEM ARTICHOKE SALAD WITH POMEGRANATE & CELERY

serves 4–6

½ lb (250 g) Jerusalem artichokes

2 Tbsp extra-virgin olive oil, plus ¼ cup (2 fl oz/60 ml)

Leaves from 2 fresh thyme sprigs

Salt and freshly ground pepper

1 pomegranate

2 celery ribs, leaves reserved

1 head radicchio, leaves separated

1 Tbsp champagne vinegar

½ cup (2 oz/60 g) crumbled ricotta salata cheese

Preheat the oven to 375°F (190°C).

Scrub the Jerusalem artichokes and cut them into slices ½ inch (12 mm) thick. Place on a roasting pan, drizzle with the 2 Tbsp oil, sprinkle with the thyme, season well with salt and pepper, and toss to combine. Spread the slices in a single layer and roast, turning once, until golden and tender, about 20 minutes. Set aside to cool.

Meanwhile, seed the pomegranate, pat the seeds dry, and set aside.

Using a mandoline or box grater, thinly slice the celery and put the slices in a large bowl along with the reserved leaves. Tear the radicchio leaves in half and add to the celery.

In a separate small bowl, combine the ¼ cup oil and the vinegar, adding the oil in a thin stream and whisking constantly until the dressing is smooth.

Add the roasted Jerusalem artichokes to the bowl with the celery and radicchio and pour the dressing over. Season with salt and pepper and toss to coat. Scatter the cheese and pomegranate seeds on top and serve.

22

Rubbing the kale and collard greens with lemon juice not only adds flavor to this salad but also helps to soften and almost "cook" the leaves. If you like, you can use all collard greens or kale, rather than a mixture, and cherry tomatoes can replace the mangoes.

LEMONY COLLARD & KALE SALAD WITH MANGO

serves 4

12 leaves cavolo nero or other kale

4 collard leaves

Zest and juice of 1 lemon, plus more if needed

Salt and freshly ground pepper

2 mangoes

2 cloves garlic, minced

¼ cup (2 fl oz/60 ml) extra-virgin olive oil

Remove the thick stems from the kale leaves. Stack the leaves, several at a time, and roll into a cylinder, then cut crosswise into ¼-inch (6-mm) strips. Transfer to a bowl. Remove the stems and ribs from the collard leaves. Stack the leaves and roll into a cylinder, then cut crosswise into ¼-inch (6-mm) strips. Add to the bowl along with the lemon juice. Using your fingers, massage the leaves to soften them, about 5 minutes. Add the lemon zest, ½ tsp salt, and ¼ tsp pepper and toss well. Let stand for up to 2–3 hours at room temperature or in the refrigerator, if desired.

Peel the mangoes. Stand the fruit, stem end up, with a narrow side toward you. Position a sharp knife about 1 inch (2.5 cm) from the stem on one side and cut down the length of the fruit, just missing the large pit. Repeat on the other side of the pit. Cut the flesh into slices.

In a large bowl, whisk together the garlic and oil. Add the kale mixture and toss well. Taste and add more lemon zest and juice, if needed, and toss again. Divide the salad among individual plates, garnish with the mangoes, and serve.

23

Lemons and olives grow in abundance in the Mediterranean, where this salad would be at home on almost any table. If you like, you can replace the duck with chicken, reducing the cooking time as needed.

WARM DUCK SALAD WITH GRILLED LEMONS & KALAMATA OLIVES

serves 4

4 lemons (1 cubed, 1 juiced, and 2 thinly sliced)

1 duck, 4½–5 lb (2.25–2.5 kg)

6 fresh rosemary sprigs

Salt and freshly ground pepper

1 Tbsp extra-virgin olive oil, plus 1 tsp

1 clove garlic, crushed

½ cup (4 fl oz/125 ml) dry white wine

12 Kalamata olives, pitted

6 cups (6 oz/185 g) mixed greens such as escarole, arugula, and radicchio, torn into bite-sized pieces

Preheat the oven to 350°F (180°C).

Tuck the lemon cubes into the duck cavity. Rub the outside of the duck with the rosemary, 1 tsp salt, and 1 tsp pepper. Tuck the rosemary into the duck cavity. Place the duck on a rack in a roasting pan and roast until the skin is crispy and the juices are slightly pink when the thigh is pierced with a knife or until a meat thermometer registers 130–140°F (54–60°C), about 1½ hours.

Transfer the duck to a cutting board and let rest for 5 minutes. Remove the skin, chopping some to add to the salad, if desired. Cut the breast, thighs, and legs into thin slices and keep warm.

In a small saucepan, warm the 1 Tbsp oil over medium heat. Add the garlic and cook, stirring frequently, until soft, about 2 minutes. Increase the heat to high, add the wine, and boil until reduced by half, about 5 minutes. Stir in the lemon juice, olives, ½ tsp salt, and ½ tsp pepper. Remove the dressing from the heat. Discard the garlic.

Preheat a stove-top grill pan over medium-high heat. Brush the lemon slices with the remaining teaspoon of oil. Place the lemon slices on the grill pan and cook, turning once or twice, until seared, about 4 minutes.

Divide the greens among individual plates. Top with the warm duck meat and the crispy skin, if desired. Drizzle with the dressing and garnish with the lemon slices. Serve.

24

A mustard vinaigrette dresses this cool-weather first-course salad, which is pleasantly sweet and tart from the mixture of grapefruit, orange, and apple. Avocado slices provide a smooth, buttery garnish, while bits of crisp bacon add a welcome salty finish.

APPLE-CITRUS SALAD WITH AVOCADO & BACON

serves 12

2 Tbsp Dijon mustard

¼ cup (2 fl oz/60 ml) cider vinegar

⅔ cup (5 fl oz/160 ml) extra-virgin olive oil

6 slices thick-cut bacon

3 heads Bibb lettuce, torn into 2-inch (5-cm) pieces

2 Granny Smith apples, cored and cut into ½-inch (12-mm) dice

2 ruby red grapefruits, peeled and segmented with a knife

2 oranges, peeled and segmented with a knife

1 bunch green onions, green part only, chopped

Salt and freshly ground pepper

3 ripe avocados, pitted, peeled, and sliced

In a small bowl, whisk together the mustard and vinegar. Add the oil in a thin stream, whisking constantly until the vinaigrette is well blended. Set aside.

In a large frying pan, cook the bacon over medium heat, turning as needed, until crispy, 7–8 minutes. Transfer to paper towels to drain. When cool enough to handle, cut the bacon into ½-inch (12-mm) pieces.

In a large bowl, combine the lettuce, apples, grapefruits, oranges, and green onions. Season with salt and pepper, drizzle with half of the vinaigrette, and toss well.

Divide the salad among individual plates. Top with the avocados and bacon. Drizzle a little of the remaining vinaigrette over each salad and serve right away.

25

BREAD SALAD WITH CHICKEN, ORANGES & ARUGULA

serves 4–6

1 Tbsp minced fresh rosemary

Salt and freshly ground pepper

2 skin-on, bone-in chicken breast halves

½ cup (4 fl oz/120 ml) extra-virgin olive oil

8 slices day-old baguette, cut into 1-inch (2.5-cm) cubes

¼ cup (2 fl oz/60 ml) balsamic vinegar

2 cloves garlic, minced

2 large navel oranges, peeled and segmented with a knife

2 cups (2 oz/60 g) baby arugula

6–8 radishes, thinly sliced

You can ready all of the components of this wintertime take on panzanella, Italy's classic bread salad that features tomatoes and basil, ahead of time and then combine them just before serving for a quick and easy main course.

Preheat the oven to 350°F (180°C).

In a small bowl, stir together the rosemary, ½ tsp salt, and ½ tsp pepper. Rub the chicken breasts all over with the mixture and place, skin side up, on a baking sheet. Roast, turning once, until the skin is crispy and the meat is opaque, 35–40 minutes. Transfer to a cutting board. When the chicken is cool enough to handle, remove the meat, discarding the skin and bones. Cut the meat into 1-inch (2.5-cm) cubes. Transfer to a bowl, cover, and refrigerate until ready to use.

In a frying pan, warm ¼ cup (2 fl oz/60 ml) of the oil over medium-high heat. Add the bread cubes and cook, shaking the pan occasionally, until golden on all sides, 4–5 minutes. Let cool. The toasted bread can be stored in a paper bag at room temperature for up to 2 days.

In a large bowl, whisk together the remaining ¼ cup (2 fl oz/60 ml) oil, the vinegar, garlic, and ½ tsp salt until the vinaigrette is well blended. Cut the orange sections crosswise into thirds and add to the bowl along with the arugula, radishes, all but 6 or 7 of the bread cubes, and half of the chicken. Stir to mix well. Transfer the salad to a platter, garnish with the remaining bread cubes and chicken, and serve.

26

WEDGE SALAD WITH FRIED OYSTERS & MIGNONETTE

serves 4

¾ cup (6 fl oz/180 ml) champagne vinegar

3 Tbsp minced shallot

Salt and freshly ground white or black pepper

Canola or other light vegetable oil for frying

2 large eggs

1 cup (5 oz/155 g) all-purpose flour

12 shucked oysters, drained and picked over for shell pieces

1 small to medium head iceberg lettuce, cut into 4 wedges

This salad is a happy cross between oysters on the half shell and an oyster poor boy sandwich, combining the luscious crispness of one and the tang of the other. The iceberg wedge takes well to the vinaigrette and complements the slightly spicy mollusks.

In a small bowl, whisk together the vinegar, shallot, and 1 Tbsp white or black pepper until the vinaigrette is well blended. Set aside.

Pour oil into a large frying pan to a depth of 1 inch (2.5 cm) and warm over medium-high heat until it registers 375°F (190°C) on a deep-frying thermometer. Line a plate with paper towels. In a shallow bowl, whisk the eggs until blended. In a second shallow bowl, stir together the flour, 1 tsp salt, and 1 tsp black pepper. Dip an oyster in the eggs, allowing the excess to drip off, and then dredge in the flour, shaking off the excess. Slide the oyster into the hot oil. Repeat with about 5 more oysters. Do not crowd the pan. Fry, turning once, until golden on both sides, about 1 minute per side. Using a slotted spoon, transfer to the paper towel–lined plate. Repeat with the remaining oysters.

Place a lettuce wedge on each individual plate, drizzle with some of the vinaigrette, and add 3 oysters to each plate. Serve right away with the remaining vinaigrette alongside.

27

Fruit salad makes a refreshing side dish for brunch or lunch, or may be served as a healthful dessert. Here, tropical fruits, which are typically in the market year-round, take center stage. When choosing mangoes and papayas, look for fruits that yield slightly to a gentle touch. A ripe pineapple will be fragrant, have deep green leaves, and give slightly when pressed.

MANGO, PINEAPPLE & PAPAYA SALAD

serves 4–6

2 papayas

1 mango

½ small pineapple, about 1 lb (500 g), peeled

Juice of 3 limes

¼ cup (⅓ oz/10 g) chopped fresh mint

Peel the papayas, cut them in half, and scoop out and discard the seeds. Cut the flesh into ½-inch (12-mm) cubes and place in a bowl.

Peel the mango. Stand the fruit stem end up with a narrow side toward you. Position a sharp knife about 1 inch (2.5 cm) from the stem on one side and cut down the length of the fruit, just missing the large pit. Repeat on the other side of the pit. Cut the flesh into ½-inch (12-mm) cubes. Add to the bowl.

Lay the pineapple on its side and cut shallow furrows in the flesh to remove the eyes. Cut the pineapple lengthwise into quarters, cut away the tough core, and cut the flesh into ½-inch (12-mm) cubes. Add to the bowl.

Pour the lime juice over the fruit, sprinkle with the mint, and turn gently to coat, then serve. The salad may also be covered and refrigerated for up to 4 hours before serving.

28

Pomelo, which is quite fragrant, is similar to grapefruit but is at least twice as large, thicker skinned, and slightly less juicy. Grapefruit is exceptionally juicy, and while it can be substituted here, the sections won't be quite as firm.

ESCAROLE SALAD WITH POMELO, RED ONION & CALAMARI

serves 4

2 pomelos, peeled and segmented with a knife

¼ cup (1¼ oz/40 g) finely diced red onion

1 head escarole, pale yellow and green inner leaves only

Salt

1 lb (500 g) cleaned squid rings and tentacles

1 Tbsp balsamic vinegar

2 Tbsp extra-virgin olive oil

1 clove garlic, minced

In a bowl, stir together the pomelo segments and onion. Arrange the escarole on a platter or on individual plates and spoon the pomelo mixture on top.

Bring a saucepan of water to a boil over medium-high heat. Add 1 tsp salt and the squid and cook until just opaque, about 2 minutes. Drain and rinse under cold running water, then drain again and pat dry. Arrange on top of the pomelo mixture.

In a small bowl, whisk together the vinegar, oil, garlic, and ¼ tsp salt until the vinaigrette is well blended. Drizzle over the salad and serve right away.

29

A wonderful mix of contrasting colors, textures, and flavors, this vibrant salad is not only fast and simple to make but is also healthful and delicious. If you are using boxed tofu, be careful when removing it from the container, as you want the block to remain intact so it can be neatly cubed.

TOFU SALAD WITH EDAMAME & SHAVED ROOT VEGETABLES

serves 4

¾ lb (375 g) firm silken tofu, cut into slices 1 inch (2.5 cm) thick

2 Tbsp light soy sauce

2 tsp toasted sesame oil

2 green onions, including tender green parts, minced

1-inch (2.5-cm) piece fresh ginger, peeled and grated

2 watermelon radishes or 6 red radishes

1 small celery root (about ¾ lb/375 g), peeled and halved lengthwise

2 carrots, peeled and halved crosswise

Salt

2 cups (12 oz/375 g) frozen shelled edamame

2 Tbsp sesame seeds, toasted

Place the tofu in a shallow baking dish. In a small bowl, whisk together the soy sauce, oil, green onions, and ginger. Pour over the tofu and marinate at room temperature for at least 1 hour or up to 3 hours.

Meanwhile, using a mandoline or a very sharp knife, shave the radishes and celery root crosswise. Reserve a few whole shavings for garnish and cut the rest into smaller pieces. Using a vegetable peeler, shave the carrots lengthwise, then cut each ribbon into 3 or 4 pieces. Set aside.

In a saucepan, bring 4 cups (32 fl oz/1 l) water to a boil over medium-high heat. Add ½ tsp salt and the edamame. Reduce the heat to medium and cook until just tender, 5–6 minutes. Drain and rinse with cold water.

Divide the edamame among individual plates. Cut the tofu into 1-inch (2.5-cm) cubes. Using a spatula, carefully remove the cubes from the marinade (they are fragile) and place on top of the edamame. Pour a little of the marinade over them. Top with the radish, celery root, and carrot pieces and sprinkle with the sesame seeds. Garnish with the reserved whole vegetable shavings and serve right away.

30

Bright and lively, this salad hits the spot during the dead of winter. Serve alongside slow-roasted pork with mojo or adobo sauce for a Latin-style meal.

WARM RUBY GRAPEFRUIT SALAD

serves 4

1 Tbsp mild olive oil or canola oil

¼ red onion, thinly sliced

½ jalapeño chile, thinly sliced

2 ruby red grapefruits, peeled and segmented with a knife

1 avocado, pitted, peeled and sliced

¼ cup (⅓ oz/10 g) chopped fresh cilantro

In a frying pan, warm the oil over medium heat. Add the onion and jalapeño and sauté until softened, about 5 minutes. Add the grapefruit segments and avocado to the pan, mix gently, and warm through. Sprinkle with cilantro and serve.

31

Most of the spiciness of a chile resides in its seeds and, to a lesser extent, the white inner membranes. Seeding the serrano will cut down sharply on its heat.

CABBAGE, PEAR & GINGER SLAW

serves 4

¼ cup (2 fl oz/60 ml) seasoned rice vinegar

1 Tbsp toasted sesame oil

1 tsp peeled and grated fresh ginger

1 tsp packed light brown sugar

1 tsp soy sauce

½ head napa cabbage

1 firm mango, peeled

1 Asian pear, halved and cored

1 red serrano chile

Salt and freshly ground pepper

In a small bowl, whisk together the vinegar, sesame oil, ginger, sugar, and soy sauce to make a dressing. Set aside.

Using a mandoline or box grater, shred the cabbage, mango, and pear. Combine in a bowl. Cut the chile into thin rings, remove the seeds, and add the rings to bowl. Add the dressing and toss to combine. Season with salt and pepper to taste and serve.

In the heart of winter, turn to cruciferous vegetables like Brussels sprouts, broccoli, and cauliflower. Shaving, shredding, or spiralizing them and tossing with an herb vinaigrette helps keep the vegetables light and bright. Take advantage of seasonal citrus fruits, like juicy oranges and sweet mandarins, which pair well with shellfish, grains, roots, and dried nuts, for flavorful salads.

february

1

SALAD OF ASIAN GREENS WITH TAMARI-GLAZED PORK BELLY

serves 6

¼ cup (2 fl oz/60 ml) tamari

½ tsp toasted sesame oil

1 Tbsp honey

2 lb (1 kg) pork belly, skin removed

3 heads small bok choy

¼–⅓ small head green cabbage, shredded

2 celery ribs, minced

Sliced green onion tops for garnish, optional

FOR THE DRESSING

2 tsp tamari

1 tsp toasted sesame oil

1 tsp honey

1 tsp sherry vinegar

Tamari, a rich version of soy sauce that, unlike regular soy sauce, includes little or no wheat, imparts a hint of smokiness that adds to the complex flavors of the grilled pork belly. The pork belly takes only about 10 minutes to grill, and the greens take even less time. Ask the butcher to remove the skin from the pork belly for you.

In a small bowl, whisk together the tamari, oil, and honey to make a marinade. Pour into a shallow baking dish, add the pork belly, and turn several times to coat. Cover and refrigerate for 3–4 hours, turning and basting occasionally with the marinade.

Cut off the dark green tops from 2 heads of the bok choy, roll the tops together into a cylinder, and thinly slice crosswise. Transfer to a large bowl. Finely chop the white part and add to the bowl along with the cabbage and celery. Set aside. Cut the other head in half lengthwise and set aside.

To make the dressing, in a small bowl, whisk together the tamari, oil, honey, and vinegar until well blended. Set aside.

Prepare a charcoal or gas grill for direct-heat cooking over medium-high heat. Alternatively, preheat a stove-top grill pan over medium-high heat. Place the bok choy halves on the grill rack or in the grill pan and cook, turning several times, until lightly charred, about 4 minutes. Transfer to a cutting board.

Remove the pork belly from the marinade, reserving the marinade. Place the pork belly on the grill rack or in the pan and cook, turning often and basting occasionally with the reserved marinade, until pork is firm to the touch and is a dark, mahogany color, »→

about 10 minutes. Transfer to a cutting board and let rest for 5 minutes, then cut crosswise into slices ¼ inch (6 mm) thick.

Chop the grilled bok choy and add to the bowl with the other vegetables. Drizzle with the dressing and toss gently to coat. Mound the salad onto individual plates and arrange the pork belly on top. Sprinkle with green onion, if desired. Serve right away.

2

WARM LENTIL SALAD WITH MUSTARD VINAIGRETTE

serves 4–6

1 cup (7 oz/220 g) green French (du Puy) lentils, picked over and rinsed

1 yellow onion, finely chopped

1 clove garlic, halved

¼ tsp dried thyme

2 fresh flat-leaf parsley sprigs, plus ½ cup (1½ oz/45 g) finely chopped

1 shallot, minced

2 tsp white wine vinegar

4½ tsp Dijon mustard

Salt and freshly ground pepper

¼ cup (2 fl oz/60 ml) extra-virgin olive oil

This is delicious as a side for herb-roasted chicken or pork tenderloin, or grilled sausages. To add more greenery, stir in a handful or two of baby spinach when you add the parsley.

In a heavy saucepan, combine the lentils with 6 cups (48 fl oz/1.5 l) water, the onion, garlic, thyme, and parsley sprigs over medium heat. Bring to a simmer, cover, and cook until the lentils are tender, about 30 minutes.

Meanwhile, transfer 2 Tbsp of the lentil-cooking liquid to a bowl and whisk in the shallot, vinegar, mustard, and salt and pepper to taste. Add the oil in a thin stream, whisking constantly until the dressing is well blended. Set the vinaigrette aside.

Drain the lentils well in a fine-mesh sieve and discard the parsley sprigs and garlic halves. Transfer the lentils to a bowl, add the vinaigrette and chopped parsley, and toss to combine. Season with salt and pepper and serve warm or at room temperature.

3

*Freshly grated
horseradish mixed
with the salmon
adds loft and texture
to the cakes, as well
as subtly imparting
its inimitable flavor.
For the greens,
use small leaves
of young spinach or
red Asian mustard
or a mixture of kale
and red or green
chard. This is an
excellent next-day
use for leftover
poached salmon.*

SALMON CAKES WITH FRESH HORSERADISH ON WILTED GREENS

serves 4

1½ lb (750 g) salmon fillet,
pin bones removed

Salt and freshly ground pepper

1 piece fresh horseradish,
2–3 inches (5–7.5 cm) long

3 Tbsp grated yellow onion

2 Tbsp Dijon mustard

½ cup (¾ oz/20 g) chopped fresh
flat-leaf parsley

2 large eggs, beaten

3 Tbsp unsalted butter

3 Tbsp vegetable oil

1½ cups (2 oz/60 g) panko

6 cups (6 oz/185 g) greens (see note)

Juice of 2 lemons

Cut the salmon into pieces as needed to fit
into a large saucepan. Cover the fish with
water, add 1 tsp salt, and bring to a boil
over medium heat, then reduce the heat to a
simmer and poach the salmon gently until
just opaque throughout, about 20 minutes.
Peel off and discard the salmon skin, put the
flesh in a large bowl, and flake with a fork.
Set aside.

Peel the horseradish, then grate on the large
holes of a box grater. You will need about
½ cup (2½ oz/75 g) for the salmon cakes.
The remaining grated horseradish can be
mixed with a little heavy cream and
mayonnaise to make a sauce.

Add the horseradish, onion, mustard, parsley,
eggs, ½ tsp salt, and 2 tsp pepper to the bowl
with the salmon. Using a fork, mash until the
ingredients come together in a mass. Shape
into 12 balls, each about the size of a small
lemon. Flatten into cakes about 2½ inches
(6 cm) in diameter. Place in a single layer on
a sheet of aluminum foil or waxed paper.

Preheat the oven to 300°F (150°C). Line a
baking sheet with paper towels. ⤳

In a large frying pan, melt 1½ Tbsp of the
butter with 1½ Tbsp of the oil over medium
heat. Spread half of the panko in a shallow
dish and sprinkle with salt and pepper. Press
both sides of 6 of the salmon cakes into the
panko. Carefully place the cakes in the pan
and cook, turning once, until crispy and
golden, about 2 minutes per side. Transfer to
the paper towel–lined baking sheet and keep
warm in the oven. Repeat with the remaining
panko and salmon cakes, using the remaining
1½ Tbsp of the butter and 1½ Tbsp oil.

4

*If shaving the
carrots lengthwise
seems too labor-
intensive or difficult,
you can shave or
thinly slice the
carrots into coins.
Meaty green olives
are delicious in this
salad, although any
olives, including
oil-cured black ones,
will impart a pleasant
briny and salty note
to the mix.*

CARROT, OLIVE & ALMOND SALAD

serves 4

½ tsp cumin seeds

1 lb (500 g) multicolored carrots

¼ cup (1½ oz/45 g) green olives, pitted

¼ cup (⅓ oz/10 g) lightly packed
fresh flat-leaf parsley leaves

1 tsp fresh lemon juice

2 Tbsp extra-virgin olive oil

Salt and freshly ground pepper

¼ cup (1 oz/30 g) unsalted roasted
almonds, chopped

In a dry frying pan, toast the cumin seeds
over medium-low heat, stirring, until fragrant
and starting to brown, 2–3 minutes. Pour
onto a plate and let cool.

Using a mandoline or a box grater, shave
the carrots lengthwise into thin ribbons.
Set aside in a bowl.

With a large knife, coarsely chop the olives
and parsley. Transfer to a small bowl, add the
lemon juice and cumin seeds, and stir with a
fork to combine. Add the oil in a thin stream,
whisking until the dressing is well blended.
Season with salt and pepper to taste.

Add the olive mixture to the carrots and
toss well. Divide the salad among individual
plates, sprinkle with the almonds, and serve.

5

WILD RICE SALAD WITH MUSHROOMS & SAGE

serves 10–12

6 celery ribs

3 Tbsp extra-virgin olive oil

½ cup (2½ oz/75 g) finely chopped yellow onion

2 cups (12 oz/375 g) wild rice

1 Tbsp minced fresh flat-leaf parsley

1 tsp minced fresh sage

Salt and freshly ground pepper

6 cups (48 fl oz/1.5 l) chicken broth

1 Tbsp unsalted butter

½ lb (250 g) cremini mushrooms, sliced

Cooking mushrooms separately and then folding them into wild rice lets them contribute their distinctive earthy flavor to this dish, but keeps their smooth and meaty texture at its best. You can use shiitakes or chanterelles in place of button mushrooms, or a mixture. This is a great dish for entertaining a crowd.

Trim the celery ribs and cut each rib crosswise into 2-inch (5-cm) lengths, then cut the pieces on the diagonal to make long slivers about ¼ inch (6 mm) thick. Set aside.

In a large saucepan, warm the oil over medium heat. Add the onion and celery and sauté until soft, 7–8 minutes. Add the wild rice, parsley, sage, ¾ tsp salt, and ½ tsp pepper and stir until the rice glistens, 1–2 minutes. Pour in the broth, raise the heat to high, and bring to a boil. Reduce the heat to medium-low, cover, and cook until the wild rice is tender, about 50 minutes.

About 5 minutes before the rice is ready, cook the mushrooms: In a frying pan, melt the butter over medium-high heat. When it foams, add the mushrooms and sauté until lightly golden, about 5 minutes. Season with ¼ tsp each salt and pepper.

When the rice is done, drain off any excess liquid and stir in the hot mushrooms. Transfer to a warmed bowl and serve hot.

6

CRAB LOUIS SALAD

serves 4–6

4 large eggs

FOR THE DRESSING

1 cup (8 fl oz/250 ml) mayonnaise

¼ cup (2 fl oz/60 ml) ketchup-style chile sauce

2 Tbsp minced green bell pepper

2 green onions, including tender green parts, minced

1 Tbsp fresh lemon juice

½ head iceberg lettuce

2 hearts of romaine lettuce

1 lb (500 g) cooked crabmeat, picked over for shell fragments

½ cup (3 oz/90 g) cherry tomatoes, halved

¼ English cucumber, thinly sliced

1 lemon, cut into wedges

This retro salad is often made with shrimp instead of crab, or with a combination of the two. Use cooked, peeled, and deveined shrimp in the size you prefer (on the West Coast, tiny bay shrimp are usually the first choice). You can also top the salad with lightly cooked asparagus.

To hard-cook the eggs, place them in a saucepan just large enough to hold them. Add cold water to cover by 1 inch (2.5 cm) and bring just to a boil over high heat. Remove the pan from the heat and cover. Let stand for 15 minutes. Drain the eggs, then transfer to a bowl of ice water and let cool before cutting into quarters.

To make the dressing, in a small bowl, whisk together the mayonnaise, chile sauce, bell pepper, green onions, and lemon juice. Cover and refrigerate until serving.

Tear the iceberg lettuce into bite-sized pieces and coarsely chop the romaine hearts. In a large bowl, toss together the lettuces. Distribute the lettuces in a thick layer on a large platter or among individual plates. Heap the crabmeat down the center of the lettuce. Arrange the tomatoes, cucumber, and quartered eggs around the crab. Garnish with the lemon wedges, and serve, passing the dressing on the side.

7

*Autumn through
spring, beets are a
highlight at farmers'
markets, especially
the golden and
pink-and-white-
striped Chioggia
varieties. In this
colorful composed
salad, crisp fennel
and creamy avocado
provide textural
contrast with the
beets, and thin
shavings of ricotta
salata cheese add
a salty tang.*

BEET & FENNEL SALAD WITH RICOTTA SALATA

serves 4

4 beets, preferably golden or Chioggia
(about 1¼ lb/625 g total weight)

1½ Tbsp fresh lemon juice

1 shallot, minced

Salt and freshly ground pepper

¼ cup (2 fl oz/60 ml) extra-virgin olive oil

1 small fennel bulb, trimmed

2 oz ricotta salata or feta cheese

½ large avocado

1 Tbsp minced fresh flat-leaf parsley

Preheat the oven to 400°F (200°C). Trim off
the leafy beet tops. Wrap the beets in foil and
roast on a baking sheet until easily pierced
with the tip of a knife, about 1 hour. Remove
from the oven and let cool in the foil.

Meanwhile, in a small bowl, whisk together
the lemon juice, shallot, and a generous pinch
of salt. Let stand for 30 minutes to allow the
shallot flavor to mellow, then add the oil
in a thin stream, whisking constantly until
the dressing is well blended. Season with
additional salt and pepper to taste.

Unwrap and peel the cooled beets, then slice
very thinly. Put them in a bowl and toss
gently with about one-third of the vinaigrette,
taking care not to break up the slices. Make
a thin bed of the beets on a large platter or
divide among individual plates.

Halve the fennel lengthwise and, using a
mandoline or a very sharp knife, slice each
half crosswise paper-thin. Put the fennel in
a bowl, add about one-half of the remaining
vinaigrette, and toss to coat. Scatter the
fennel over the beets. With a vegetable peeler,
shave the cheese evenly over the fennel.

Peel and pit the avocado and slice thinly
crosswise. Arrange the avocado slices
attractively on top of the salad. Drizzle
the salad with as much of the remaining
vinaigrette as desired (you may not need
it all). Top with the parsley and serve.

8

*True, February is
not tomato season,
but tiny grape
tomatoes are often
quite decent even in
the wintertime and
can satisfy that late-
winter hankering for
the fresh fruit.*

ARUGULA SALAD WITH PINE NUTS, AVOCADO & HEARTS OF PALM

serves 4

6 cups (6 oz/185 g) baby arugula leaves

1 basket grape tomatoes, halved

⅓ cup (2 oz/60 g) pine nuts

4 stalks jarred hearts of palm,
cut on a slight diagonal into ½-inch
(12-mm) slices

1 avocado, pitted, peeled,
and cut into thin slices

FOR THE LEMON DRESSING

2 Tbsp fresh lemon juice

Salt and freshly ground pepper

6 Tbsp (3 fl oz/90 ml) extra-virgin
olive oil

Parmesan cheese for shaving

In a serving bowl, toss together the
arugula, tomatoes, pine nuts, hearts of
palm, and avocado.

To make the dressing, in a small bowl,
whisk together the lemon juice and salt and
pepper to taste. Add the oil in a thin stream,
whisking constantly until the dressing is
smooth. Pour over the salad and toss well.
Using a vegetable peeler, shave the cheese
over the salad and serve.

9

LENTIL SALAD WITH MOZZARELLA & PROSCIUTTO

serves 6

Salt and freshly ground pepper

1¼ cups (9 oz/280 ml) green French (du Puy) lentils, picked over and rinsed

¼ cup (2 fl oz/60 ml) red wine vinegar

2 Tbsp minced red onion

¼ cup (⅓ oz/10 g) julienned fresh basil leaves, plus small whole leaves for garnish

¼ lb (125 g) paper-thin prosciutto slices, cut into strips 1 inch (2.5 cm) wide

3 Tbsp extra-virgin olive oil

5 oz (155 g) fresh mozzarella cheese, torn into generous pieces

This is a great dish to bring to a potluck, as it holds up well and absorbs more flavor as it sits. If you're transporting it, tear up the mozzarella, then return it to the liquid in which it came. This will keep it fresh and moist. Just before serving, add the mozzarella and the garnishes to the platter.

In a saucepan, combine 4 cups (32 fl oz/1 l) water and ½ tsp salt and bring to a boil. Add the lentils, reduce the heat to medium-low, cover, and cook until the lentils are tender but still hold their shape, 20–25 minutes. Remove from the heat and drain well. Let cool to room temperature.

In a large bowl, using a fork, stir together the vinegar, ½ tsp pepper, the onion, the julienned basil, and all but one-fourth of the prosciutto. Add the oil in a thin stream, stirring constantly until the dressing is well blended. Add the lentils and toss to mix.

Spoon the lentils onto a platter. Tuck the cheese into the lentils. Sprinkle the basil leaves and the remaining prosciutto over the lentils and serve.

10

BUTTER LETTUCE WITH SHEEP'S MILK CHEESE & HAZELNUTS

serves 4–6

¾ cup (4 oz/125 g) hazelnuts

1 large or 2 medium heads butter lettuce

3 Tbsp extra-virgin olive oil

1 Tbsp white balsamic vinegar

1 Tbsp champagne vinegar

2 tsp honey

Salt

4 oz (125 g) aged sheep's milk cheese, crumbled

If you can find it, the creamy, tart-rinded Ossau-Iraty cheese from the Pyrenees region of France is delicious in contrast with the sweet honey and crunchy nuts in this salad. Aged pecorino or Manchego is a nice pick too. Serve with a crisp, dry rosé.

In a dry frying pan, toast the hazelnuts over medium-low heat, stirring, until fragrant and starting to brown, about 5 minutes. Wrap the hazelnuts in a towel and rub to remove the skins. Pour onto a plate to cool slightly, then chop coarsely and set aside.

Tear the larger leaves of lettuce into several pieces, but keep the medium and small leaves whole. You should have 4–5 cups (4–5 oz/125–155 g).

In a large serving bowl, whisk together the oil, the white balsamic and champagne vinegars, the honey, and ½ tsp salt. Add the lettuce leaves and toss to coat well. Add half of the cheese and half of the hazelnuts and toss well. Top with the remaining cheese and nuts and serve.

11

FRISÉE & APPLE SALAD WITH HERB-CRUSTED GOAT CHEESE

serves 4

1 log (8 oz/250 g) fresh goat cheese

1 Tbsp finely chopped shallot

1 tsp Dijon mustard

1½ Tbsp champagne vinegar

1 tsp fresh lemon juice

¼ cup (2 fl oz/60 ml) walnut oil

½ cup (4 fl oz/125 ml) canola oil

2 Tbsp chopped fresh chives, plus extra for garnish (optional)

Salt and freshly ground pepper

2 large eggs

1 cup (2 oz/60 g) fresh bread crumbs, lightly toasted

2 Tbsp chopped fresh flat-leaf parsley

1 large head frisée, pale yellow inner leaves only, cut into 1- to 2-inch (2.5- to 5-cm) pieces

1 Gala apple, cored and cut into ⅛-inch (3-mm) slices

This classic vinaigrette pairs beautifully with the bitterness of the frisée, the sweetness of the apples, and the tanginess of the goat cheese. If you can't find frisée, mesclun, sometimes labeled "spring mix," is a good alternative.

Cut the cheese into 8 equal rounds and transfer to a plate. Cover and freeze until firm, about 15 minutes.

Meanwhile, in a small bowl, whisk together the shallot, mustard, vinegar, and lemon juice. Add the walnut oil and 2 Tbsp of the canola oil in a thin stream, whisking constantly until the vinaigrette is well blended. Stir in the chives and season with salt and pepper. Set aside.

In a shallow bowl, whisk the eggs until blended and season lightly with salt and pepper. In a second shallow bowl, stir together the bread crumbs and parsley, and season with salt and pepper. Dip each cheese round into the eggs, letting the excess drip off, then coat with the bread crumbs.

In a sauté pan, warm the remaining 6 Tbsp (3 fl oz/90 ml) canola oil over medium-high heat. Add the cheese rounds and fry, turning once, until golden brown, 1–2 minutes per side. Transfer to a plate.

In a large bowl, combine the frisée and apple and toss with enough vinaigrette to lightly coat. Divide among individual plates and place 2 cheese rounds alongside each salad. Sprinkle with chopped chives, if desired. Serve right away.

12

COUSCOUS SALAD WITH MANDARINS & HARISSA VINAIGRETTE

serves 4–6

1 cup (6 oz/185 g) instant couscous

1 cup (8 fl oz/250 ml) boiling water

Salt and freshly ground pepper

3 Tbsp extra-virgin olive oil

3 Tbsp fresh lemon juice

½ tsp minced garlic

½ tsp harissa

2 or 3 mandarin oranges, peeled, segmented, and seeded

½ cup (3 oz/90 g) raisins

½ cup (2½ oz/75 g) slivered almonds

¼ cup (⅓ oz/10 g) finely chopped fresh flat-leaf parsley

8 romaine lettuce leaves, coarsely chopped

Couscous, small pasta pellets typically treated like a grain, makes an excellent base for seasonal salads of all kinds. In summer, tomatoes and cucumbers can replace the mandarins and raisins used here, and in fall, persimmons and pomegranate seeds can be substituted.

In a heatproof bowl, combine the couscous, boiling water, and ½ tsp salt and stir until blended. Cover tightly and let stand until all of the water has been absorbed, about 20 minutes. Uncover and let the couscous cool to room temperature, about 15 minutes.

In a small bowl, whisk together the oil, lemon juice, garlic, ¼ tsp salt, ½ tsp pepper, and the harissa until the vinaigrette is well blended.

Cut the mandarin segments in half and add to the couscous along with the raisins, almonds, and parsley. Drizzle with the vinaigrette and stir to mix well.

Arrange the lettuce leaves on a platter, mound the couscous salad on top, and serve.

13

KALE SALAD WITH CREAMY LEMON DRESSING

serves 4

2 cups (4 oz/125 g) torn country-style bread (½-inch/12-mm pieces)

Olive oil for drizzling

Salt and freshly ground pepper

1 lb (500 g) cavolo nero kale

½ cup (4 fl oz/125 ml) mayonnaise

1½ Tbsp fresh lemon juice

2 cloves garlic, minced

1 tsp anchovy paste

½ tsp Dijon mustard

¼ tsp lemon zest

1 cup (6 oz/185 g) halved cherry tomatoes

Shaved Parmesan cheese for garnish

This nutritious and delicious salad calls for deep green, ruffled Tuscan kale (also known as cavolo nero, dinosaur, or Lacinato kale), which is milder flavored and more tender than other kale varieties. Torn croutons add a rustic touch to the dish.

Preheat the oven to 350°F (180°C). Line a baking sheet with parchment paper.

Spread the bread pieces on the prepared baking sheet. Drizzle with oil, season with salt and pepper, and toss to coat. Bake until golden brown, about 20 minutes. Let cool.

Remove the thick stems from the kale leaves. Stack the leaves, several at a time, and roll into a cylinder, then cut crosswise into very thin strips. Transfer to a large bowl.

In a bowl, whisk together the mayonnaise, 2 Tbsp water, the lemon juice, garlic, anchovy paste, mustard, and lemon zest until the dressing is well blended. Season with pepper.

Toss the kale with enough dressing to coat. Top with the croutons and tomatoes and garnish with cheese. Serve the remaining dressing alongside.

14

SPINACH SALAD WITH ORANGES & ROASTED BEETS

serves 6

4 small beets (about ½ lb/250 g total weight)

FOR THE SHALLOT DRESSING

1 Tbsp fresh lemon juice, plus more as needed

1 shallot, minced

Salt and freshly ground pepper

3 Tbsp extra-virgin olive oil

2 large navel oranges

6 cups (6 oz/185 g) baby spinach

Plump, sweet navel oranges turn up frequently in winter salads—and not just fruit salads. They add appealing color and zing to this mix of beets and spinach, a good prelude to a main course of pork chops or duck. Red-fleshed blood oranges, at their delicious peak during winter, can be used in place of the navel oranges.

Preheat the oven to 375°F (190°C). Trim off the leafy beet tops. Wrap the beets in foil and roast on a baking sheet until easily pierced with the tip of a knife, 45–60 minutes. Remove from the oven and let cool in the foil.

Meanwhile, in a small bowl, combine the lemon juice and shallot. Season with salt and pepper. Let stand for 30 minutes to allow the shallot flavor to mellow, then add the oil in a thin stream, whisking constantly until the dressing is well blended.

Cut a slice off the top and bottom of each orange. Stand each upright and, following the contour of the fruit, cut away all the peel and white pith. Cut along both sides of each segment to free it from the membrane.

When the beets are cool enough to handle, peel and cut them into wedges about the size of the orange segments. Put the beet wedges in a bowl and toss with just enough of the dressing to coat them lightly.

Put the spinach in a large bowl and add the orange segments. Add the remaining dressing and toss to coat. Taste and adjust the seasoning with salt, pepper, and lemon juice.

Divide the spinach and oranges among individual plates. Arrange the beets on top and serve.

15

HERBED CRAB & CUCUMBER SALAD WITH BASIL VINAIGRETTE

serves 4

Here, the classic chunky crab salad is given a Thai accent with the addition of chile paste, basil, and cilantro as background flavors. Cucumber balances the heat. This salad can also be made with shrimp in place of the crabmeat.

FOR THE BASIL VINAIGRETTE

3 Tbsp coconut oil, melted

½ tsp honey

1 Tbsp rice vinegar

Salt and freshly ground pepper

¼ cup (⅓ oz/10 g) finely chopped fresh Thai basil or Italian green or purple basil

FOR THE SALAD

1 Tbsp mayonnaise

1 tsp Thai chile paste

1 lb (500 g) cooked crabmeat, picked over for shell fragments and squeezed to remove excess water

1 bunch fresh chives, finely chopped

½ cup (½ oz/15 g) fresh flat-leaf parsley leaves, chopped

½ cup (½ oz/15 g) fresh cilantro leaves, stems removed

Salt and freshly ground pepper

12 butter lettuce leaves

1 cucumber, peeled, seeded, and cut into 2-inch (5-cm) matchsticks

4 fresh Thai basil or Italian green or purple basil sprigs

To make the vinaigrette, in a small bowl, whisk together the coconut oil and honey until the honey dissolves. Add the vinegar, ⅛ tsp salt, and ⅛ tsp pepper and whisk until the vinaigrette is well blended. Stir in the basil and set aside.

To make the salad, in a medium bowl, stir together the mayonnaise and chile paste. Add the crabmeat, chives, parsley, cilantro, ¼ tsp salt, and ¼ tsp pepper and gently stir to mix. Some of the crab should still be in largish lumps. Taste and adjust the seasonings.

Arrange 3 lettuce leaves on each individual plate and mound the salad on top. Scatter the cucumber over the salads and drizzle with the vinaigrette. Garnish each with a basil sprig and serve.

16

BROCCOLI & CAULIFLOWER SLAW WITH RAISINS & NUTS

serves 4–6

An old-fashioned mayonnaise dressing made with a hint of sugar and vinegar gives this contemporary salad the feel of comfort food. Adjust the creaminess by adding more or less mayonnaise and milk. For a variation, currants, dried cherries, or dried cranberries could be used instead of raisins.

3 heads of broccoli, cut into quarters, stem end intact, tough stems peeled

½ head cauliflower

1 cup (6 oz/185 g) pine nuts

1½ cups (9 oz/280 g) raisins

½ cup (4 fl oz/125 ml) mayonnaise

¼ cup (2 fl oz/60 ml) milk

2 tsp sugar

2–3 tsp red wine vinegar

Using a mandoline or box grater, thinly slice the broccoli quarters. Cut the pieces in half. Do the same with the cauliflower.

In a small frying pan, toast the pine nuts over medium-low heat until just turning golden brown, 3–4 minutes. Pour onto a plate to let cool.

In a bowl, combine the broccoli, cauliflower, raisins, and pine nuts. In another bowl, mix together the mayonnaise, milk, sugar, and vinegar to taste. Pour the dressing over the salad, toss to coat, and serve.

17

WALDORF SALAD

serves 6–8

The traditional Waldorf salad gets a fresh twist with the addition of dried cranberries, a drizzling of sherry vinegar, and a splash of fragrant walnut oil.

½ cup (2 oz/60 g) walnuts

4 large Granny Smith apples, left unpeeled

2 Tbsp fresh lemon juice

1 cup (5 oz/155 g) chopped celery

2 green onions, including tender green parts, chopped

½ cup (3 oz/90 g) dried cranberries

⅓ cup (3 fl oz/80 ml) walnut oil

3 Tbsp sherry vinegar

In a small frying pan, toast the walnuts over medium-low heat, stirring, until fragrant and starting to brown, about 5 minutes. Pour onto a plate to cool and then chop coarsely.

Halve and core the apples, cut into ½-inch (12-mm) pieces, and add to a large bowl with the lemon juice. Add the celery, green onions, cranberries, and toasted walnuts. Add the walnut oil and vinegar, toss to mix, and serve.

THAI BEEF SALAD

serves 4

FOR THE SPICY DRESSING

3 Tbsp Asian fish sauce

3 Tbsp fresh lime juice

2 tsp sugar

1–2 tsp minced Thai chiles with seeds

1 flank steak, ¾–1 lb (375–500 g)

Salt and freshly ground pepper

2 tsp peanut oil

1 large head butter lettuce, torn into bite-sized pieces

1 cup (5 oz/155 g) thinly sliced English cucumber

½ cup (2 oz/60 g) thinly sliced sweet onion or red onion

½ cup (2½ oz/75 g) red bell pepper strips

½ cup (¾ oz/20 g) lightly packed torn fresh mint leaves

½ cup (¾ oz/20 g) lightly packed torn fresh cilantro leaves

¼ cup (⅓ oz/10 g) lightly packed torn fresh Thai or regular basil leaves

This salad, popular on Thai-restaurant menus, is easy to prepare at home. Fish sauce, essential to creating authentic Southeast Asian flavor, is widely available at well-stocked supermarkets or Asian groceries. The low-fat vinaigrette and lean meat make this a healthful main-course salad.

To make the dressing, in a large bowl, stir together the fish sauce, lime juice, sugar, and chiles until well blended. Set aside.

Preheat the broiler or prepare a charcoal or gas grill for direct-heat cooking over high heat. Sprinkle the steak evenly with salt and pepper and rub into the meat. Brush lightly on both sides with the oil.

To cook the steak, place it on a broiler pan and slide it under the broiler about 4 inches (10 cm) from the heat source, or place it on the grill rack. Cook, turning once, until the meat is seared on the outside and cooked rare to medium-rare in the center, about 4 minutes per side. Transfer the steak to a cutting board and let rest for 20 minutes.

Cut the steak across the grain into very thin slices, then cut each slice in half lengthwise if needed. Add the slices of meat to the dressing and toss to coat. Add the lettuce, cucumber, onion, bell pepper, mint, cilantro, and basil, toss to coat, and serve.

CANNELLINI BEAN, FENNEL & SHRIMP SALAD

serves 6

1½ cans (15 oz/470 g each) cannellini or other white beans, drained and rinsed

1 fennel bulb (about 1 lb/500 g), trimmed, fronds reserved

½ tsp fennel seeds

3 Tbsp red wine vinegar

½ tsp minced garlic

Salt and freshly ground pepper

¼ cup (2 fl oz/60 ml) extra-virgin olive oil

1 lb (500 g) cooked medium shrimp, peeled and deveined

½ cup (2 oz/60 g) thinly sliced red onion

Frozen shrimp is reliably good in quality, and you can keep it on hand in the freezer for pulling together a salad like this one. Thaw the shrimp overnight in the refrigerator, and then let it come to room temperature for at least 30 minutes before adding it to the warm beans.

Put the beans in a saucepan and place over medium-low heat. Stir occasionally until warm. Remove from the heat and cover to keep warm.

Have ready a bowl of ice water. Quarter the fennel bulb lengthwise. Add the fennel to the ice water and let soak for 30 minutes. Drain well and thinly slice crosswise. Finely chop ½ cup (¾ oz/20 g) of the reserved fennel fronds.

In a mortar, coarsely crush the fennel seeds with a pestle. In a large bowl, whisk together the vinegar, crushed fennel seeds, garlic, ½ tsp salt, and pepper to taste. Add the oil in a thin stream, whisking constantly until the dressing is well blended.

Put the shrimp in a bowl and add the fennel, chopped fennel fronds, beans, and onion. Fold gently until all the ingredients are evenly distributed and serve.

JICAMA-MANGO SALAD WITH CILANTRO DRESSING

serves 4

½ cup (3 oz/90 g) minced red onion

FOR THE CILANTRO DRESSING

6 Tbsp (½ oz/15 g) chopped fresh cilantro

¼ cup (2 fl oz/60 ml) plus 2 tsp extra-virgin olive oil

3 Tbsp fresh lime juice

3 Tbsp fresh orange juice

4 tsp honey

¼ tsp chili powder

Salt and freshly ground pepper

5 small mangoes (about 3½ lb/1.75 kg total weight)

1 small jicama (about 1 lb/500 g total weight)

Chili powder for garnish

Crisp jicama and sweet, silky mango are enlivened by a honeyed, slightly tart vinaigrette in this refreshing salad with tropical Latin flavors. Pungent, lemony cilantro adds complexity, and chili powder brings subtle heat.

In a small bowl, soak the onion in cold water to cover for 15 minutes.

To make the dressing, in a food processor or blender, combine the cilantro, oil, lime juice, orange juice, honey, chili powder, a scant ½ tsp salt, and a few grindings of pepper and purée until smooth. Taste and adjust the seasonings.

Peel the mangoes. Stand a fruit stem end up with a narrow side toward you. Position a sharp knife about 1 inch (2.5 cm) from the stem and cut down the length of one side, just missing the large pit. Repeat on the other side of the pit. Cut the flesh into ½-inch (12-mm) pieces. Repeat with the remaining mangoes. Peel the jicama and cut the flesh into ½-inch pieces.

Drain the onion in a fine-mesh sieve and transfer to a bowl. Add the mango, jicama, ½ tsp salt, and ¼ tsp pepper. Drizzle with the dressing and toss well. Taste and adjust the seasonings.

Divide the salad among plates. Garnish each serving with a light dusting of chili powder and serve.

GARLICKY PASTA SALAD WITH CRAB & SHRIMP

serves 4

1½ lb (750 g) asparagus, tough ends trimmed

Salt and freshly ground pepper

¾ lb (375 g) penne, fusilli, or tubetti

1 clove garlic, minced

3 Tbsp balsamic vinegar

1 tsp Dijon mustard

2 Tbsp prepared aioli

¼ cup (2 fl oz/60 ml) extra-virgin olive oil

¼ lb (125 g) cooked crabmeat, picked over for shell fragments

¼ lb (125 g) cooked small shrimp, peeled and deveined

2 tsp finely chopped fresh tarragon

1 small head green- or red-leaf lettuce, leaves torn into bite-sized pieces

The ingredients that you add to a pasta salad can be as varied as the shape of pasta you choose. Replace the crab, shrimp, and asparagus in this recipe with shredded poached chicken and shelled peas, or experiment with your own combinations of meat, poultry, or seafood and vegetables.

If the asparagus spears are thick, peel them to within about 2 inches (5 cm) of the tips. Cut the spears on the diagonal into pieces.

Bring a large pot of salted water to a boil. Add the pasta and cook, stirring occasionally to prevent sticking, until al dente, according to package directions. About 4 minutes before the pasta is finished cooking, add the asparagus to the boiling water and cook until crisp-tender, 3–4 minutes. Drain the pasta and asparagus, rinse under cold running water to halt the cooking, and drain again.

In a large bowl, whisk together the garlic, vinegar, mustard, aioli, ½ tsp salt, and a pinch of pepper. Add the oil in a thin stream, whisking constantly until smooth. Add the pasta and asparagus to the dressing and toss to coat evenly.

Add the crabmeat (breaking it up slightly), shrimp, and tarragon to the pasta and toss to combine. Arrange the lettuce on plates, top with the pasta salad, and serve.

22

*Woodsy, aromatic
thyme pairs
beautifully with
the hearty flavors
of winter. Here, it
enhances brown
lentils topped with
crisp bacon, sweet
roasted carrots and
sautéed onions,
and earthy kale.*

LENTIL & KALE SALAD WITH BACON

serves 6

6 small carrots, peeled and finely chopped

4 Tbsp (2 fl oz/60 ml) extra-virgin olive oil

Salt and freshly ground pepper

1 large red onion, thinly sliced

1 large bunch kale, stemmed and thinly sliced crosswise

4 large cloves garlic

10 fresh thyme sprigs

1 cup (7 oz/220 g) brown lentils, picked over and rinsed

4 cups (32 fl oz/1 l) chicken broth

6 slices bacon

1 tsp sherry vinegar

Preheat the oven to 400°F (200°C). Line a rimmed baking sheet with foil. Put the carrots on the prepared sheet, drizzle with 2 Tbsp of the oil, sprinkle with ¾ tsp salt and ¼ tsp pepper, and toss to coat evenly. Spread the carrots in a single layer and roast until tender, about 15 minutes, stirring once or twice. Let cool to room temperature.

Meanwhile, in a nonstick frying pan, warm the remaining 2 Tbsp oil over medium heat. Add the onion, ¼ tsp salt, and several grindings of pepper and sauté until the onion is soft and lightly caramelized, about 15 minutes. Set aside.

Bring a saucepan two-thirds full of water to a boil over high heat. Add 1 Tbsp salt and the sliced kale and cook until tender, about 6 minutes. Drain and set the saucepan aside.

Place the garlic and thyme on a square of cheesecloth, bring the corners together, and secure with kitchen string. In the same saucepan you used to cook the kale, combine the lentils, broth, ½ tsp salt, ¼ tsp pepper, and the cheesecloth sachet and bring to a boil over high heat. Reduce the heat to medium and simmer, uncovered, until the lentils are tender but not mushy, 15–20 minutes. ⟫

While the lentils are cooking, in a large frying pan, cook the bacon over medium heat, turning once, until crisp and browned, about 7 minutes. Transfer to paper towels to drain. Let cool, and then coarsely chop.

Drain the lentils, discard the sachet, and return the lentils to the saucepan. Stir in the kale, vinegar, and ½ tsp salt. Taste and adjust the seasonings. Transfer the lentil mixture to a serving bowl. Top with the sautéed onion, roasted carrots, and bacon, and serve.

23

*Slaws come in many
guises, from creamy
cabbage based to
vinegary zucchini,
and are usually
served as side dishes,
but they also make
excellent toppings
and fillings. Try this
one alongside or
stuffed into fried-
oyster sandwiches,
hamburgers, hot
dogs, or even a
grilled cheese
sandwich.*

FENNEL & CELERY ROOT SLAW

serves 4

1 fennel bulb

1 small celery root (about ¾ lb/375 g), peeled

2 Tbsp extra-virgin olive oil

2 tsp fresh lemon juice

½ tsp red wine vinegar

Salt and freshly ground pepper

2 Tbsp minced fresh flat-leaf parsley

1½ Tbsp minced red onion

½ tsp Dijon mustard

Cut the stalks off the fennel bulb and discard, reserving some of the feathery fronds for garnish. Remove and discard any tough, discolored outer layers. Cut the bulb lengthwise into slices ¼ inch (6 mm) thick, then cut the slices lengthwise again ¼ inch (6 mm) thick. Cut the celery root crosswise into slices ¼ inch (6 mm) thick, then cut the slices lengthwise again ¼ inch (6 mm) thick.

In a bowl, whisk together the oil, lemon juice, vinegar, ½ tsp salt, ¼ tsp pepper, the parsley, onion, and mustard until the vinaigrette is well blended. Add the fennel and celery root and stir to coat well. Cover and refrigerate for at least 1 hour or up to 6 hours before serving.

Transfer the slaw to a serving bowl, garnish with the reserved fennel fronds, and serve.

24

GRILLED CHICKEN CAESAR SALAD

serves 4

FOR THE CAESAR DRESSING

1 large egg (see note) or 1 Tbsp mayonnaise

2 cloves garlic, minced

1–3 anchovy fillets, finely chopped (optional)

2 tsp Dijon mustard

Juice of 1 lemon

1 tsp Worcestershire sauce

1 tsp red wine vinegar

4 Tbsp (2 fl oz/60 ml) extra-virgin olive oil

Salt and freshly ground pepper

1¼ lb (625 g) skinless, boneless chicken breast halves, pounded lightly to an even thickness

Olive oil, for brushing

3 romaine lettuce hearts

Parmesan cheese for shaving

Pounding the chicken breasts lightly before cooking helps them cook more evenly. Place each breast between two sheets of wax paper or plastic wrap and pound gently with a meat mallet to an even thickness. Repeat with the remaining breasts.

To make the dressing, in a blender, combine the egg or mayonnaise, garlic, anchovies to taste (if using), mustard, lemon juice, Worcestershire sauce, vinegar, extra-virgin olive oil, ½ tsp salt, and a generous grinding of pepper. Purée until smooth, and set aside.

Prepare a charcoal or gas grill for direct-heat cooking over high heat. Alternatively, preheat a stove-top grill pan over high heat. Brush both sides of the chicken breasts with oil and season generously with salt and pepper. Place the chicken on the grill rack or in the grill pan and cook, turning once, until opaque throughout, 4–5 minutes per side. Transfer to a cutting board and let stand for 5–7 minutes. Cut on the diagonal into slices.

Meanwhile, in a large bowl, combine the lettuce and dressing and toss to coat evenly. Arrange the lettuce on individual plates and top with the chicken slices. Using a vegetable peeler, shave the cheese over each salad and serve.

Note: Raw egg can carry salmonella. The risks involved in salmonella poisoning are greatest for children, the elderly, pregnant women, and anyone with a compromised immune system.

25

BABY SPINACH WITH GINGER-GLAZED SCALLOPS

serves 4

FOR THE CITRUS VINAIGRETTE

1 Tbsp minced shallot

½ cup (4 fl oz/125 ml) fresh grapefruit juice

1½ Tbsp fresh lime juice

1½ tsp fresh lemon juice

1½ tsp grapeseed oil

Salt

2½ Tbsp soy sauce

1½ Tbsp peeled and grated fresh ginger

1½ tsp honey

½ tsp Dijon mustard

¾ lb (375 g) baby spinach leaves

8 sea scallops, tough muscles removed

2½ tsp grapeseed oil

Grapefruit and scallops are excellent partners. Play up this affinity by adding a few segments of carefully peeled grapefruit to each plate. For a more pronounced ginger flavor, pound the ginger in a mortar, or crush it as you would a garlic clove with the flat side of a chef's knife.

To make the vinaigrette, in a small saucepan, combine the minced shallot and the grapefruit juice and let stand for about 10 minutes. Add the lime and lemon juices and place the pan over medium-high heat. Bring to a boil and cook until the liquid is reduced slightly, to about ½ cup (4 fl oz/125 ml), 1–2 minutes. Remove and whisk in the 1½ tsp oil in a thin stream until well blended. Stir in ¼ tsp salt and set aside.

In a small bowl or cup, stir together the soy sauce, ginger, honey, and mustard and set aside.

Just before beginning to cook the scallops, put the spinach in a bowl and pour the vinaigrette over it. Toss well. Divide the dressed spinach among individual plates.

Pat the scallops dry. In a frying pan large enough to hold all the scallops in a single layer, warm the 2½ tsp oil over medium-high heat. When it is hot, add the scallops and sear, turning once, until golden, about 30 seconds on each side. Add the soy sauce mixture, reduce the heat to low, and turn the scallops in the sauce for about 45 seconds. They will become a deep mahogany brown.

Divide the scallops among the plates, placing them on the spinach. Drizzle with any sauce remaining in the pan and serve.

26

COUSCOUS SALAD WITH DRIED FRUIT & PINE NUTS

serves 4

½ cup (3 oz/90 g) pine nuts

⅛ tsp saffron threads

1½ Tbsp extra-virgin olive oil

1½ cups (9 oz/280 g) instant whole-wheat couscous

⅓ cup (2 oz/60 g) thinly slivered dried apricots

¼ cup (1½ oz/45 g) golden raisins

Salt and freshly ground pepper

¼ tsp ground cinnamon

½ cup (¾ oz/20 g) chopped fresh mint leaves

1 tsp grated orange zest

¼ cup (2 fl oz/60 ml) fresh orange juice

¼ cup (2 fl oz/60 ml) fresh lemon juice

Tangy citrus, dried fruit, and toasted pine nuts flavor this savory Middle Eastern salad. It s hearty enough for a main course, and it also makes a delicious side dish to accompany simple broiled fish or roast chicken. You can substitute regular couscous, Israeli couscous, or fregola, a Sardinian pasta similar to Israeli couscous, for the whole-wheat couscous.

In a small frying pan, toast the pine nuts over medium-low heat, stirring, until starting to brown, 3–4 minutes. Pour onto a plate to cool. In the same frying pan, shake the saffron threads over medium heat until fragrant and a shade darker, about 1 minute. Transfer to a small bowl and, when cool, crumble with your fingertips.

In a large heatproof bowl, drizzle the oil over the couscous and mix well to coat. Scatter the couscous with the apricots and raisins.

In a small saucepan, bring 2 cups (16 fl oz/500 ml) water to a boil. Stir in the saffron, ½ tsp salt, and the cinnamon and pour over the couscous. Cover the bowl tightly with foil and let stand until the couscous is tender and the liquid is absorbed, about 5 minutes.

Remove the foil and fluff the couscous grains well with a fork. Stir in the mint, pine nuts, orange zest, orange juice, and lemon juice. Season with pepper and additional salt and serve.

27

BRUSSELS SPROUT & ARUGULA SALAD WITH WALNUTS

serves 4

1 lb (500 g) Brussels sprouts, trimmed

½ cup (2 oz/60 g) chopped walnuts

1½ Tbsp walnut oil

1 Tbsp cider vinegar

Salt and freshly ground pepper

1 cup (1 oz/30 g) arugula leaves

Walnut oil has a rather short shelf life, only about 6–8 months. To forestall spoilage, check the date of the pressing on the label to make sure it's fairly fresh, and store the oil in the refrigerator.

Using a mandoline, thinly shave the Brussels sprouts lengthwise.

In a small frying pan, toast the walnuts over medium-low heat, stirring, until starting to brown, about 5 minutes. Let cool.

Put the shaved Brussels sprouts in a bowl. Add the walnut oil, vinegar, and season to tate with salt and pepper. Toss to mix.

Divide the arugula among individual plates. Spoon the Brussels sprouts and their juices over the arugula, garnish with the walnuts, and serve.

28

CARROT & MEDJOOL DATE SALAD WITH GORGONZOLA

serves 4

¼ cup Gorgonzola or other mild blue cheese, crumbled

⅓ cup (3 fl oz/80 ml) extra-virgin olive oil

¼ cup (2 fl oz/60 ml) champagne vinegar

Freshly ground pepper

1 lb (500 g) carrots, peeled and grated

8 Medjool dates, pitted and diced

Dandelion leaves or arugula for garnish

Here, the sharp, salty character of Gorgonzola and the natural sweetness of carrots and dates come together to create an explosion of perfectly suited flavors. Medjool dates are exceptionally large and sweet, but another date variety, such as Deglet Noor or Bahri, can be substituted.

In a large bowl, combine the cheese, oil, vinegar, and ½ tsp pepper. Using a fork, mash the cheese and then whisk until the dressing is smooth and well blended. Add the carrots and dates and stir to coat well.

Transfer the salad to a serving bowl or individual plates. Garnish with the dandelion leaves and serve right away.

With signs of the frost waning, ease into spring with young greens such as dandelion, mâche, fava leaves, and baby arugula and spinach. Try them in simple, fresh combinations, topped with tangy cheese, toasted nuts, or a tender salmon fillet served cold or warm. Or, lightly dress spring greens, like pea shoots and watercress, with lemon juice, herbs, and shallots. Seasonal favorites like peas, haricots verts, new potatoes, and asparagus make perfect toppings.

march

1

Plan to serve this salad as soon as you're done tossing it, as the artichokes will start turning brown fast. Artichokes are notoriously hard to pair with wine, but a light pinot noir would match nicely with the blue cheese.

SHAVED ARTICHOKE & BLUE CHEESE SALAD

serves 4

⅓ cup (2 oz/60 g) almonds

1 or 2 lemons

8 small to medium artichokes

4 Tbsp (2 fl oz/60 ml) extra-virgin olive oil

¼ cup (½ oz/15 g) frisée

Salt and freshly ground pepper

2 Tbsp crumbled blue cheese

In a small frying pan, toast the almonds over medium-low heat, stirring, until fragrant and starting to brown, about 5 minutes. Pour onto a plate to cool, chop coarsely, and set aside.

Squeeze the juice of 1 lemon half into a large bowl of cold water. Snap off the tough outer leaves of each artichoke until you reach the pale green inner leaves. Trim the stem flush with the base and trim away the dark green portions from the base. Cut off the top one-third of the artichokes, removing the pointed tips. Halve each artichoke lengthwise and, using a small spoon, remove the fuzzy choke. As each artichoke is trimmed, immerse it in the lemon water.

Using a mandoline or a very sharp knife, slice the artichokes thinly lengthwise. Put in a bowl, drizzle with 2 Tbsp of the olive oil, and toss well. Add the frisée, season with salt and pepper, drizzle with the remaining 2 Tbsp olive oil, and squeeze in the juice from 1 lemon half. Toss gently and season with salt and with more lemon juice, if needed. Scatter with the cheese and almonds and serve.

2

In this perfect spring salad, salmon and its pan juices become a topping for a tangle of sprightly greens dressed with a tangy lemon vinaigrette. Pea shoots, the clippings from young pea plants, have a mild pealike flavor. Look for them at well-stocked grocery stores, farmers' markets, or Asian markets—or substitute additional watercress.

PAN-SEARED SALMON WITH PEA SHOOTS & WATERCRESS

serves 8

FOR THE DRESSING

⅓ cup (3 fl oz/80 ml) fresh Meyer lemon or regular lemon juice

3 shallots, minced

Salt and freshly ground pepper

⅔ cup (5 fl oz/160 ml) extra-virgin olive oil

8 salmon fillets, each about ⅓ lb (155 g) and ½ inch (12 mm) thick, pin bones removed

½ cup (4 fl oz/125 ml) dry white wine

8 Tbsp (4 fl oz/125 ml) fresh lemon juice

5 cups (5 oz/155 g) watercress leaves

5 cups (5 oz/155 g) pea shoots

To make the dressing, in a large bowl, combine the lemon juice, shallots, ½ tsp salt, and ½ tsp pepper. Whisk until the salt dissolves, then let stand for 30 minutes to allow the shallot flavor to mellow. Add the oil in a thin stream, whisking constantly until the dressing is well blended.

Meanwhile, to prepare the salmon, sprinkle 1½ tsp salt in a wide, heavy frying pan and place over medium-high heat until nearly smoking. Add the salmon fillets and sear for 2 minutes on one side. Turn and sear for 1 minute on the second side. Sprinkle with 1 tsp pepper. Reduce the heat to low, then pour in the white wine and 2 Tbsp of the lemon juice. Cover and cook until the juices are nearly absorbed and the fish is halfway cooked, about 3 minutes. Uncover and pour in 2 more Tbsp of the lemon juice and 3 Tbsp water. Re-cover and cook just until the fish flakes easily with a fork, about 3 minutes. Most of the pan juices will have been absorbed.

Whisk the dressing to recombine. Add the watercress and pea shoots to the dressing and toss gently to coat, then divide the greens among individual plates. Place a salmon fillet on each mound of greens.

Raise the heat under the frying pan to high, add the remaining 4 Tbsp (2 fl oz/60 ml) lemon juice and 1 Tbsp water, and stir to scrape up any browned bits on the pan bottom. Pour the pan juices evenly over the fish and serve.

SPRING RICE SALAD WITH DILL-LEMON DRESSING

serves 6–8

1 cup (7 oz/220 g) long-grain white rice or basmati rice

2½ cups (20 fl oz/625 ml) vegetable broth or water

Salt and freshly ground pepper

1 large fennel bulb, trimmed and cut lengthwise into slices ¼ inch (6 mm) thick

½ lb (250 g) sugar snap peas or snow peas, trimmed

½ lb (250 g) thin asparagus, tough ends trimmed and spears cut into 1-inch (2.5-cm) lengths

FOR THE DILL-LEMON DRESSING

4 Tbsp (2 fl oz/60 ml) fresh lemon juice

4 Tbsp (⅓ oz/10 g) chopped fresh dill

1 clove garlic, minced

½ cup (4 fl oz/125 ml) extra-virgin olive oil

Lemon wedges for garnish

Fresh dill sprigs for garnish

This light and colorful salad makes a terrific first course. If any of the vegetables are unavailable in the market, you can substitute green beans, zucchini, broccoli, or even fresh peas with equally delicious results.

If using basmati rice, rinse well and drain.

In a heavy saucepan, combine the broth and ½ tsp salt and bring to a boil. Slowly add the rice, reduce the heat to low, cover, and cook for 20 minutes. After 20 minutes, uncover and check to see if the rice is tender and the water is absorbed. If not, re-cover and cook for a few minutes until the rice is done. Remove from the heat, fluff the grains with a fork, and transfer to a bowl to cool.

Bring a saucepan three-fourths full of salted water to a boil. Add the fennel and the peas and blanch for 2 minutes. Using a slotted spoon, transfer the vegetables to a bowl and let cool. Add the asparagus to the same water and cook just until tender, 3–4 minutes. Drain and let cool with the other vegetables.

To make the dressing, in a large bowl, whisk together the lemon juice, dill, garlic, and salt and pepper to taste. Add the oil in a thin stream, whisking constantly until the dressing is smooth. Add the cooled rice and vegetables and toss together. Garnish with lemon wedges and dill sprigs and serve.

FAVA GREENS WITH CHICKEN, PECANS & KUMQUATS

serves 4

30 kumquats (½–¾ lb/250–375 g)

¼ cup (2 fl oz/60 ml) blood orange–infused olive oil or extra-virgin olive oil

1 Tbsp honey

½ tsp ground ginger

2 Tbsp champagne vinegar

4 cups (4 oz/125 g) young fava leaves or baby spinach leaves, loosely packed

½ cup (2 oz/60 g) pecans

2 cups (¾ lb/375 g) chopped roasted chicken meat

In early spring, start checking your local farmers' market for fava greens, which are the leaves from the fava bean plant. They are a boon to fava bean lovers who often avoid the legume for its highly demanding prep. They taste milder than the beans and are delicious in salads, contributing a touch of sweetness and acidity.

Cut 20 of the kumquats crosswise into thin slices, removing any seeds as you go. Set aside and quarter the remaining kumquats lengthwise.

In a serving bowl, combine the oil and honey and whisk until the honey dissolves. Stir in the ginger and vinegar. Add the fava leaves, half the pecans, and the chicken and toss to combine. Divide among individual plates. Garnish with the remaining pecans and the sliced and quartered kumquats and serve.

5

CRISPY SWEETBREAD, RADISH & ARUGULA SALAD

serves 4–6

This salad is full of straightforward flavors. Radishes and arugula share a peppery profile, and the unique taste of warm breaded sweetbreads heightens the other textures and flavors in the salad. The sweetbreads are time-consuming to prepare but are well worth the effort. They can be readied a day ahead and refrigerated until it's time to bread and fry them.

2½–3 lb (1.25–1.5 kg) sweetbreads

¾ cup (6 fl oz/180 ml) fresh lemon juice or distilled white vinegar, plus 2 Tbsp

FOR THE DRESSING

¼ cup (2 fl oz/60 ml) fresh lemon juice

¼ cup (2 fl oz/60 ml) extra-virgin olive oil

Salt and freshly ground pepper

½ tsp sweet paprika

2 large eggs

⅓ cup (1 oz/20 g) fine fresh bread crumbs

½ tsp dried thyme

Salt and freshly ground pepper

¼ cup (2 fl oz/60 ml) grapeseed or safflower oil

3 cups (3 oz/90 g) baby arugula

2 bunches radishes, thinly sliced

Put the sweetbreads in a large bowl and add cold water to cover along with ¼ cup (2 fl oz/60 ml) of the lemon juice. Let soak for about 1 hour. Drain. Using your fingers, separate the lobes and remove the filmy white filaments. Repeat the soaking process twice, using fresh water and lemon juice each time. After the last soaking, drain the sweetbreads and rinse under cold running water.

Put the sweetbreads in a large saucepan and add cold water to cover along with the 2 Tbsp lemon juice. Bring almost to a boil over medium-high heat, reduce the heat to medium-low, and poach for 15 minutes, until opaque and somewhat firm to the touch. Drain and let cool to room temperature. The sweetbreads are now ready for breading and frying, or can be stored in an airtight container in the refrigerator for up to 36 hours.

To make the dressing, in a small bowl, whisk together the lemon juice, olive oil, ½ tsp salt, 1 tsp pepper, and the paprika until the dressing is well blended. Taste and adjust the seasonings. ⤜

Cut the sweetbreads into bite-sized pieces. In a small, shallow bowl, whisk the eggs until blended. In a second small, shallow bowl, stir together the bread crumbs, thyme, ½ tsp salt, and 2 tsp pepper.

Line a baking sheet with paper towels. In a frying pan, warm the grapeseed oil over high heat until it just begins to smoke. Reduce the heat to medium. Dip the sweetbread pieces, a few at a time, into the eggs, allowing the excess to drip off, and then roll in the bread crumb mixture. Add the sweetbreads to the pan and cook, turning once, until golden brown, 1–2 minutes per side. Transfer to the paper towel–lined baking sheet. Repeat with the remaining sweetbreads.

In a large bowl, combine the arugula and radishes. Add the warm sweetbreads and the dressing and toss well. Serve right away.

6

BUTTER LETTUCE WITH DIJON VINAIGRETTE

serves 4–6

At bistros in France, you'll often find a simple green salad like this one on the menu. Usually the butter lettuce leaves are served atop several spoonfuls of thick, mustard-laced vinaigrette in an individual bowl. It's the perfect simple side salad for any time of year.

1 large or 2 medium heads butter lettuce

2 Tbsp red wine vinegar

2 tsp Dijon mustard

Salt

¼ cup (2 fl oz/60 ml) extra-virgin olive oil

Separate the heads of lettuce into individual leaves. Tear the larger leaves into several pieces; keep the medium and small leaves whole. You should have 4–5 cups (4–5 oz/125–155 g). Rinse the leaves, spin dry, and set aside.

In a large bowl, whisk together the vinegar, mustard, and ½ tsp salt. Add the oil in a thin stream, whisking constantly until the mixture is thick. Add the lettuce leaves and toss well to coat. Divide the salad among individual plates and serve.

7

This salad of seared beef with spicy watercress and paper-thin slices of onion is popular in both Cambodia and Vietnam. Fresh, peppery watercress and marinated raw onions are tossed with a lime vinaigrette, and the warm beef and pan juices are poured over the salad for an effect that is both cooling and crisp, savory and sweet.

WARM BEEF & WATERCRESS SALAD

serves 4–6

FOR THE MARINADE

1 Tbsp peanut oil

3 cloves garlic, minced

1 Tbsp Asian fish sauce

½ tsp sugar

Freshly ground pepper

1 lb (500 g) beef tenderloin, cut into 1-inch (2.5-cm) cubes

FOR THE SAUCE

2 Tbsp fresh lime juice

1 Tbsp rice vinegar

1 Tbsp light soy sauce

1 Tbsp Asian fish sauce

1 tsp sugar

½ small yellow onion, sliced paper-thin

1 Tbsp peanut oil

2 green onions, including tender green parts, thinly sliced on the diagonal

3 cloves garlic, minced

2 cups (2 oz/60 g) loosely packed watercress, tough stems removed

To make the marinade, in a large bowl, combine the oil, garlic, fish sauce, sugar, and ⅛ tsp pepper and stir to mix well. Add the beef and stir to coat thoroughly. Cover and refrigerate for at least 2 hours or overnight.

To make the sauce, in a small bowl, whisk together the lime juice, vinegar, soy sauce, fish sauce, sugar, and ⅛ tsp pepper. Put the onion slices in a small bowl and drizzle with 1 Tbsp of the sauce. Set the onions and the remaining sauce aside.

In a large wok or frying pan, warm the oil over high heat. Add the beef and stir-fry until browned, 4–5 minutes. Add the green onions and garlic and stir-fry just until fragrant, a few seconds. Remove the pan from the heat, pour in the remaining sauce, and toss to mix.

To serve, toss the watercress with the marinated sliced onions and mound on a platter. Using a slotted spoon, spoon the beef over the greens, drizzle the pan juices over the beef, and serve.

8

Carrots and jicama, both of them crunchy and sweet, are a winning combination in this tangy, low-calorie salad. Serve as an accompaniment to a smoked turkey sandwich, or grilled chicken, shrimp, or fish.

CARROT & JICAMA SALAD WITH LIME VINAIGRETTE

serves 4–6

2 tsp ground cumin

3 Tbsp fresh lime juice

1 Tbsp seeded and minced jalapeño chile

1 tsp minced garlic

Salt

2 Tbsp grapeseed oil

1 large or 2 medium jicamas, about ¾ lb (375 g)

3 carrots (about 10 oz/315 g total weight), peeled

¼ cup (⅓ oz/10 g) minced fresh cilantro

In a small frying pan over medium-low heat, warm the cumin just until fragrant, about 20 seconds. Transfer to a small bowl. Add the lime juice, jalapeño, garlic, and ½ tsp salt and whisk. Add the oil in a thin stream, whisking constantly until the vinaigrette is smooth. Set aside.

Using a sharp knife, trim the stem and root ends from the jicama(s), then cut into 4 or 6 manageable wedges. Cut and lift up a small piece of the brown skin near the stem end and pull down to remove. Use a vegetable peeler to remove any stubborn remnants of skin and the tough layer underneath.

Using a food processor fitted with the shredding disk or the largest holes of a box grater, shred the carrots and jicama(s). In a large bowl, combine the carrots, jicama(s), and cilantro. Pour the vinaigrette over the vegetables and toss gently to mix. Divide the salad among individual plates and serve.

9

FARRO SALAD WITH SUGAR SNAPS, SPRING PEAS & MEYER LEMON

serves 6–8

Welcome spring with this eye-catching salad that combines garden-fresh English and sugar snap peas with Italian farro, a hearty ancient grain related to wheat. Bits of diced Meyer lemon contribute a bright, tangy flavor. To blanch the vegetables, add them to a pot of boiling salted water for 1 minute, then transfer to a bowl of ice water to stop the cooking, drain well, and pat dry with paper towels.

Salt and freshly ground pepper

½ lb (250 g) sugar snap peas, trimmed

1 cup (5 oz/155 g) shelled English peas

7 Tbsp (3½ fl oz/110 ml) extra-virgin olive oil

2 cups (12 oz/375 g) farro

2 Meyer lemons

3 Tbsp coarsely chopped fresh dill

Crumbled feta cheese for serving (optional)

Bring a large saucepan three-fourths full of salted water to a boil over high heat. Meanwhile, prepare a large bowl of ice water. Add the sugar snap peas to the boiling water and blanch for 1 minute. Using a strainer, scoop out the snap peas and immerse them in the ice water. Scoop them out with the strainer.

Using the same boiling water, blanch the English peas for 1 minute. Drain the peas and immerse them in the ice water, then drain again. Cut the snap peas in half on the diagonal. Set aside.

In a saucepan, warm 1 Tbsp of the oil over medium-high heat. Add the farro and cook, stirring, until fragrant, 2–3 minutes. Add 3½ cups (28 fl oz/875 ml) water and bring to a boil. Season with salt, reduce the heat to low, cover, and simmer until the farro is tender, about 18 minutes. Drain through a fine-mesh sieve, then spread the farro out on a baking sheet and let cool.

Meanwhile, zest the lemons and set the zest aside. Working over a bowl, segment the lemons, reserving the juice. Squeeze the juice from the peels and the remaining pulp and strain the juice. Cut the lemon segments into small pieces.

In a small bowl, whisk together 3 Tbsp of the lemon juice and the dill. Add the remaining 6 Tbsp (3 fl oz/90 ml) oil in a thin stream, whisking constantly until the vinaigrette is well blended. ⇥

In a large bowl, toss together the farro, sugar snap peas, English peas, lemon segments, lemon zest, and vinaigrette. Season with salt and pepper. Sprinkle with cheese, if using, and serve.

10

PASTA SALAD WITH ROASTED BROCCOLI & ANCHOVIES

serves 4–6

Orecchiette with broccoli rabe and anchovies is a classic southern Italian pasta dish. Here, similar ingredients have been tapped to create a salad. To emphasize their distinctive flavor, the anchovies are chopped rather than used in a sauce. Roasting the broccoli brings out its natural sweetness, which creates a good counterpoint to the salty fish.

4 cups (8 oz/250 g) broccoli florets (from about 4 heads)

¼ cup (2 fl oz/60 ml) extra-virgin olive oil, plus 2 Tbsp

Salt and freshly ground black pepper

¾ lb (375 g) orecchiette pasta

8 olive oil–packed anchovy fillets, chopped

½ tsp red pepper flakes

2 Tbsp red wine vinegar

1 tsp fresh lemon juice

Place the broccoli in a single layer on a baking sheet. Drizzle with the 2 Tbsp oil, sprinkle with ½ tsp salt, and toss to coat well. Roast, turning once, until crispy and golden on the edges, 10–12 minutes. Let cool.

Bring a large pot of water to a boil over medium-high heat. Add 1 tsp salt and the pasta, stir well, and cook according to the package directions until the pasta is al dente, about 14 minutes. Drain and transfer to a bowl.

Add the ¼ cup (2 fl oz/60 ml) oil, the anchovies, red pepper flakes, vinegar, lemon juice, ½ tsp salt, and ¼ tsp black pepper to the pasta and stir to coat well. Let stand for 15 minutes to blend the flavors. Taste and adjust the seasonings. Gently stir in the broccoli and transfer the salad to a platter. Serve warm or at room temperature.

11

SPRING SALAD WITH RADISHES & FRESH HERBS

serves 4-6

1 loaf (½ lb/250 g) sweet batard, crust removed, bread torn into 1-inch (2.5-cm) pieces

¾ cup (6 fl oz/180 ml) extra-virgin olive oil, plus 2 Tbsp

Salt and freshly ground pepper

¼ cup (2 fl oz/60 ml) champagne vinegar

1½ tsp fresh lemon juice

1½ tsp Dijon mustard

8 cups (10 oz) mesclun

1 cup (1 oz/30 g) fresh herbs such as parsley and chervil leaves, dill fronds, snipped chives, and torn basil leaves

5 radishes, very thinly sliced

Shaved ricotta salata cheese for serving

Spring-fresh mesclun greens, crunchy radishes, and a brightly flavored vinaigrette come together in this simple toss-and-serve salad you'll be craving all season long. A scattering of croutons and of shaved ricotta salata adds texture and a hint of salt to the finished salad.

Preheat the oven to 350°F (180°C).

In a large bowl, toss the bread pieces with the 2 Tbsp oil and season with salt and pepper. Spread the pieces on a baking sheet and bake until golden brown and crisp, 12–15 minutes. Let cool.

In a small bowl, whisk together the vinegar, lemon juice, and mustard. Add the ¾ cup (6 fl oz/180 ml) oil in a thin stream, whisking constantly until the vinaigrette is well blended. Season with salt and pepper.

In a large bowl, toss together the mesclun, herbs, and radishes with enough vinaigrette to lightly coat. Top with the croutons and cheese and serve right away.

12

SEARED SCALLOP, ORANGE & RED ONION SALAD

serves 4

½ red onion, thinly sliced

1½ Tbsp rice vinegar

3 oranges

½ cup (2½ oz/75 g) pitted mild green olives

2 Tbsp extra-virgin olive oil

1 lb (500 g) sea scallops, tough muscles removed

Salt and freshly ground pepper

2 Tbsp coarsely chopped fresh mint leaves

This salad makes a nice main-course lunch dish or a light supper, pairing nicely with a dry Riesling or a light-bodied red wine such as a pinot noir or Chianti.

Rinse the onion slices under cold running water, then drain. In a bowl, combine them with the rice vinegar and set aside.

Grate the zest of 1 orange to yield 1 tsp zest, and reserve. Cut a slice off the top and bottom of each orange. Stand each upright and, following the contour of the fruit, cut away all the peel and white pith. Slice the oranges in half lengthwise, then slice crosswise into thin half-rounds. In a bowl, combine the orange slices with the olives, reserved zest, and 1 Tbsp of the olive oil.

Pat the scallops dry and season them lightly with salt and pepper. In a large nonstick frying pan, warm the remaining 1 Tbsp oil over medium-high heat. Add the scallops and cook, turning once, until browned on both sides and opaque in the center, 4–5 minutes total. Take care not to overcook the scallops, as they go quickly from perfectly tender to overcooked and tough.

Add the onion (including the vinegar), the mint, a pinch of salt, and a few grindings of pepper to the orange mixture and mix gently. Divide the orange salad among dinner plates, top with the warm scallops, and serve.

13

DANDELION GREENS WITH CROUTONS & ANCHOVY DRESSING

serves 4

Here is a salad for anyone who appreciates assertive flavors. Salty, oil-rich anchovies are mashed with garlic and olive oil to form a thick dressing that complements sturdy, slightly bitter dandelion greens. Look for young, tender dandelion greens and be sure to trim away any tough stems.

8 slices baguette

½ cup (4 fl oz/125 ml) extra-virgin olive oil, plus 1 Tbsp

6 olive oil–packed anchovy fillets

2 cloves garlic, minced

Freshly ground pepper

1 bunch dandelion leaves

Preheat the oven to 400°F (200°C).

Brush the baguette slices on both sides with the 1 Tbsp oil and place on a baking sheet. Bake until golden on the bottom, about 6 minutes, then turn and bake until golden on the other side, 4–5 minutes. Let cool.

In a bowl, mash together the anchovies and garlic with the back of a fork or wooden spoon. Add the ½ cup (4 fl oz/125 ml) oil in a thin stream, whisking constantly until the dressing is well blended, then whisk in ½ tsp pepper. Set aside.

Trim the tough stems from the dandelion leaves. Coarsely chop the large leaves, leaving any small ones whole. Add to the bowl with the dressing and toss to coat. Divide the salad among individual plates and serve with the croutons.

14

LENTIL & PARSLEY SALAD WITH DUCK BREAST

serves 4

A satisfying main-course salad, this dish has it all, nutritionally speaking: protein from the duck, calcium and iron from the lentils, and vitamins A and C from the frisée.

1½ cups (10½ oz/330 g) green French (du Puy) lentils, picked over and rinsed

2 fresh bay leaves, or 1 dried bay leaf

Salt and freshly ground pepper

½ tsp dried thyme

½ tsp ground juniper berries

1 duck breast, about ¾ lb (375 g)

1 Tbsp fresh lemon juice

3 Tbsp extra-virgin olive oil

¼ cup (⅓ oz/10 g) chopped fresh flat-leaf parsley, plus 1 Tbsp

2 small heads frisée, torn pale inner leaves only

Put the lentils in a saucepan with 5 cups (40 fl oz/1.25 l) water, the bay leaves, and 1 tsp salt. Bring to a boil, reduce the heat to low, and simmer, uncovered, until tender, 20–30 minutes. Drain and let cool. Discard the bay leaves.

Preheat the oven to 450°F (230°C). Rub and press the thyme, juniper, ¼ tsp salt, and ¼ tsp pepper into the duck breast. Place on a baking sheet, skin side up. Roast until the skin is crisp but the meat is still pink at the center, 20–25 minutes. Let cool slightly, remove the skin, and cut the breast crosswise on the diagonal into very thin slices; set aside.

In a bowl, whisk together the lemon juice and ¼ tsp each salt and pepper. Add the oil in a thin stream, whisking constantly until the dressing is smooth. Mix in the ¼ cup parsley and the lentils; taste and adjust the seasonings.

Divide the frisée among individual plates and top with the lentils. Arrange the sliced duck over the lentils, garnish with the 1 Tbsp parsley, and serve.

15

WHITE ANCHOVY, PARMESAN & GRILLED BREAD SALAD

serves 4

1 small fennel bulb, trimmed and shaved crosswise into thin slices

1 carrot, shaved crosswise into thin slices

2 celery ribs, shaved crosswise into thin slices

½ cup (½ oz/14 g) loosely packed fresh flat-leaf parsley leaves

¼ cup (¾ oz/20 g) chopped green onion tops

Juice of 1 lemon

2 tsp champagne vinegar or white wine vinegar

3 Tbsp extra-virgin olive oil, plus more for brushing

Salt and freshly ground pepper

4 slices country-style bread (about 1 inch/2.5 cm thick)

1 cup (4 oz/120 g) Parmesan cheese shavings

12–16 olive oil–packed white anchovy fillets

This salad is finished with white anchovies and shaved Parmigiano-Reggiano cheese, pungent flavors that pair well with a crisp Alsatian Riesling. For the best result, look for a country loaf with an open crumb and a thick, crisp crust. Serve the salad as a first course or a light lunch.

In a large bowl, combine the fennel, carrot, celery, ¼ cup (¼ oz/7 g) of the parsley, the green onions, lemon juice, vinegar, and oil. Season with salt and pepper and stir until blended. Set aside.

Prepare a charcoal or gas grill for direct-heat cooking over medium-high heat. Alternatively, preheat a stove-top grill pan over medium-high heat.

Brush both sides of the bread slices with oil and season with salt and pepper. Place the bread on the grill rack or in the grill pan and cook, turning once, until crispy and golden, 2–3 minutes per side. Transfer to a cutting board and let cool slightly, then cut the bread into ½- to ¾-inch (12-mm–2-cm) cubes.

Add the bread to the bowl with the vegetable mixture along with ½ cup (2 oz/60 g) of the cheese. Let stand, stirring occasionally, for 12–15 minutes. Taste and adjust the seasonings.

Divide the salad among individual bowls and garnish with the anchovies. Sprinkle with the remaining ¼ cup (¼ oz/7 g) parsley and ½ cup (2 oz/60 g) cheese and serve.

16

SALAD OF NEW POTATOES, SPRING PEAS & MINT

serves 4

¼ cup (2 fl oz/60 ml) extra-virgin olive oil

¼ cup (2 fl oz/60 ml) raspberry vinegar

Salt

4 Tbsp (⅓ oz/10 g) chopped fresh mint, plus sprigs for garnish

12 small new potatoes such as red rose or Yukon gold (about 1½ lb/750 g total weight)

1 cup (5 oz/155 g) shelled English peas (about 1 lb/500 g unshelled)

½ cup (4 fl oz/125 ml) low-sodium chicken broth

8–12 butter lettuce leaves

Explosive flavors abound in this simple salad. A bouquet of spring mint is combined with raspberry vinegar and olive oil to coat warm new potatoes and peas. More mint, added just before serving, intensifies the vinegar-infused mint of the dressing.

In a small bowl, whisk together the oil, vinegar, ½ tsp salt, and 2 Tbsp of the mint until the vinaigrette is well blended. Set aside.

Put the potatoes in a saucepan and cover with water by 2 inches (5 cm). Bring to a boil over high heat, reduce the heat to medium, and cook until tender when pierced with a knife, about 20 minutes. Drain the potatoes and, when cool enough to handle, peel them, if desired. If the potatoes are quite small, leave them whole; if not, halve or quarter them. Transfer to a large bowl.

Meanwhile, in a small saucepan, combine the peas and broth. Bring to a simmer over medium heat and cook just until the peas are warmed through and bright green, about 1 minute. Do not overcook. Drain and add to the bowl with the potatoes.

Drizzle the vinaigrette over the potato salad and let stand for 10–15 minutes, stirring gently several times.

Line individual plates with the lettuce leaves. Mound the potato salad on the lettuce. Sprinkle with the remaining 2 Tbsp mint, garnish each with a mint sprig, and serve.

17

RADISH, CUCUMBER & FENNEL SALAD

serves 4-6

3 Tbsp champagne vinegar

1 tsp Dijon mustard

½ tsp honey

1 tsp minced fresh chives

1 tsp minced fresh dill

Salt and freshly ground pepper

¼ cup (2 fl oz/60 ml) olive oil

4 radishes, trimmed

2 fennel bulbs, trimmed, halved, and cored

1 English cucumber, ends trimmed

¼ cup (¼ oz/7 g) fresh flat-leaf parsley leaves

You can thinly slice the vegetables for this refreshing spring salad with a sharp chef's knife, but a mandoline will make the task easier and will guarantee uniform slices. For the prettiest result, seek out brightly colored radishes, such as watermelon radishes, at your local farmers' market, though any mildly flavored radishes will work.

In a small bowl, whisk together the vinegar, mustard, honey, chives, and dill, and season with salt and pepper. Add the oil in a thin stream, whisking constantly until the vinaigrette is well blended. Set aside.

Using a mandoline or a sharp knife, thinly slice the radishes. Transfer to a large bowl. Thinly slice the fennel and cucumber and add to the bowl. Add the parsley and toss to combine.

Drizzle the vinaigrette over the salad and toss to coat. Season with salt and pepper and serve right away.

18

CLASSIC SALADE NIÇOISE

serves 6

4 large eggs

1 lb (500 g) haricots verts, stem ends trimmed

1 lb (500 g) new potatoes

4 tomatoes

1 head butter lettuce, leaves separated

1 can (7 oz/220 g) tuna, preferably Italian olive oil–packed

12 anchovy fillets

⅓ cup (2 oz/60 g) Niçoise olives

¼ cup (2 fl oz/60 ml) extra-virgin olive oil

2 Tbsp red wine vinegar

Salt and freshly ground pepper

Although it has many versions, the classic salad of Nice, France, typically includes haricots verts—slender, young green beans—along with boiled potatoes, hard-cooked eggs, and lettuce. The most authentic version calls for canned olive oil–packed tuna, rather than fresh or water-packed tuna, and Niçoise olives.

To hard-cook the eggs, place them in a saucepan just large enough to hold them. Add cold water to cover by 1 inch (2.5 cm) and bring just to a boil over high heat. Remove the pan from the heat and cover. Let stand for 15 minutes. Have ready a bowl of ice water. Drain the eggs, then transfer to the ice water and let cool.

Meanwhile, bring another saucepan of water to a boil over medium-high heat. Add the haricots verts and cook until tender, 3–4 minutes. Using a strainer, scoop out the beans and transfer them to a colander. Rinse under running cold water. Add the potatoes to the boiling water and cook until tender, 5–10 minutes depending on size. Drain and rinse under running cold water until cool enough to handle. Cut the potatoes into halves or quarters.

Cut the tomatoes into quarters. Peel the hard-cooked eggs and cut in half lengthwise. Arrange the lettuce leaves on a large platter. Make small mounds of the haricots verts, potatoes, tomatoes, tuna, and egg halves on and around the lettuce. Scatter the anchovies and olives over the potatoes.

Drizzle the salad with the olive oil and vinegar. Sprinkle with ½ tsp each salt and pepper and serve.

19

ORZO SALAD WITH SHRIMP, FETA & FRESH HERBS

serves 4–6

Tiny, rice-shaped orzo pasta serves as a palette for the honest flavors of fresh herbs and shrimp. Precooked high-quality shrimp make this salad quick to assemble. The cheese adds an extra richness to the finished dish.

Salt and freshly ground pepper

1½ cups (10½ oz/330 g) orzo pasta

¼ cup (⅓ oz/10 g) chopped fresh flat-leaf parsley

3 Tbsp chopped fresh dill

3 Tbsp chopped fresh chives

2 celery ribs, finely chopped

¼ cup (2 fl oz/60 ml) extra-virgin olive oil

1 Tbsp fresh lemon juice, plus more if needed

1 lb (500 g) cooked bay shrimp

2–3 oz (60–90 g) feta cheese, crumbled

In a saucepan, bring 4 cups (32 fl oz/1 l) water to a boil over medium-high heat. Add 1 tsp salt and the orzo and cook according to the package directions. Drain well.

In a large bowl, combine the parsley, dill, chives, celery, and ½ tsp salt. Add the oil, 1 Tbsp lemon juice, and ½ tsp pepper and whisk until the vinaigrette is well blended. Add the orzo and stir to coat well, then stir in the shrimp. Taste and add more lemon juice, if needed.

Transfer the salad to a serving bowl, sprinkle with the cheese, and serve.

20

ASPARAGUS & SMOKED SALMON SALAD WITH TARRAGON CREAM

serves 4

This salad combines two iconic ingredients of spring: asparagus and tarragon. The cream-enriched dressing is kept light and bright by the acidic tang of cider vinegar as well as lemon juice.

FOR THE TARRAGON CREAM

1 cup (8 fl oz/250 ml) heavy cream

2 Tbsp cider vinegar

1 tsp fresh lemon juice

Salt and freshly ground pepper

2 Tbsp minced fresh tarragon

1½ lb (750 g) asparagus, tough ends trimmed

⅓ lb (155 g) smoked salmon, thinly sliced

1½ tsp fresh lemon juice

Fresh tarragon sprigs for garnish

To make the tarragon cream, put the cream in a small bowl, then whisk in the cider vinegar, 1 tsp lemon juice, ¼ tsp each salt and pepper, and the 2 Tbsp tarragon. Set aside. The cream will curdle and thicken within 4–5 minutes.

If the asparagus spears are thick, peel them to within about 2 inches (5 cm) of the tips. Arrange the asparagus in a steamer basket and place over boiling water. (The water should not touch the bottom of the basket.) Cover and steam just until tender to the bite, 3–4 minutes. Transfer the asparagus to a colander and immediately place under cold running water to stop the cooking and preserve the bright green color. Slice the spears on the diagonal about ½ inch (12 mm) thick. Set aside. (At this point, the tarragon cream and asparagus may be chilled before serving, if desired.)

Arrange the salmon on a platter or individual plates. Drizzle evenly with the 1½ tsp lemon juice. Top with the asparagus, and drizzle the tarragon cream over all. Garnish with the tarragon sprigs and serve.

21

Poaching tuna in olive oil is a delicate treatment that renders the fish so silky smooth it melts in your mouth. Baby spinach wilts quickly, so if you opt to replace the spinach with sturdy greens, such as kale or escarole, they will need to be cooked and chopped. If the beans are prepared ahead, let them stand in the broth (refrigerated if overnight) and then reheat them before assembling the salad.

WARM GIGANTE BEAN & SPINACH SALAD WITH POACHED TUNA

serves 4

1½ cups (10½ oz/330 g) dried Gigante beans such as Royal Corona, picked over for stones or grit and rinsed

2 bay leaves

Salt and freshly ground pepper

1 red onion, cut crosswise into slices ¼ inch (6 mm) thick

½ cup (4 fl oz/125 ml) extra-virgin olive oil, or as needed, plus 1–2 Tbsp

1 lb (500 g) sushi-grade ahi tuna (about 2 inches/5 cm thick)

4 cups (4 oz/125 g) baby spinach

1–2 Tbsp fresh lemon juice

2 Tbsp chopped fresh flat-leaf parsley

In a large saucepan, combine the beans and 8 cups (64 fl oz/2 l) water. Bring to a boil over medium heat, then boil for 15–20 minutes. Reduce the heat to low, add the bay leaves, cover, and simmer for 1 hour. Add 2 tsp salt, re-cover, and simmer until the beans are tender to the bite, 30–45 minutes longer, adding more water if needed. Let the beans stand in their cooking liquid.

Preheat the oven to 350°F (180°C).

Spread the onion slices in a single layer on a baking sheet. Drizzle with the 1–2 Tbsp oil, and sprinkle with ¼ tsp salt and ¼ tsp pepper. Roast, turning occasionally, until soft and beginning to turn golden, about 20 minutes. Don't be concerned if some of the rings separate. Remove from the oven and cover to keep warm.

Pour oil into a small, shallow saucepan to a depth of ½ inch (12 mm) and heat over medium-high heat until the oil reaches 325°F (165°C) on a deep-frying thermometer. Season the tuna with ½ tsp salt and ½ tsp pepper. Using tongs, place it in the hot oil and cook until the first ½–¾ inch (12 mm–2 cm) is opaque, 3–4 minutes. Using tongs and a spatula if necessary, gently turn the tuna and cook until about ½ inch (12 mm) of the midsection is still pink, 3–4 minutes longer. Transfer to a cutting board, reserving the poaching oil. Cut the tuna into generous ¼-inch thick slices. »→

In a frying pan, warm ¼ cup (2 fl oz/60 ml) of the bean cooking liquid over high heat. Add the spinach and cook, tossing gently, until wilted but still bright green, about 2 minutes. Set aside.

In a small bowl, whisk together ¼ cup (2 fl oz/60 ml) of the poaching oil, the lemon juice, ¼ tsp salt, ¼ tsp pepper, and all but 2 tsp of the parsley until the vinaigrette is well blended.

Drain the beans and transfer to a large bowl. Add the spinach and half of the vinaigrette and stir gently. Taste and adjust seasonings with salt and pepper. Divide the bean mixture among warmed individual plates or shallow bowls. Top with the tuna and garnish with the onion slices. Drizzle with the remaining vinaigrette, sprinkle with the reserved parsley, and serve.

22

Fresh English peas, full of natural sugars, are a hallmark of spring. Look for young, tender pods that are plump with whole peas that will need only brief cooking. This simple salad showcases them with complementary flavors of fried pancetta, aromatic mint, and ricotta salata cheese.

SPRING PEAS WITH PANCETTA, MINT & RICOTTA SALATA

serves 4–6

Salt and freshly ground pepper

5 lb (2.5 kg) English peas in the pod, shelled

2 thin slices pancetta, chopped

1 tsp raspberry vinegar

1 Tbsp extra-virgin olive oil

2 Tbsp minced fresh mint, plus sprigs for garnish

4 oz (125 g) ricotta salata cheese, crumbled

Bring a large pot three-fourths full of salted water to a boil over high heat. Add the peas and cook until barely tender, about 2 minutes. Drain, place under cold running water until cool, and drain again. Set aside.

In a frying pan, sauté the pancetta over medium heat until lightly crisped, 4–5 minutes. Using a slotted spoon, transfer to paper towels to drain.

In a large bowl, whisk together the vinegar and ½ tsp each salt and pepper. Add the oil in a thin stream, whisking constantly. Add the peas, pancetta, and chopped mint and toss to coat. Stir in half of the cheese. Garnish with the remaining cheese and the mint sprigs, then serve.

23

The secret to the old-fashioned flavor of this salad is the addition of a little sweet pickle juice and sliced pimiento-stuffed olives, along with the more traditional ingredients like mayonnaise, onions, and hard-cooked eggs. Make this in abundance for a springtime family gathering.

OLD-FASHIONED MACARONI SALAD WITH SWEET PICKLES

serves 6

3 cups (10½ oz/330 g) elbow macaroni

Salt and freshly ground pepper

FOR THE DRESSING

⅓ cup (3 fl oz/80 ml) mayonnaise

¼ cup (2 oz/60 g) sour cream

1 tsp Dijon mustard

1–2 tsp sweet pickle juice

½ white onion, finely chopped

3 celery ribs, finely chopped, leaves reserved and finely chopped

3 sweet pickles, finely chopped

2 hard-cooked eggs, chopped

½ cup (2½ oz/75 g) pimiento-stuffed green olives, chopped

½ bunch fresh chives, snipped

Bring a pot of salted water to a boil over high heat. Reduce the heat to medium, add the macaroni, and cook until tender, according to package directions. Drain and rinse under cold running water and set aside to drain.

To make the dressing, in a serving bowl, combine the mayonnaise, sour cream, mustard, pickle juice, ½ tsp salt and ½ tsp pepper Stir to mix well.

Add the onion, celery, and pickles and stir to mix again. Add the macaroni and turn to coat. Add the hard-cooked eggs, green olives, and celery leaves and turn once again. Taste and adjust the seasoning with salt, if needed. Transfer to a serving bowl, garnish with the snipped chives, and serve.

24

It takes a certain amount of work to prepare fava beans, but your effort will be rewarded when you serve this elegant salad. Look for bright green fava pods with medium to smallish beans inside, as these will be the most tender.

FAVA BEAN & POACHED SALMON SALAD

serves 4

2 lb (1 kg) fava beans in the pod, shelled

1 Tbsp extra-virgin olive oil

Salt and freshly ground pepper

½ cup (4 fl oz/125 ml) dry white wine

1 bay leaf

1 fresh thyme sprig

2 fresh flat-leaf parsley sprigs

3 lemons (2 sliced, 1 cut into 4 wedges)

4 salmon fillets (each about 6 oz/185 g and 1 inch/2.5 cm thick), skin on and pin bones removed

¼ cup (2 oz/60 g) crème fraîche

¼ cup (⅓ oz/10 g) chopped fresh chives

Bring a pot of water to a boil over high heat. Add the fava beans and blanch for about 30 seconds; do not overcook. Drain and rinse under cold running water. Pinch each fava bean to pop it from its skin. Transfer the beans to a bowl. Add the oil, ½ tsp salt, and ¼ tsp pepper and stir gently. Set aside.

In a large frying pan, combine ½ cup (4 fl oz/125 ml) water, the wine, bay leaf, thyme, parsley, and lemon slices. Add the salmon and sprinkle with ½ tsp salt and ¾ tsp pepper. Bring to a simmer over medium-high heat, reduce the heat to low, cover, and simmer until the fish flakes easily with a fork, 7–10 minutes. Remove from the heat and let stand, uncovered, for 5 minutes to finish cooking. Transfer the salmon to a plate and let cool to room temperature.

Spoon the fava beans onto individual plates. Slide a spatula under a salmon fillet, between the flesh and skin, and gently separate, leaving the skin behind. Place on the fava beans. Repeat with the remaining fillets. Top each fillet with a spoonful of crème fraîche. Sprinkle the chives over the beans, crème fraîche, and salmon. Garnish each with a lemon wedge and serve.

25

ASPARAGUS, BEET & GOAT CHEESE SALAD

serves 8

1½ lb (750 g) beets, trimmed

¼ cup (2 fl oz/60 ml) extra-virgin olive oil, plus 2 Tbsp

Salt and freshly ground pepper

2 Tbsp minced shallot

¼ cup (2 fl oz/60 ml) fresh orange juice

2½ Tbsp fresh lemon juice

½ lb (250 g) asparagus, tough ends trimmed

2 Tbsp fresh flat-leaf parsley leaves

2 Tbsp fresh chervil leaves

¼ lb (125 g) fresh goat cheese, crumbled

2 Tbsp finely chopped fresh chives

At its peak in springtime, asparagus is tender enough to eat uncooked. Here, slender ribbons of raw asparagus are tossed with a tangy citrus vinaigrette and arranged on top of a bed of lightly dressed beet slices. The beets can be roasted and sliced up to 2 days in advance and refrigerated in an airtight container.

Preheat the oven to 400°F (200°C).

Place the beets in a roasting pan, toss with the 2 Tbsp oil, and season with salt and pepper. Cover the pan with aluminum foil and roast until the beets are easily pierced with a knife, about 1 hour. Let the beets cool to room temperature, then peel. Using a mandoline or a very sharp knife, cut the beets into thin slices. Set aside.

In a small bowl, combine the shallot, orange juice, and lemon juice and let stand for 5 minutes. Add the ¼ cup (2 fl oz/60 ml) oil in a thin stream, whisking constantly until the vinaigrette is well blended. Season with salt and pepper.

Divide the beet slices among individual plates, overlapping them to form a ring. Drizzle with a little of the vinaigrette.

Using a vegetable peeler, peel the asparagus into long strips and place in a bowl. Add the parsley, chervil, and the remaining vinaigrette and toss to coat.

Mound the asparagus mixture on top of the beets. Sprinkle the cheese around the asparagus and beets, garnish with the chives, and serve.

26

GRILLED LAMB & COUSCOUS SALAD

serves 4

1¼ lb (625 g) boneless leg of lamb, cut into thick slices

2 Tbsp extra-virgin olive oil, plus ¼ cup (2 fl oz/60 ml)

Salt and freshly ground pepper

¼ tsp dried thyme

1 Tbsp grapeseed oil

1 small yellow onion, finely chopped

1½ cups (9 oz/280 g) Israeli couscous

2 cups (16 fl oz/500 ml) chicken broth

¼ cup (⅓ oz/10 g) minced fresh mint

Juice of 1 lemon

2 cups (2 oz/60 g) mixed baby greens

If you can't find Israeli couscous, substitute 1½ cups (9 oz/280 g) instant couscous: place in a heatproof bowl; bring 2¾ cups (22 fl oz/680 ml) chicken broth to a boil with the onion, salt, and pepper; pour over the couscous and stir to combine; cover and let stand for 15 minutes. Or, boil 10 oz (315 g) orzo pasta until al dente, drain, and toss with the cooked onion, salt, pepper, oil, mint, and lemon juice.

Place the lamb in a large baking dish and brush both sides with the 2 Tbsp olive oil. Season generously with salt and pepper and the thyme. Let stand for up to 1 hour at room temperature or up to 2 hours in the refrigerator (and let return to room temperature before cooking).

In a saucepan over medium heat, warm the grapeseed oil. Add the onion and cook, stirring occasionally, until softened, about 5 minutes. Add the couscous and cook, stirring, until just beginning to brown, about 6 minutes. Add the broth, 1 tsp salt, and a pinch of pepper. Bring to a boil, reduce the heat to low, cover, and simmer until the couscous is tender and all the liquid is absorbed, about 8 minutes. Remove from the heat and stir in the ¼ cup olive oil and the mint.

Prepare a gas or charcoal grill for direct-heat cooking over high heat. Alternatively, preheat a stove-top grill pan over high heat. Place the lamb slices on the grill rack or in the grill pan and cook, turning once, until rare or medium-rare, 2–3 minutes per side. Transfer to a cutting board and let rest for 5 minutes before cutting into thin strips. Add most of the lemon juice to the couscous. Taste and adjust the seasoning with salt, pepper, and lemon juice, then fluff again. Spoon the couscous onto plates and surround with the salad greens. Top with the lamb and serve.

27

SOBA NOODLE SALAD WITH SUGAR SNAP PEAS & SOY-PEANUT DRESSING

serves 4

Pairing soba, the Japanese buckwheat noodle, with delicate spring vegetables and crisp herbs counterbalances the dense, rich texture of the noodles. The peanut dressing binds the whole together to create a hearty main dish.

1 lb (500 g) dried soba noodles or whole-wheat spaghetti

1 cup (1/3 lb/155 g) sugar snap peas, trimmed and cut in half on the diagonal

3 or 4 small carrots, peeled and julienned

1/2 cup (2/3 oz/20 g) chopped fresh cilantro leaves

1/2 cup (2/3 oz/20 g) chopped fresh mint leaves

FOR THE SOY-PEANUT DRESSING

1 tsp canola or peanut oil

1-inch (2.5-cm) piece fresh ginger, peeled and minced

2 cloves garlic, minced

1 Tbsp soy sauce

4 tsp rice vinegar

1/2 tsp red pepper flakes

1/3 cup (3 oz/90 g) chunky peanut butter

1/2 cup (4 fl oz/125 ml) chicken or vegetable broth

Salt

In a large pot of boiling water, cook the noodles until tender, according to package directions. Two minutes before the noodles are ready, add the snap peas and carrots. After 2 minutes, drain the noodles and vegetables and place in a large bowl along with the cilantro and mint.

To make the dressing, in a saucepan, heat the oil over medium-high heat. Add the ginger and garlic and stir. Add the soy sauce, vinegar, red pepper flakes, peanut butter, broth, and salt to taste. Stir until the mixture is smooth, then reduce the heat to low and simmer until thick, 5–7 minutes.

Pour the dressing over the noodles, vegetables, and herbs and gently turn to coat well. Let cool to room temperature before serving.

28

FRIED POTATO SALAD WITH BACON

serves 6

Here is a new twist on the classic potato salad. The potatoes are cooked in a pressure cooker until almost tender, then fried in bacon fat until browned and crispy. Mixing in crumbled bacon just before serving adds a savory, crunchy touch. This hearty salad is the perfect partner for barbecued ribs or grilled meats.

2 lb (1 kg) baby red potatoes

Salt and freshly ground pepper

6 slices thick-cut bacon

1 Tbsp brown mustard

1 Tbsp red wine vinegar

2 Tbsp extra-virgin olive oil

1/3 cup (1/2 oz/15 g) chopped fresh flat-leaf parsley

1/3 cup (1 oz/30 g) sliced green onion, including tender green parts

Put the potatoes in a saucepan and cover with salted water by 2 inches (5 cm). Bring to a boil over high heat, reduce the heat to medium, and cook until just underdone, about 15 minutes. Drain the potatoes, cover, and refrigerate until thoroughly chilled, at least 1 hour or up to overnight. Cut the potatoes into 1/4-inch (6-mm) slices. Set aside.

In a large frying pan, cook the bacon over medium-high heat, turning as needed, until crispy, 7–10 minutes. Using a slotted spoon, transfer to paper towels to drain, reserving the bacon fat in the pan. When cool enough to handle, crumble the bacon. Set aside.

Transfer 1 Tbsp of the bacon fat to a small bowl and set aside. Reserve 3 Tbsp of the fat in the pan; discard the remaining fat. Arrange the potato slices in a single layer in the pan, set over medium-high heat, and cook, turning once, until browned and crispy, about 2 minutes per side. Transfer to a large bowl.

Whisk the mustard and vinegar into the bowl with the reserved bacon fat, and season with salt and pepper. Add the oil in a thin stream, whisking constantly until the dressing is well blended. Pour the dressing over the potatoes. Add the bacon, parsley, and green onion and stir gently to combine. Taste and adjust the seasonings. Serve right away.

29
MÂCHE, RADISH, BLUE CHEESE & SUGARED PECAN SALAD

serves 4

Mâche is a tender, nutty-flavored salad leaf that is sold in ready-to-use bags in the produce section of many supermarkets. For a substitute, use field greens or a mixture of baby or wild arugula and baby spinach leaves. You can make the sugared pecans up to 1 week in advance and store them in an airtight container at room temperature.

FOR THE VINAIGRETTE

1 shallot, minced

2 Tbsp red wine vinegar

1 tsp Dijon mustard

Salt and freshly ground black pepper

⅓ cup (3 fl oz/80 ml) olive oil

½ cup (2 oz/60 g) pecan halves

1 tsp sugar

¼ tsp dry mustard

Pinch of cayenne pepper

4 oz (125 g) mâche or field greens

8 radishes, thinly sliced

4 oz (125 g) blue cheese, crumbled

Preheat the oven to 350°F (180°C).

To make the vinaigrette, in a small bowl, whisk together the shallot, vinegar, and Dijon mustard. Season to taste with salt and black pepper. Let stand at room temperature for 30 minutes to allow the shallot flavor to mellow, then add the oil in a thin stream, whisking constantly until the dressing is smooth and thick.

Rinse the pecans in a sieve and set aside to drain. In a small bowl, combine the sugar, dry mustard, and cayenne and mix well. Add the pecans and toss until evenly coated. Spread the pecans on a nonstick rimmed baking sheet and toast in the oven until dark brown, about 10 minutes. Transfer the pecans to a plate to let cool, and set aside.

To serve, combine the mâche leaves and radish slices in a serving bowl. Whisk the vinaigrette to recombine, if needed. Drizzle the mâche with the vinaigrette and toss until evenly coated. Top with the cheese and the pecans and serve.

30
ARUGULA SALAD WITH PECORINO & PINE NUTS

serves 4–6

If pecorino, a sheep's milk cheese, is unavailable, use Parmesan instead. Young, tender baby arugula leaves are best for this salad. If you can find only larger leaves, trim off the stems.

1 Tbsp balsamic vinegar

1 tsp red wine vinegar

Salt and freshly ground pepper

3 Tbsp extra-virgin olive oil

4–5 cups (4–5 oz/125–155 g) baby arugula

Pecorino cheese for shaving

3 Tbsp lightly toasted pine nuts

In a large serving bowl, whisk together the vinegars and ½ tsp each salt and pepper. Add the oil in a thin stream, whisking constantly until the dressing is smooth. Add the arugula and toss to coat evenly.

Divide the arugula among plates. Using a vegetable peeler, shave the cheese over the salads. Sprinkle with the nuts and serve.

31
WHOLE-WHEAT PASTA SALAD WITH TUNA & FRESH HERBS

serves 6–8

This main dish salad, loaded with fresh herbs and the taste of the Mediterranean, is equally at home on your dinner table or toted to a potluck. To ensure the best result, do not stint on the tuna. Look for good-quality olive–oil packed tuna, which will have a firm texture and a rich flavor.

Salt and freshly ground pepper

½ lb (250 g) whole-wheat penne pasta

2 Tbsp extra-virgin olive oil

2 Tbsp fresh lemon juice

2 tsp capers, rinsed

¼ cup (⅓ oz/10 g) chopped fresh flat-leaf parsley

¼ cup (⅓ oz/10 g) chopped fresh basil

¼ cup (⅓ oz/10 g) chopped fresh cilantro

½ cup (4 oz/125 g) oil-cured black olives, pitted

2 cans (6 oz/185 g each) olive oil–packed tuna, drained and broken into chunks

Bring a large pot of water to a boil over high heat. Add 1 tsp salt and the pasta, stir well, and cook until al dente, about 12 minutes. Drain and transfer to a large bowl.

Add the oil, lemon juice, ½ tsp salt, and ½ tsp pepper to the hot pasta and stir well. Mix in the capers, parsley, basil, cilantro, olives, and tuna. Taste and adjust the seasonings. Cover and refrigerate for at least 1 hour or up to overnight before serving. Serve at room temperature.

As the sun shines brighter and the days grow longer, artichokes, asparagus, peas, and fava beans proliferate at the market. These hardly need more than a light simmer before scattering them into countless fresh combinations. Olive oil, shaved Parmesan, and prosciutto are simple but flavorful adornments. Enliven classic salads with verdant spring herbs: chives for egg salad, tarragon for chicken, and dill for tender new potatoes.

april

1

BABY BEET SALAD WITH SUGARED WALNUTS

serves 6

Seek out baby beets in an array of colors, such as golden yellow, pale pink, and magenta red, for an eye-catching presentation. If you can find them, blood oranges contrast nicely with the earthy beets.

3 bunches mixed baby beets
(3–4 lb/1.5–2 kg total weight), trimmed

FOR THE SUGARED WALNUTS

½ cup (2 oz/60 g) walnut pieces

1 tsp grapeseed oil

2 tsp confectioners' sugar

1 tsp Dijon mustard

3 Tbsp balsamic vinegar

⅓ cup (3 fl oz/80 ml) plus 2 Tbsp extra-virgin olive oil

5 oranges, preferably blood oranges

Salt and freshly ground pepper

3 cups (3 oz/90 g) arugula leaves, stemmed

1 red onion, thinly sliced

2 Tbsp chopped fresh flat-leaf parsley

Preheat the oven to 375°F (190°C). Wrap the beets in squares of foil and roast on a baking sheet until easily pierced with the tip of a knife, 30–40 minutes. Let cool in the foil, then unwrap and peel. Cut each beet in half or into wedges and set aside.

To make the sugared walnuts, in a bowl, toss the walnuts with the grapeseed oil. Add the sugar and toss to coat evenly. Heat a small frying pan over medium heat. Add the walnuts and sauté just until they start to brown and the sugar begins to caramelize, about 3 minutes. Transfer to a small plate and let cool.

In a bowl, whisk together the mustard and vinegar. Add the olive oil in a thin stream, whisking constantly until the vinaigrette is smooth. Grate the zest from 1 of the oranges and add to the dressing, then season to taste with salt and pepper. Add the beets, toss to coat, and let stand at room temperature for 2–4 hours.

Using a small, sharp knife, cut a slice off both ends of each of the remaining 4 oranges to reveal the flesh. Stand an orange upright on a cutting board and thickly slice off the peel and pith in strips, following the contour of the fruit. Holding the orange in one hand over a bowl, cut along either side of each section to release it from the membrane, »→

letting the sections drop into the bowl. Repeat with the remaining oranges. Pour any juice in the bowl over the beets.

Scatter the arugula over a platter. Using a slotted spoon, remove the beets from the vinaigrette and arrange over the greens along with the orange sections, onion slices, and walnuts. Drizzle a little of the vinaigrette over the top and toss to combine. Add more vinaigrette if needed to lightly coat the greens (you may not need it all). Garnish with parsley and serve.

2

RHUBARB & AVOCADO SALAD WITH WATERCRESS

serves 4

Marinating the rhubarb in a little sugar tames enough of its tartness to use it raw in this colorful salad. The creamy avocado contrasts nicely with the crisp rhubarb, and the avocado oil blends with the slightly sweet balsamic to make a dressing that complements all of the other ingredients.

3 or 4 ribs red rhubarb

2 Tbsp sugar

2 Tbsp avocado oil

1 Tbsp balsamic vinegar

1 large bunch watercress, tough stems removed

1 avocado, pitted, peeled, and diced

Trim away any leaves from the rhubarb and cut the ribs on the diagonal into ¼-inch (6-mm) slices. Place in a bowl, sprinkle with the sugar, and let stand for 15 minutes, stirring occasionally.

In a small bowl, whisk together the oil and vinegar until the vinaigrette is well blended. Fold in the watercress, the rhubarb, and avocado oil mixture. Gently fold in about half of the avocado.

Divide the salad among individual plates. Garnish with the remaining avocado and serve.

3

GRILLED LAMB & WILTED SPINACH SALAD WITH CHARRED BREAD

serves 4

This grill-friendly salad is quick and easy to make. Everything is cooked on the grill except the spinach, which is wilted in a frying pan with the jus from the carved lamb. For a shortcut, arrange the raw spinach on the salad plates, then top them with the hot ingredients and drizzle with the jus. The warmth of the other components will wilt the spinach.

1 lb (500 g) boneless lamb sirloin, about 1 inch (2.5 cm) thick

½ tsp dried oregano

½ tsp dried thyme

½ tsp salt

½ tsp freshly ground pepper

3 bunches green onions, root end trimmed

2 Tbsp extra-virgin olive oil

4 oz (125 g) crustless, soft inner part of country-style bread, such as ciabatta or baguette, torn into bite-sized pieces

8 cups (8 oz/250 g) packed baby spinach

¼ cup (1¼ oz/40 g) crumbled feta cheese

Rub the lamb with the oregano, thyme, salt, and pepper. Place the green onions on a plate, drizzle with the oil, and turn to coat.

Prepare a charcoal or gas grill for direct-heat cooking over medium-high heat and preheat a grill basket. Alternatively, preheat a stove-top grill pan over medium-high heat. Place the green onions in the grill basket or lay crosswise on the grill, or place in the grill pan. Cook, turning once, until lightly golden and slightly charred, 4–5 minutes. Transfer to a cutting board.

Place the lamb on the grill or in the pan and cook, turning once, until an instant-read thermometer inserted into the thickest part registers 135°F (57°C), about 5 minutes per side. Transfer to a cutting board, cover loosely with aluminum foil, and let rest for 5–10 minutes. Place the bread in the grill basket or in the pan and cook, turning once or twice, until lightly charred, 3–4 minutes. Transfer to a bowl.

Chop the green onions, both white and green parts. Cut the lamb into thin slices, reserving the jus.

Pour the lamb jus into a frying pan and place over medium-high heat. Add the spinach, cover, and cook, shaking the pan occasionally, until the spinach is just wilted, about 2 minutes. »→

Divide the spinach among individual plates. Top with the green onions and lamb. Tuck in equal amounts of the bread, sprinkle with the cheese, and serve.

4

CELERY ROOT & KOHLRABI SLAW WITH MEYER LEMON DRESSING

serves 4–6

Celery root and kohlrabi are especially good candidates for slaw. Knobby, juicy kohlrabi, a popular vegetable in northern Europe, tastes a bit like its brassica kin, while celery root, with its gnarly brown exterior and ivory interior, has a flavor reminiscent of its namesake cousin. Once you remove the tough outer skin from both vegetables, you are rewarded with crisp flesh perfect for grating.

½ cup (4 fl oz/125 ml) fresh Meyer lemon juice, or another lemon variety with 1 tsp sugar added

1 tsp ground cumin

⅛ tsp ground turmeric

Salt and freshly ground pepper

2 Tbsp chopped fresh flat-leaf parsley

1 celery root (about ¾ lb/375 g), peeled

3 kohlrabi, peeled

1 Tbsp minced fresh dill

In a large bowl, whisk together the lemon juice, cumin, turmeric, ⅛ tsp salt, ¼ tsp pepper, and 1 Tbsp of the parsley until the dressing is well blended. Set aside.

Using a mandoline or a very sharp knife, thinly slice the celery root and the kohlrabi crosswise (the thinner, the better). Then cut the slices into very thin slices lengthwise. Add to the bowl with the dressing and stir to coat well.

Mound the slaw on a platter or in a serving bowl. Garnish with the remaining 1 Tbsp parsley and the dill and serve.

5

Cornichons are tart, salty, and full of pickled flavor. Along with the mustard, they add zip to the tender waxy potatoes and crunchy radishes and celery in this salad. A spoonful of crème fraîche on individual servings tempers the salad's tanginess and adds a luxurious touch.

NEW POTATO & RADISH SALAD WITH MUSTARD-DILL VINAIGRETTE

serves 6

FOR THE VINAIGRETTE

6 Tbsp (3 fl oz/90 ml) cider vinegar

7 cornichons, minced

¼ cup minced fresh dill

1 shallot, minced

3 Tbsp Dijon mustard

1 Tbsp sugar

Salt

½ cup (4 fl oz/125 ml) plus 1 Tbsp extra-virgin olive oil

2 lb (1 kg) red new potatoes

4 celery ribs, finely chopped

8 large radishes, trimmed and finely chopped

2 Tbsp coarsely chopped fresh dill

⅓ cup (3 oz/80 g) crème fraîche or sour cream

To make the vinaigrette, in a large bowl, whisk together the vinegar, cornichons, minced dill, shallot, mustard, sugar, and ½ tsp salt until the salt and sugar dissolve. Add the oil in a thin stream, whisking constantly until the dressing is well blended. Taste and adjust the seasonings.

Have ready a bowl of ice water. In a large saucepan, combine the potatoes, 1 Tbsp salt, and water to cover by 1 inch (2.5 cm) and bring to a boil over high heat. Reduce the heat to medium, cover partially, and simmer until the potatoes are just tender when pierced with the tip of a paring knife, about 10 minutes.

Drain the potatoes in a colander and then plunge them into the ice water. Let cool, then drain again and pat dry. Cut each potato into halves or quarters.

Whisk the vinaigrette to recombine, then add the potatoes to the bowl. Add the celery and radishes and toss gently. Taste and adjust the seasonings. Sprinkle the salad with the chopped dill. Serve, passing the crème fraîche at the table.

6

A chopped salad is a good way to use up leftover salad vegetables and small pieces of cheese. Create new combinations with your favorite ingredients. Try chopped chicken, crumbled blue cheese, chopped apples, and toasted walnuts with a cider vinegar–walnut oil vinaigrette.

CHOPPED SALAD OF CHICKEN, WATERCRESS & RICOTTA SALATA

serves 4–6

2 cups (¾ lb/375 g) bite-sized pieces roasted chicken meat

2 cups (¾ lb/375 g) cherry tomatoes, cut in half lengthwise

1 large cucumber, peeled, seeded, and cut into ½-inch (12-mm) pieces

1 bunch watercress, tough stems removed and leaves coarsely chopped

4 oz (125 g) ricotta salata or feta cheese, crumbled

2 green onions, including tender green parts, chopped

¼ cup (1½ oz/45 g) chopped pitted black Mediterranean olives

2 Tbsp fresh lemon juice

1 clove garlic, crushed through a press

Salt and freshly ground pepper

½ cup (4 fl oz/125 ml) extra-virgin olive oil

In a serving bowl, combine the chicken, tomatoes, cucumber, watercress, cheese, green onions, and olives.

In a small bowl, whisk together the lemon juice, garlic, and salt and pepper to taste. Add the oil in a thin stream, whisking constantly until the dressing is well blended.

Pour the dressing over the salad, mix gently, and serve.

WHEAT BERRY SALAD WITH SNOW PEAS & CARROTS

serves 6

1 cup (5 oz/155 g) wheat berries

Salt

FOR THE VINAIGRETTE

¼ cup (2 fl oz/60 ml) peanut oil

1 tsp toasted sesame oil

2 Tbsp rice vinegar

1 Tbsp honey or sugar

1–2 tsp soy sauce

4 carrots, peeled and very thinly sliced

½ lb (250 g) snow peas, trimmed and cut on the diagonal into thin slices

Handful of radish sprouts or other sprouts

This simple salad is very healthful and high in fiber. Wheat berries are whole kernels of wheat, and their mild flavor lets this savory Asian-inspired dressing shine. Carrots and snow peas mark this as a springtime dish. Look for interesting varieties of carrots in different colors, and use a mandoline to slice them paper-thin.

In a saucepan, combine the wheat berries and 6 cups (48 fl oz/1.5 l) water. Bring to a simmer over medium-high heat. Cook, uncovered, until the grain is tender, about 1 hour, adding more water if needed. When almost done, add 1 tsp salt. When tender, drain and rinse briefly under cold running water. Drain again and allow to cool in the colander.

Meanwhile, to make the vinaigrette, in a small bowl, whisk together the peanut and sesame oils, vinegar, honey, and 1 tsp soy sauce. Taste and add more soy sauce if desired. Put the drained wheat berries in a bowl and add the vinaigrette, gently mixing. Let stand at room temperature for 1–2 hours, if possible, before adding the vegetables.

For the carrots and peas, bring a saucepan of water to a boil over medium-high heat. Have ready a bowl of ice water. Add the carrots and blanch until just tender but still slightly crunchy, 2–3 minutes. Add the peas during the last 30 seconds. Drain and plunge the vegetables into the ice water, then remove and pat dry.

Add the vegetables to the wheat berries and toss gently. Garnish with the radish sprouts and serve.

LOBSTER SALAD WITH CUCUMBER & DILL

serves 4

1 lb (500 g) fresh-cooked lobster meat (from about 2 lb/1 kg lobster in the shell)

1 cucumber, peeled, seeded, and chopped

1 tsp grated lemon zest

2½ Tbsp fresh lemon juice

1 small shallot, minced

Salt and freshly ground pepper

½ cup (4 fl oz/125 ml) extra-virgin olive oil

2 Tbsp minced fresh dill

4 cups (4 oz/125 g) loosely packed watercress, tough stems removed

Fresh lobster is available year-round, but if you aren't sure about its quality, choose frozen lobster tails. Serve this elegant salad with toasted brioche slices and a chilled chardonnay.

Pick the lobster over for shell fragments and cut the meat into bite-sized chunks. In a bowl, combine the lobster and chopped cucumber. Set aside.

In a small bowl, whisk together the lemon zest and juice, shallot, and salt and pepper to taste. Add the olive oil in a thin stream, whisking constantly until the dressing is well blended. Stir in the dill, then taste and adjust the seasonings.

Pour the dressing over the lobster and toss to coat evenly. Cover the salad and refrigerate to chill and marinate for at least 30 minutes or up to several hours.

Divide the watercress among individual plates, top with the lobster salad, and serve.

9

WATERCRESS & RADISH SALAD WITH GRAPEFRUIT

serves 10–12

3 Tbsp red wine vinegar

1 Tbsp whole-grain mustard

Salt and freshly ground pepper

6 Tbsp (3 fl oz/90 ml) olive oil

3 pink grapefruits, peeled and segmented with a knife

4 bunches watercress, tough stems removed

6 large radishes, trimmed and thinly sliced lengthwise

Here, pink grapefruits, which deliver a tart-sweet flavor, are paired with peppery green watercress and piquant radishes in a colorful salad fit for a dinner party.

In a large, shallow serving bowl, whisk together the vinegar, mustard, and ½ tsp each salt and pepper. Add the oil in a thin stream, whisking constantly until the dressing is smooth.

Just before serving, add the grapefruit sections, watercress, and radishes to a large bowl. Drizzle in the dressing and toss gently to coat. Serve right away.

10

CALAMARI & WHITE BEAN SALAD

serves 4

Salt and freshly ground pepper

¼ cup (2 fl oz/60 ml) white wine vinegar, or as needed

3 Tbsp fresh lemon juice

1 Tbsp minced garlic

½ cup (4 fl oz/125 ml) extra-virgin olive oil

1 lb (500 g) cleaned squid, cut into bite-sized rings and tentacles

1 can (15 oz/470 g) cannellini beans or other white beans, rinsed and drained

2 jarred roasted red bell peppers, cut into strips

1 cup (4 oz/125 g) thinly sliced red onion

2 Tbsp capers, rinsed

⅓ cup (2 oz/60 g) green olives, pitted and chopped

Fresh flat-leaf parsley leaves for garnish

Enjoying this salad, it won't be hard to imagine you are in coastal Italy, sipping a glass of crisp vino bianco while enjoying a mix of fresh calamari, velvety white beans, and sweet roasted peppers tossed in a citrus-and-garlic dressing.

In a large pot, bring 4 qt (4 l) salted water to a boil over medium-high heat. Have ready a bowl of ice water.

In a large bowl, combine the vinegar, lemon juice, garlic, 1 tsp salt, and ¼ tsp pepper and let stand for 5 minutes. Add the olive oil in a thin stream, whisking constantly until the dressing is well blended.

Add the squid to the boiling water and cook until just tender, about 1 minute. Drain the squid and plunge into the ice water to stop the cooking. Drain well and pat dry.

Add the cooked squid, beans, peppers, onion, capers, and olives to the dressing and mix well. Cover and refrigerate for 2–4 hours to blend the flavors.

Just before serving, taste the salad and adjust the vinegar and seasonings. Divide among individual plates, garnish with parsley leaves, and serve.

11

This is a delicious Provençal-style main-course salad. Roast the meat just for the salad, or keep the recipe in your repertoire when looking for ways to use up leftover beef, lamb, or chicken roasts.

SALAD OF GRILLED LAMB, POTATOES & AIOLI

serves 6

2 lb (1 kg) small red potatoes, left unpeeled

2 Tbsp olive oil

Salt and freshly ground pepper

FOR THE AIOLI

1 egg yolk

1 tsp Dijon mustard

5 Tbsp (3 fl oz/80 ml) olive oil

⅓ cup (3 fl oz/80 ml) grapeseed oil

Juice of ½ lemon

2 or 3 cloves garlic, minced

3–3¼ lb (1.5–1.65 kg) leg of lamb, trimmed, boned, and butterflied

2 Tbsp olive oil

3 jarred roasted red bell peppers, cut lengthwise into thick strips (optional)

Preheat the oven to 375°F (190°C). Prepare a charcoal or gas grill for direct-heat cooking over high heat, or preheat the broiler.

Arrange the potatoes in a single layer in a baking dish. Add the oil and salt and pepper to taste, and turn the potatoes to coat evenly. Cover with foil and bake until tender, 40–50 minutes. Remove from the oven and uncover.

Meanwhile, to make the aioli, in a bowl, whisk together the egg yolk, mustard, and 1 Tbsp of the olive oil until thoroughly blended. In a cup, combine the remaining 4 Tbsp olive oil and the grapeseed oil. Gradually add the oils to the egg yolk mixture in a thin, steady stream, whisking constantly until the mixture thickens. Add the lemon juice, garlic, and salt and pepper to taste. Whisk in 2 Tbsp warm water to make the aioli barely fluid. Cover and refrigerate.

Rub the lamb with the 2 Tbsp olive oil and salt and pepper to taste. About 10 minutes after placing the potatoes in the oven, place the lamb on the grill rack or a broiler pan. Grill or broil 4–6 inches (10–15 cm) from the heat source until an instant-read thermometer inserted into the thickest portion registers 130–135°F (54–57°C) for medium-rare, ⟫→

about 15 minutes on each side. Transfer to a cutting board and cover loosely with foil. Let rest for 10 minutes before carving.

Meanwhile, place the potatoes on the grill rack or broiler pan and grill or broil, turning occasionally, until hot and well marked, about 10 minutes.

Cut the lamb across the grain into thin slices and arrange on a platter with the potatoes and roasted bell peppers, if using. Serve the aioli on the side.

12

This classic Tuscan salad is made as soon as fava beans ripen in the spring garden. Use a slightly aged pecorino, which will hold its shape better when cut.

FAVA BEAN SALAD WITH PECORINO

serves 4

Salt and freshly ground pepper

3 lb (1.5 kg) fava beans in the pod, shelled

6 oz (185 g) pecorino cheese

¼ cup (2 fl oz/60 ml) extra-virgin olive oil

Bring a pot three-fourths full of lightly salted water to a boil. Add the shelled beans and blanch for 1–2 minutes. Drain, rinse under cold running water, and drain again. Pinch each bean to pop it from its skin. Transfer the beans to a serving bowl.

Cut the cheese into ½-inch (12-mm) cubes and add the cubes to the bowl of favas. Add the olive oil, a light sprinkling of salt, and pepper to taste. Toss all the ingredients together and serve.

13

PASTA SALAD WITH SPRING ASPARAGUS & SNAP PEAS

serves 6

Salt and freshly ground pepper

8 oz (250 g) asparagus

8 oz (250 g) sugar snap peas, trimmed

¾ lb (375 g) penne or other shaped pasta

5 Tbsp (3 fl oz/80 ml) extra-virgin olive oil

1 orange

2 Tbsp red wine vinegar

3 Tbsp finely chopped fresh chives

For a more substantial dish, add fresh fava beans to this bright-tasting salad. Shell them and blanch in a pot of boiling water for 1–2 minutes. Drain, and when cool enough to handle, pinch each bean to pop it out of its skin.

In a large pot over high heat, bring 5 qt (5 l) salted water to a boil. Trim the tough ends from the asparagus and, if the spears are thick, peel them to within 2 inches (5 cm) of the tips. Cut on the diagonal into 1½-inch (4-cm) pieces. Boil the asparagus until tender, 4–5 minutes. Using a strainer, remove the asparagus, drain, and let cool completely in the refrigerator.

Add the sugar snap peas to the boiling water and cook until tender, 1–2 minutes. Drain and let cool completely in the refrigerator.

Add the penne to the boiling water and cook until al dente, according to package directions. Drain the penne and toss immediately with 1 Tbsp of the oil. Cover and let cool completely in the refrigerator, 1–24 hours.

Grate the zest of the uncut orange, then juice the orange. In a large bowl, whisk together the orange zest, orange juice, vinegar, and salt and pepper to taste. Add the remaining 4 Tbsp (2 fl oz/60 ml) oil in a thin stream, whisking constantly until the dressing is well blended. Add the penne, asparagus, sugar snap peas, and chives. Toss to mix well and serve at room temperature.

14

SHRIMP, CRAB & MÂCHE SALAD

serves 4–6

1 watermelon radish or daikon radish

¼ cup (2 oz/60 g) plain yogurt

3 Tbsp mayonnaise

4½ tsp Dijon mustard

Grated zest and juice of 1 lemon

2 Tbsp minced fresh chives

6 oz (185 g) mâche or field greens

½ lb (250 g) cooked shrimp, peeled with tail segments left intact and deveined

½ lb (250 g) cooked crabmeat, picked over for shell fragments

This salad is simple but elegant, perfect served as a first course at a brunch or luncheon. You can mix up the type of seafood: try bay shrimp, lobster, or even smoked fish.

Using a mandoline or a very sharp knife, thinly slice the radish. Set aside.

In a small bowl, whisk together the yogurt, mayonnaise, mustard, lemon zest and juice, and chives to make a dressing.

Divide the mâche among individual plates and top with the shrimp, crabmeat, and radish slices. Drizzle with the dressing and serve.

GLASS-NOODLE SALAD WITH SHRIMP, CHICKEN & MINT

serves 4

½ cup (4 fl oz/125 ml) chicken broth

6 oz (185 g) ground chicken

Salt and freshly ground pepper

6 oz (185 g) shrimp, peeled with tail segments left intact and deveined

¼ lb (125 g) bean thread noodles, soaked in warm water for 15 minutes and drained

FOR THE DRESSING

Juice of 2 limes

3 Tbsp Asian fish sauce

2 tsp sugar

1 Tbsp roasted chile paste

2 large red Fresno or serrano chiles, seeded and finely chopped

1 green onion, including tender green parts, chopped

3 Tbsp coarsely chopped fresh cilantro

1 Tbsp finely shredded fresh mint

4 large red-leaf lettuce leaves, torn into pieces

2 Tbsp fried shallot garnish *(left)*

To make the fried shallot garnish, slice 4 shallots into very thin slices, then separate the slices. Pour canola oil to a depth of about 1 inch (2.5 cm) in a small frying pan, place over medium heat, and heat to 325°F (165°C) on a deep-frying thermometer. Add the slices and fry until they turn light golden brown, about 5 minutes. Drain and let cool on paper towels.

In a saucepan, bring the broth to a gentle boil over medium heat. Add the chicken and cook, stirring to break up the meat, until the meat turns opaque and has a crumbled texture, about 3 minutes. Using a wire skimmer, transfer the chicken to a bowl. Season with salt and pepper and let cool.

Raise the heat under the boiling broth to medium-high, add the shrimp, and boil until they turn bright orange-pink, about 30 seconds. Drain well and let cool, then add to the bowl with the chicken.

Bring a saucepan three-fourths full of salted water to a boil over high heat. Add the noodles and cook until they are translucent, about 1 minute. Pour into a colander and rinse under cold running water. Drain well and transfer to a bowl. ⤳

To make the dressing, in a large bowl, combine the lime juice, fish sauce, sugar, roasted chile paste, and chiles. Stir together until the sugar dissolves. Add the chicken-shrimp mixture and the noodles to the dressing and toss to mix. Mix in the green onion, cilantro, and mint.

Divide the lettuce among individual salad bowls and mound the noodle salad on top. Garnish with the fried shallots. Serve at room temperature.

LEMON CHICKEN SALAD WITH TARRAGON

serves 4

1 lemon

2 skinless, boneless chicken breast halves (about 1 lb/500 g total weight)

Salt and freshly ground pepper

1 Tbsp grapeseed oil

½ fennel bulb, trimmed, quartered lengthwise, and finely chopped

1 green onion, including tender green parts, finely chopped

¾ tsp chopped fresh tarragon

⅓ cup (3 oz/80 g) mayonnaise

Tarragon and fennel are classic and delicious additions to chicken salad, but feel free to try other herb-and-vegetable combinations. One idea: chopped dill and diced Belgian endive for a Scandinavian-inspired version.

Grate ½ tsp zest from the lemon, then halve and squeeze 1 tsp juice. Set the zest and juice aside.

Place the chicken breast halves between 2 sheets of wax paper and pound them with a meat mallet to an even thickness. Pat dry.

Season both sides of the chicken breast halves with salt and pepper. In a large frying pan, warm the oil over medium heat. Add the chicken and cook until golden brown and opaque throughout, 4–5 minutes per side. Transfer to a cutting board and let stand for 5 minutes.

In a bowl, combine the lemon zest and juice, the fennel, green onion, tarragon, mayonnaise, ¾ tsp salt, and pepper to taste and mix until smooth. Chop the chicken finely and add to the fennel mixture. Toss until thoroughly blended and serve.

17

SEASONED BEAN SPROUT SALAD

serves 4–6

1 Tbsp sesame seeds

1½ lb (750 g) mung bean sprouts

2 Tbsp rice vinegar

1 Tbsp peanut oil

2 tsp toasted sesame oil

2 green onions, including tender green parts, minced

3 cloves garlic, minced

½ tsp chili powder

Salt

This salad, Korean in origin, is often served as one of many side dishes offered along with the usual steamed short-grain rice and soup. The salad may be made a day in advance. Mung bean sprouts release water as they marinate, so be sure to drain any excess liquid before serving the salad.

In a small frying pan, toast the sesame seeds over medium-low heat, stirring, until fragrant and starting to brown, about 2 minutes. Pour onto a plate and let cool.

Put the bean sprouts in a saucepan and add water to just cover. Bring to a boil over high heat and cook for 1 minute. Remove the pan from the heat, cover, and let stand for 2 minutes. Drain the sprouts and rinse under cold running water. Drain again, then gently squeeze the excess water from the sprouts. Transfer the sprouts to a clean kitchen towel, wring gently, and pat dry. Put the dry sprouts in a large bowl.

Put the vinegar in a bowl and add the peanut and sesame oils in a thin stream, whisking constantly until well blended. Add the green onions, garlic, sesame seeds, chili powder, and 1½ tsp salt and stir to mix well. Taste and adjust the seasonings. Pour the dressing over the bean sprouts and toss to coat thoroughly. Let stand at room temperature for 30 minutes before serving, or cover and refrigerate for at least 1 hour or up to overnight. Serve at room temperature or chilled.

18

INSALATA DI CAMPO

serves 4

1 bunch dandelion greens, or 12 large arugula leaves

1 head escarole, pale inner leaves only

½ small head radicchio

1 head frisée, pale yellow inner leaves only

¼ cup (1 oz/30 g) walnuts, coarsely chopped

4 Tbsp (2 fl oz/60 ml) extra-virgin olive oil

1 Tbsp red wine vinegar

1–2 Tbsp balsamic vinegar, depending upon age and intensity

Salt and freshly ground pepper

4 oz (125 g) thick slices pancetta, finely chopped

Parmesan cheese for shaving

An Italian favorite, this salad is full of the sharp, bitter flavors of chicories and dandelion greens. The more varied the greens, the better. Use the commonly available greens in this recipe, or look for specialty Italian chicories at farmers' markets and Italian produce markets. You should have about 6 cups (6 oz/185 g) of greens to make 4 salads.

Stem about 12 dandelion leaves, coarsely chop, and set aside. Tear the large leaves of escarole, radicchio, and frisée into bite-sized pieces, but leave small ones whole.

In a small frying pan, toast the walnuts over medium-low heat, stirring, until fragrant and starting to brown, about 5 minutes. Pour onto a plate to cool.

In a serving bowl, combine the oil and the vinegars and whisk well to make a vinaigrette. Stir in ½ tsp each salt and pepper. Taste and adjust the seasonings if needed. Set aside.

In a frying pan, cook the pancetta over medium-high heat until lightly browned, 3–4 minutes. Remove and set aside.

Just before serving, add the greens to the vinaigrette and toss. Divide among individual plates, topping each with pancetta and walnuts. Using a vegetable peeler, shave the cheese over the salad and serve.

19

BULGUR SALAD WITH LEMON, PEAS & MINT

serves 4

1 cup (6 oz/185 g) bulgur wheat

Salt and freshly ground pepper

2 tsp extra-virgin olive oil, plus 1 Tbsp

⅔ lb (315 g) sugar snap peas, trimmed and sliced on diagonal (about 2 cups)

⅓ cup (½ oz/15 g) minced fresh mint, plus sprigs for garnish

1 Tbsp fresh lemon juice

1 Tbsp capers, rinsed and chopped

2 oil-packed sun-dried tomatoes, chopped

Bulgur, the featured grain in the classic Mediterranean salad tabbouleh, is sometimes confused with cracked wheat. Bulgur comes in a variety of grinds, from fine to coarse, and is the better choice for salads. (Cracked wheat is crushed, and is better used as an addition to breads or in cereals.)

In a saucepan, bring 2 cups (16 fl oz/500 ml) water to a boil. Add the bulgur and ½ tsp salt. Return to a boil, then reduce the heat to low. Cover and cook until the bulgur is tender and the water is absorbed, about 20 minutes.

Combine the bulgur and the 2 tsp oil in a bowl, turning gently to coat and fluff the grains. Let cool to room temperature.

Add the sugar snap peas, minced mint, lemon juice, capers, sun-dried tomatoes, ½ tsp salt, ½ tsp pepper, and the 1 Tbsp oil to the bulgur. Stir well to blend. Garnish with the mint sprigs and serve at room temperature.

20

CRAB SUNOMONO

serves 4

1 large English cucumber, or 2 or 3 Japanese cucumbers

Salt

1 tsp sesame seeds

½ lb (250 g) cooked crabmeat, picked over for shell fragments

¼ cup (2 fl oz/60 ml) seasoned rice vinegar

1 Tbsp sake

1 tsp sugar

1 tsp soy sauce

¼ tsp toasted sesame oil

In Japanese, su means "vinegar," and mono means "thing." So this delicious dish literally translates to "vinegared thing." Pickled crab and cucumber salad is a healthful, simple salad that is the perfect start to a meal of sushi or other fish entrée. You can try thinly sliced daikon or raw asparagus in place of the cucumber.

Using a mandoline or box grater, slice the cucumber into very thin slices. Sprinkle with 1 tsp salt and toss to combine. Place in a fine-mesh sieve and let stand at room temperature until most of the liquid has drained out, about 10 minutes. Discard the liquid and squeeze the cucumbers to remove any remaining moisture.

Meanwhile, in a small frying pan, toast the sesame seeds over medium-low heat, stirring, until they are fragrant and starting to brown, about 2 minutes. Pour onto a plate and let cool.

In a bowl, combine the crabmeat and cucumber slices. In a separate small bowl, combine the vinegar, sake, sugar, soy sauce, and sesame oil and whisk until well combined. Pour the vinegar mixture over the cucumber and crab mixture and toss to combine.

Divide the crab mixture among individual plates and sprinkle with the sesame seeds before serving.

21

ASPARAGUS SALAD WITH LEMON & SHAVED PARMESAN

serves 6

3½ lb (1.75 kg) pencil-thin asparagus

Salt and freshly ground pepper

1 large lemon

2 Tbsp extra-virgin olive oil

Parmesan cheese for shaving

In this simple first course, salty, nutty-tasting Parmesan provides a suitably bold contrast to the natural acidity of lemon and the grassiness of asparagus. Extra-virgin olive oil, preferably a fruity one, binds together all of the elements nicely.

Bring a large saucepan two-thirds full of water to a boil over high heat. Have ready a bowl of ice water.

Trim off the tough end of each asparagus spear and cut the spears on the diagonal into 1½-inch (4-cm) lengths.

Add 1 Tbsp salt and the asparagus pieces to the boiling water and cook until the asparagus is crisp-tender and bright green, about 2½ minutes. Drain and then immediately plunge the asparagus into the ice water. Let stand until cool, about 2 minutes, then drain again and pat dry. Transfer to a serving platter.

Finely grate 1 Tbsp zest from the lemon, then halve and squeeze 1 Tbsp juice. In a small bowl, whisk together the lemon zest and juice, ¼ tsp salt, and ¼ tsp pepper. Add the oil in a thin stream, whisking constantly until the dressing is well blended. Taste and adjust the seasonings. Drizzle the dressing evenly over the asparagus. Using a vegetable peeler, shave the cheese over the asparagus and serve.

22

BITTER GREENS WITH DUCK BREAST & CHERRIES

serves 4

FOR THE CHAMPAGNE VINAIGRETTE

3 Tbsp fresh lemon juice

1 tsp champagne vinegar

Salt and freshly ground pepper

2 Tbsp extra-virgin olive oil

2 small heads radicchio

1 cup (1 oz/30 g) baby arugula leaves

½ cup (½ oz/15 g) torn bitter greens *(see note)*

2 Tbsp chopped fresh flat-leaf parsley

1 whole boneless duck breast

1 cup (¼ lb/125 g) fresh cherries, pitted and halved, or ¼ cup (1½ oz/45 g) dried tart cherries

For the bitter greens in this recipe, try red Asian mustard greens, watercress, or dandelion leaves torn into bite-sized pieces, or a blend. You can also use additional whole baby arugula leaves.

To make the vinaigrette, in a large bowl, whisk together the lemon juice, vinegar, ½ tsp salt, and ¼ tsp pepper. Add the oil in a thin stream, whisking constantly until the dressing is well blended. Set aside.

Using a sharp knife, cut away the hard white core from the base of the radicchio. Cut the head lengthwise into slices ¼ inch (6 mm) thick, then separate the layers and remove the hard V-shaped core. Put the cut radicchio into the bowl holding the vinaigrette. Add the arugula, bitter greens, and parsley and gently mix. Set aside.

Pat the duck breast dry. In a frying pan, warm ½ tsp salt over high heat. When it is hot, add the duck breast, skin side down. Reduce the heat to medium-high and cook until crisp and golden brown on the first side, 6–7 minutes. Turn and cook the other side until lightly browned, about 4 minutes. Cover the pan and cook until the duck breast is medium-rare, another 3–4 minutes. Transfer to paper towels to drain briefly.

Place the duck breast on a cutting board and separate the breast halves. Cut each half crosswise into slices ¼ inch (6 mm) thick.

Heap the dressed radicchio mixture onto a platter and arrange the duck slices and cherries on top of it. Serve warm.

23

ISRAELI COUSCOUS SALAD WITH FAVA BEANS & OLIVES

serves 6

3 cups (24 fl oz/750 ml) chicken broth

½ cup (4 fl oz/125 ml) fresh lemon juice

Salt

4 Tbsp (2 fl oz/60 ml) extra-virgin olive oil

2⅓ cups (¾ lb/375 g) Israeli couscous

2½ lb (1.25 kg) fava beans in the pod, shelled

4 carrots, peeled and finely chopped

¾ cup (1 oz/30 g) coarsely chopped fresh flat-leaf parsley

24 oil-cured black olives, pitted and coarsely chopped

5 oz (155 g) feta cheese, crumbled

If you prefer mild olives, try a large, meaty bright green Italian variety—Castelvetrano or Cerignola. They can be found jarred in most well-stocked supermarkets.

In a small saucepan, combine the broth, lemon juice, and ½ tsp salt and bring to a boil over high heat. Meanwhile, in a saucepan, warm 2 Tbsp of the olive oil over medium heat. Add the couscous and cook, stirring occasionally, until light golden brown, about 4 minutes.

Pour the hot broth mixture over the couscous, raise the heat to high, and bring to a boil. Cover immediately, reduce the heat to medium-low, and simmer until all of the liquid has been absorbed, about 15 minutes. Drizzle the remaining 2 Tbsp olive oil over the couscous, stir to mix, and transfer to a large bowl. Let cool to room temperature.

While the couscous cools, fill a saucepan three-fourths full with salted water and bring to a boil over high heat. Have ready a bowl of ice water. Add the fava beans to the boiling water and blanch just until tender, about 2 minutes. Use a slotted spoon to remove the beans and immediately transfer them to the ice water. Let stand until cool, then lift out the beans with the slotted spoon. Add the carrots to the boiling salted water and cook until crisp-tender, about 2 minutes. Transfer the carrots to the ice water. Let stand until cool, then drain again.

Pinch each fava bean to pop it from its skin. You should have about 1¼ cups skinned beans. Add the fava beans, carrots, parsley, olives, and cheese to the bowl with the couscous, toss well, and serve.

24

CLASSIC EGG SALAD

serves 4

8 eggs

¼ cup (2 fl oz/60 ml) mayonnaise

1 Tbsp Dijon mustard

1 Tbsp chopped fresh tarragon

1 Tbsp chopped fresh chives

2 tsp chopped fresh dill

¼ cup (1 oz/30 g) thinly sliced celery

Salt and freshly ground pepper

What's more comforting than a classic, creamy egg salad sandwiched between two slices of toasted bread? Or a few spoonfuls accompanied with slices of fresh tomato and some crisp lettuce? If you ever have a carton of eggs that are about to expire, this salad is a most delicious way to use them up.

To hard-cook the eggs, place them in a saucepan just large enough to hold them. Add cold water to cover by 1 inch (2.5 cm) and bring just to a boil over high heat. Remove the pan from the heat and cover. Let stand for 15 minutes. Have ready a bowl of ice water. Drain the eggs, then transfer to the ice water and let cool.

Peel the eggs and slice them into a bowl. Then, using 2 table knives, scissor-cut them into smaller pieces. Add the mayonnaise, mustard, herbs, celery, salt to taste, and a few grindings of pepper, and mix to combine evenly. Serve.

25

ARTICHOKE & WHITE BEAN SALAD

serves 8

This salad makes enough for a crowd and is great for festive spring gatherings, alongside a pork roast or grilled chicken. You can make the salad in advance and keep it covered in the refrigerator for up to 24 hours. Remove from the refrigerator 30 minutes before serving.

FOR THE DRESSING

¼ cup (2 fl oz/60 ml) fresh lemon juice

1 clove garlic, thinly sliced

1 tsp Dijon mustard

¼ tsp red pepper flakes

1 tsp ground fennel seeds

Salt and freshly ground pepper

½ cup (4 fl oz/125 ml) extra-virgin olive oil

½ lemon (if using fresh artichokes)

6 baby artichokes, or 1 package (8 oz/250 g) frozen quartered artichoke hearts, thawed and brought to room temperature

2 cans (15 oz/470 g each) white beans, rinsed and drained

1 small red onion, chopped

2 celery ribs, thinly sliced

2 Tbsp chopped fresh oregano

To make the dressing, in a large bowl, whisk together the lemon juice, garlic, mustard, red pepper flakes, and fennel seeds. Season with salt and pepper to taste. Add the oil in a thin stream, whisking constantly until the dressing is well blended.

If using fresh artichokes, squeeze the lemon half into a large bowl of cold water. Trim the artichoke stems, leaving about ½ inch (12 mm). Cut ½ inch off the tops. Peel off the tough outer leaves until you reach the tender, pale green leaves. Cut each artichoke lengthwise into 6 wedges and immerse in the lemon water. Bring a pot three-fourths full of salted water to a boil. Add the artichokes and cook until tender, about 15 minutes. Drain and let cool to room temperature.

In a large bowl, combine the artichokes, beans, onion, celery, and oregano and toss well. Let stand for at least 30 minutes or refrigerate for up to 4 hours to allow the flavors to blend before serving.

26

GREEN BEAN SALAD WITH SWEET & SOUR MUSTARD VINAIGRETTE

serves 6

In this delicious riff on the everyday green bean salad, the beans are combined with nutrient-rich chickpeas, crunchy radishes, and crisp bacon and then tossed with a sweet-tart mustardy vinaigrette. It's the ideal side dish for a seaside picnic or a backyard barbecue. For a vegetarian version, omit the bacon.

Salt and freshly ground pepper

1½ lb (750 g) green beans, trimmed and halved crosswise

4 slices bacon (optional)

¼ cup (2 fl oz/60 ml) cider vinegar

6 Tbsp (3 oz/90 g) packed light brown sugar

6 Tbsp (3 oz/90 g) whole-grain mustard

2 Tbsp Dijon mustard

½ cup (3/4 oz/20 g) chopped fresh chives

1 can (15 oz/470 g) chickpeas, drained and rinsed

8 radishes, thinly sliced

Bring a large saucepan three-fourths full of salted water to a boil over high heat. Meanwhile, prepare a large bowl of ice water. Add the green beans to the boiling water and cook until crisp-tender, about 4 minutes. Using a strainer, scoop out the green beans and immerse them in the ice water, then drain and set aside.

If using the bacon, in a frying pan, cook the bacon over medium heat, turning as needed, until crispy, 7–8 minutes. Transfer to paper towels to drain. When cool enough to handle, crumble the bacon.

In a small bowl, whisk together the vinegar, brown sugar, mustards, and chives until the vinaigrette is well blended. Season with salt and pepper.

In a large bowl, toss together the green beans, chickpeas, radishes, and bacon (if using). Drizzle with the vinaigrette and toss well to combine. Taste and adjust the seasonings and serve.

27

POTATO SALAD WITH FAVA BEANS, GREEN GARLIC & CRÈME FRAÎCHE

serves 4–6

Strictly seasonal, green garlic and spring onions are the season's gems. Green garlic is milder than its mature relative and looks like a slightly larger green onion. True spring onions resemble green onions but have an oversized white bulb close to the size of a conventional white onion.

1 lb (500 g) young fava beans in the pod, shelled (about 1 cup)

6 stems green garlic

4 spring onions

2½ lb (1.25 kg) small waxy potatoes such as Yukon Gold, Yellow Finn, or Red Rose

Salt and freshly ground pepper

½ cup (4 fl oz/125 ml) mayonnaise

½ cup (4 oz/125 g) crème fraîche

2 tsp Dijon mustard

2 tsp fresh lemon juice

1 Tbsp minced fresh tarragon, plus ½ tsp

1 Tbsp minced fresh flat-leaf parsley, plus ½ tsp

Bring a saucepan of water to a boil over medium-high heat. Blanch the shelled favas just until the skin plumps, about 20 seconds. Drain and pinch each bean to pop it from its skin. Set the beans aside.

Remove the tough outer skin from each green garlic stem. Finely chop the bulbs and set aside.

Trim the spring onions, leaving about 2 inches (5 cm) of light green, and finely chop. Set aside.

In a saucepan, combine the potatoes with water to cover by 2 inches (5 cm) and add 1 tsp salt. Bring to a boil over medium-high heat, then reduce the heat to medium and cook, uncovered, until tender and easily pierced with a fork, 20–25 minutes. Drain, and when just cool enough to handle, peel and cut into ½-inch (12-mm) cubes. Place the still-warm potatoes in a large bowl.

In a bowl, combine the mayonnaise, crème fraîche, mustard, lemon juice, ½ tsp salt, and ½ tsp pepper. Mix well. Taste and adjust the seasoning. Spoon this dressing over the warm potatoes, turning gently. Add the green garlic, spring onions, the 1 Tbsp each tarragon and parsley, and the fava beans, reserving a few for garnish. Turn well.

Garnish with the remaining tarragon, parsley, and fava beans before serving.

28

GRILLED ASPARAGUS & RADISH SALAD

serves 4

The asparagus absorbs a subtle smoky flavor and a bit of char from its relatively brief time on the grill, which together enhance its natural grassy flavor. Finishing the salad with a squeeze of juice from grilled lemon halves adds the perfect tart accent.

1 bunch asparagus, tough ends trimmed

1 tablespoon extra-virgin olive oil, plus more for drizzling

1 clove garlic, minced

1 tablespoon chopped fresh flat-leaf parsley

Zest and juice of 1 lemon

Salt and freshly ground pepper

1 large shallot, thinly sliced

2 lemons, halved

6 radishes, very thinly sliced

5 oz (155 g) baby arugula

Prepare a charcoal or gas grill for direct-heat cooking over medium-high heat and preheat a grill basket. Alternatively, preheat a stove-top grill pan over medium-high heat.

Cut the asparagus on the diagonal into 1-inch (2.5-cm) pieces. In a small bowl, combine the olive oil, garlic, parsley, lemon zest, lemon juice, and season with salt and pepper. In a large bowl, combine the asparagus, shallots, and lemon-oil mixture and toss to coat.

Put the asparagus mixture in the grill basket. Place the lemons, cut side down, directly on the grill and cover the grill. Or place the asparagus mixture and lemons in the grill pan. Cook for 5 minutes, then transfer the lemons to a bowl. Add the radishes to the grill basket or pan and cook, tossing occasionally, until the radishes are slightly softened and start to look transparent, 1–2 minutes.

Divide the arugula among individual plates. Top with the asparagus mixture and drizzle with oil. Finish with a squeeze of the grilled lemons and serve.

29

MÂCHE, PURSLANE & GREEN ONION SALAD

serves 4–6

Purslane, a succulent with a slightly sour taste, is a bright and flavorful green to use in salads. Here, a mix of purslane and the milder mâche strikes just the right flavor balance, and is delicious with a citrusy vinaigrette.

FOR THE LEMON-THYME VINAIGRETTE

Grated zest and juice of ½ lemon

¼ cup (2 fl oz/60 ml) white wine vinegar

1½ tsp fresh thyme leaves

Salt and freshly ground pepper

½ cup (4 fl oz/125 ml) extra-virgin olive oil

4 cups (4 oz/125 g) mâche or field greens

4 cups (4 oz/125 g) purslane, thick stems removed, or baby arugula

4 green onions, including tender green parts, cut into 1-inch (2.5-cm) pieces (on the diagonal if thick)

To make the vinaigrette, in a large bowl, whisk together the lemon zest and juice, vinegar, thyme, and salt and pepper to taste. Add the oil in a thin stream, whisking constantly until the dressing is well blended.

Add the mâche, purslane, and green onions to the bowl and toss with the vinaigrette. Season with salt and pepper to taste and serve.

30

CHARRED ASPARAGUS SALAD WITH POACHED EGG & KUMQUAT VINAIGRETTE

serves 4

Kumquat dressing might sound counterintuitive because the fruit is so small. However, its zest, which holds the fruit's essential oils, carries a bold flavor, so only a few kumquats are needed to transform a classic asparagus and poached egg dish into something special.

24–32 asparagus spears, ends trimmed

3½ Tbsp extra-virgin olive oil

1½ tsp sea salt

½ tsp freshly ground pepper

8 kumquats

1 tsp white wine vinegar

4 large eggs

Place the asparagus in a shallow baking dish, drizzle with 1 Tbsp of the oil, ¼ teaspoon of the salt, and ¼ teaspoon of the pepper, and turn to coat well.

Peel 4 of the kumquats by making an incision lengthwise from top to bottom, then remove the peel with your fingers. Finely chop the peel and set aside. Squeeze the juice from the kumquat flesh into a small bowl, removing the seeds. Discard the pulp. Thinly slice the remaining 4 kumquats crosswise and remove the seeds. Set aside.

Add the remaining 2½ Tbsp oil, ¼ tsp salt, and ¼ tsp pepper to the bowl with the kumquat juice and chopped peel and whisk until the vinaigrette is well blended. Set aside.

Prepare a charcoal or gas grill for direct-heat cooking over medium-high heat. Alternatively, preheat a stove-top grill pan over medium-high heat. Place the asparagus on the grill rack or in the grill pan and cook, turning several times, until charred, bright green, and tender but not soft, 3–4 minutes. Transfer to a plate.

In a large frying pan, pour in water to within 1 inch (2.5 cm) of the rim. Bring to a simmer over medium-high heat, add 1 tsp salt and the vinegar, and reduce the heat to low. Working quickly, crack the eggs one at a time into a small bowl and slide each into the simmering water. Cover the pan, remove from the heat, and let the eggs sit for 4–5 minutes, until the whites are just set and the yolks are still soft.

Arrange 6–8 asparagus spears on each salad plate. Drizzle a little of the dressing over them. Using a slotted spatula, remove the eggs one at a time and place on the asparagus. Drizzle with the remaining vinaigrette. Garnish with the kumquat slices and serve.

Now is the right time of year to enjoy alfresco lunches of crisp young greens, shoots, and edible flowers drizzled with a bright vinaigrette. For main-course salads, partner grilled salmon with crisp spears of asparagus, or roast beef with tender leeks, for a satisfying meal. Sprightly lemons add their signature flavor to the best of this season's dressings, especially when accented with fresh herbs such as dill, tarragon, and mint.

may

PEA & ASPARAGUS SALAD WITH MEYER LEMON DRESSING

serves 6–8

Salt and freshly ground pepper

2 cups (10 oz/315 g) fresh shelled English peas (about 2 lb/1 kg unshelled)

2 lb (1 kg) thin asparagus tips

2 cups (2 oz/60 g) pea shoots

Shredded zest and juice of 1 Meyer lemon or regular lemon

¼ cup (2 fl oz/60 ml) extra-virgin olive oil

¼ tsp sugar, if needed

An all-green salad makes a bold statement that spring has arrived, but you can also use a mix of asparagus colors— green, white, and purple—for a very pretty combination. Shaved Parmesan or pecorino can be added for a rich, nutty note, and any leftover salad can be stirred into risotto, pasta, or omelettes.

Bring a saucepan three-fourths full of salted water to a boil. Meanwhile, prepare a large bowl of ice water. Add the peas to the boiling water and blanch for 1 minute. Using a strainer, scoop out the peas and refresh them in the ice water. Scoop them out of the ice water with the strainer, and set aside.

Using the same boiling water, cook the asparagus until tender, 3 minutes. Add more ice to the bowl of ice water, if needed. Drain the asparagus and refresh in the same bowl of ice water. Drain again, slice in half lengthwise, and set aside.

In a bowl, combine the peas, asparagus, pea shoots, lemon zest and juice, and oil, and toss to combine. Add the sugar if not using Meyer lemon juice. Season with salt and pepper to taste. Transfer to a platter or divide among individual plates and serve.

CHEF'S SALAD WITH SOPRESSATA, FONTINA & PICKLED PEPPERS

serves 6

5 thick slices day-old country-style bread

2 Tbsp extra-virgin olive oil

Salt and freshly ground pepper

FOR THE OREGANO VINAIGRETTE

¼ cup (2 fl oz/60 ml) extra-virgin olive oil

1 Tbsp minced shallot

2 Tbsp red wine vinegar

2 Tbsp chopped fresh oregano

12–15 cherry tomatoes, halved

1½ heads romaine lettuce, torn into bite-sized pieces (about 6 cups/6 oz/185 g)

18 slices sopressata or salami, cut into triangles

6 oz (185 g) fontina cheese, thinly sliced and cut into strips ½ inch (12 mm) wide

8 oz (250 g) peperoncini, coarsely chopped

1 Tbsp chopped fresh oregano

Think of this as an antipasto platter transformed into a chef's salad with the addition of lettuce and a dressing, and this will help you to create your own variations. Different cured meats, such as salami or bresaola, could be used, or cheeses such as pecorino or mozzarella.

Preheat the oven to 400°F (200°C).

Cut the bread into 1-inch (2.5-cm) cubes. Put them on a baking sheet just large enough to hold the cubes in a single layer, drizzle with the 2 Tbsp oil, and toss several times to coat. Sprinkle with ½ tsp salt. Bake, turning several times, until golden, 10–15 minutes. Set the croutons aside.

To make the vinaigrette, in the bottom of a large bowl, combine the ¼ cup oil, shallot, vinegar, 2 Tbsp oregano, ¼ tsp salt, and ¼ tsp pepper. Mix well with a fork or whisk.

Add the tomatoes to the vinaigrette and press them slightly with the back of a fork to release their juices. Just before serving, add the lettuce and half the croutons and toss.

Divide the dressed salad evenly among individual bowls. Divide and arrange the sopressata, cheese, peperoncini, and remaining croutons on each salad. Sprinkle with the 1 Tbsp oregano and serve.

3

To make this dish into a pasta salad, simply toss about ¾ lb (375 g) cooked and drained fettuccine with the prepared salad. As a pasta salad, the recipe will yield 8 to 10 servings.

SALAD OF SPRING BEANS, PEAS & ZUCCHINI RIBBONS

serves 4

Salt and freshly ground pepper

1 cup (5 oz/155 g) fresh shelled English peas (about 1 lb/500 g unshelled)

2 lb (1 kg) fava beans in the pod, shelled

½ lb (250 g) haricots verts or other young, tender green beans, stem ends trimmed

4 zucchini (about 1 lb/500 g total weight)

FOR THE BASIL MARINADE

2 cloves garlic

⅓ cup (3 fl oz/80 ml) extra-virgin olive oil

3 Tbsp fresh lemon juice

⅓ cup (½ oz/15 g) julienned fresh basil leaves

15 anchovy fillets

½ cup (2 oz/60 g) Parmesan cheese shavings

Bring a saucepan three-fourths full of salted water to a boil over medium-high heat and add the peas. Boil until just tender, 3–5 minutes. Do not overcook. Using a strainer, scoop out the peas and place them under cold running water to stop the cooking. Drain again and set aside.

Add the fava beans to the same boiling water. Blanch until just tender, about 2 minutes. Drain and let cool, then pinch each bean to pop it from its skin. Set aside.

Arrange the green beans in a steamer basket, pour out most of the water from the saucepan, return it to the heat, and place the basket over the boiling water. (The water should not touch the bottom of the basket.) Cover and steam just until the beans are tender, 3–4 minutes for haricots verts and 5–7 minutes for larger beans. Lift out the basket and place under cold running water to stop the cooking. Drain and set aside.

Using a vegetable peeler, peel the zucchini. Then, still using the vegetable peeler, cut the flesh of the zucchini into long, thin, fettuccinelike ribbons. Set aside. ↠

To make the marinade, in a bowl or mortar, combine the garlic and ½ tsp salt. Using a fork or a pestle, crush them into a paste. Using a fork, stir vigorously as you add the oil in a thin stream, and then stir in the lemon juice and ½ tsp pepper. Pour this mixture into a large bowl and add the peas, favas, green beans, zucchini ribbons, and the basil. Turn until well coated, cover, and refrigerate for at least 1½ hours or up to 5 hours.

To serve, gently mix all but 4 or 5 of the anchovy fillets into the vegetables. Transfer the mixture to a serving bowl or a platter and top with the remaining anchovies. Scatter the cheese shavings over the vegetables and anchovies and serve.

4

The acid in the lemon juice "cooks" the fish in this quick-to-assemble ceviche, leaving it moist and tender. Look for specialty dried tomatoes, such as Sungolds or Sweet 100s, or dry your own: halve them, place cut side up on a parchment paper–lined baking sheet, drizzle very lightly with olive oil, sprinkle with salt and pepper, and place in a 225°F (110°C) oven until shriveled but still slightly moist, 2 to 3 hours, depending on the size of the tomatoes.

CEVICHE SALAD CUPS WITH SUN-DRIED TOMATOES & GINGER

serves 4

1 lb (500 g) true cod or other firm white fish, diced

¼ cup (2 fl oz/60 ml) fresh lime juice, plus 2 limes, quartered

2 tsp peeled and grated fresh ginger

2 Tbsp minced sun-dried tomatoes

2 Tbsp chopped fresh cilantro

2 Tbsp minced shallot

8 butter lettuce leaves

In a bowl, combine the fish, lime juice, ginger, and sun-dried tomatoes and stir gently to mix. Let stand for 10 minutes, then stir in the cilantro and shallot. Cover and refrigerate until the fish is opaque, at least 1 hour or up to 4 hours before serving.

Tuck 2 lettuce leaves together to make each lettuce cup. Mound the ceviche into the cups, garnish with the lime wedges, and serve.

5

BULGUR SALAD WITH ZUCCHINI, ASPARAGUS & GREEN ONIONS

serves 6

For a spring twist on tabbouleh, this salad gives you the chance to fire up the grill and embrace the warmer weather. Bursting with green vegetables and herbs of spring— asparagus, zucchini, green onions, and mint and parsley— the salad is fresh and bright-tasting. Serve alongside grilled lamb chops for a quick and healthful dinner.

8–10 spears asparagus, tough ends trimmed

2 zucchini, cut on diagonal into slices ¼ inch (6 mm) thick

1 tsp olive oil

1½ cups (9 oz/280 g) bulgur wheat

FOR THE LEMON-CARDAMOM DRESSING

2 tsp grated lemon zest

2 Tbsp fresh lemon juice

2 tsp ground cumin

½ tsp ground turmeric

½ tsp cardamom seeds, crushed

Salt and freshly ground pepper

3 Tbsp extra-virgin olive oil

1 cup (7 oz/220 g) canned chickpeas, drained and rinsed

2 green onions, including tender green parts, thinly sliced

1 bunch fresh mint leaves, minced

2 Tbsp minced fresh flat-leaf parsley

Prepare a charcoal or gas grill for direct-heat cooking over medium heat.

If the asparagus spears are thick, peel them to within about 2 inches (5 cm) of the tips. Put the asparagus and zucchini in a heatproof bowl, pour boiling water over to cover, and let stand for 2 minutes to soften slightly. Drain, let cool, and toss with the 1 tsp oil. If desired, put them in a grill basket.

When the grill is ready, put the bulgur in a heatproof bowl and add boiling water to cover by 2 inches (5 cm). Let stand for 10 minutes. Meanwhile, grill the asparagus and zucchini, turning often, until lightly browned and crisp-tender, 4–5 minutes. Remove to a platter and let cool slightly. Cut the asparagus spears on the diagonal into thirds.

To make the dressing, in a bowl, whisk together the lemon zest and juice, cumin, turmeric, cardamom, 1 tsp salt, and several grindings of pepper. Add the 3 Tbsp oil in a thin stream, whisking constantly until the dressing is smooth. ⤛

Pour the dressing into a saucepan, add the chickpeas, and warm over medium heat for a couple of minutes, stirring occasionally.

Drain the bulgur. Combine the bulgur, grilled vegetables, green onions, mint, parsley, and chickpeas with the dressing in a serving bowl and toss to coat evenly. Serve warm or at room temperature.

6

FAVA BEAN & CORN SALAD WITH FRESH MINT

serves 4

Sweet young corn and buttery fresh fava beans make an irresistible pair in this simple salad. Even after shelling, fava beans have a second skin that needs to be peeled away in all but the youngest, most tender beans. Serve with warm sourdough bread and sweet butter.

Salt and freshly ground pepper

2 cups (12 oz/375 g) fresh or thawed frozen corn kernels (from about 2 ears of corn)

1½ lb (750 g) fava beans in the pod, shelled

2 Tbsp extra-virgin olive oil

1½ Tbsp cider vinegar

8 radishes, trimmed and thinly sliced

2 Tbsp coarsely chopped fresh mint leaves

Bring a large pot of salted water to a boil. Add the corn and cook for 1 minute. Using a strainer, scoop out the corn and set aside.

Add the fava beans to the boiling water and cook until just tender, about 2 minutes. Drain and rinse under cold running water. Pinch each fava bean to pop it from its skin.

In a bowl, whisk together the oil and vinegar until well blended. Stir in the corn, favas, radishes, and mint. Season with ½ tsp salt and a few grindings of pepper. Serve at once, or cover and refrigerate for up to 4 hours and serve chilled.

WARM FARRO SALAD WITH HERBS

serves 4–6

Farro is a great base for salads as the seasons change. It is both hearty and nutty, pairing nicely with spring's fresh herbs, new onions, and lemon juice. Serve the salad warm if there is still chill in the air, or at room temperature if you venture out on a picnic.

4 Tbsp (2 fl oz/60 ml) extra-virgin olive oil

1 bay leaf

1 fresh rosemary sprig

1 cup (6 oz/185 g) farro

2 cups (16 fl oz/500 ml) chicken broth

Salt and freshly ground pepper

Grated zest and juice of 1 lemon

¼ cup (½ oz/15 g) chopped fresh chives

¼ cup (⅓ oz/10 g) chopped fresh chervil

¼ cup (⅓ oz/10 g) chopped fresh flat-leaf parsley

¼ cup (¾ oz/20 g) chopped green onion, including tender green parts

1½ tsp chopped fresh tarragon

In a large saucepan, warm 2 Tbsp of the olive oil over medium heat. Add the bay leaf, rosemary, and farro and cook, stirring, for 1 minute. Add the broth, 2 cups (16 fl oz/ 500 ml) water, 1 tsp salt, and several grindings of pepper. Bring to a boil, then cover, reduce the heat, and simmer until the farro is tender and the liquid is absorbed, about 20 minutes. Remove from the heat and let cool slightly.

Discard the bay leaf and rosemary and transfer the farro to a bowl. Add the lemon zest and juice, the remaining 2 Tbsp olive oil, the chives, chervil, parsley, green onion, and tarragon and toss to combine. Season with salt and serve warm.

SPRING GREENS & FLOWERS SALAD

serves 6

Celebrate spring with this colorful, simple-to-make salad. You can buy edible, pesticide-free flowers at many greengrocers and farmers' markets, or grow some in your garden at home. Other pretty, edible flowers include pansies, violets, hibiscuses, and scented geraniums.

4 cups (4 oz/125 g) baby spinach leaves

4 cups (4 oz/125 g) oakleaf lettuce leaves

1 cup (1 oz/30 g) mâche or field greens

½ cup (¾ oz/20 g) garlic chive flowers, or 2 Tbsp minced fresh chives

¼ cup (2 fl oz/60 ml) rice vinegar

2 Tbsp peeled and minced fresh young ginger or 1 Tbsp mature fresh ginger

1 clove garlic, minced

½ cup (4 fl oz/125 ml) safflower oil

Salt and freshly ground pepper

12 nasturtiums or other edible flowers

In a large bowl, combine the spinach, oakleaf lettuce, mâche, and chive flowers. Toss gently to mix and set aside.

In a small bowl, combine the rice vinegar, ginger, and garlic. Add the oil in a thin stream, whisking constantly until the vinaigrette is well blended. Season with salt and pepper to taste.

Drizzle the vinaigrette over the greens and toss to mix well. Transfer to a serving bowl, garnish with the nasturtiums, and serve.

9

WARM GOAT CHEESE & CHICKEN SALAD

serves 4

½ cup (2 oz/60 g) fine dried bread crumbs or panko

Salt and freshly ground pepper

1 large egg

8 oz (250 g) fresh goat cheese, cut into 8 thick rounds

Grated zest and juice of 1 lemon

1 tsp tarragon mustard or Dijon mustard

5 Tbsp (2½ fl oz/75 ml) olive oil

2 tsp finely chopped fresh tarragon

6 oz (185 g) mixed baby salad greens

3 cups (18 oz/560 g) shredded roasted chicken

2 Tbsp grapeseed oil

This salad is also delicious without the chicken, as a classic goat cheese side salad. Serve with a crisp white wine like sauvignon blanc or pinot gris.

In a shallow bowl, combine the bread crumbs and a pinch each of salt and pepper. Lightly beat the egg in another shallow bowl. Dip 1 flat surface of each cheese round into the egg, letting the excess egg drip back into the bowl. Then dip the egg-coated surface of each in the bread crumbs, patting the crumbs in place. Leave the second side and the rims of the cheese rounds uncoated. Set aside.

In a large bowl, whisk together the lemon zest and juice, mustard, ¼ tsp salt, and a pinch of pepper. Add the olive oil in a thin stream, whisking constantly until the dressing is smooth. Stir in the tarragon.

Add the mixed greens and the chicken to the dressing and toss to coat evenly. Arrange on individual plates. In a large nonstick frying pan, warm the grapeseed oil over medium-high heat until it shimmers. Working in batches if needed, add the cheese rounds and cook on the crumbed side until just beginning to soften but not melt, about 45 seconds. Carefully flip the rounds and cook for about 30 seconds on the other side. Top the salads with the cheeses and serve.

10

POTATO SALAD WITH ARTICHOKES, FETA CHEESE & OLIVE RELISH

serves 4–6

FOR THE OLIVE RELISH

5 Tbsp (2½ fl oz/75 ml) olive oil

2½ Tbsp white wine vinegar

1 large clove garlic, minced

1½ tsp dried oregano

Salt and freshly ground pepper

6 large Greek or Sicilian green olives, pitted and chopped

6–8 brine-cured black Mediterranean olives, pitted and chopped

½ cup (2½ oz/75 g) chopped fennel

3 large green onions, including green parts, chopped

12 small multicolored potatoes (about 2½ lb/1.25 kg total weight)

1 can (14 oz/440 g) quartered artichoke hearts in water

5 oz (155 g) feta cheese, coarsely crumbled

Although feta originated in Greece, French feta, milder and less salty, is better for this salad because of the saltiness of the olive relish. You can make the olive relish up to a day in advance. Cover and refrigerate, stirring occasionally, until ready to use.

To make the olive relish, combine the oil, vinegar, garlic, oregano, and ¼ tsp pepper in a bowl. Whisk to blend. Stir in the olives, fennel, and two-thirds of the green onions.

Bring a large pot of salted water to a boil. Add the potatoes and cook until tender when pierced with a small knife, about 25 minutes. Drain and let stand until cool to the touch, about 20 minutes. Cut the potatoes in half, then transfer to a large bowl. Sprinkle with salt and pepper to taste. Add the artichokes and olive relish. Toss to blend. Stir in most of the cheese, reserving some for sprinkling on top.

Sprinkle the remaining green onions and the remaining cheese over the salad and serve.

SPRING HERB SALAD WITH WALNUT-CRUSTED GOAT CHEESE

serves 6

6 Tbsp (3 fl oz/90 ml) champagne vinegar

2 shallots, minced

1 Tbsp honey

Salt and freshly ground pepper

½ cup (4 fl oz/125 ml) plus 2 Tbsp walnut oil

3 cups (12 oz/375 g) walnuts

2 logs (9 oz/280 g each) fresh goat cheese

¼ cup (2 fl oz/60 ml) extra-virgin olive oil

7 cups (7 oz/220 g) mâche, field greens, baby arugula, baby spinach, or a combination

½ cup (¾ oz/20 g) coarsely chopped fresh dill

1 cup (1½ oz/45 g) coarsely chopped fresh flat-leaf parsley

½ cup (¾ oz/20 g) minced fresh chives

Goat cheese crusted with nuts and baked until warm is a delicious topping for a fresh herb salad with a slightly sweet, acidic dressing. If you like, serve with a basket of garlic-rubbed crostini and spread the goat cheese on top.

Preheat the oven to 350°F (180°C).

In a small bowl, whisk together the vinegar, shallots, honey, 2 pinches of salt, and several grindings of pepper. Add the walnut oil in a thin stream, whisking constantly until the vinaigrette is well blended. Taste and adjust the seasonings. Set aside.

In a small frying pan, toast the walnuts over medium-low heat, stirring, until fragrant and starting to brown, about 5 minutes. Pour onto a plate to cool, then finely chop. In a bowl, stir together the chopped walnuts and ¼ tsp salt.

Season each cheese log with salt and pepper. Using a thin-bladed knife, cut each log crosswise into 6 equal slices. Coat the slices on all sides with the walnuts, pressing gently so that the nuts adhere. Transfer to a rimmed baking sheet and drizzle lightly with the olive oil. Bake until warm, about 5 minutes.

Meanwhile, in a large bowl, toss together the mâche, dill, parsley, chives, 2 pinches of salt, and several grindings of pepper. Whisk the vinaigrette to recombine, then drizzle one-third of it over the greens and toss well. Taste and adjust the seasonings. Divide the dressed greens among individual plates. Top each serving with 2 warm cheese rounds. Pass the remaining dressing at the table for drizzling.

CELERY & MUSHROOM SALAD WITH SHAVED PARMESAN

serves 6–8

4–6 celery ribs

½ lb (250 g) very firm white button mushrooms

3 Tbsp minced fresh flat-leaf parsley

3–4 Tbsp extra-virgin olive oil

1–2 Tbsp fresh lemon juice

Salt and freshly ground pepper

¼-lb (125-g) piece Parmesan cheese

Celery makes an excellent light yet full-flavored salad. For the best results, use firm fresh mushrooms for this recipe, with tightly closed caps revealing not a hint of the gills. Take care with cutting each ingredient, as texture is an important element of this salad.

Using a small knife, peel back the celery strings, starting at the base of each celery rib. Discard the strings. Using a mandoline or a very sharp knife, cut the celery into paper-thin slices.

Trim ¼ inch (6 mm) off each mushroom stem. Using a mandoline or a very sharp knife, cut the mushrooms lengthwise into paper-thin slices.

In a large bowl, whisk together the parsley, oil, lemon juice, ½ tsp salt, and ½ tsp pepper until the dressing is well blended. Add the celery and mushrooms and toss gently. Taste and adjust the seasonings.

Using a cheese slicer or a vegetable peeler, scrape along the largest surface of the cheese to yield 8–12 curls. Reserve remaining Parmesan for another use.

Divide the salad among individual plates or a platter and garnish with the cheese.

13

Baby artichokes grow lower down on the stalk than the larger variety. They do not have chokes, which saves on prep time. Drop them into a bowl of water mixed with the juice of a lemon to slow discoloration after cutting them.

PASTA SALAD WITH BABY ARTICHOKES & GRILLED TUNA

serves 4–6

Salt and freshly ground pepper

1 lb (500 g) cavatappi, penne, or fusilli pasta

9 Tbsp (5 fl oz/160 ml) extra-virgin olive oil, plus more for coating

1 lemon

About 20 baby artichokes

3 cloves garlic, very thinly sliced

½ cup (4 fl oz/125 ml) dry white wine

3 ripe tomatoes, peeled, seeded, and finely chopped

1 lb (500 g) tuna steak, about 1½ inches (4 cm) thick

½ red onion, very thinly sliced

Grated zest and juice of 1 large orange

Leaves from 5–6 large sprigs fresh mint

Leaves from 5–6 large sprigs fresh marjoram, coarsely chopped

Bring a large pot of salted water to a boil. Add the pasta and cook until al dente, according to package directions. Drain and rinse under cold water to stop the cooking. Drain well, transfer to a large bowl, and toss with 3 Tbsp of the oil. Set aside.

Halve and squeeze the lemon into a large bowl of cold water. Trim the artichoke stems, leaving about ½ inch (12 mm). Cut ½ inch off the tops. Peel off the tough outer leaves until you reach the tender, pale green leaves. Halve each artichoke lengthwise and immerse in the lemon water.

In a frying pan, warm 3 Tbsp of the oil over medium heat. Drain the artichokes well, pat dry, and add them, along with the garlic, to the pan. Season with salt and pepper to taste. Sauté until they are just turning golden at the edges, about 5 minutes. Add the white wine and let it boil away. Add ½ cup (4 fl oz/125 ml) warm water and simmer, uncovered, on medium-low heat until the artichokes are tender, about 5 minutes (if the liquid evaporates before the artichokes are tender, add a little extra warm water). Turn off the heat and add the tomatoes, tossing gently.

Prepare a charcoal or gas grill for direct-heat cooking over high heat. Alternatively, heat a stove-top grill pan over high heat. »→

Coat the tuna lightly with oil and season with salt and pepper to taste. Place the tuna on the grill or in the grill pan and sear on one side without moving it until you can see the edges are nicely browned, about 4–5 minutes. Turn and sear the other side, about 4 minutes, or until it just starts to flake when prodded with a fork; the center should be slightly pink. Let cool and cut into small chunks.

Add the artichoke mixture, onion, orange zest and juice, and herbs to the pasta. Add the tuna, the remaining 3 Tbsp oil, and salt and pepper to taste. Toss gently and serve, or let sit at room temperature for up to 2 hours.

14

Sweeter than regular Lisbon or Eureka lemons, Meyer lemons add an intriguing taste to this California-style lobster salad.

LOBSTER & AVOCADO SALAD WITH SHAVED MEYER LEMONS

serves 4

1 very firm Meyer lemon or Valencia orange

¼ cup (2 fl oz/60 ml) extra-virgin olive oil

1 Tbsp minced shallot

2 Tbsp champagne vinegar

Salt and freshly ground pepper

3 cooked, shelled lobster tails, cut into 1-inch (2.5-cm) chunks

1 head butter lettuce, torn into pieces

1 cup (1½ oz/45 g) fresh flat-leaf parsley leaves

½ cup (¾ oz/20 g) fresh cilantro leaves

½ cup (¾ oz/20 g) fresh chives, cut into ½-inch (12-mm) lengths

2 avocados, pitted, peeled, and diced

Using a mandoline or a very sharp knife, slice the lemon as thinly as possible. Set aside.

In a large bowl, combine the oil, shallot, vinegar, and ¼ tsp each salt and pepper. Mix well with a fork.

Add the lobster chunks to the vinaigrette, then remove and set aside. Just before serving, add the lettuce and parsley to the vinaigrette. Also add the cilantro and chives, reserving a little of each for garnish. Toss the salad and divide among individual plates. Top each salad with an equal portion of the lobster chunks, Meyer lemon slices, and diced avocado. Garnish with a sprinkling of the reserved cilantro and chives and serve.

15

Even if you're not a fan of the sturdier greens like chard and kale, look for baby chard in spring. The leaves are picked when they are small and tender, but they still offer the array of benefits found in this nutritional powerhouse.

GREEN BEAN SALAD WITH MUSTARD SEEDS, HERBS & BABY CHARD

serves 4

Salt

²/₃ lb (315 g) young, tender green beans, preferably haricots verts

1 cup (5 oz/155 g) fresh shelled English peas

3 Tbsp olive oil

1 tsp black mustard seeds

½ small red onion, finely chopped

1 jalapeño or serrano chile, seeded and minced

1 clove garlic, minced

Grated zest of 1 lemon

1 Tbsp chopped fresh tarragon

1 Tbsp chopped fresh flat-leaf parsley

1 cup (1 oz/30 g) baby chard or spinach leaves

Bring a large saucepan three-fourths full of salted water to a boil over high heat. Meanwhile, prepare a large bowl of ice water. Add the green beans to the boiling water and cook until crisp-tender, about 4 minutes. Using a strainer, scoop out and immerse them in the ice water, then drain and pat dry. Put the green beans in a large bowl.

Return the water in the saucepan to a boil, add the peas, and cook for 1 minute. Using the strainer, scoop out and immerse them in the ice water, then drain and pat dry and add to the bowl with the green beans.

In a small saucepan over low heat, warm the oil with the mustard seeds until the seeds begin to pop. Add the mixture to the bowl with the vegetables. Add the red onion, chile, garlic, lemon zest, tarragon, and parsley to the bowl and stir to mix well. Season to taste with salt. Just before serving, gently fold in the chard leaves.

16

Little Gem is a small, compact lettuce, upright like romaine, but with ruffled leaves like a butter lettuce head, that hold up well when cut into wedges. Green Goddess dressing, full of the herbs that give the dressing its name, is exceptionally flavorful.

LITTLE GEM WEDGES WITH RADISHES & GREEN GODDESS DRESSING

serves 4

FOR THE DRESSING

1 cup (8 fl oz/250 ml) mayonnaise

½ cup (4 oz/125 g) sour cream

1 clove garlic, minced

5 anchovy fillets, minced

½ cup (¾ oz/20 g) minced fresh chives

⅓ cup (½ oz/15 g) minced fresh flat-leaf parsley

3 Tbsp minced fresh tarragon

1 Tbsp fresh lemon juice

1 Tbsp champagne vinegar

Salt and freshly ground pepper

4–6 heads Little Gem lettuce, or more if very small

8 radishes, red or white tipped, trimmed

To make the dressing, combine the mayonnaise, sour cream, garlic, anchovies, chives, parsley, tarragon, lemon juice, vinegar, ½ tsp salt, and ¼ tsp pepper and mix well. Set aside.

Halve the Little Gems lengthwise and thinly slice the radishes crosswise.

Arrange the Little Gems on a serving platter or distribute among salad plates. Sprinkle with the radish slices, drizzle with the dressing, and serve.

17

GRILLED SALMON, POTATO & ASPARAGUS SALAD

serves 4

1 lb (500 g) salmon fillet,
pin bones removed

Olive oil

Salt and freshly ground pepper

1 lb (500 g) small, multicolored potatoes

¾ lb (375 g) asparagus,
tough ends trimmed

FOR THE VINAIGRETTE

4 dry-packed sun-dried tomato halves

3 Tbsp fresh lemon juice

1 Tbsp minced fresh flat-leaf parsley

1 Tbsp minced fresh dill

1 tsp grated orange zest

½ tsp minced garlic

¼ cup (2 fl oz/60 ml) extra-virgin olive oil

10 oz (315 g) mixed baby greens

3 green onions, including tender
green tops, thinly sliced

Perfect for a light supper or a special lunch, this salad can be prepared quickly just before serving, or the salmon, potatoes, and asparagus can be prepared up to a day ahead, then combined with the dressing at the last minute.

Prepare a charcoal or gas grill for direct-heat cooking over high heat. Alternatively, preheat a stove-top grill pan over high heat. Brush the salmon with oil and season with salt and pepper. Place the fillet on the grill rack or in the pan and grill, turning once, until opaque throughout, about 4 minutes per side.

Transfer the salmon to a plate and let cool to room temperature. Meanwhile, put the potatoes in a large saucepan with water to cover. Bring to a boil over high heat, reduce the heat to medium-low, cover, and simmer until the potatoes are tender when pierced with a knife, about 15 minutes. Drain, cut in half, and set aside to cool completely.

Place the asparagus in a steamer basket over boiling water in a saucepan, cover the pan, and cook until crisp-tender, about 3 minutes. Rinse the asparagus under cold running water until cool. Pat dry and set aside.

To make the vinaigrette, put the sun-dried tomatoes in a heatproof bowl, pour in boiling water to cover, and let stand for 5 minutes. Drain and cut into ¼-inch (6-mm) pieces. In a small bowl, whisk together the chopped tomatoes, lemon juice, parsley, dill, orange zest, garlic, 2 Tbsp water, ½ tsp salt, and ⟩⟩

a grinding of pepper. Add the oil in a thin stream, whisking constantly until the dressing is well blended.

In a large bowl, toss the salad greens with 2 Tbsp of the vinaigrette. Peel off the salmon skin. Cut the flesh into 4 pieces. Divide the salmon, asparagus, potatoes, and greens evenly among 4 plates and drizzle with the remaining vinaigrette. Sprinkle with the green onions and serve.

18

BABY ARTICHOKE, PARMESAN & ARUGULA SALAD

serves 4

½ lemon

6 baby artichokes

FOR THE LEMON VINAIGRETTE

2 Tbsp fresh lemon juice

Salt

¼ cup (2 fl oz/60 ml) extra-virgin olive oil

1 bunch arugula, stemmed and shredded

Parmesan cheese for shaving

Freshly ground pepper

This classic salad appears on Italian menus in early spring when baby artichokes are in season. If you wish to make the salad with larger artichokes, trim and quarter the artichokes, cut out the chokes, and blanch in boiling water for about 5 minutes. Let cool, then toss with the greens and serve.

Squeeze the lemon into a large bowl of cold water. Trim the artichoke stems, leaving about ½ inch (12 mm). Cut ½ inch off the tops. Peel off the tough outer leaves until you reach the tender, pale green leaves. Halve each artichoke lengthwise and then thinly slice. Immerse in the lemon water.

To make the vinaigrette, in a small bowl, combine the lemon juice and salt to taste. Add the oil in a thin stream, whisking constantly until the dressing is smooth. Taste and adjust the seasoning with salt.

Put the arugula in a serving bowl. Drain the artichoke slices and pat dry. Add to the greens and toss gently. Drizzle the dressing over the salad and, using a vegetable peeler, shave the cheese over the salad. Season generously with pepper and serve.

19

FENNEL, CHICKPEA & SUN-DRIED TOMATO SALAD WITH MOZZARELLA

serves 6

Sun-dried tomatoes offer the concentrated essence of ripe tomatoes and have a chewy, meaty texture. In this salad, their intensity is kept in check by nutty chickpeas and mild-tasting fresh mozzarella. Slices of fennel add crunch and a licorice flavor, while fresh dill and oregano bring fragrant, herbal hints.

1 can (15 oz/470 g) chickpeas, drained and rinsed

1 cup (5 oz/155 g) drained olive oil–packed sun-dried tomatoes, coarsely chopped

7 Tbsp (3½ fl oz/105 ml) extra-virgin olive oil

⅔ cup (1 oz/30 g) minced fresh dill

1 tsp minced fresh oregano

1 tsp fresh lemon juice, plus ¼ cup (2 fl oz/60 ml)

Salt and freshly ground pepper

1 tsp sugar

2 small fennel bulbs, trimmed and thinly sliced

1 head romaine lettuce, leaves torn into bite-sized pieces

6 oz (185 g) bocconcini (small fresh mozzarella balls), cut into quarters

In a bowl, toss together the chickpeas, sun-dried tomatoes, 1 Tbsp of the olive oil, 2 Tbsp of the dill, the oregano, the 1 tsp lemon juice, ¼ tsp salt, and several grindings of pepper. Let stand at room temperature for 15 minutes.

In a small bowl, whisk together the ¼ cup lemon juice, the sugar, ¼ tsp salt, and several grindings of pepper until the sugar dissolves. Add the remaining 6 Tbsp (3 fl oz/90 ml) olive oil in a thin stream, whisking constantly until the dressing is well blended. Taste and adjust the seasonings.

In a large bowl, toss together the fennel, lettuce, the remaining dill, ¼ tsp salt, and several grindings of pepper. Whisk the dressing to recombine, then drizzle it over the fennel-lettuce mixture and toss well. Taste and adjust the seasonings. Divide the dressed mixture among individual plates. Top with the chickpea mixture and the cheese and serve.

20

ISRAELI COUSCOUS WITH CELERY & SUN-DRIED TOMATOES

serves 4-6

Plump Israeli couscous granules the size of peas make a sturdy salad base that can easily carry the intense flavors of the eastern Mediterranean used here. Toasted almonds and celery give the salad loft and texture, while a bounty of fresh herbs and spices balances the dressing.

Salt and freshly ground pepper

1 cup (6 oz/185 g) Israeli couscous

4 celery ribs, cut into ¼-inch (6-mm) dice

6 drained oil-packed sun-dried tomatoes, minced

1 cucumber, peeled, seeded, and finely chopped

¼ cup (⅓ oz/10 g) chopped fresh flat-leaf parsley

1 Tbsp fresh lemon juice

½ tsp dried oregano

¼ cup (2 fl oz/60 ml) extra-virgin olive oil

¼ cup (1 oz/30 g) toasted almonds, chopped

In a saucepan, bring 2 cups (16 fl oz/500 ml) water to a boil over medium-high heat. Add ½ tsp salt and the couscous. Reduce the heat to low, cover, and simmer until most of the water has been absorbed, about 10 minutes.

Drain the couscous and transfer to a bowl. Add the celery, sun-dried tomatoes, cucumber, parsley, lemon juice, oregano, oil, ¼ tsp salt, and ½ tsp pepper. Taste and adjust the seasonings. Sprinkle the toasted almonds on top and serve.

21

LEMONY QUINOA SALAD WITH RADISHES, AVOCADO & BASIL

serves 6

Crisp, peppery radishes are one of the hallmarks of springtime. Their texture and flavor are highlighted here, contrasted against creamy avocado, bright-tasting citrus segments, and nutty, mild quinoa.

1 cup (6 oz/185 g) quinoa, well rinsed

2 lemons

2 small avocados, peeled, pitted, and cut into thin slices

2 cloves garlic, minced

2 bunches radishes, trimmed and halved lengthwise

½ cup (2½ oz/75 g) crumbled feta cheese

Leaves from 1 bunch fresh basil, torn into pieces

1 Tbsp ground coriander

¼ tsp red pepper flakes

⅓ cup (3 fl oz/80 ml) extra-virgin olive oil

Salt and freshly ground black pepper

Drain the quinoa and combine it in a pot with 3 cups (24 fl oz/750 ml) water. Bring to a boil, then reduce the heat to low, cover, and simmer until the grains are tender and the water is absorbed, about 15 minutes. Remove from the heat, fluff the quinoa, and let cool completely.

Peel the lemons with a knife. Working over a bowl, cut between the membranes to release the segments into the bowl. Squeeze the juice from the membranes into the bowl. Add the avocado slices and toss to coat with the lemon juice. Transfer the quinoa to the bowl and add the garlic, radishes, cheese, and torn basil and toss gently to mix well without breaking up the avocado.

In a small bowl, whisk together the coriander, red pepper flakes, oil, ½ tsp salt, and ¼ tsp pepper. Pour the dressing over the salad, toss gently, and serve.

22

GREEN MANGO & GRILLED SHRIMP SALAD

serves 4–6

A slawlike salad composed of green mangoes, carrots, and chopped chile is the base of this Vietnamese salad. Grilled shrimp sit atop, and the savory, citrusy, slightly sweet dressing draws everything together. Serve on a hot day with light beer.

½ lb (250 g) large shrimp, peeled and deveined

1 Tbsp peanut oil

Salt and freshly ground pepper

FOR THE DRESSING

1 large clove garlic

1 fresh red chile, seeded

¼ cup (2 fl oz/60 ml) fresh lime juice

5 Tbsp (2½ fl oz/75 ml) Asian fish sauce

3 Tbsp sugar

2 Tbsp grated carrot

2 green mangoes, peeled and grated

1 carrot, peeled and finely grated

1 Tbsp chopped fresh Thai basil or cilantro leaves

1 red Fresno or serrano chile, seeded and chopped

Prepare a charcoal or gas grill for direct-heat cooking over high heat. In a bowl, toss the shrimp with the oil, ½ tsp salt, and pepper to taste. If desired, put them in a grill basket.

To make the dressing, in a mortar, pound together the garlic and red chile with a pestle until puréed. Mix in the lime juice, fish sauce, sugar, and 6 Tbsp (3 fl oz/90 ml) water. Pour into a bowl and add the 2 Tbsp carrot.

Place the shrimp over the hottest part of the fire and grill, turning as needed, until they turn bright orange-pink and feel firm to the touch, about 2 minutes. Transfer to a plate and set aside to cool.

In a large bowl, combine the mangoes, carrot, basil, chile, and ¼ cup (2 fl oz/60 ml) of the dressing and toss well.

Arrange the salad on a platter and top with the shrimp. Drizzle with more dressing (you may not need all of it) and serve.

WATERCRESS & DUCK SALAD WITH GINGERED STRAWBERRY DRESSING

serves 4

This springtime salad features the classic pairing of fruit with crisp-skinned duck. Crystallized ginger lends sweetness and a spiced flavor to a strawberry dressing that balances the duck's richness.

2 baskets (1 lb/500 g) large strawberries, stemmed and hulled

1½ tsp minced crystallized ginger

1½ tsp fresh lemon juice

1 tsp sugar

Salt and freshly ground pepper

4 Tbsp (2 fl oz/60 ml) walnut oil

2 boneless duck breast halves (about ¾ lb/375 g each)

¾ cup (3 oz/90 g) pecans

2 small bunches watercress, tough stems removed

Preheat the oven to 400°F (200°C). Put 4 or 5 of the berries in a blender. Add the ginger, lemon juice, sugar, and a pinch each of salt and pepper and process until smooth. Pour through a fine-mesh sieve into a small bowl. Add 1 Tbsp of the walnut oil in a thin stream, whisking constantly until the dressing is well blended. Taste and adjust the seasonings and set aside. Quarter the remaining berries lengthwise and set aside.

Using a sharp, thin-bladed knife, score the skin of each duck breast half in a ½-inch (12-mm) crosshatch pattern, being careful not to cut into the meat. Season each duck breast on both sides with salt and pepper.

Warm a large, heavy, ovenproof frying pan over medium-low heat for 2 minutes. Add the duck breasts, skin side down, and cook without disturbing until the skin is crisp and medium brown, about 5 minutes. Remove the duck from the pan, pour off and discard all but 2 Tbsp of the fat, and return the duck, skin side up, to the pan. Place the pan in the oven and cook until an instant-read thermometer inserted into the center of each breast registers 130°F (54°C) for medium-rare, 10–12 minutes, or until cooked to your liking. Transfer the duck to a cutting board, tent with foil, and let rest for 5 minutes.

In a small frying pan, toast the pecans over medium-low heat, stirring, until fragrant and starting to brown, about 5 minutes. Pour onto a plate to cool, then coarsely chop. ≫→

In a small bowl, stir together the toasted pecans and a pinch of salt.

In a large bowl, combine the watercress and the quartered strawberries, drizzle with the remaining 3 Tbsp walnut oil, and season with a scant ¼ tsp each of salt and pepper. Toss well. Divide the greens and berries among individual plates.

Thinly slice the duck breasts on the diagonal. Fan an equal amount of duck on top of the greens on each plate. Drizzle each serving with the dressing, sprinkle with the pecans, and serve.

TABBOULEH WITH FETA CHEESE

serves 4

For this recipe, look for bulgur labeled fine, which will marry best with the other ingredients in this intensely green salad. Letting the salad stand to soak up the lemon dressing is also important. Traditional tabbouleh is made with more parsley than bulgur, so don't skimp on the amount called for here.

1 cup (8 fl oz/250 ml) boiling water

½ cup (3 oz/90 g) fine bulgur

Leaves of 1 large bunch fresh flat-leaf parsley, most minced, a few left whole and reserved for garnish

Leaves of 1 bunch fresh spearmint, minced

½ cup (2½ oz/75 g) finely chopped red onion

2 cups (¾ lb/375 g) cherry tomatoes, quartered

1 cup (5 oz/155 g) crumbled feta cheese

Juice of 1 large lemon

2 Tbsp extra-virgin olive oil

Salt and freshly ground pepper

In a large bowl, pour the boiling water over the bulgur. Let stand for 30 minutes, uncovered, until the bulgur has absorbed all of the liquid and has softened.

Add the chopped parsley, mint, and onion to the bulgur and mix with a fork to combine.

Put the tomatoes in a colander and work them with your fingers to drain off some of their liquid and eliminate some of the seeds. Add the drained tomatoes and crumbled cheese to the salad.

Pour the lemon juice and oil over the tabbouleh and mix well. Season with salt and pepper to taste. Cover and refrigerate for at least 2 hours or up to 24 hours before serving to let the flavors blend. Let the salad return to room temperature, garnish with the whole parsley leaves, and serve.

25

Sturdy and easily transportable, this is a great salad to make for potlucks, picnics, or cookouts. The orzo and dressing will pair well with almost any combination of ingredients, so try other options with veggies you have on hand.

ORZO SALAD WITH ARTICHOKES, PINE NUTS & GOLDEN RAISINS

serves 8

FOR THE DRESSING

¼ cup (2 fl oz/60 ml) fresh lemon juice

1 Tbsp Dijon mustard

2 cloves garlic

½ cup (½ oz/15 g) fresh basil leaves

½ cup (4 fl oz/125 ml) extra-virgin olive oil

Salt and freshly ground pepper

1 lb (500 g) orzo pasta

Extra-virgin olive oil

½ lemon (if using fresh artichokes)

12 baby artichokes or 1 package (1 lb/500 g) frozen quartered artichoke hearts, thawed and brought to room temperature

⅓ cup (2 oz/60 g) pine nuts

¾ cup (4½ oz/140 g) golden raisins

½ cup (½ oz/15 g) fresh basil leaves, julienned

3 green onions, including tender green tops, thinly sliced on the diagonal

To make the dressing, in a food processor or blender, combine the lemon juice, mustard, garlic, basil leaves, and oil and purée until smooth. Season with salt and pepper to taste. Transfer to a small bowl and set aside.

Bring a large pot three-fourths full of salted water to a boil over high heat. Add the orzo and cook until al dente, according to package directions. Rinse well in cold water to remove any excess starch and drain in a colander. Transfer to a large bowl and toss lightly with a little oil to prevent the pasta from sticking together.

If using fresh artichokes, squeeze the lemon half into a large bowl of cold water. Trim the artichoke stems, leaving about ½ inch (12 mm). Cut ½ inch off the tops. Peel off the tough outer leaves until you reach the tender, pale green leaves. Cut each artichoke lengthwise into 6 wedges and immerse in the lemon water. Bring a pot three-fourths full of salted water to a boil. Add the artichokes and cook until tender, about 14 minutes. Drain and let cool to room temperature. ⤳

In a small frying pan, toast the pine nuts over medium-low heat, stirring, until fragrant and starting to brown, 3–4 minutes. Pour onto a plate to cool.

Add the artichokes, pine nuts, raisins, basil, and green onions to the bowl containing the orzo. Whisk the dressing to recombine and drizzle it over the orzo. Toss to coat evenly. Taste and adjust the seasonings and serve.

26

This is an excellent way to use leftover grilled or roast beef—or purchased roast beef from the deli. The spicy vinaigrette brings together the mild flavor of the leeks and the robust flavor of the meat.

ROAST BEEF SALAD WITH LEEKS & CREAMY MUSTARD VINAIGRETTE

serves 4–6

16 small leeks

¼ cup (2 fl oz/60 ml) extra-virgin olive oil

2–3 Tbsp Dijon mustard

1½ Tbsp sherry vinegar

2 tsp minced shallot

Salt and freshly ground pepper

1½ lb (750 g) lean roast beef, such as flank steak or tri-tip roast, cut against the grain into slices at least ¼ inch (6 mm) thick

Trim the leeks, leaving the root end intact and keeping about half of the dark greens. Prepare a bowl of ice water. Place the leeks in a large frying pan with about 1 inch (2.5 cm) of water. Bring to a boil over medium heat, cover, reduce the heat to low, and cook, adding more water if needed, until just fork-tender, about 10 minutes. Transfer to the ice water, and let cool. Remove and pat dry.

In a small bowl, whisk together the oil and mustard. Whisk in the vinegar, shallot, and salt and pepper to taste.

Lay the leeks together on a cutting board, side by side. Cut into 2-inch (5-cm) lengths and place them on a platter, still arranged together. Drizzle with half the vinaigrette. Top with the sliced beef, drizzle with the remaining dressing, and serve.

27

For a pretty presentation, after grilling the asparagus, try making bundles by wrapping spears with the prosciutto strips. Plate the greens and then nestle a bundle of asparagus on top of each serving.

GRILLED ASPARAGUS & PROSCIUTTO SALAD

serves 4

1¼ lb (625 g) asparagus, tough ends trimmed

7 Tbsp (3½ fl oz/105 ml) olive oil

Salt and freshly ground pepper

1 clove garlic, minced

2 Tbsp red wine vinegar

1 tsp tarragon mustard or Dijon mustard

1 Tbsp minced fresh chives

6 oz (185 g) mixed baby greens

3 oz (90 g) thinly sliced prosciutto, cut into strips

Parmesan cheese for shaving

Prepare a gas or charcoal grill for direct-heat cooking over medium-high heat. Alternatively, preheat a stove-top grill pan over medium-high heat. If the asparagus spears are thick, use a vegetable peeler to pare away the tough skins to within about 2 inches (5 cm) of the tips. Brush the asparagus with 1 Tbsp of the oil and season with salt and pepper. Place the spears on the grill rack, in a grill basket, or in the pan and grill, turning occasionally with tongs, until slightly charred and tender, about 8 minutes.

In a large bowl, whisk together the garlic, vinegar, mustard, ¼ tsp salt, and a pinch of pepper. Add the remaining 6 Tbsp (3 fl oz/ 90 ml) oil in a thin stream, whisking constantly until smooth. Stir in the chives.

Add the greens and prosciutto to the vinaigrette and toss to coat evenly. Arrange the asparagus on individual plates and top with the greens. Using a vegetable peeler, shave the cheese over the salads and serve.

28

If serving this salad as a starter, use tarragon and, if you like, serve the fruit over spinach with a lemony dressing. Or, use mint for a refreshing dessert salad.

STRAWBERRY & CHERRY SALAD

serves 4

Hazelnuts or walnuts for garnish

2 cups (8 oz/250 g) strawberries, hulled and halved

2 cups (8 oz/250 g) cherries, pitted and halved

Juice of 1 lemon

5–10 fresh tarragon or mint leaves, chopped

In a small frying pan, toast the hazelnuts over medium-low heat, stirring, until fragrant and starting to brown, about 5 minutes. Wrap the hazelnuts in a towel and rub to remove the skins. Pour onto a plate to cool. Chop coarsely, and set aside.

In a bowl, toss the strawberries and cherries with the lemon juice. Add the tarragon and toss gently. Garnish with the chopped nuts and serve.

29

Dark, jammy berries are a delicious match with creamy, rich Gorgonzola and peppery arugula. If you can't find nice-looking berries, substitute fresh or dried cherries, currants, or cranberries.

ARUGULA SALAD WITH BERRIES & GORGONZOLA

serves 4–6

2 Tbsp balsamic vinegar

Salt and freshly ground pepper

3 Tbsp extra-virgin olive oil

6 cups (6 oz/185 g) baby arugula

8 oz (250 g) Gorgonzola or other blue cheese, crumbled

1 cup (4 oz/125 g) fresh blackberries or blueberries

In a large bowl, whisk together the vinegar and salt and pepper to taste. Add the oil in a thin stream, whisking constantly until the dressing is smooth.

Add the arugula to the dressing and toss to coat. Add the cheese and toss gently. Divide among plates, top with the berries, and serve.

ROASTED BEET SALAD WITH GOAT CHEESE & WALNUTS

serves 6

3 golden beets (about 1 lb/500 g), trimmed

6 red beets (about 2 lb/1 kg total weight), trimmed

½ cup (4 fl oz/125 ml) olive oil

Salt and freshly ground pepper

2 Tbsp fresh lemon juice

5 Tbsp (2½ oz/75 g) crème fraîche

1 Tbsp chopped fresh dill

2 tsp minced shallot

3 bunches watercress

¼ lb (125 g) fresh goat cheese, crumbled

⅓ cup (1¼ oz/40 g) toasted chopped walnuts

Red and golden beets are combined with watercress, creamy goat cheese, and crunchy walnuts to create this vivid winter salad. If you purchased the beets with their greens attached, cut off the tops and reserve them for another use. They are delicious lightly sautéed in olive oil with garlic and red pepper flakes.

Preheat the oven to 350°F (180°C).

Place the golden and red beets on a baking sheet. Coat the beets with 3 Tbsp of the oil and season with salt and pepper. Cover the baking sheet with aluminum foil and roast until the beets are easily pierced with a knife, about 1 hour. When the beets are cool enough to handle, peel and cut into 1-inch (2.5-cm) wedges. Set aside.

Meanwhile, in a small bowl, whisk together the lemon juice, crème fraîche, dill, and shallot. Add the remaining 5 Tbsp (3 fl oz/80 ml) oil in a thin stream, whisking constantly until well blended. Season with salt and pepper. Separate the watercress into leaves and small sprigs, discarding the stems.

Arrange the beet wedges in a layer on a platter and top with the watercress. Garnish with the cheese and walnuts. Drizzle the vinaigrette over the salad and serve at once.

CHOPPED CHICKEN SALAD WITH LEMON-TARRAGON DRESSING

serves 2

1 skinless, boneless chicken breast half, about ½ lb (250 g)

1½ cups (12 fl oz/375 ml) chicken broth, or as needed

FOR THE LEMON-TARRAGON DRESSING

1½ Tbsp fresh lemon juice, plus more if needed

2 tsp minced fresh tarragon

1 tsp Dijon mustard

1 small clove garlic, minced

2½ Tbsp olive oil

Salt and freshly ground pepper

¼ lb (125 g) romaine lettuce heart, chopped

¼ small fennel bulb, trimmed and chopped

6 small fresh mushrooms, chopped

5 radishes, chopped

1 small carrot, peeled and chopped

¼ small head radicchio, chopped

¼ small red onion, chopped

This versatile salad can accommodate the odds and ends of raw vegetables that tend to accumulate in the refrigerator bin. Instead of fennel, mushrooms, or radishes, try cucumber, zucchini, celery, or cauliflower. Or, eliminate the chicken to make a vegetarian version.

In a small saucepan over medium heat, combine the chicken breast half and the 1½ cups (12 fl oz/375 ml) broth, or as needed to cover. Bring to a simmer, adjust the heat to keep the broth just below a simmer, and cook, uncovered, until the chicken is just cooked through, about 10 minutes. Using a slotted spoon, transfer the chicken breast to a cutting board. When the chicken is cool, cut it into small, neat pieces.

To make the dressing, in a bowl, whisk together the 1½ Tbsp lemon juice, tarragon, mustard, and garlic. Add the olive oil in a thin stream, whisking constantly until the dressing is well blended. Season with salt and pepper to taste. Set aside to allow the flavors to blend.

In a large bowl, combine the romaine, fennel, mushrooms, radishes, carrot, radicchio, and red onion.

Add the chicken to the dressing and stir to coat. Add the chicken and all the dressing to the vegetables and toss well. Taste and adjust the seasoning with lemon juice and serve.

This month, spring's greenery makes way for the colorful bounty of summer fruits—melons, stone fruits, and berries—all delicious when simply tossed with basil or mint. The vegetable harvest also begins in earnest, with summer squash ready for grilling and bell peppers for roasting, each blending smoky flavor with June's signature freshness. Sun-ripened garden tomatoes also get star treatment, paired simply with basil or mixed with grains or cheese.

1
CHICKEN, ROASTED RED PEPPER & GREEN BEAN SALAD
page 130

2
CHERRY TOMATO SALAD WITH BURRATA & PESTO
page 130

3
GRILLED SUMMER SQUASH SALAD
page 133

8
MACARONI SALAD
page 135

9
CHIPOTLE BEEF & CORN SALAD
page 136

10
GRILLED LAMB SALAD
page 136

15
FRESH STRAWBERRY & SPINACH SALAD
page 141

16
POACHED SALMON SALAD WITH PRESERVED LEMON & GARLIC
page 141

17
CHICKEN TOSTADA SALAD
page 142

22
POTATO SALAD WITH GREEN BEANS & CUCUMBER-YOGURT DRESSING
page 145

23
FARMERS' MARKET SALAD WITH TOMATO-BASIL VINAIGRETTE
page 147

24
STONE FRUIT SALAD WITH HAZELNUTS & BLUE CHEESE
page 147

29
PAN-ROASTED CORN SALAD WITH TOMATOES & FETA
page 150

30
GRILLED SQUASH & ORZO SALAD WITH PINE NUTS & MINT
page 150

june

1

CHICKEN, ROASTED RED PEPPER & GREEN BEAN SALAD

serves 4

Beans and lean poultry make this high in protein and low in saturated fat, for a main-course salad that is as satisfying as it is healthful. Sweet, slightly floral sherry vinegar creates a vibrant salad dressing, which doubles as a glaze for the tender strips of chicken.

2 large red bell peppers
(about 1 lb/500 g total weight)

Salt and freshly ground pepper

½ lb (250 g) green beans, trimmed

FOR THE SHERRY-THYME VINAIGRETTE

3 Tbsp sherry vinegar

1 Tbsp chopped fresh thyme

½ tsp minced garlic

¼ cup (2 fl oz/60 ml) extra-virgin olive oil

1 tsp olive oil

¾ lb (375 g) skinless, boneless chicken breast halves, cut lengthwise into strips 1 inch (2.5 cm) wide

1 small red onion

2 celery ribs

10 oz (315 g) mixed baby salad greens

Preheat the broiler. Place the peppers on a baking sheet and slide under the broiler about 6 inches (15 cm) from the heat source. Broil, turning often, until the skins are blackened on all sides, 10–15 minutes. Transfer to a covered bowl or seal in a paper bag. Let the peppers steam until cool, about 10 minutes. Rub and peel off the charred skins. Cut the peppers in half lengthwise, remove the seeds and membranes, and cut lengthwise into strips 1 inch (2.5 cm) wide. Set aside.

Bring a saucepan three-fourths full of salted water to a boil, add the green beans, and boil until tender, 4–7 minutes; the timing will depend on their size. Drain and immerse in a bowl of ice water. Drain and set aside.

To make the vinaigrette, in a small bowl, whisk together the vinegar, thyme, garlic, ½ tsp salt, and a grinding of pepper. Add the extra-virgin olive oil in a thin stream, whisking constantly until well blended.

Brush a large, nonstick frying pan with the 1 tsp olive oil. Place over medium heat and heat until hot enough for a drop of water to sizzle and then immediately evaporate. Add the chicken, a few pieces at a time, and cook for 2 minutes. ⤳

Turn the chicken pieces, whisk the vinaigrette to recombine, and drizzle 2 Tbsp of the vinaigrette on the chicken. Continue to cook for 2 minutes; the chicken should be opaque throughout. Turn the chicken to coat it well with the vinaigrette and remove the pan from the heat. Let the chicken stand in the pan.

Cut the onion in half through the stem end. Place cut side down and thinly slice lengthwise until you have about ½ cup (2 oz/60 g). Reserve the remainder for another use. Cut the celery ribs on the diagonal into ¼-inch (6-mm) slices.

In a large bowl, combine the salad greens and 1 Tbsp of the vinaigrette. Toss to coat the greens. Spread the greens in a layer on a large platter. In the same bowl, combine the roasted bell peppers, green beans, cooked chicken and any pan juices, onion, celery, and remaining vinaigrette. Toss to mix. Spoon on top of the greens and serve.

2

CHERRY TOMATO SALAD WITH BURRATA & PESTO

serves 4–6

Burrata is a moist, fresh ball of mozzarella filled with curds and cream, which slowly ooze out with each forkful.

3 Tbsp prepared basil pesto

1½ Tbsp red wine vinegar

¼ cup (2 fl oz/60 ml) extra-virgin olive oil

Salt and freshly ground pepper

About 4 cups (1½ lb/750 g) mixed red, yellow, and orange cherry tomatoes

1 burrata cheese

Small fresh basil leaves for garnish

In a bowl, whisk together the pesto and vinegar. Add the oil in a thin stream, whisking constantly until the dressing is well blended. Season with salt and pepper to taste.

Slice the tomatoes in half, add to the bowl, and toss gently. Season with salt and pepper and use a slotted spoon to mound them on a serving platter. Nestle the cheese in the center and drizzle with some pesto dressing from the bowl. Garnish with the basil leaves and serve.

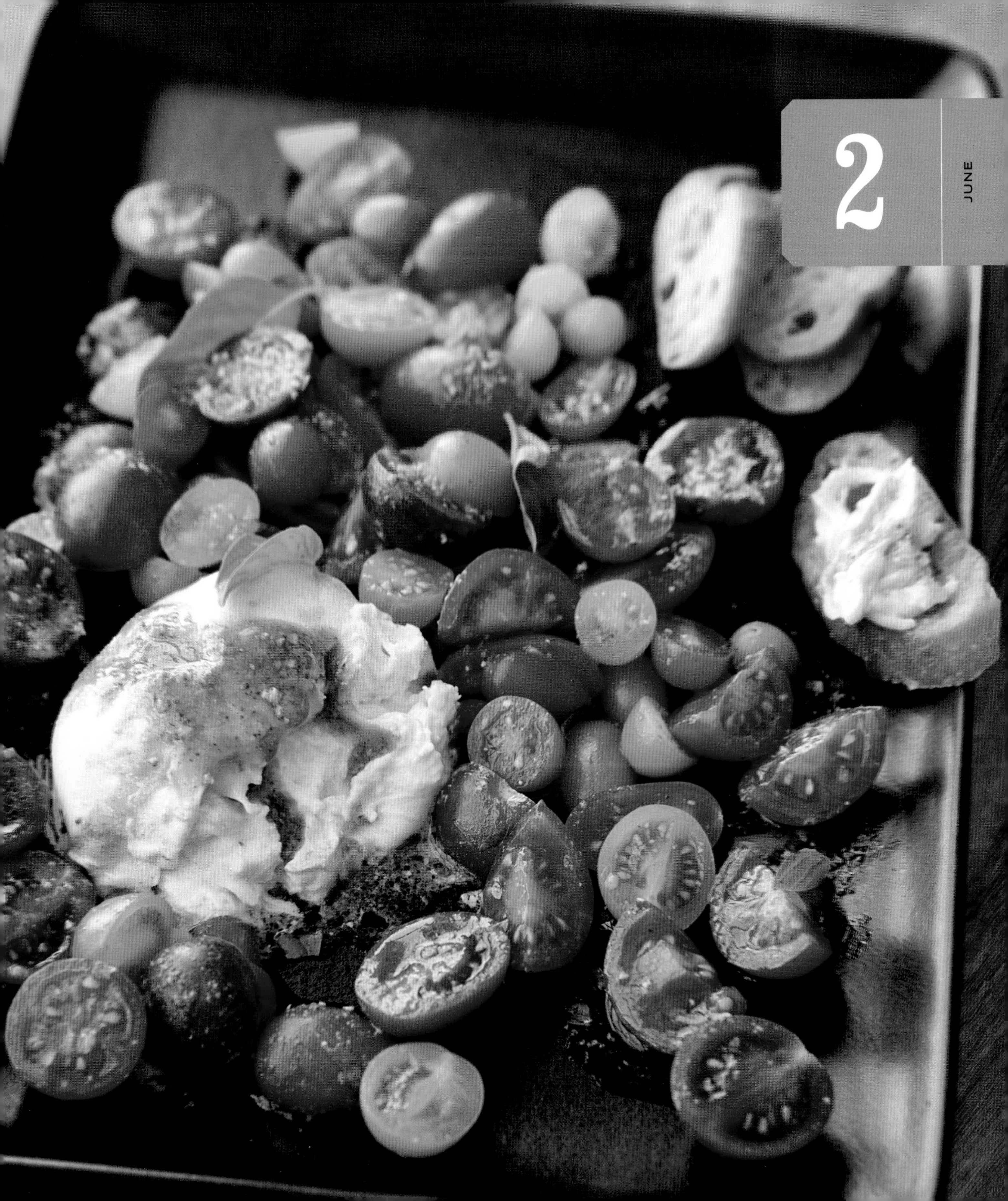

3

GRILLED SUMMER SQUASH SALAD

serves 6

Zucchini, crookneck, and pattypan squashes are all terrific grilled and lightly dressed with a tomato-basil vinaigrette. When shopping for squashes, choose an eye-catching variety of shapes, colors, and sizes.

FOR THE TOMATO-BASIL VINAIGRETTE

5–6 fresh basil leaves

2 oil-packed sun-dried tomatoes, drained

1 Tbsp balsamic vinegar

1 Tbsp red wine vinegar

1 Tbsp maple syrup

1 Tbsp Dijon mustard

½ cup (4 fl oz/125 ml) grapeseed oil

¼ cup (2 fl oz/60 ml) extra-virgin olive oil

Salt and freshly ground pepper

¼ cup (1½ oz/45 g) pine nuts

5–6 small to medium zucchini
(about 2 lb/1 kg total weight)

5–6 yellow crookneck squashes
(about 2 lb/1 kg total weight)

10 pattypan squashes
(about 2 lb/1 kg total weight)

2 plum tomatoes, cored,
quartered, and seeded

½ cup (4 fl oz/125 ml) extra-virgin olive oil

1 Tbsp minced fresh marjoram

2 Tbsp minced fresh flat-leaf parsley

5 cups (5 oz/155 g) field greens
or baby lettuce leaves

To make the vinaigrette, roll the basil leaves together lengthwise and slice crosswise into thin ribbons. In a blender or food processor, combine the sun-dried tomatoes, balsamic and red wine vinegars, maple syrup, and mustard. Pulse several times to chop the sun-dried tomatoes and incorporate ingredients into a thick, red paste. With the motor running, add the oils in a thin, steady stream. Add the basil, 1 tsp salt, and pepper to taste; pulse once to incorporate.

In a dry frying pan, toast the pine nuts over medium-low heat, stirring, until fragrant and starting to brown, 3–4 minutes. Pour onto a plate to cool.

Prepare a charcoal or gas grill for indirect-heat cooking over medium-high heat. Cut the zucchini and squashes in half lengthwise, and then cut each half into wedges about ¾ inch (2 cm) thick. In a large bowl, combine the squash wedges, tomatoes, ½ cup olive oil, and marjoram and toss to coat. ⟫⟶

Season with 2 tsp salt and 1 tsp pepper. If desired, put them in a grill basket. Grill the squashes and tomatoes, turning as needed, until lightly charred on all sides, 8–10 minutes. Move the vegetables to the side of the grill where the heat is less intense, cover, and grill until cooked through, 5–6 minutes.

Transfer the grilled vegetables back to the bowl. Stir in the pine nuts and parsley. Taste and adjust the seasonings.

In a separate medium bowl, season the field greens with salt and pepper and dress with 2 Tbsp of the vinaigrette. Divide the greens among individual plates, arrange the grilled vegetables on top, and serve. Pass the remaining vinaigrette at the table.

4

MELON, JICAMA & PINEAPPLE SALAD

serves 8-10

Combining cubed sweet fruits with a spicy citrus dressing is common in Latin America and in Latin American communities in the United States. The seasoned mix of fruits is often sold from carts or street stands in takeaway cups, but it is also easy to make at home. Serve this salad alongside tacos, arepas, empanadas, or other Latin-inspired dishes.

8 oz (250 g) seedless watermelon,
peeled and thinly sliced

8 oz (250 g) cantaloupe, peeled
and thinly sliced

8 oz (250 g) honeydew melon, peeled
and thinly sliced

8 oz (250 g) Crenshaw, Haogen,
or other specialty melon, peeled
and thinly sliced

8 oz (250 g) fresh pineapple, peeled
and thinly sliced

1 medium jicama, peeled and cut
into matchstick-size pieces

Zest of 1 lime plus juice of 3 limes

Juice of 1 lemon

½–1 tsp red pepper flakes

Salt

¼ cup (⅓ oz/10 g) chopped fresh cilantro

In a large bowl, combine the melons, pineapple, and jicama. In a small bowl, whisk together the lime zest, lime juice, lemon juice, red pepper flakes, and ½ tsp salt until well blended. Drizzle over the salad and stir gently to mix. Cover and refrigerate for 2 hours. Just before serving, gently stir in the cilantro, reserving about ⅓ for garnish.

Transfer the salad to a platter and garnish with the reserved cilantro. Serve right away.

5

FARRO SALAD WITH GRAPE TOMATOES & RICOTTA SALATA

serves 4

1 cup (6 oz/185 g) farro

Salt and freshly ground pepper

2 Tbsp extra-virgin olive oil

1 Tbsp fresh lemon juice

1 cup (6 oz/185 g) grape or cherry tomatoes, stemmed and halved

½ cup (2 oz/60 g) crumbled ricotta salata cheese

2 green onions, including tender green tops, thinly sliced

¼ cup (⅓ oz/10 g) shredded fresh basil

Farro, an ancient form of wheat, is cultivated primarily in the regions of Tuscany and Umbria. The light brown grains have a full, nutty flavor that is delicious in soups and salads. Salty ricotta, juicy tomatoes, and a handful of fresh basil unite in this rustic Italian salad.

In a large saucepan, combine the farro and 2 qt (2 l) water. Place the pan over medium-high heat, bring to a boil, and add 1 tsp salt. Reduce the heat to medium or medium-low, so the farro simmers steadily, and cook, uncovered, until tender yet still slightly firm and chewy, about 30 minutes. Remove from the heat and drain well in a fine-mesh sieve.

In a serving bowl, whisk together the olive oil and lemon juice until well blended. Whisk in salt and pepper to taste. Add the farro and toss well. Gently stir in the tomatoes, cheese, green onions, and basil until all the ingredients are evenly distributed. Serve at room temperature.

6

LOBSTER, POTATO & GREEN BEAN SALAD WITH PESTO VINAIGRETTE

serves 6

12–18 small red potatoes or Yellow Finn potatoes (about 2 lb/1 kg total weight)

Salt and freshly ground pepper

2 Tbsp pine nuts or chopped walnuts

1½ lb (750 g) green beans, trimmed and cut into 2-inch (5-cm) lengths

1 cup (1½ oz/45 g) tightly packed fresh basil leaves

1 tsp minced garlic

About ¾ cup (6 fl oz/180 ml) olive oil

¼ cup (2 fl oz/60 ml) red wine vinegar

Butter lettuce for lining plates

4 cooked, shelled lobster tails, cut into 1-inch (2.5-cm) chunks

Cherry tomatoes for garnish

Summer means seafood, and tender hunks of lobster make this salad special enough for an outdoor party. Accompany with crusty bread and Champagne or prosecco. The pesto vinaigrette can be made a day ahead and stored in the refrigerator. Bring to room temperature before using.

Put the potatoes in a saucepan with salted water to cover and bring to a boil over high heat. Reduce the heat to medium and simmer, uncovered, until the potatoes are cooked through but still firm, 10–20 minutes. Drain and rinse under cold water.

In a dry frying pan, toast the pine nuts over medium-low heat, stirring, until fragrant, 3–4 minutes. Pour onto a plate to cool.

Bring a large pot three-fourths full of salted water to a boil. Drop in the green beans and cook until crisp-tender, 2–4 minutes. Drain the beans and plunge them into ice water to stop the cooking. Drain again and set aside.

In a food processor, combine the basil leaves, garlic, and nuts. Pulse to combine. Add about ½ cup (4 fl oz/125 ml) of the olive oil and process to form a coarse purée. Transfer to a bowl and stir in the vinegar and enough of the remaining oil to make a spoonable vinaigrette. Season with salt and pepper.

To serve, cut the potatoes into slices ¼ inch (6 mm) thick. In a large bowl, combine the potatoes and green beans with half of the vinaigrette. Toss to coat. Line individual plates with lettuce leaves. Divide the potato mixture among the plates, top with the lobster meat, and drizzle with the remaining vinaigrette. Garnish with cherry tomatoes and serve.

CHINESE CHICKEN SALAD

serves 4–6

FOR THE VINAIGRETTE

1 Tbsp minced shallot

¼ cup (2 fl oz/60 ml) rice vinegar

1 Tbsp *each* soy sauce and honey

½ cup (4 fl oz/125 ml) canola or peanut oil

FOR THE FRIED WONTON STRIPS

Canola or peanut oil for frying

10 wonton wrappers, cut into ⅛-inch (3-mm) strips

Salt

FOR THE CHICKEN

3 Tbsp rice vinegar

2 Tbsp soy sauce

1 Tbsp Sriracha chile sauce

2 green onions, white part only, halved crosswise

1 clove garlic, smashed

½-inch (12-mm) piece fresh ginger, smashed

¼ cup (2 fl oz/60 ml) canola oil, plus 2 Tbsp

2 skinless, boneless chicken breast halves (about 6 oz/185 g each), thinly sliced

1 head napa cabbage (about ¾ lb/375 g), thinly sliced

2 carrots, peeled and julienned

2 green onions, green part only, thinly sliced

1 red bell pepper, seeded and julienned

1 cup (2 oz/60 g) bean sprouts

Salt and freshly ground pepper

¼ cup (¼ oz/7 g) fresh cilantro leaves

To make the vinaigrette, in a bowl, whisk together the shallot, vinegar, soy sauce, and honey. Gradually add the oil, whisking constantly until well blended. Set aside.

To make the wonton strips, pour oil into a large saucepan to a depth of 2 inches (5 cm) and heat over medium-high heat until it registers 350°F (180°C) on a deep-frying thermometer. Line a baking sheet with paper towels. Working in batches, fry the wonton strips until crispy and golden, about 1 minute per batch. Using a slotted spoon, transfer to the paper towel–lined baking sheet and season with salt. Set aside.

To make the chicken, in a bowl, whisk together the vinegar, soy sauce, Sriracha, green onions, garlic, ginger, and the ¼ cup (2 fl oz/60 ml) oil. Pour into a resealable ⟫

plastic bag, add the chicken, and seal the bag. Let stand at room temperature for 30 minutes. Remove the chicken from the marinade.

In a sauté pan, warm the 2 Tbsp oil over medium-high heat. Add the chicken and cook, stirring occasionally, until opaque throughout, 1–2 minutes. Transfer to a plate and let cool.

In a large bowl, combine the cabbage, carrots, green onions, bell pepper, bean sprouts, and chicken. Season with salt and pepper. Drizzle with some of the vinaigrette and toss to coat, adding more vinaigrette to taste. Transfer to a platter, garnish with the fried wonton strips and cilantro, and serve.

MACARONI SALAD

serves 4–6

Salt and freshly ground pepper

½ lb (250 g) elbow macaroni

2 celery ribs, finely diced

¼ cup (1¼ oz/40 g) finely diced red onion

½ red bell pepper, seeded and finely diced

2 Tbsp chopped fresh chives

2 large egg yolks (see note)

1 tsp Dijon mustard

½ cup (4 fl oz/125 ml) canola oil

¼ cup (2 oz/60 g) whole-grain mustard

2 Tbsp finely chopped fresh flat-leaf parsley

½ tsp sweet paprika

Bring a pot of salted water to a boil over high heat. Add the macaroni and cook until al dente, according to package directions. Drain, rinse with cold water, and drain again.

In a large bowl, stir together the macaroni, celery, onion, bell pepper, and chives. Set aside.

In a medium bowl, combine the egg yolks and Dijon mustard. Using an immersion blender, process until well mixed. With the blender running, gradually add the oil until thick and emulsified, then blend in 2 Tbsp water. Stir in the whole-grain mustard, parsley, and paprika. Season with salt and pepper.

Pour the dressing over the macaroni mixture and stir to mix. Taste and adjust the seasonings and serve.

7

Fried wonton strips add crunchiness to this full-meal salad, which is loaded with an interesting assortment of vegetables and with chicken that is marinated in a heady brew before cooking. An Asian-inspired vinaigrette nicely marries the rich mix of ingredients.

8

For the dressing in this version of an all-American favorite, homemade mayonnaise is seasoned with paprika and two kinds of mustard. Please note that raw egg can carry salmonella. The risks involved in salmonella poisoning are greatest for children, the elderly, pregnant women, and anyone with a compromised immune system.

9

CHIPOTLE BEEF & CORN SALAD

serves 4

1¼ lb (625 g) boneless sirloin or rib-eye steak, about 1½ inches (4 cm) thick

2 Tbsp olive oil, plus ¼ cup (2 fl oz/60 ml)

Salt and freshly ground pepper

¼ cup (1½ oz/45 g) canned chipotle chiles in adobo, with sauce

Juice of 2 limes

1 Tbsp white wine vinegar

1 large clove garlic, sliced

2 cups (12 oz/375 g) corn kernels (from about 2 ears of corn)

6 radishes, chopped

4 plum tomatoes, chopped

¼ cup (⅓ oz/10 g) minced fresh cilantro

2 heads romaine lettuce, pale inner leaves only, torn into bite-sized pieces

Grilled steak, corn, and romaine get a smoky infusion from dried chiles in this dressing. Chipotle chiles, which are dried and smoked jalapeños, are commonly sold in cans, preserved in a spicy, vinegary tomato sauce called adobo. Transfer unused chiles and sauce to a glass jar with a tight cap and refrigerate for up to 6 months.

Place the steak on a plate, brush both sides with the 2 Tbsp oil, and season both sides generously with salt and pepper. Let stand for 30 minutes.

Meanwhile, in a blender, combine the chipotle chiles with their sauce, the ¼ cup oil, half of the lime juice, the vinegar, garlic, 1 Tbsp water, ¼ tsp salt, and a pinch of pepper. Process until smooth.

In a bowl, toss together the corn, radishes, tomatoes, cilantro, the remaining lime juice, and ¼ tsp salt.

Prepare a gas or charcoal grill for direct-heat cooking over medium-high heat. Alternatively, preheat a stove-top grill pan over medium-high heat. Place the steak on the grill rack or in the grill pan and cook, turning every 4 minutes, about 16 minutes total for medium-rare. Transfer to a cutting board and let stand for 5–10 minutes. Cut the steak on the diagonal across the grain into thin slices. Arrange the lettuce on plates and top with the beef and corn mixture. Drizzle with the dressing and serve.

10

GRILLED LAMB SALAD

serves 4

FOR THE SPICY YOGURT DRESSING

1 cup (8 oz/250 g) plain yogurt

Salt and freshly ground black pepper

¼ tsp paprika

¼ tsp ground cumin

⅛ tsp cayenne pepper

1 tsp fresh lemon juice

1 cucumber, peeled, seeded, and chopped

6 oil-packed sun-dried tomatoes, chopped

1½ lb (750 g) boneless leg of lamb, trimmed and cut into 1-inch (2.5-cm) cubes

2 Tbsp extra-virgin olive oil

1 tsp paprika

½ cup (½ oz/15 g) fresh mint leaves

½ cup (½ oz/15 g) fresh flat-leaf parsley leaves

1 heart of romaine lettuce, torn into bite-sized pieces

2 cucumbers, peeled and cut into slices ¼ inch (6 mm) thick

2 cups (12 oz/375 g) cherry tomatoes, halved

This recipe draws inspiration from gyros, the popular Middle-Eastern street food. Instead of wrapping the lamb and greens in a flatbread, here it is served as a plated salad. Serve with lightly grilled pita triangles alongside.

To make the dressing, combine the yogurt, ¼ tsp salt, ½ tsp pepper, the ¼ tsp paprika, the cumin, cayenne, lemon juice, cucumber, and sun-dried tomatoes in a blender or food processor and purée. Taste and adjust the seasonings. Refrigerate, covered, until ready to use.

Put the lamb cubes in a bowl and add the oil, 1 tsp salt, ½ tsp pepper, and the 1 tsp paprika. Turn and let marinate for at least 30 minutes or up to several hours.

Prepare a charcoal or gas grill for direct-heat cooking over high heat. Thread the lamb onto 8 skewers. When the grill is hot, place the skewers on the grill rack and cook, turning several times, until lightly charred, 6–8 minutes for medium-rare. For medium, cook for 2–3 minutes more. Remove from the heat and let rest briefly.

In a bowl, combine the mint and parsley and the romaine. Divide among individual plates, and add slices of cucumber and the cherry tomatoes. Drizzle with the dressing, top each salad with 2 skewers of lamb, and serve.

11

CHOPPED SHRIMP SALAD WITH FRESH HERBS

serves 4

1½ lb (750 g) cooked medium shrimp, peeled, deveined, and finely chopped

2 celery ribs, minced

1 shallot, minced

2 tsp minced fresh chives

1 tsp minced fresh tarragon

1 Tbsp extra-virgin olive oil

½ tsp fresh lemon juice

¼–½ tsp cayenne pepper

Salt

2 Tbsp mayonnaise

16 small hearts of romaine lettuce leaves or Belgian endive leaves

Sweet paprika for garnish

This simple salad, which can be made several hours in advance of serving, shows off the flavor of shrimp, keeping other ingredients to a minimum. You can transform this tasty shrimp mixture into an appetizer by omitting the lettuce and serving it on crackers or crostini.

In a bowl, combine the shrimp, celery, shallot, chives, tarragon, oil, lemon juice, cayenne, and ½ tsp salt and stir to mix well. Taste and adjust the seasonings, then stir in the mayonnaise.

Arrange the lettuce leaves on individual plates, top with the shrimp mixture, and sprinkle with a little paprika. Serve chilled or at room temperature. The salad can be assembled ahead and refrigerated up to 8 hours in advance.

12

CHICKEN & MANGO SALAD WITH CHUTNEY VINAIGRETTE

serves 4

½ cup (2½ oz/75 g) cashews

½ red onion

2 ripe mangoes

4 cups (1½ lb/750 g) shredded cooked chicken meat

2 celery ribs, thinly sliced

4 cups (4 oz/125 g) sliced romaine lettuce

⅓ cup (3 fl oz/80 ml) peanut or grapeseed oil

¼ cup (2 fl oz/60 ml) champagne vinegar

1 Tbsp Dijon mustard

2–3 tsp Asian chile oil or Sriracha chile sauce (optional)

2 cloves garlic, minced

½ cup (5 oz/155 g) mango chutney

Leftover roast chicken finds a home in this bright, tangy salad, studded with tropical mangoes and cashews. It's good enough that you may want to pick up a rotisserie bird just for the purpose. Or, the next time you roast a chicken, roast two and create leftovers.

In a dry frying pan, toast the cashews over medium-low heat, stirring, until fragrant and starting to brown, about 5 minutes. Pour onto a plate to cool, then chop coarsely and set aside.

Thinly slice the onion half lengthwise. Rinse the onion under cold running water and drain well. Peel and pit the mangoes and cut the flesh into 1-inch (2.5-cm) chunks. Put the onion and mangoes in a large bowl with the chicken, celery, and lettuce.

In a food processor, combine the oil, vinegar, mustard, and chile oil, if using, and process until blended. Add the garlic and chutney and process until smooth.

Pour the dressing over the salad and toss gently. Serve at once, or chill for up to 4 hours and mix well before serving. Garnish with the cashews and serve.

13

CAESAR SALAD WITH CHIPOTLE CHILE DRESSING

serves 4–6

It is widely believed that the classic Caesar salad was first created by an Italian-born cook, Césare Cardini, who lived in Tijuana, Mexico. This modern version accentuates the salad's Mexican heritage with the addition of chipotle chiles in the dressing, chile-dusted croutons, and queso añejo cheese on top.

FOR THE CHILE-DUSTED CROUTONS

3 Tbsp extra-virgin olive oil

½ tsp ancho chile powder

Salt and freshly ground pepper

2 cups (4 oz/125 g) cubed sourdough or other country-style bread (1-inch/2.5-cm cubes)

FOR THE CHIPOTLE DRESSING

1 large egg (see Note), or 1 Tbsp mayonnaise

3 cloves garlic

3 tsp fresh lime juice

1 canned chipotle chile in adobo, plus 2 tsp sauce

⅓ cup (3 fl oz/80 ml) extra-virgin olive oil

2 hearts of romaine lettuce, separated into leaves

Queso añejo or Parmesan cheese shavings

To make the croutons, preheat the oven to 350°F (180°C). In a large bowl, combine the 3 Tbsp oil, chile powder, ½ tsp salt, and ½ tsp pepper. Add the bread cubes to the bowl and toss to coat. Spread the bread cubes on a baking sheet and bake, turning once or twice, until golden, about 15 minutes. Remove the croutons from the oven and let cool on the baking sheet.

To make the dressing, in a blender, combine the egg or mayonnaise, the garlic, lime juice, chipotle chile and sauce, ½ tsp salt, and ½ tsp pepper. Blend until well mixed, then with the motor on low speed, slowly drizzle in the ⅓ cup oil and process until thick and smooth.

Transfer the dressing to a large serving bowl. Add the lettuce leaves and three-fourths of the croutons to the bowl with the dressing and mix to coat the leaves thoroughly with the dressing. Top with the remaining croutons. Scatter the cheese over and serve.

Note: Raw egg can carry salmonella. The risks involved in salmonella poisoning are greatest for children, the elderly, pregnant women, and anyone with a compromised immune system.

14

ARUGULA, OAKLEAF LETTUCE & BASIL SALAD

serves 4–6

Sometimes nothing beats a simple leafy green salad with a terrific vinaigrette. Here, cherry tomatoes are roasted until the skins blister and the tomatoes burst, giving the finished dressing a sweet, slightly caramelized flavor.

FOR THE ROASTED-TOMATO DRESSING

8 red or yellow cherry tomatoes

Salt and freshly ground pepper

¼ cup (2 fl oz/60 ml) red wine vinegar

4 fresh basil leaves

½ cup (4 fl oz/125 ml) extra-virgin olive oil

4 cups (4 oz/125 g) arugula leaves, stemmed

4 cups (4 oz/125 g) spotted, red, or green oakleaf lettuce

Fresh purple or green basil leaves, larger leaves torn

To make the dressing, preheat the oven to 400°F (200°C). Place the tomatoes on a small rimmed baking sheet and season well with salt and pepper. Roast until the skins are well blistered and the tomatoes burst, about 25 minutes. Drizzle the vinegar over the tomatoes and roast for 5 minutes. Remove from the oven and let cool completely.

Transfer the roasted tomatoes and vinegar to a food processor and add the 4 basil leaves and the olive oil. Process until smooth, about 1 minute. Season with salt and pepper to taste.

In a large serving bowl, combine the arugula, lettuce, and basil and toss with some of the vinaigrette. Season with salt and pepper to taste, add more vinaigrette as needed (you may not need all of it), and serve.

15

FRESH STRAWBERRY & SPINACH SALAD

serves 6

¼ cup (1 oz/30 g) pecans

FOR THE POPPY-SEED VINAIGRETTE

¼ cup (2 fl oz/60 ml) rice vinegar

2 Tbsp sugar

2 tsp poppy seeds

½ tsp dry mustard

Salt and freshly ground pepper

¾ cup (6 fl oz/180 ml) grapeseed oil

6 cups (6 oz/185 g) baby spinach leaves

2 cups (8 oz/250 g) strawberries, hulled and halved

It is easy to love this popular combination. Light, healthful, and delicious, it is best prepared when strawberries are at their early-summer peak. The dressing is slightly sweet, and the poppy seeds and chopped pecans add nice texture. Goat cheese, ricotta salata, or feta cheese would make a great addition.

In a dry frying pan, toast the pecans over medium-low heat, stirring, until fragrant and starting to brown, about 5 minutes. Pour onto a plate to cool, then coarsely chop and set aside.

To make the vinaigrette, in a small bowl, whisk together the vinegar, sugar, poppy seeds, dry mustard, and a pinch each of salt and pepper. Add the oil in a thin stream, whisking constantly until the dressing is well blended.

In a large bowl, toss together the spinach, strawberries, and pecans. Add half of the vinaigrette and toss gently to coat. Add more vinaigrette as needed (you may not need all of it), and serve.

16

POACHED SALMON SALAD WITH PRESERVED LEMON & GARLIC

serves 4–6

1 lb (500 g) salmon fillet, pin bones removed

Salt and freshly ground pepper

1 garlic clove, mashed to a paste

2 green onions, minced

Rind of 1 small preserved lemon, minced

¼ cup (2 fl oz/60 ml) extra-virgin olive oil, plus 1 Tbsp

Juice of 1 lemon

1 head butter lettuce, leaves torn

Use a mortar to crush the garlic for this boldly flavored salad. Preserved lemons, which are salted and then pickled in their own juices, can be found jarred in specialty food shops, Middle Eastern markets, or online.

Cut the salmon into pieces as needed to fit into a large saucepan. Cover the fish with water, add 1 tsp salt, and bring to a boil over medium heat, then reduce the heat to a simmer and poach the salmon gently until just opaque throughout, about 20 minutes.

Peel off and discard the salmon skin, put the flesh in a bowl, and break up into pieces with a fork. Add the mashed garlic, green onions, preserved lemon rind, and the ¼ cup oil to the bowl and toss to mix. Season to taste with pepper and set aside.

In a small bowl, whisk together the lemon juice and the 1 Tbsp oil and season to taste with salt and pepper. Put the lettuce leaves in a large bowl, drizzle with the lemon dressing, and toss to mix. Distribute the greens among individual plates and top with some of the salmon salad. Season to taste with salt and pepper and serve.

17

CHICKEN TOSTADA SALAD

serves 4

FOR THE LIME VINAIGRETTE

Grated zest and juice of 2 limes

1 clove garlic, minced

Salt and freshly ground pepper

⅔ cup (5 fl oz/160 ml) olive oil

1 can (15 oz/470 g) black beans, drained and rinsed

2 cups (12 oz/375 g) fresh corn kernels (from about 2 ears of corn, grilled if desired)

2 cups (12 oz/375 g) cherry tomatoes, halved

4 canned green chiles, chopped

1 cup (8 fl oz/250 ml) corn oil

4 corn tortillas, each 6 inches (15 cm) in diameter, halved

1 small head romaine lettuce, cut into bite-sized pieces

2 cups (¾ lb/375 g) shredded cooked chicken meat

1 avocado, peeled, pitted and sliced

Fresh cilantro leaves and sliced green onion for garnish (optional)

This is a refreshed version of the ubiquitous taco salad, with lean chicken and chopped vegetables piled high on a crispy tortilla. For a shortcut, omit frying the tortillas and serve the chicken salad over large handfuls of good-quality corn tortilla chips.

To make the vinaigrette, in a bowl, whisk together the lime zest and juice, garlic, ¼ tsp salt, and ⅛ tsp pepper. Add the oil in a thin stream, whisking constantly until the vinaigrette is smooth.

Transfer 3 Tbsp of the vinaigrette to a large bowl and add the beans, corn, tomatoes, and chiles; mix gently. Reserve the remaining vinaigrette. Let the salsa stand for at least 10 minutes to blend the flavors.

Meanwhile, in a frying pan, warm the corn oil over medium-high heat. When it is hot, slip 3 tortilla halves into the oil and cook until golden and almost crisp, 1–2 minutes. Using tongs, transfer to paper towels to drain. Repeat with the remaining tortilla halves.

Add the lettuce to the reserved vinaigrette and toss to coat. Place 2 fried tortilla halves on each of 4 plates and divide the lettuce among them. Spoon the salsa over the lettuce, top with the chicken and avocado, garnish with the cilantro and green onion, if desired, and serve.

18

PEACH, ARUGULA & GOAT CHEESE SALAD

serves 4

½ cup (4 fl oz/125 ml) balsamic vinegar, plus 2 Tbsp

2 peaches

2 Tbsp firmly packed light brown sugar

2 cups (2 oz/60 g) arugula leaves, stemmed

2 Tbsp grapeseed oil

Salt and freshly ground pepper

4 oz (125 g) fresh goat cheese, crumbled

This salad showcases ripe peaches in season. Sample local varieties at the farmers' market, including white or yellow peaches, or smaller, flatter, donut peaches. Balsamic vinegar reduces to a syrupy consistency to make a simply delicious condiment for grilled fruit and salads.

In a small, heavy saucepan, bring the ½ cup vinegar to a boil over medium-high heat. Reduce the heat to a simmer and cook the vinegar down until it is thick enough to coat the back of a spoon. Let cool.

Cut the peaches in half lengthwise; remove and discard the pits. Cut each half into 6 wedges. Place the wedges in a shallow dish, sprinkle with the brown sugar, and drizzle with the 2 Tbsp vinegar.

Prepare a charcoal or gas grill for direct-heat cooking over medium-high heat. Oil the grill rack or a grill basket. Grill the peaches, turning once, until grill marks appear, about 1 minute per side.

In a large bowl, combine the arugula and the oil and toss to coat. Season with salt and pepper to taste. Put the arugula in a large serving bowl or divide among individual plates. Arrange the grilled peaches on top of the arugula. Drizzle with the balsamic reduction and sprinkle with the cheese. Top with a few grindings of pepper and serve.

19

Lentils, which cook quickly and have a faintly earthy flavor, make up the base of this multicolored salad that also boasts slivers of red tomato and cubes of white feta cheese. For a vegetarian option, substitute lightly toasted walnuts for the chicken.

LENTIL SALAD WITH SUN-DRIED TOMATOES, CHICKEN & FETA

serves 4

1 cup (7 oz/220 g) green French (du Puy) lentils, picked over and rinsed

Salt

8 drained oil-packed sun-dried tomatoes, minced, 3 Tbsp oil reserved

1 clove garlic, minced

3 Tbsp minced fresh flat-leaf parsley

¼ lb (125 g) feta cheese, cut into ½-inch (12-mm) cubes

1½ cups (9 oz/280 g) slivered roasted chicken

In a large saucepan, combine the lentils, 6 cups (48 fl oz/1.5 l) water, and 1 tsp salt. Bring to a boil over medium-high heat, reduce the heat to low, and simmer, uncovered, until the lentils are tender, 30–40 minutes.

Drain the lentils well and transfer to a large bowl. Add ½ tsp salt, the sun-dried tomatoes and oil, garlic, and parsley and stir gently to mix.

Mound the lentils on a platter. Top with the cheese and chicken and serve.

20

Quinoa, a mild grain that originated in Peru, can provide a backdrop for many different flavors. This salad combines it with bold Mediterranean ingredients: garlic, basil, vinegar, and blistered peppers.

ROASTED BELL PEPPER & QUINOA SALAD

serves 4–6

1 cup (6 oz/185 g) quinoa

2 red bell peppers

2 yellow bell peppers

Grated zest of 1 lemon

2 Tbsp fresh lemon juice

1 medium tomato, coarsely chopped

1 clove garlic, chopped

½ cup (½ oz/15 g) loosely packed fresh basil leaves, plus small leaves for garnish

1 tsp sherry vinegar or white wine vinegar

1 Tbsp extra-virgin olive oil

Salt and freshly ground pepper

In a dry frying pan, toast the quinoa over medium heat, stirring, until fragrant with a nutty aroma, 2–3 minutes. Transfer to a fine-mesh sieve and rinse under cold running water until the water runs clear. Drain thoroughly and put in a pot with 3 cups (24 fl oz/750 ml) water. Bring to a boil, then reduce the heat to low, cover, and simmer until the water is absorbed and the grains are translucent, about 15 minutes. Remove from the heat, fluff the quinoa, and let cool completely.

Preheat the broiler. Place the peppers on a baking sheet and slide under the broiler 4–6 inches (10–15 cm) from the heat source. Broil, turning often, until the skins are blackened on all sides, 10–15 minutes. Remove to a covered bowl or seal in a paper bag. Let the peppers steam until cool, about 10 minutes. Rub and peel off the charred skins. Cut the peppers in half lengthwise, reserving their juices, remove the seeds and membranes, and chop finely.

In a blender or food processor, combine the reserved juice from the peppers, lemon zest, lemon juice, tomato, garlic, the ½ cup basil, vinegar, olive oil, 2 Tbsp water, 1 tsp salt, and several grindings of pepper and process until smooth. Add to the cooled quinoa along with the bell peppers and toss. Season with salt and pepper to taste.

Mound on a platter or divide among plates. Garnish with basil leaves and serve.

21

A traditional salade verte is a tangle of greens coated in a mustardy vinaigrette. In France, it is typically served after the main course, frequently alongside a cheese plate. The best versions include seasonal greens and a smattering of fragrant herbs.

SALADE VERTE

serves 4–6

FOR THE VINAIGRETTE

2 tsp white wine vinegar

3 or 4 drops balsamic vinegar

Salt and freshly ground pepper

½ tsp Dijon, champagne, tarragon, or other mustard, or to taste

3 Tbsp extra-virgin olive oil or equal parts extra-virgin olive oil and walnut or hazelnut oil

5 or 6 large handfuls mixed torn greens, such as frisée, mâche, arugula, dandelion greens, butter lettuce, Belgian endive, and/or baby romaine

1 shallot, thinly sliced or chopped

1 Tbsp chopped fresh chives

1 tsp chopped fresh chervil

1 tsp chopped fresh tarragon

Thin slices of country-style bread for serving (optional)

To make the vinaigrette, in a large serving bowl, whisk together the vinegars and a pinch of salt until the salt dissolves, then stir in the mustard. Add the oil in a thin stream, whisking constantly until the vinaigrette is smooth. Season with pepper, then taste and adjust the seasonings.

Add the mixed greens and shallot to the vinaigrette and toss until the leaves are well coated. Add the chives, chervil, and tarragon and toss again to distribute the herbs evenly. Divide the salad among individual plates and serve with the bread alongside, if desired.

22

This salad provides two sides in one by combining a fresh green vegetable with filling potatoes. Serve as an accompaniment to grilled or roasted meat. The summery cucumber-yogurt dressing may be prepared a day in advance, covered, and refrigerated.

POTATO SALAD WITH GREEN BEANS & CUCUMBER-YOGURT DRESSING

serves 6

FOR THE CUCUMBER-YOGURT DRESSING

⅔ cup (5 oz/155 g) plain whole-milk yogurt

⅓ cup (3 fl oz/80 ml) mayonnaise

¼ cup (⅓ oz/10 g) minced fresh dill

½ tsp dried oregano

Salt and freshly ground pepper

¾ cup (4 oz/125 g) peeled, seeded, and finely chopped cucumber (from about one 3½-inch/9-cm piece)

5 Yukon Gold potatoes (about 1¾ lb/875 g total weight), peeled, halved lengthwise, and cut crosswise into slices ⅓ inch (9 mm) thick

½ lb (250 g) green beans, trimmed and cut into 2-inch (5-cm) pieces

½ Tbsp white wine vinegar

To make the dressing, in a bowl, whisk together the yogurt, mayonnaise, dill, oregano, ½ tsp salt, and ½ tsp pepper. Stir in the cucumber. Set aside.

To steam the potatoes, pour water to a depth of 1 inch (2.5 cm) into a large pot and bring to a boil. Put the potatoes in a steamer basket and set the basket over the boiling water. (The water should not touch the bottom of the steamer basket.) Cover and steam until the potatoes are tender when pierced with a knife, about 14 minutes. Transfer the potatoes to a large bowl. Let cool for 5 minutes, then sprinkle lightly with salt and pepper.

In the same steamer, cook the green beans until just crisp-tender, about 5 minutes. Transfer the green beans to the bowl with the potatoes. Sprinkle with salt and pepper and let cool to lukewarm, about 20 minutes.

Using a slotted spoon, transfer the cucumbers from the yogurt mixture to the bowl with the potatoes and beans. Mix the vinegar into the yogurt mixture. Stir enough of the dressing into the salad to coat generously and serve.

23

JUNE

FARMERS' MARKET SALAD WITH TOMATO-BASIL VINAIGRETTE

serves 4

Although you can serve this salad as is, you can take it up a step with a topping of crispy garlic chips. If you don't have a spiralizer or a mandoline, use a sharp knife and cut the zucchini and summer squash lengthwise into thin slices, then cut again into long julienne strips.

FOR THE GARLIC CHIPS (OPTIONAL)

¼ cup (1½ oz/45 g) very thinly sliced garlic

¼ cup (2 fl oz/60 ml) olive oil

Salt

1 plum tomato, peeled, cored, and seeded

1 small clove garlic, minced

1 Tbsp champagne vinegar

¼ cup (2 fl oz/60 ml) extra-virgin olive oil

1½ Tbsp chopped fresh basil

Salt and freshly ground pepper

Pinch of sugar (optional)

2 zucchini, ends trimmed

2 summer squash, ends trimmed

4 radishes, very thinly sliced

1 shallot, very thinly sliced

1 cup (6 oz/185 g) cherry tomatoes, halved

1 cup (5 oz/155 g) crumbled cotija or feta cheese

If making the garlic chips, in a small sauté pan, combine the garlic and oil. Place over medium heat and gently fry, stirring occasionally, until the garlic is golden, about 2 minutes. Using a fine-mesh strainer, transfer the chips to a paper towel–lined plate and sprinkle with salt. Reserve the garlicky oil for sautéing or salad dressing.

In a mini food processor, purée the plum tomato. Transfer to a small bowl. Add the minced garlic, vinegar, oil, and basil and whisk until the vinaigrette is well blended. Season with salt and pepper. Taste and add the sugar, if needed.

Using a spiralizer fitted with the small shredder blade, cut the zucchini and squash into spaghetti-like spiral strands, stopping to cut the curls with kitchen shears every 3 or 4 rotations. Alternatively, using a mandoline, slice the zucchini into long julienne strips.

Transfer the zucchini and squash to a large bowl. Add the radishes, shallot, and cherry tomatoes. Drizzle with vinaigrette to taste and toss to coat evenly. Top with the cheese and the garlic chips, if using, and serve.

24

JUNE

STONE FRUIT SALAD WITH HAZELNUTS & BLUE CHEESE

serves 6

Stone fruits— peaches, plums, apricots—have a special affinity for nuts, as their pits themselves carry a bitter almond flavor. A sprinkling of savory blue cheese balances the sweetness of the fruit and the bitter edge of the hazelnuts, making this a sophisticated summertime salad.

¼ cup (1½ oz/45 g) hazelnuts

2 Tbsp rice vinegar

1 tsp honey

Salt and freshly ground pepper

½ cup (4 fl oz/125 ml) extra-virgin olive oil

6 cups (6 oz/185 g) baby arugula leaves

2 small plums, halved, pitted, and cut into ¼-inch (6-mm) slices

2 small apricots, halved, pitted, and cut into ¼-inch (6-mm) slices

1 firm peach, halved, pitted, and cut into ¼-inch (6-mm) slices

¼ cup (1½ oz/45 g) crumbled blue cheese

In a dry frying pan, toast the hazelnuts over medium-low heat, stirring, until fragrant and starting to brown, about 5 minutes. Wrap the hazelnuts in a towel and rub to remove the skins. Pour onto a plate to cool, then chop coarsely and set aside.

In a small bowl, whisk together the vinegar, honey, and a pinch each of salt and pepper. Add the olive oil in a thin stream, whisking constantly until the vinaigrette is smooth.

In a large bowl, gently toss together the arugula, plums, apricots, peach, and hazelnuts. Add half of the vinaigrette and toss gently, adding more as needed to lightly coat the arugula. Sprinkle with the cheese and serve.

147

25

To hard-cook the eggs, place them in a saucepan just large enough to hold them. Add cold water to cover by 1 inch (2.5 cm) and bring just to a boil over high heat. Remove the pan from the heat and cover. Let stand for 15 minutes. Have ready a bowl of ice water. Drain the eggs, then transfer to the ice water and let cool before peeling.

SALADE NIÇOISE WITH SEARED WILD SALMON

serves 6

FOR THE OLIVE-ANCHOVY DRESSING

2 Tbsp chopped pitted niçoise olives

2 or 3 olive oil–packed anchovy fillets

5 Tbsp (2½ fl oz/75 ml) extra-virgin olive oil

3 Tbsp white wine vinegar

2 Tbsp minced fresh chives

¾ tsp sugar

¼ tsp Dijon mustard

2 lb (1 kg) small red potatoes, quartered

Salt and freshly ground pepper

¾ lb (375 g) haricots verts or other young, tender green beans, stem ends trimmed

6 wild salmon fillets (6 oz/185 g each), pin bones removed

1 Tbsp grapeseed oil

1 head romaine lettuce, thinly sliced

3½ cups (21 oz/655 g) cherry tomatoes, halved

6 eggs, hard-cooked *(left)* and cut into quarters

2 Tbsp minced fresh chives

To make the dressing, in a food processor, combine the olives and anchovies and process until smooth, about 10 seconds. Add the olive oil, vinegar, chives, sugar, and mustard and process until the dressing is smooth. Set aside.

Have ready a bowl of ice water. In a large saucepan, combine the potatoes, 1 Tbsp salt, and water to cover by 1 inch (2.5 cm) and bring to a boil over high heat. Reduce the heat to medium, cover partially, and simmer until the potatoes are just tender when pierced with the tip of a paring knife, 5–7 minutes. Drain and immediately transfer the potatoes to the ice water. Let stand until cool, then transfer the potatoes to a large bowl.

Fill a saucepan two-thirds full of water and bring to a boil over high heat. Have ready another bowl of ice water. Add 1 Tbsp salt and the haricots verts to the boiling water and cook until crisp-tender, about 3 minutes. Drain and transfer to the ice water. Let stand until cool and drain. Add the beans to the bowl with the potatoes. ⟫⟫

Season the salmon fillets on both sides with salt and pepper. In a large nonstick frying pan, warm the oil over medium-high heat until shimmering. Working in batches, add the salmon to the pan, skin side up, and cook until golden brown, about 2 minutes. Turn the salmon over and cook until just opaque at the center, 2–3 minutes. Transfer to a large plate, remove the skin, and tent with foil.

Add the lettuce, ¾ tsp salt, and several grindings of pepper to the potatoes and beans and toss to mix. Drizzle with half of the vinaigrette and toss again. In a bowl, toss the tomatoes with ¼ tsp salt.

Divide the mixture among individual plates. Top each serving with some of the tomatoes, and then with a piece of salmon. Arrange 4 egg quarters on each serving and sprinkle them lightly with salt. Sprinkle each salad with chives and serve, passing the remaining vinaigrette at the table.

26

Cool cucumbers shine through in this quintessential summer salad. It comes together quickly for an outdoor supper, but would be equally charming with toasted bagels and slices of smoked salmon for brunch. For a touch of heat, add a pinch of cayenne pepper.

CUCUMBER SALAD WITH YOGURT-DILL SAUCE

serves 4

4 English cucumbers, peeled and thinly sliced

Salt and ground white pepper

⅔ cup (5 oz/155 g) plain yogurt

1 Tbsp fresh lemon juice

2 Tbsp minced fresh dill

3 cloves garlic, minced

3 Tbsp extra-virgin olive oil

Place the cucumber slices in a single layer on a plate. Salt lightly and let stand for about 1 hour. Drain off the excess liquid.

In a large bowl, combine the yogurt, lemon juice, dill, and garlic. Season with salt and white pepper to taste and whisk to combine. Add the oil in a thin stream, whisking constantly until the dressing is well blended.

Add the drained cucumber slices to the bowl and toss with the dressing. Refrigerate for 1 hour, then serve chilled.

27

SMOKY SHRIMP & PASTA SALAD

serves 4–6

This hearty summer salad combines smoky grilled shrimp with bell peppers, onions, and pasta. Using a mesh pan on the grill rack ensures that no shrimp or pepper pieces will slip through the rack into the fire. Other types of short pasta, such as penne or rotini, can be substituted for the fusilli.

Salt and freshly ground pepper

½ lb (250 g) fusilli pasta

2 Tbsp sherry vinegar

2 tsp smoked paprika

6 Tbsp (3 fl oz/90 ml) olive oil

1 lb (500 g) medium shrimp, peeled and deveined

3 cloves garlic, sliced

4 bell peppers (a mixture of red, yellow, and orange), seeded and diced

1 small red onion, diced

6 green onions, including tender green parts, thinly sliced

2 Tbsp minced fresh flat-leaf parsley

Bring a large pot of water to a boil over medium-high heat. Add 1 tsp salt and the pasta. Stir well. Reduce the heat to medium and cook until al dente or according to the package directions. Drain and set aside.

Meanwhile, in a small bowl, whisk together the vinegar, paprika, and 2 Tbsp of the oil until the vinaigrette is well blended. Reserve half of the vinaigrette. In a medium bowl, combine the shrimp, the remaining vinaigrette, and one-third of the garlic. Season with salt and pepper and toss to coat. Cover and refrigerate for 20–30 minutes.

In a large bowl, stir together the bell peppers, red onion, the remaining garlic, and the remaining 4 Tbsp (2 fl oz/60 ml) oil. Season with salt and pepper. Set aside.

Prepare a charcoal or gas grill for direct-heat cooking over medium-high heat and preheat a grill basket. Alternatively, preheat a stove-top grill pan over medium-high heat.

Place the bell pepper mixture in the grill basket or in the grill pan. Cook, stirring occasionally, until just softened, about 15 minutes, adding the green onions during the last minutes of cooking. Transfer to a bowl.

Place the shrimp in the grill basket or in the pan and cook, turning once, until just opaque, 3–5 minutes per side. Add to the bowl with the bell pepper mixture. Add the pasta, parsley, and the reserved vinaigrette and stir to combine. Serve warm.

28

GREEN PAPAYA SALAD

serves 4–6

Sriracha sauce is a tantalizing combination of sun-ripened chiles ground up with garlic into a paste. Along with fish sauce and rice vinegar, it adds spice and piquancy to shreds of crunchy papaya in this classic Southeast Asian salad.

1 large green papaya, about 1½ lb (750 g)

1 carrot

4 shallots, thinly sliced, plus 1 Tbsp chopped

1 red Fresno chile, cut into thin rings and seeded

2 Tbsp chopped fresh cilantro

2 cloves garlic, chopped

1 tsp sugar

¼ cup (2 fl oz/60 ml) rice vinegar

¼ cup (2 fl oz/60 ml) Asian fish sauce

2 Tbsp fresh lime juice

2 Tbsp Sriracha chile sauce

3 Tbsp canola oil

Using a vegetable peeler, peel the papaya. Cut the papaya in half lengthwise and then scoop out and discard the seeds. Using the largest holes on a box grater or a mandoline, and holding each papaya half lengthwise, shred the flesh into long, thin strips. Peel the carrot and shred into long, thin strips.

In a large bowl, combine the papaya, carrot, sliced shallots, chile, and cilantro and toss gently to mix well.

In a mini food processor or mortar, combine the chopped shallot, garlic, and sugar and process or grind with a pestle until a smooth paste forms. Add 1–2 tsp water if needed to facilitate the grinding. Transfer the garlic paste to a bowl and whisk in the vinegar, fish sauce, lime juice, and Sriracha sauce. Add the oil in a thin stream, whisking constantly until the dressing is well combined.

Pour the dressing over the papaya mixture and toss to coat thoroughly. Refrigerate for at least 2 hours or up to overnight before serving. Serve chilled.

29

Make this simple salad in the summertime, when ears of corn and juicy tomatoes fill local market bins. Tart lime juice and salty feta are the perfect counterpoints to the naturally sweet seasonal produce. Serve as a light lunch with a crusty baguette or as a side dish to grilled chicken or lamb skewers.

PAN-ROASTED CORN SALAD WITH TOMATOES & FETA

serves 4

4 ears of corn, husks and silk removed

2 Tbsp unsalted butter

4 Tbsp (2 fl oz/60 ml) extra-virgin olive oil

1 clove garlic, minced

1 tsp coarsely chopped fresh thyme

1 bunch green onions, green part only, thinly sliced on the diagonal

Salt and freshly ground pepper

2–3 cups (12–18 oz/375–560 g) halved cherry tomatoes

½ lb (250 g) feta cheese, cut into ½-inch (12-mm) cubes

Juice of ½ lime, plus more if needed

2 Tbsp finely slivered fresh basil

Hold each ear of corn upright in a large bowl. Using a sharp knife, cut straight down between the kernels and the cob, rotating the ear about a quarter turn after each cut.

In a large nonstick sauté pan, melt half of the butter with 1 Tbsp of the oil over medium-high heat until almost smoking. Add half of the garlic and cook, stirring constantly, for 20–30 seconds. Add half of the corn and cook, stirring occasionally, until golden and just tender, 3–4 minutes. Add half each of the thyme and green onions and cook, stirring occasionally, for about 1 minute. Season with salt and pepper and transfer to a large bowl. Repeat with the remaining butter, 1 Tbsp of the oil, and the remaining garlic, corn, thyme, and green onions. Transfer to the bowl. Let cool to room temperature, stirring occasionally, about 30 minutes.

In a medium bowl, combine the tomatoes, cheese, and the remaining 2 Tbsp oil. Season with salt and pepper and toss gently to mix. Add the tomato mixture, lime juice, and basil to the corn mixture and toss to combine. Taste and adjust the seasonings, adding more lime juice if needed, and serve.

30

Early in the summer, seek out baby squashes in a variety of shapes. Combining these with halved larger squash makes a beautiful presentation on a bed of pasta. Use a grill basket so you don't lose any cherry tomatoes and baby squash, if using.

GRILLED SQUASH & ORZO SALAD WITH PINE NUTS & MINT

serves 4

2 lb (1 kg) mixed yellow squash and zucchini

1½ Tbsp olive oil

Salt and freshly ground pepper

½ lb (250 g) orzo pasta

½ cup (2½ oz/75 g) pine nuts

3 Tbsp fresh lemon juice

1 Tbsp champagne vinegar or white wine vinegar

3 Tbsp chopped fresh mint leaves

Parmesan cheese for shaving (optional)

Trim and cut the squash lengthwise into slices ¼ inch (6 mm) thick. Put in a bowl and add ½ Tbsp of the oil, ½ tsp salt, and a few grindings of pepper. Mix to coat.

Prepare a charcoal or gas grill for direct-heat cooking over medium-high heat. Grill the squash, turning once, until tender, 5–8 minutes total. Let cool and cut into 1½-inch (4-cm) pieces, and put in a large bowl.

Bring a pot of salted water to a boil. Add the orzo and cook until al dente, according to package directions. Drain and rinse under cold running water.

Meanwhile, in a dry frying pan, toast the pine nuts over medium-low heat, stirring, until fragrant and starting to brown, 3–4 minutes. Pour onto a plate to cool.

Add the orzo to the squash along with the remaining 1 Tbsp oil, lemon juice, vinegar, and pine nuts and toss to combine. Season with salt and pepper to taste. Garnish with the mint. Just before serving, use a vegetable peeler to shave the cheese over the salad, if using, and serve.

High summer means high season for sun-loving corn and tomatoes. Toss a handful of corn kernels into salads to add a sweet, fresh bite. Heirloom tomatoes are at their best when freshly sliced and simply dressed, and green tomatoes shine when breaded and lightly fried. Make good use of the outdoor grill this season, too: fish, steak, and corn love a bed of leafy greens. Or, create innovative chopped salads of charred eggplant, yellow squash, and zucchini.

4
EGGPLANT SALAD WITH OLIVES & SHERRY VINAIGRETTE
page 157

5
GREEN BEAN & YELLOW TOMATO SALAD WITH MINT
page 158

6
CLASSIC GREEK SALAD
page 158

7
SPINACH, TOMATO & CORN SALAD
page 159

11
CAPRESE SALAD WITH FRIED GREEN TOMATOES
page 163

12
JAPANESE CUCUMBER SALAD
page 163

13
RICE SALAD WITH PESTO & GRILLED SHRIMP
page 164

14
CHICKEN & ROASTED TOMATO SALAD
page 164

18
FATTOUSH SALAD
page 166

19
CREAMY COLESLAW
page 168

20
YELLOW SQUASH & FARRO SALAD
page 168

21
CRISPY EGGPLANT, MISO BUTTER & CHARRED SUNGOLD TOMATO SALAD
page 169

25
GRILLED STEAK, PEPPER & ONION SALAD WITH ROMESCO DRESSING
page 172

26
FRESH FIG & GOAT CHEESE SALAD
page 172

27
LOBSTER SALAD WITH TARRAGON & CHAMPAGNE VINAIGRETTE
page 173

28
CELERY SALAD WITH BLUE CHEESE & LEMON
page 173

july

1

HEIRLOOM TOMATO SALAD WITH BLUE CHEESE DRESSING

serves 4

Ripe summer tomatoes need no more than a sprinkle of sea salt or a classic vinaigrette, but a creamy dressing enriched with crumbled blue cheese only improves on a good thing. Serve with a light white wine such as sauvignon blanc or pinot grigio.

1½ lb (750 g) heirloom tomatoes, in a variety of sizes and colors

FOR THE BLUE CHEESE DRESSING

¼ cup (2 fl oz/60 ml) mayonnaise

¼ cup (2 fl oz/60 ml) buttermilk

1 clove garlic, thinly sliced

2 tsp champagne vinegar, or more to taste

2 oz (60 g) blue cheese, plus extra for crumbling

Salt and freshly ground pepper

2 Tbsp minced green onion, including tender green parts

1 Tbsp minced fresh flat-leaf parsley

Core large tomatoes and cut them into wedges or slices. Cut cherry tomatoes in half. Arrange all the tomatoes attractively on a serving platter.

To make the dressing, in a food processor or a blender, combine the mayonnaise, buttermilk, garlic, the 2 tsp vinegar, and the cheese and process until smooth. Transfer to a bowl and stir in salt to taste and more vinegar if desired.

In a small bowl, combine the green onion and parsley, mixing well.

Drizzle the dressing over the tomatoes, using as much as you like (you may not need it all), then garnish with the green onion–parsley mixture and several grindings of pepper. If desired, crumble extra cheese over the salad and serve.

2

QUICK GRILLED SQUID SALAD

serves 4–6

If you can't find squid readily at your grocer, this fresh seafood salad would be equally appealing with shrimp. Purchase 1 lb (16 oz/500 g) medium-sized shrimp; peel and devein them, then thread 4–6 on a skewer and grill or broil them until they turn pink and curl slightly.

Juice of 2 limes

¼ cup (⅓ oz/10 g) lightly packed fresh mint leaves

¼ cup (⅓ oz/10 g) coarsely chopped fresh cilantro

2 red Thai chiles, seeded and minced

4 Tbsp (2 fl oz/60 ml) olive oil

1 lb (500 g) cleaned squid, cut into bite-sized rings and tentacles

Salt and freshly ground pepper

Lemon wedges for squeezing

Prepare a charcoal or gas grill for direct-heat cooking over medium-high heat.

In a bowl, whisk together the lime juice, mint, cilantro, and chiles. Add 2 Tbsp of the olive oil in a thin stream, whisking constantly until the dressing is smooth. Set aside.

In a bowl, toss the squid with the remaining 2 Tbsp olive oil and season lightly with salt and pepper.

Put the squid in a grill basket and grill, turning once, until opaque and lightly charred on the edges, about 1 minute per side.

Toss the squid with the dressing, and serve hot or at room temperature, with the lemon wedges alongside.

3

GIGANTE BEAN SALAD WITH PEPPERS & CHORIZO

serves 4

This salad takes its cue from Spanish tapas. Beans, chorizo, and small, whole peppers are common tapas ingredients used on their own or in combination, frequently drizzled with olive oil. Peppers and chorizo are also popular as bite-sized pinxtos (spikes), Basque-style snacks speared on bread.

FOR THE BEANS

1½ cups (10½ oz/330 g) dried Gigante beans, picked over for stones and rinsed

2 bay leaves

Salt

FOR THE TOMATO VINAIGRETTE

3 plum tomatoes, halved lengthwise

1½ Tbsp extra-virgin olive oil, plus 1 tsp

4 cloves garlic, minced

Salt and freshly ground pepper

1½ Tbsp red wine vinegar

¼ tsp smoked paprika

12–15 Padrón or shishito peppers

½ lb (250 g) fresh chorizo, casing removed

To make the beans, in a large saucepan, combine the beans and 8 cups (64 fl oz/2 l) water. Bring to a boil over medium heat, then boil for 15–20 minutes. Reduce the heat to low, add the bay leaves, cover, and simmer for 1 hour. Add 2 tsp salt, cover, and simmer until the beans are tender to the bite, 30–45 minutes longer. Drain and set aside.

Meanwhile, make the vinaigrette: Preheat the oven to 325°F (165°C). In a bowl, toss the tomatoes with the 1 tsp oil, garlic, and ¼ tsp salt. Place the tomatoes, cut sides down, on a baking sheet. Roast until tender, 45–60 minutes. Let cool. Slip off the skins and discard. In a blender, combine the tomatoes, garlic, the 1½ Tbsp oil, the vinegar, ¼ tsp pepper, and the paprika and purée until smooth. Taste and adjust the seasonings.

Preheat a stove-top grill pan over medium-high heat. Place the peppers in the pan and cook, turning often, until softened and charred in spots, about 5 minutes. Transfer to a cutting board. Stem and coarsely chop 4 or 5 of the peppers. Keep the others whole.

Crumble the chorizo into a frying pan. Cook over medium-high heat, stirring, until crisp, about 10 minutes. Drain on paper towels.

Divide beans among 4 bowls. Sprinkle with chorizo and chopped peppers. Drizzle with vinaigrette and toss to mix. Garnish with the reserved whole peppers and serve.

4

EGGPLANT SALAD WITH OLIVES & SHERRY VINAIGRETTE

serves 6

Do not skip the step of salting the eggplant cubes and letting them stand for an hour. The salt does two things: it draws out the bitter juices and it collapses the flesh slightly, so it will absorb less oil when it is fried. Serve plenty of fresh country-style bread with this salad for soaking up the delicious juices.

2 large eggplants, peeled and cut into 1-inch (2.5-cm) cubes

Salt and freshly ground pepper

Olive oil for frying

¼ tsp ground coriander

⅔ cup (5 fl oz/160 ml) extra-virgin olive oil

1 clove garlic, minced

¼ cup (2 fl oz/60 ml) sherry vinegar

⅓ cup (3 fl oz/80 ml) fresh orange juice

¼ cup (1¼ oz/40 g) pine nuts, toasted

½ cup (2½ oz/75 g) pitted and slivered Kalamata olives

1 small red onion, shaved or thinly sliced

½ cup (¾ oz/20 g) torn fresh flat-leaf parsley, plus more for garnish

In a large bowl, toss the eggplant with enough salt to lightly coat. Transfer to a colander set in a sink. Let stand for about 1 hour. Rinse the eggplant thoroughly under cold running water, drain well, and pat dry.

Pour olive oil into pot to a depth of 2 inches (5 cm) and heat over medium heat until it registers 350°F (180°C) on a deep-frying thermometer. Line a plate with paper towels. Working in batches, fry the eggplant until tender and golden, about 2 minutes. Using a slotted spoon, transfer to the paper towel–lined plate. Repeat with the remaining eggplant. Transfer to a bowl.

In a small saucepan, toast the coriander over medium-low heat, stirring, until fragrant, about 30 seconds. Add olive oil and increase the heat to medium-high. Add the garlic and cook, stirring frequently, just until golden, about 1 minute. Remove from the heat. Whisk in the vinegar and orange juice. Pour half of the vinaigrette over the eggplant, stir to mix well, and let cool.

In a second large bowl, mix the pine nuts, olives, onion, and parsley. Stir in half of the remaining vinaigrette and season with salt and pepper. Gently fold in the eggplant mixture. Add more vinaigrette to taste.

Transfer the salad to a large platter or divide among individual plates. Garnish with a pinch of parsley and serve right away.

5

GREEN BEAN & YELLOW TOMATO SALAD WITH MINT

serves 4

Salt and freshly ground pepper

1 lb (500 g) long, slender green beans, stem ends trimmed

½ cup (¾ oz/20 g) chopped fresh mint

2 Tbsp extra-virgin olive oil

1 or 2 yellow tomatoes

½ cup (2 oz/60 g) thin red onion wedges

2 tsp red wine vinegar, or to taste

You can't go wrong with simple salad pairings of sun-loving vegetables, like fresh beans and tomatoes. Yellow tomatoes have a sweeter, less acidic flavor than red, but use any color or combination you like. Just reduce the amount of red wine vinegar to taste if you use tart varieties.

Bring a large pot three-fourths full of salted water to a boil. Add the beans to the boiling water and cook until tender, 5–7 minutes. Drain.

In a large serving bowl, combine the hot beans, mint, oil, and ½ tsp salt and toss to mix. Set aside to cool to room temperature, about 20 minutes.

Cut the tomatoes into wedges about ½ inch (12 mm) thick. Just before serving, add the tomatoes, onion, 2 tsp vinegar, and a grinding of pepper to the bean mixture and toss to mix. Taste and add more vinegar, if needed. Serve at room temperature.

6

CLASSIC GREEK SALAD

serves 4

Juice of 1 lemon

1 clove garlic, minced

Freshly ground pepper

¼ cup (2 fl oz/60 ml) extra-virgin olive oil, plus 2 Tbsp

4 rounds pita bread

½ tsp dried oregano

2 hearts of romaine lettuce, coarsely chopped

1 English cucumber, halved crosswise and thickly sliced

2 tomatoes, cut into wedges

1 cup (5 oz/155 g) assorted brine-cured olives

8 oz (250 g) feta cheese, crumbled

8 green onions, including tender green parts, thinly sliced

In Greece you'll find this salad both with and without the lettuce, but what is crucial is using the freshest ingredients and ripest tomatoes you can find. Seek out authentic Greek feta cheese, which is creamy and salty. Kalamata olives are the favorite choice.

In a large bowl, whisk together the lemon juice, garlic, and a generous amount of pepper. Add the ¼ cup olive oil in a thin stream, whisking constantly until the dressing is smooth.

Preheat the oven to 300°F (150°C). Cut each pita round into 4 wedges. Arrange on a baking sheet and brush both sides with the 2 Tbsp oil. Sprinkle with the oregano and place in the oven to warm for about 10 minutes.

Meanwhile, add the lettuce, cucumber, and tomatoes to the dressing and toss to coat evenly. Arrange on plates and top with the olives, cheese, and green onions. Place the warm pita wedges alongside the salads and serve.

7

SPINACH, TOMATO & CORN SALAD

serves 4

Baby spinach gains even more fresh flavor with chopped basil, mint, parsley, and dill, and a pinch of toasted cumin enlivens ordinary vinaigrette. Fresh sweet corn does not require cooking; look for the freshest young ears you can find, at a farmers' market or roadside farm stand.

2 ears corn, husks and silk removed

1 large tomato, chopped

½ cup (2½ oz/75 g) chopped English cucumber

½ cup (2 oz/60 g) chopped sweet onion such as Vidalia

2 Tbsp *each* chopped fresh basil, mint, flat-leaf parsley, and dill

1 tsp chopped garlic

1 tsp ground cumin

¼ cup (2 fl oz/60 ml) extra-virgin olive oil

2 Tbsp red wine vinegar

Salt and freshly ground pepper

5 oz (155 g) baby spinach leaves

Hold each ear of corn upright, stem end down, in the center of a wide, shallow bowl and cut off the kernels.

Add the tomato, cucumber, and onion to the corn. Add the basil, mint, parsley, dill, and garlic.

In a small, dry frying pan over medium-low heat, warm the cumin just until fragrant, about 20 seconds. Transfer to a small bowl. Add the olive oil, vinegar, ½ tsp salt, and a grinding of pepper and whisk until a smooth dressing forms.

Add the dressing to the corn-tomato mixture and toss to coat. Add the spinach, toss again, and serve.

8

OLD-FASHIONED POTATO SALAD

serves 8

Easy-to-handle red potatoes and common pantry staples define this creamy classic, essential at backyard barbecues. Every family has their own favorite recipe, so don't hesitate to add coarsely chopped olives, sliced hard-boiled eggs, chopped pickles, or flaked tuna, according to your tradition.

3 lb (1.5 kg) red-skinned potatoes

Salt and freshly ground pepper

3 Tbsp white wine vinegar

1 cup (8 fl oz/250 ml) mayonnaise

2 Tbsp whole-grain mustard

4 celery ribs, finely chopped

4 green onions, including green parts, chopped

2 Tbsp minced fresh flat-leaf parsley

Place the unpeeled potatoes in a large saucepan, add salted water to cover by 1 inch (2.5 cm), cover the pan, and bring to a boil over high heat. Set the lid askew, reduce the heat to medium-low, and cook at a brisk simmer until the potatoes are tender, about 25 minutes. Drain, then rinse the potatoes under cold running water until they are cool enough to handle.

Cut the potatoes into chunks about ½ inch (12 mm) thick and place in a large bowl. Sprinkle with the vinegar. Let cool completely.

In a small bowl, mix together the mayonnaise and mustard. Add to the potatoes along with the celery, green onions, and parsley and mix gently. Season with salt and pepper to taste. Cover and refrigerate until chilled, at least 2 hours. Serve chilled.

9

QUINOA SALAD WITH GRILLED VEGETABLES & FETA

serves 6–8

¾ cup (6 fl oz/180 ml) olive oil

2 cups (12 oz/375 g) quinoa, well rinsed

3½ cups (28 fl oz/875 ml) water or vegetable stock

Salt and freshly ground pepper

1 red onion, cut into ¼-inch (6-mm) slices

2 zucchini, cut lengthwise into ¼-inch (6-mm) slices

2 summer squash, cut lengthwise into ¼-inch (6-mm) slices

2 cups (12 oz/375 g) grape tomatoes, halved

¼ cup (2 fl oz/60 ml) fresh lemon juice

⅓ cup (⅓ oz/10 g) fresh basil leaves, larger leaves torn

⅓ cup (⅓ oz/10 g) fresh mint leaves, larger leaves torn

¼ lb (125 g) feta cheese, crumbled

A perfect showcase for summer squashes, this vibrant salad yields a good-size amount, making it ideal for entertaining. Prep is simple, too, with the vegetables cooked on a stove-top grill pan, eliminating the need to fire up the grill. To bring out the nutty flavor of the quinoa, it is lightly toasted before it is simmered in liquid until tender.

In a saucepan, warm 1 Tbsp of the oil over medium-high heat. Add the quinoa and cook, stirring, until lightly toasted, 2–3 minutes. Add the water, season with salt, and bring to a boil. Reduce the heat to medium-low, cover, and simmer until the grains are tender and the water is absorbed, about 15 minutes. Let the quinoa cool.

Prepare a charcoal or gas grill for direct-heat cooking over medium-high heat. Alternatively, preheat a stove-top grill pan over medium-high heat.

In a large bowl, combine the onion, zucchini, squash, and 3 Tbsp of the oil and toss gently to coat. Season with salt and pepper. Place the vegetables on the grill rack or in the grill pan and cook, turning once, until nicely grill-marked and tender, 3–4 minutes per side. Transfer to a cutting board and let cool slightly, then cut into rough ¼-inch (6-mm) dice. Add the vegetables and the tomatoes to the pot with the quinoa and stir gently to combine.

In a small bowl, whisk together the remaining ½ cup (4 fl oz/125 ml) oil and the lemon juice until blended. Season with salt and pepper. Drizzle the vinaigrette over the quinoa. Add the basil, mint, and half of the cheese and stir to combine. Top with the remaining cheese and serve.

10

GRILLED PLUOT SALAD WITH GOAT CHEESE & WILD ARUGULA

serves 6

9 or 10 pluots, about 1½ lb (750 g), halved and pitted

5 Tbsp (2½ fl oz/75 ml) extra-virgin olive oil

2 Tbsp sugar

2 Tbsp champagne vinegar

Salt and freshly ground pepper

2–3 cups (2–3 oz/60–90 g) arugula leaves, stemmed

½ head butter lettuce, torn into bite-sized pieces (about 2 cups/2 oz/60 g)

4 oz (125 g) fresh goat cheese, crumbled

1 tsp minced fresh thyme blossoms or leaves

Like all stone fruits, the pluot, a cross between a plum and an apricot, grills well. The heat caramelizes the surface, intensifying the sweet-tart flavor. A mix of peppery arugula, tender butter lettuce, and tangy goat cheese complements the beautiful grilled fruit halves.

Place the pluot halves in a baking dish, drizzle with 2 Tbsp of the oil, and turn to coat. Sprinkle with the sugar and turn again. Set aside.

In a serving bowl, combine the remaining 3 Tbsp oil, the vinegar, ½ tsp salt, and ¼ tsp pepper and mix well. Add the arugula and butter lettuce and set aside without tossing. (This can be done up 30 minutes in advance of serving.)

Prepare a charcoal or gas grill for direct-heat cooking over medium-high heat, or preheat a stove-top grill pan over medium-high heat. When ready, place the pluots directly on the grill or in the grill pan, cut side down. Cook until lightly golden and grill marked, about 2 minutes. Turn and cook on the other side until the skin shrinks slightly, about 1 minute. Do not overcook.

Toss the salad and divide among individual plates. Top each salad with a few grilled pluot halves, crumbles of cheese, and a sprinkling of thyme, and serve.

11

CAPRESE SALAD WITH FRIED GREEN TOMATOES

serves 4

Crunchy, well-seasoned green tomatoes layered between creamy slices of fresh mozzarella is a surprise alternative to the popular caprese salad made with ripe red tomatoes. Any green tomato can be used for this dish, as all green tomatoes, regardless of variety, are firm enough to fry.

Vegetable oil for frying

1 cup (5 oz/155 g) all-purpose flour

2 large eggs

½ cup (4 fl oz/125 ml) buttermilk

½ cup (2½ oz/75 g) cornmeal

½ cup (1 oz/60 g) fresh bread crumbs

Salt and freshly ground pepper

⅛ tsp sweet paprika

4 medium to large green (unripe) tomatoes, cut into ½-inch (12-mm) slices

¾ lb (375 g) fresh mozzarella cheese, cut into slices ¼–½ inch (6–12 mm) thick

1 cup (1 oz/30 g) fresh basil leaves, torn in half if large

¼ cup (2 fl oz/60 ml) extra-virgin olive oil

Pour vegetable oil into a large frying pan to a depth of ½ inch (12 mm) and heat over medium-high heat until it registers 375°F (190°C) on a deep-frying thermometer, or until it sizzles when a few bread crumbs are dropped in. Line a baking sheet with paper towels.

Preheat the oven to 275°F (135°C).

Spread the flour on a plate. In a shallow bowl, whisk together the eggs and buttermilk. In a second shallow bowl, stir together the cornmeal, bread crumbs, 2 tsp salt, 1 tsp pepper, and the paprika. Dredge a tomato slice in the flour, shaking off the excess; then dip into the egg mixture, allowing the excess to drip off; and finally dredge in the cornmeal mixture. Gently slip the tomato into the hot oil. Repeat until the pan is full but not crowded. Fry, turning once, until golden and crisp, about 3 minutes per side. Using a slotted spoon, transfer to the paper towel–lined baking sheet. Keep warm in the oven while frying the remaining tomatoes.

Transfer the tomatoes to a platter. Insert the cheese slices and basil between the tomatoes. Drizzle with the olive oil and serve at once.

12

JAPANESE CUCUMBER SALAD

serves 4

1 lb (500 g) Japanese cucumber, peeled, halved lengthwise, and seeded

Salt and freshly ground pepper

3 Tbsp rice vinegar

½ tsp sugar

1 tsp toasted sesame oil

2 Tbsp thinly sliced green onion, white and green parts (cut on the diagonal)

1 Tbsp thinly sliced fresh shiso leaves or mint

1 Tbsp black or white sesame seeds

This recipe calls for jagged-edge-leafed shiso (also known as perilla), an herb widely used in Japanese cooking. Its flavor is reminiscent of mint and basil, and mint can be substituted if shiso is not available. Look for deep green, long, slender, mild-flavored Japanese cucumbers in Asian groceries or farmers' markets. Persian or English cucumbers can be used in their place.

Using a mandoline or a very sharp knife, cut the cucumber into ⅛-inch (3-mm) slices. Transfer to a colander and sprinkle with ½ tsp salt. Let stand for 10 minutes.

In a small bowl, whisk together the vinegar, sugar, and oil until the vinaigrette is well blended. In a medium bowl, combine the cucumber, green onion, shiso, and sesame seeds. Drizzle with the vinaigrette and stir to combine. Season with salt and pepper. Serve the salad right away, or cover and refrigerate for up to 12 hours before serving. Serve chilled or at room temperature.

13

Although combining shellfish and cheese is frowned on in traditional Italian cooking, that taboo is gradually disappearing as chefs and home cooks discover that the pairing can result in a tasty dish. This Italian-inspired salad, in which chopped grilled shrimp is added to pesto-laden rice and then finished with a heaping spoonful of grated cheese, is proof of that successful marriage.

RICE SALAD WITH PESTO & GRILLED SHRIMP

serves 4

1 cup (7 oz/220 g) Arborio rice

Salt and freshly ground pepper

1 clove garlic, chopped

Coarse sea salt

1 cup (1 oz/30 g) tightly packed fresh basil leaves, plus sprigs for garnish

2 Tbsp pine nuts or walnuts

¼ cup (2 fl oz/60 ml) extra-virgin olive oil, plus 2 Tbsp

24 large shrimp, peeled and deveined

¼ cup (1 oz/30 g) grated Asiago cheese

In a saucepan, bring 2 cups (16 fl oz/500 ml) water to a boil over medium-high heat. Add the rice and 1 tsp salt. Reduce the heat to low, cover, and simmer until the rice is tender and all of the water has been absorbed, about 20 minutes. Remove from the heat (keep covered) and let the rice cool completely. The rice can be stored in an airtight container in the refrigerator for up to 1 day.

In a mortar, combine the garlic and ¼ tsp coarse sea salt. With a pestle, crush the garlic to make a paste. Add the basil and pine nuts and crush them into the paste; this will take about 5 minutes. Slowly drizzle in the ¼ cup (2 fl oz/60 ml) oil, stirring constantly until incorporated. Alternatively, make the pesto in a food processor or blender. The pesto can be stored in an airtight container, drizzled with oil, in the refrigerator for up to 1 day.

In a bowl, combine the shrimp, the 2 Tbsp oil, ½ tsp salt, and ½ tsp pepper and toss to coat. Prepare a charcoal or gas grill for direct-heat cooking over medium-high heat. Alternatively, preheat a stove-top grill pan over medium-high heat. Place the shrimp in a grill basket on the grill rack or in the grill pan and cook until almost opaque, about 2 minutes. Turn and cook until the shrimp curl a bit and are opaque throughout, 1–2 minutes. Do not overcook.

Transfer the shrimp to a cutting board. Chop 8 of the shrimp. Keep the remaining shrimp whole.

Put 2 cups (10 oz/315 g) rice in a bowl and, using your fingers, separate the grains. Reserve the remaining rice for another use. ⟫

Add the pesto and stir until thoroughly incorporated, then fold in the chopped shrimp. Divide the rice among individual plates. Garnish each with 4 whole shrimp, a basil sprig, and a sprinkling of the cheese and serve.

- -

14

In the dry heat of the oven, tomatoes shrink into sweet, juicy concentrations of themselves, becoming the perfect partners for chicken and arugula. But for ease, you can substitute sun-dried tomatoes. Oil-packed tomatoes can be taken straight from the jar and chopped. Dry-packed tomatoes should be soaked in hot water for about 20 minutes, then drained and chopped.

CHICKEN & ROASTED TOMATO SALAD

serves 4

1½ lb (750 g) plum tomatoes, halved lengthwise and seeded

6 Tbsp (3 fl oz/90 ml) olive oil

1 Tbsp fresh thyme leaves

Salt and freshly ground pepper

1¼ lb (625 g) skinless, boneless chicken breast halves, pounded lightly to an even thickness

2 Tbsp unsalted butter

1 Tbsp safflower oil

6 oz (185 g) arugula leaves, stemmed

1½ Tbsp balsamic vinegar

Parmesan cheese for shaving

Preheat the oven to 350°F (180°C). Oil a large rimmed baking sheet. Arrange the tomatoes, cut side up, on the prepared sheet in a single layer. Brush with 2 Tbsp of the olive oil, sprinkle with thyme, and season with salt and pepper. Roast the tomatoes until shriveled on top but still juicy underneath, about 50 minutes. Let cool on the baking sheet. Cut the tomatoes in half again.

Season both sides of each chicken breast with salt and pepper. In a large frying pan over medium heat, melt the butter with the safflower oil. Add the chicken and cook, turning once, until golden brown and firm, 4–5 minutes per side. Transfer to a cutting board and let stand for 5 minutes.

Place the arugula in a large bowl, drizzle with the remaining 4 Tbsp (2 fl oz/60 ml) olive oil, and toss to coat evenly. Sprinkle with the vinegar, ¼ tsp salt, and a pinch of pepper, and toss again. Arrange the arugula on plates. Cut the chicken on the diagonal into slices and place on the arugula. Top with the roasted tomatoes. Use a vegetable peeler to shave cheese over the salads and serve.

15

Feast on summer seafood with big flakes of salmon and charred corn straight off the grill. To boil potatoes, put them in a large pot and cover with plenty of salted water. Bring to a boil, reduce the heat to medium-high, and cook the potatoes until tender when pierced with a small, sharp knife, about 20 minutes. Drain and let cool to the touch, about 15 minutes.

GRILLED SALMON, YELLOW POTATO & CORN SALAD

serves 4

4 salmon fillets, about 5 oz (155 g) each, skin on and pin bones removed

1 cup (2 oz/60 g) tightly packed fresh basil leaves

½ cup (4 fl oz/125 ml) olive oil, plus more for brushing

Salt and freshly ground pepper

4 ears corn, husks and silk removed

½ lemon

½ lb (250 g) yellow all-purpose potatoes such as Yukon Gold or Yellow Finn, boiled until tender and chopped *(left)*

2 Tbsp finely chopped sweet onion such as Vidalia or Maui

1 cup (6 oz/185 g) yellow cherry tomatoes, halved

Put the salmon fillets, skin side down, in a shallow dish. Combine the basil, ½ cup oil, ¼ cup (2 fl oz/60 ml) water, ½ tsp salt, and several grindings of pepper in a blender or food processor and process until smooth. Set aside half of the basil mixture for the dressing. Brush the other half over the flesh sides of the salmon. Cover and refrigerate for 30 minutes or up to 6 hours. Remove from the refrigerator 15 minutes before grilling.

Prepare a charcoal or gas grill for direct-heat cooking over medium-high heat. Brush the corn with olive oil. Grill, turning often, until the corn is lightly browned and crisp-tender, about 15 minutes. Transfer to a platter and let cool.

If using a charcoal grill, let the coals burn down to medium-low. If using a gas grill, reduce the heat. Arrange the fish in an oiled grill basket or place on a sheet of oiled heavy-duty foil, skin side down. Place the basket or slide the foil onto the grill. Cover the grill and cook until white droplets start to appear on the surface of the fish, about 8 minutes. Turn carefully and grill just until nicely seared, about 2 minutes. Transfer the fish to a platter, squeeze the lemon half over, tent with foil, and let stand for 5 minutes. ⟫

Cut the kernels from the corn cobs and put them in a large bowl. Add the potatoes, onion, tomatoes, and reserved basil mixture. Toss gently to distribute and coat evenly. Remove and discard the skin from the salmon and flake the flesh into large chunks and add to the bowl. Toss again gently, taking care not to break up the salmon further. Taste and adjust the seasoning and serve.

16

JULY

Ripe seasonal fruit comes alive with a sprinkle of mint and a drizzle of syrup. To make simple syrup, combine equal parts sugar and water in a saucepan and place over low heat. Stir until the sugar is completely dissolved. Remove from the heat and let cool to room temperature. Pour into a clean jar or other airtight container, and refrigerate for up to 2 months.

MINTED FRUIT SALAD

serves 8–10

1¼ cups (10 fl oz/310 ml) simple syrup *(left)*

3 Tbsp fresh lime juice

1 large papaya, about 2 lb (1 kg)

1 mango

6 cups (1½ lb/750 g) mixed raspberries, strawberries, and blackberries

2 cups (¾ lb/375 g) chopped pineapple

½ cup (½ oz/15 g) fresh mint leaves

1 Tbsp dark rum (optional)

Put the syrup in a saucepan over low heat, cover, and bring just to a simmer. Pour into a heatproof bowl, stir in the lime juice, and set aside to cool to room temperature. Cover and refrigerate until well chilled, at least 2 hours.

Prepare the fruits for the salad: Peel and seed the papaya and cut it into 1-inch (2.5-cm) chunks. Peel and pit the mango, and cut it into 1-inch chunks as well. Hull and halve the strawberries and quickly rinse all of the berries. In a large glass or ceramic bowl, combine the papaya, mango, berries, and pineapple and toss to mix. Coarsely chop the mint, setting aside a few nice small leaves for garnish. Drizzle with the syrup, scatter with the chopped mint, and toss very gently. If desired, drizzle with the rum. Garnish with the reserved mint leaves and serve.

17

SHAVED ZUCCHINI SALAD WITH PECORINO & ALMONDS

serves 4–6

½ cup (2½ oz/75 g) raw almonds

1 Tbsp balsamic vinegar

1 tsp red wine vinegar

Salt and freshly ground pepper

3 Tbsp extra-virgin olive oil

2 small zucchini and/or summer squash, about 4 inches (10 cm) long and 1 inch (2.5 cm) in diameter, trimmed

Pecorino cheese for shaving

Zucchini can be overly abundant at this time of year. If you feel like you've cooked it in every way imaginable, try thinly shaving it for this fresh raw salad. An aged pecorino cheese, nutty but still light, is delicious in this salad, but any cheese hard enough to be shaved may be used, such as Parmesan, grana padano, or aged goat cheese.

In a dry frying pan, toast the almonds over medium-low heat, stirring, until fragrant and lightly golden, 5 minutes. Pour onto a plate to cool, coarsely chop, and set aside.

In a large bowl, whisk together the vinegars and ½ tsp each salt and pepper. Add the oil in a thin stream, whisking constantly until the vinaigrette is smooth. Set aside.

Using a mandoline or very sharp chef's knife, slice the zucchini lengthwise into thin ribbons. Pat the zucchini dry on paper towels.

Add the zucchini to the bowl with the vinaigrette and toss to coat well. Divide the salad among individual plates. Using a vegetable peeler, shave the cheese over the salads in thin curls. Scatter the toasted almonds over the top and serve.

18

FATTOUSH SALAD

serves 4

2 pita bread rounds, cut into 1-inch (2.5-cm) triangles

6 Tbsp (3 fl oz/90 ml) olive oil, plus more for brushing

Salt and freshly ground pepper

2 Tbsp red wine vinegar

2 Tbsp fresh lemon juice

1 Tbsp honey

2 tsp ground sumac

2 Tbsp chopped fresh flat-leaf parsley

5 oz (155 g) mesclun

½ English cucumber, cut into 1/16-inch (2-mm) half-moons

½ red onion, very thinly sliced

1 can (15 oz/470 g) chickpeas, drained and rinsed

1/3 cup (1 3/4 oz/55 g) pitted Kalamata olives, halved

2½ oz (75 g) feta cheese, crumbled

Fattoush, a classic Levantine salad, combines a medley of chopped vegetables and herbs with toasted pita chips. For a complete meal, top the salad with the protein of your choice, such as grilled shrimp or roasted or grilled chicken or lamb. To mellow the bite of the raw red onion, place the slices in a bowl, cover with cold water, and let stand for 10 minutes, then drain and pat dry.

Preheat the oven to 350°F (180°C).

Place the pita triangles on a baking sheet. Brush both sides with oil and sprinkle with salt. Bake, turning them over halfway through, until golden and crisp, 10–15 minutes. Let cool.

Meanwhile, in a small bowl, whisk together the vinegar, lemon juice, honey, sumac, and parsley. Add the oil in a thin stream, whisking constantly until the vinaigrette is well blended. Season with salt and pepper.

In a large bowl, toss together the mesclun, cucumber, onion, chickpeas, olives, cheese, and pita triangles. Drizzle with some of the vinaigrette and toss to coat well, adding more vinaigrette to taste. Serve right away.

19

CREAMY COLESLAW

serves 6–8

1 head green cabbage (about 2 lb/1 kg)

2 celery ribs

1 Granny Smith apple

1 small yellow or red onion

2 small carrots, peeled

2 Tbsp cider vinegar, or as needed

2 Tbsp minced fresh flat-leaf parsley

1¼ cups (10 fl oz/310 ml) mayonnaise

Salt and freshly ground pepper

This crunchy-creamy classic is essential for barbecues, alongside burgers and dogs, or piled on top of a pulled pork sandwich. If you don't have a food processor, prep the vegetables by hand with a chef's knife and the large holes of a box grater. Thinly sliced red bell pepper and cucumber would be nice additions.

Cut the cabbage through the stem end into wedges, and cut out the core. Using a food processor fitted with the thin slicing attachment, slice the cabbage into thin slivers. Transfer to a large bowl. Slice the celery crosswise in the same way and add it to the cabbage.

Replace the slicing attachment with the shredding attachment. Halve and core the apple but do not peel. Cut the apple and the onion into wedges. Shred the apple, onion, and carrots, and add to the cabbage and celery.

Sprinkle the vegetables with the vinegar and toss to coat evenly. Add the parsley and mayonnaise and mix well. Season with salt and pepper to taste. Cover and refrigerate until chilled, at least 2 hours. Taste and adjust the seasoning with more vinegar, salt, and pepper before serving. Serve chilled.

20

YELLOW SQUASH & FARRO SALAD

serves 6

1½ cups (9 oz/280 g) farro

Salt

2 Tbsp extra-virgin olive oil, plus ½ cup (4 fl oz/125 ml)

1 lb (500 g) yellow squash, cut into ½-inch (12-mm) chunks

1 clove garlic

¼ cup (2 fl oz/60 ml) fresh lemon juice

1 small cucumber, about ½ lb (250 g), peeled and cut into ½-inch (12-mm) chunks

5 green onions, including tender green parts, cut on the diagonal into ¼-inch (6-mm) pieces

¼ cup (⅓ oz/10 g) chopped fresh basil

¼ cup (⅓ oz/10 g) chopped fresh mint

5 oz (155 g) feta cheese, crumbled

Nutty farro quickly soaks up liquids and flavors, in this case lemon and garlic. Because of this, just be sure to add the dressing when you're ready to serve, to prevent the grain from becoming dry. Crumbled feta, goat cheese, or ricotta salata would all be delicious alongside the crisp cucumber and sweet squash.

Rinse and drain the farro, then transfer to a large saucepan and add 3 cups (24 fl oz/750 ml) cold water. Stir in 1 teaspoon salt and bring to a boil over high heat. Reduce the heat to medium-low, cover partially, and simmer until the farro is tender but still chewy, about 20 minutes. Drain thoroughly and set aside.

In a large frying pan over medium-high heat, warm the 2 Tbsp oil. Add the squash, season with salt, and sauté until crisp-tender, 3–4 minutes. Transfer to a plate and let cool.

To make the dressing, mash the garlic into a paste with a pinch of salt. In a small bowl, stir together the garlic and lemon juice and let stand for 10 minutes. Add the remaining ½ cup oil in a thin stream, whisking constantly until the dressing is smooth.

Put the farro, squash, cucumber, green onions, basil, mint, and feta in a large bowl. Drizzle with the dressing and toss. Season to taste with salt and serve.

21

Eggplant is amenable to nearly any flavor profile, easily adapting to the cook's choice of seasonings and accompaniments. Miso, Japanese fermented soybean paste with an earthy, rich flavor and aroma, gives this quick noodle salad, finished with fresh basil, a Japanese flair.

CRISPY EGGPLANT, MISO BUTTER & CHARRED SUNGOLD TOMATO SALAD

serves 4

4 Tbsp (2 oz/60 g) unsalted butter, at room temperature

2 Tbsp miso paste

Salt

3–4 oz (90–125 g) Japanese noodles or thin spaghetti

2–3 Tbsp coconut oil

1 medium globe eggplant or 2 Asian eggplants, cut into ½-inch (12-mm) cubes

2 cups (12 oz/375 g) Sungold tomatoes

¼ cup (¼ oz/7 g) tightly packed fresh purple or green basil leaves, cut into thin strips

In a small bowl, mash together the butter and miso paste until well blended. Set aside.

Bring a pot of water to a boil over high heat. Add 1 tsp salt and the noodles, reduce the heat to medium-high, and cook until they are tender to the bite, about 10 minutes. Drain well and transfer to a bowl. Add 1 Tbsp of the miso butter and toss to coat. Set aside.

In a large frying pan, warm 2 tablespoons of the coconut oil over medium heat. Add the eggplant cubes, sprinkle with ½ tsp salt, and cook, turning several times, until golden and crispy, about 7 minutes, adding more oil as needed. Set aside.

Prepare a charcoal or gas grill for direct-heat cooking over medium-high heat and preheat a grill basket. Alternatively, preheat a stove-top grill pan over medium-high heat.

Place the tomatoes in the grill basket or in the grill pan. Cook until charred, 1–2 minutes, turning once or twice.

Add the eggplant and 2 Tbsp of the miso butter to the bowl with the noodles and toss well. Transfer to a platter and add the tomatoes, tucking some into the noodles. Garnish with the basil and the remaining miso butter and serve.

22

Fresh corn is best between the months of July and September, making it a popular vegetable for summer barbecue. Try it grilled and folded into this salad with bright cherry tomatoes and tangy feta cheese.

GRILLED CORN SALAD

serves 8

Juice of 3 limes

2 tsp ground cumin

1 tsp mild chili powder

¾ cup (6 fl oz/180 ml) olive oil, plus more for brushing

Salt and freshly ground pepper

2 tsp cumin seeds, toasted and lightly crushed

6 ears corn, husks and silk removed

3 cups (18 oz/560 g) cherry tomatoes, stems removed and halved

½ cup (2 oz/60 g) chopped red onion

½ cup (¾ oz/20 g) chopped fresh cilantro

4 oz (125 g) feta cheese, diced

In a bowl, whisk together the lime juice, ground cumin, and chili powder. Add the ¾ cup oil in a thin stream, whisking constantly until the vinaigrette is smooth. Season with salt and pepper to taste.

In a small dry frying pan, toast the cumin seeds over medium-low heat, stirring, until fragrant, about 2 minutes. Pour onto a plate and let cool.

Prepare a gas or charcoal grill for direct-heat cooking over medium-high heat. Brush a little olive oil on each ear of corn. Grill the corn, turning the ears often so that they cook evenly, until lightly charred, about 10 minutes.

Cut the kernels off the corn cobs and put them in a large bowl. Add the tomatoes, onion, cilantro, feta, and the vinaigrette and toss to coat evenly. Transfer the salad to a platter, sprinkle with the toasted cumin seeds, and serve.

23

GRILLED PLANTAIN, MANGO & CHARRED SHRIMP SALAD

serves 4

2 mangoes

20 medium shrimp, peeled and deveined

3 Tbsp coconut oil, melted

Salt and freshly ground pepper

½ tsp ground turmeric

¼ tsp ground cumin

2 Tbsp fresh lime juice

2 Tbsp honey

2 plantains, peeled and halved lengthwise

¼ cup (⅓ oz/10 g) chopped fresh cilantro

Hot and sweet, this salad is a delicious reminder of the wealth of fruits that thrive in places with a tropical climate. Pineapple, melon, or papaya can be added with, or substituted for, the fruits used here.

Peel the mangoes. Stand the fruit, stem end up, with a narrow side toward you. Position a sharp knife about 1 inch (2.5 cm) from the stem on one side and cut down the length of the fruit, just missing the large pit. Repeat on the other side of the pit. Dice the flesh and set aside.

Prepare a charcoal or gas grill for direct-heat cooking over medium-high heat. Alternatively, preheat a stove-top grill pan over medium-high heat.

In a bowl, combine the shrimp, 1 Tbsp of the coconut oil, ½ tsp salt, and ¼ tsp pepper and toss to coat well.

In a small bowl, whisk together 1½ Tbsp of the coconut oil, ¼ tsp salt, the turmeric, cumin, lime juice, and honey until the dressing is well blended. Taste and adjust the seasonings. Set aside.

Brush the plantains with the remaining ½ Tbsp coconut oil.

Place the plantains, cut side down, on the grill rack or in the grill pan and cook, turning once, until slightly golden, about 3 minutes per side. Transfer to a cutting board.

Place the shrimp on the grill rack or in the pan and cook, turning once, until slightly charred and opaque throughout, about 5 minutes total. Transfer to a plate.

Cut the plantains into 1-inch (2.5-cm) pieces and mound them on a platter. Top with the mangoes and drizzle with the dressing. Surround with the shrimp, garnish with the cilantro, and serve.

24

WATERMELON RADISH SALAD WITH ROMAINE & AVOCADO

serves 4

1 shallot, minced

1½ Tbsp fresh lemon juice, plus more if needed

1½ Tbsp white wine vinegar

Salt

¼ cup (2 fl oz/60 ml) extra-virgin olive oil

1 avocado, pitted, peeled, and cubed

2 heads romaine lettuce, leaves cut crosswise into ½-inch (12-mm) strips

1 watermelon radish or daikon radish, thinly sliced

Cousins of the daikon radish, watermelon radishes are a humble greenish-white on the outside, but contain a burst of bright pink at their centers. Here, they are gorgeous thinly sliced and drizzled with a creamy, citrusy avocado dressing.

In a small bowl, stir together the shallot, 1½ Tbsp lemon juice, vinegar, and a pinch of salt. Add the oil in a thin stream, whisking constantly until the vinaigrette is smooth. Gently stir in the avocado, season with salt, and let stand for 10 minutes.

In a large bowl, combine the romaine and radish. Spoon the vinaigrette and avocado over the salad, toss gently, taste, and adjust the seasoning with salt and additional lemon juice. Serve.

25

GRILLED STEAK, PEPPER & ONION SALAD WITH ROMESCO DRESSING

serves 6

Spanish smoked paprika is rich with earthy nuances of chiles and cocoa. In this recipe, it lends a robust smokiness and gorgeous red color to a steak marinade and romesco-style dressing. It's an apt seasoning for a dish brimming with charred flavors from the grill.

½ cup (4 fl oz/125 ml) extra-virgin olive oil, plus 2 Tbsp

⅓ cup (3 fl oz/80 ml) sherry vinegar

2 Tbsp fresh orange juice

1 Tbsp Spanish sweet smoked paprika

5 cloves garlic, minced

1½ Tbsp fresh oregano leaves

2¾ lb (1.4 kg) flank steak

2 small red onions

3 bell peppers, in assorted colors

Salt and freshly ground pepper

FOR THE ROMESCO DRESSING

2 Tbsp extra-virgin olive oil

1 Tbsp fresh orange juice

2 Tbsp sherry vinegar

¼ tsp Spanish sweet smoked paprika

2 cloves garlic, minced

3 jarred piquillo peppers or roasted red peppers

1½ Tbsp chopped blanched almonds

½ large head green-leaf lettuce, leaves torn into bite-sized pieces

2 Tbsp chopped fresh flat-leaf parsley

In a large baking dish, combine the ½ cup oil, the vinegar, orange juice, paprika, garlic, and oregano. Lay the steak in the baking dish and turn a few times to coat it with the marinade. Cover and refrigerate for at least 2 hours or preferably overnight, turning once or twice.

About 1 hour before cooking, remove the flank steak from the refrigerator. Cut the onions crosswise into rounds ½ inch (12 mm) thick (do not separate the layers). Stem, seed, and derib the bell peppers, then cut into wide strips. Brush the vegetables with the 2 Tbsp oil and season lightly with salt and pepper.

Prepare a charcoal or gas grill for direct-heat cooking over medium-high heat.

Meanwhile, to make the dressing, in a food processor or blender, combine the oil, orange juice, vinegar, paprika, garlic, piquillo peppers, almonds, a scant ½ tsp salt, and a few ⟫⟫

grindings of pepper. Process until relatively smooth. Taste and adjust the seasonings. Set aside.

Grill the onions and peppers, turning once, until softened and lightly charred on both sides, 7–10 minutes for the onions and about 15 minutes for the peppers. Transfer to a plate. Remove the steak from the marinade and season both sides with salt and pepper. Grill, turning once, until the steak is browned on both sides and an instant-read thermometer inserted into the thickest part registers 130°F (54°C) for medium-rare, 10–15 minutes total, or until cooked to your liking. Transfer to a board and tent with foil. Cut the peppers into ½-inch (12-mm) strips and separate the onion slices into rings.

In a bowl, toss the lettuce with ⅛ tsp salt. Divide the lettuce among individual plates. Thinly slice the steak on the diagonal. Top each mound of lettuce with a portion of the steak, onions, and peppers. Spoon the dressing over each salad, sprinkle with a little parsley, and serve.

26

FRESH FIG & GOAT CHEESE SALAD

serves 4

Fresh figs only appear in markets briefly, so pair them with your best ingredients: a lush goat cheese and a high-quality balsamic vinegar—a thick, aged one that's so good, you reserve it for drizzling on salads like this one.

8 purple figs, stemmed

2 tsp extra-virgin olive oil, plus 3 Tbsp

1 Tbsp red wine vinegar

Salt and freshly ground pepper

2 cups (2 oz/60 g) mixed baby greens

3 oz (90 g) soft goat cheese, cut into 4 pieces

½ tsp balsamic vinegar

Coat the figs with the 2 tsp oil, then cut them lengthwise into quarters.

In a serving bowl, combine all but a few drops of the 3 Tbsp oil with the red wine vinegar. Add ¼ tsp salt, ¼ tsp pepper, and the greens and toss well to coat.

Divide the dressed greens among individual plates. Arrange 8 fig quarters on each and top with a piece of cheese. Drizzle the cheese with the remaining oil and a few drops of balsamic vinegar and serve.

27

LOBSTER SALAD WITH TARRAGON & CHAMPAGNE VINAIGRETTE

serves 8–10

You can use either whole lobsters or lobster tails to make this elegant salad, worthy of a special occasion. Serve it on a bed of fresh herbs for maximum flavor, or if you prefer, substitute equal portions of field greens and baby arugula leaves.

Salt and freshly ground pepper

1½ lb (750 g) cooked lobster meat, or 5 frozen lobster tails, thawed and halved lengthwise

2½ Tbsp champagne vinegar

2 tsp fresh lemon juice

2 tsp minced fresh tarragon

3½ Tbsp olive oil

2–2½ cups (2–2½ oz/60–75 g) mixed delicate fresh herbs and greens such as whole tarragon leaves, baby arugula, flat-leaf parsley leaves, watercress leaves, and small chervil sprigs

If using frozen lobster tails, bring a large pot three-fourths full of salted water to a boil over high heat. Add the lobster tails and boil them until the shells are bright red and the meat is almost opaque throughout, about 8 minutes.

Meanwhile, ready a large bowl full of ice. When the lobster tails are done, transfer them immediately to the bowl and cover with ice. (This quick cooling causes the flesh to pull away from the shell, making it easier to remove the meat.) Leave in the ice for 30 minutes. Remove the meat from the tails.

Cut the cooked lobster meat into generous bite-sized pieces. Set aside.

In a large bowl, whisk together 2 Tbsp of the vinegar, the lemon juice, ½ tsp salt, ½ tsp pepper, and the minced tarragon. Add 2 Tbsp of the oil in a thin stream, whisking constantly until the vinaigrette is smooth. Add the lobster meat and gently turn the pieces in the vinaigrette until well coated.

Divide the mixed herbs and greens among individual plates. Mound the lobster salad on each bed of herbs. Stir together the remaining 1½ Tbsp olive oil and ½ Tbsp vinegar, drizzle a little over each serving, and serve.

28

CELERY SALAD WITH BLUE CHEESE & LEMON

serves 4

Celery stars in this super simple, crunchy salad with hits of flavor from the blue cheese and lemon. If you have leftover roasted poultry, dice it and stir it into this salad for a heartier dish.

3 celery hearts, including some of the leafy tops, thinly sliced crosswise

7 green onions, including tender green parts, thinly sliced

Grated zest of 1 lemon

1½ Tbsp fresh lemon juice

3 Tbsp extra-virgin olive oil

Salt and freshly ground pepper

⅔ cup (3½ oz/105 g) crumbled blue cheese

In a bowl, combine the celery hearts and leaves, green onions, lemon zest and juice, and oil. Season to taste with salt and pepper and toss well. Fold in the cheese and serve.

29

WHITE NECTARINE & MINT SALAD

serves 4

You can just as easily use peaches or yellow nectarines in this fruit salad. For color, add cherries, raspberries, or blackberries to the mix.

Grated zest and juice of 1 lemon

1 tsp honey

4 nectarines, pitted and cut into wedges

2 Tbsp minced fresh mint

In a small saucepan, heat the lemon zest and juice with the honey until the honey melts. Set aside to cool to room temperature.

Put the nectarines in a bowl, pour the lemon-honey mixture over the fruit, and toss to coat evenly. Sprinkle with the mint, toss to mix, and serve.

30

MIXED GREENS WITH CORN FRITTERS & PIMIENTO DRESSING

serves 4–6

The Spanish prepare a salad similar to this one, but the fritters, or croquetas, are made with salt cod instead of corn. Crispy on the outside and a little creamy on the inside, they add a pleasing hot contrast to the cool dressing and the slightly chilled greens.

FOR THE PIMIENTO DRESSING

1 Tbsp extra-virgin olive oil

½ cup (4 oz/125 g) sour cream

¼ cup (2 oz/60 g) canned pimiento strips, drained

Salt

Whole milk or half-and-half as needed

4 ears white or yellow corn, husks and silk removed

1¼ cups (6½ oz/200 g) all-purpose flour

½ tsp baking powder

Coarse sea salt and freshly ground pepper

1 large egg, lightly beaten

½ cup (4 fl oz/125 ml) whole milk

Extra-virgin olive oil for frying

4 cups (4 oz/125 g) mesclun

To make the dressing, in a food processor, combine the oil, sour cream, pimientos, and ¼ tsp salt. Pulse until thickened. Transfer to a bowl and add milk, starting with 1–2 tsp, until the dressing is pourable. Set aside.

Cut the kernels from the corn cobs and place in a bowl. Mix in the flour, baking powder, 1 tsp salt, and ¼ tsp pepper. Add the egg and ¼ cup (2 fl oz/60 ml) of the milk. Stir to blend, adding more milk if needed.

Pour oil into a large frying pan to a depth of ¼ inch (6 mm) and heat over medium-high heat. Line a baking sheet with paper towels. For each fritter, drop a heaping 1 Tbsp of the corn mixture into the hot oil, spacing them well apart. Press down gently with a spatula and fry until golden on the first side, about 2 minutes. Turn and fry the second side for about 1 minute. Transfer the fritters to the paper towel–lined baking sheet. Repeat to fry the remaining fritters, adding more oil if needed and reducing the heat if necessary to prevent scorching.

Place the mesclun in a bowl, drizzle with half of the dressing, and toss to coat. Mound the salad on individual plates and divide the fritters among them. Drizzle the fritters with the remaining dressing and serve.

31

GRILLED FLANK STEAK SALAD WITH TOMATOES

serves 6

Flank steak is a great choice for salads, as it is full flavored but must be tenderized by thinly slicing across the grain—letting you toss it easily with other ingredients. Look for cherry tomatoes in mixed sizes and colors for visual interest.

FOR THE MUSTARD-HERB VINAIGRETTE

⅓ cup (3 fl oz/80 ml) balsamic vinegar

1½ Tbsp chopped fresh thyme

1½ Tbsp chopped fresh marjoram

1½ Tbsp Dijon mustard

2 large cloves garlic, minced

Salt and freshly ground pepper

¾ cup (6 fl oz/180 ml) extra-virgin olive oil

1 flank steak, about 1½ lb (750 g) and 1–1½ inches (2.5–4 cm) thick

1 red onion, cut into wedges

1 large head romaine lettuce, leaves torn into bite-sized pieces

2–3 tomatoes, preferably heirloom, cut into wedges, plus a handful of mixed cherry tomatoes, halved

To make the vinaigrette, in a small bowl, whisk together the vinegar, thyme, marjoram, mustard, garlic, and ¾ tsp each salt and pepper. Add the oil in a thin stream, whisking constantly until the vinaigrette is well blended.

Place the steak in a shallow dish. Pour half of the vinaigrette over the steak and turn to coat both sides. Cover and refrigerate for at least 4 hours or for up to 24 hours, turning occasionally. Cover and refrigerate the remaining vinaigrette. Remove the steak from the refrigerator 30 minutes before grilling.

Prepare a charcoal or gas grill for direct-heat cooking over high heat. Remove the steak from the marinade, reserving the marinade, and grill the steak, turning once or twice and brushing with the reserved marinade for up to 5 minutes before the steak is done, until nicely charred and cooked to your liking, 10–12 minutes total for medium-rare. Let the steak rest for 5–10 minutes.

While the steak is resting, place the onion wedges on the grill and cook until softened and nicely grill-marked, about 5 minutes. Thinly slice the steak across the grain, reserving any juices that accumulate. Toss the lettuce with the reserved vinaigrette, and divide among individual plates. Top with the steak, onion wedges, and tomatoes. Drizzle the steak with the meat juices and serve.

Scorching days inspire light suppers of seafood and fresh vegetables. Whether or not you can make it to the shore this time of year, indulge in shrimp and scallops tossed with avocado, lobster nestled in a pasta salad, and calamari marinated with harissa and served hot from the grill. It's time now for picnics, so make room for easy-to-pack salads like orzo with grilled corn and tomatoes, sliced watermelon with feta, and shaved zucchini simply dressed with lemon and mint.

august

1

WATERMELON, FETA & MINT SALAD

serves 6

¾ cup (¾ oz/20 g) fresh mint leaves

1 Tbsp sugar

1 serrano chile, seeded and chopped (optional)

2 Tbsp rice vinegar

1 Tbsp fresh lime juice

3 Tbsp extra-virgin olive oil

Salt and freshly ground pepper

1 small seedless watermelon, about 3 lb (1.5 kg), peeled, and cut into wedges or cubes

6 oz (185 g) feta cheese, crumbled into pieces

Salty and tangy, feta cheese is a delicious match with sweet, luscious watermelon in this salad. The chile adds an interesting hit of heat, but you can leave it out with equally good results. A refreshing dressing with just enough acid from the vinegar and lime juice completes this ultimate summer side dish.

Process ½ cup (½ oz/15 g) of the mint leaves and the sugar in a food processor until well blended. Add the chile (if using), vinegar, and lime juice and process again. With the motor running, drizzle in the olive oil. Transfer the vinaigrette to a bowl and season with a pinch each of salt and pepper.

Arrange the watermelon and cheese on individual plates and drizzle with the vinaigrette. Garnish with the remaining mint and serve.

2

GREEK-STYLE BEEF SALAD

serves 4–6

FOR THE MINT VINAIGRETTE

Juice of 2 lemons

3 Tbsp chopped fresh mint

1 large clove garlic, minced

Salt and freshly ground pepper

½ cup (4 fl oz/125 ml) extra-virgin olive oil

1 tri-tip roast (about 1 lb/500 g)

1 large bunch watercress, tough stems removed

1 red onion, halved lengthwise and thinly sliced

1 cucumber, halved lengthwise, seeded, and thinly sliced crosswise

1 cup (6 oz/185 g) grape or cherry tomatoes, halved

¾ cup (3 oz/90 g) Kalamata or other Mediterranean black olives, pitted

4 oz (125 g) feta cheese, crumbled

This versatile Mediterranean mix of cucumber and tomato is joined with grilled steak for summer. Rotisserie chicken could easily take its place on a weeknight, or lamb would pair beautifully with the minty vinaigrette. Serve with warm pita bread.

To make the vinaigrette, in a small bowl, whisk together the lemon juice, 2 Tbsp of the mint, and the garlic. Season with about ½ tsp each salt and pepper. Add the oil in a thin stream, whisking constantly until the dressing is smooth.

Prepare a gas or charcoal grill for direct-heat cooking over medium-high heat. Season the tri-tip generously with salt and pepper. Let stand at room temperature for 10 minutes.

Place the tri-tip over the hottest part of the fire. Cover the grill and cook, turning once or twice with tongs, for about 30 minutes total for medium-rare, or until cooked to your liking. Transfer to a carving board and let rest 5–10 minutes before slicing.

While the tri-tip is resting, in a bowl, toss the watercress with about half of the vinaigrette. Thinly slice the tri-tip across the grain. Arrange the beef, onion, cucumber, tomatoes, olives, and cheese on top of the watercress and gently toss. Divide the salad among individual plates. Drizzle with the remaining vinaigrette, sprinkle with the remaining mint, and serve.

3

EDAMAME, CORN & TOMATO SALAD

serves 4

¾ cup (5 oz/155 g) fresh or frozen corn kernels (from about 1 ear)

1½ cups (9 oz/280 g) frozen shelled edamame

12 cherry tomatoes, halved

1 large avocado, pitted, peeled, and cubed

2 Tbsp fresh lime juice

Salt and freshly ground pepper

1 Tbsp canola oil

8 dark outer leaves romaine lettuce

2 Tbsp chopped fresh cilantro

Edamame is the Japanese word for fresh soybeans. Simply steamed or boiled and sprinkled with salt, they make a delicious snack. Here, they pair with classic summer produce for a fresh-tasting salad that can accompany anything hot off the grill.

Bring a saucepan of water to a boil and have ready a bowl of ice water. Add the corn and the edamame and cook for 3 minutes. Using a slotted spoon, transfer to the bowl of ice water. Drain the corn and edamame, place in a large bowl, and add the tomatoes and avocado to the bowl.

In a small bowl, whisk together the lime juice, 1 tsp salt, and ⅛ tsp pepper. Add the oil in a thin stream, whisking constantly until the dressing is smooth. Pour the dressing over the salad and gently toss to combine. Arrange the lettuce leaves on a serving platter and spoon the salad onto the leaves. Garnish with the cilantro and serve.

4

PEACH SALAD WITH MINT & INDIAN SPICES

serves 6

6 medium-ripe peaches

2 tsp fresh lemon juice

½ tsp cumin seeds

Lettuce leaves for serving

1½ tsp chaat masala *(left)*, or 1 tsp cumin seeds

½ tsp salt

½ tsp finely grated lemon zest

¼ cup (⅓ oz/10 g) loosely packed fresh mint leaves

8 blackberries or 16 raspberries (optional)

In India, the word chaat is used both for snacks in general and for this fruit salad designed to pique the appetite. Its primary seasoning is chaat masala, a spice blend that includes roasted cumin, asafetida, black salt, mango powder, cayenne pepper, and black pepper. Look for it in Indian markets, or substitute toasted cumin seeds.

Bring a large saucepan three-fourths full of water to a boil and fill a large bowl with ice water. Using a sharp knife, cut an X in the bottom of each peach and immerse the peaches in the boiling water for 30 seconds. Using a slotted spoon, transfer to the bowl of ice water to cool, then peel off the skin. Pit and thinly slice the peaches. Immediately place the peach slices and lemon juice in a bowl and toss to coat the slices with the juice to prevent them from discoloring.

In a small dry frying pan over high heat, toast the cumin seeds, tossing and shaking the pan, until they turn very dark brown, almost black, about 5 minutes. Remove from the heat and let cool for a few minutes, then lightly bruise them. (You can do this with a mortar and pestle or by putting the seeds in a paper or plastic bag on a work surface and running a rolling pin over them.)

Line a platter with lettuce leaves. Sprinkle the chaat masala, salt, lemon zest, and half of the mint over the peaches, toss well, and transfer to the platter. Scatter the cumin seeds, berries (if using), and the remaining mint leaves over the top. Serve.

5

August is the perfect time of year for an all-out barbecue, where coleslaw is mandatory. This version lightens up the old-fashioned recipe with tangy buttermilk, enlivened with fresh herbs and sweet golden raisins.

BUTTERMILK COLESLAW

serves 4

½ cup (3 oz/90 g) golden raisins

FOR THE BUTTERMILK DRESSING

¾ cup (6 fl oz/180 ml) mayonnaise

½ cup (4 fl oz/125 ml) buttermilk

¼ cup (2 oz/60 g) sour cream

½ bunch fresh flat-leaf parsley, stemmed and minced

½ bunch fresh chives, minced

Salt and ground white pepper

1 large carrot, peeled

½ red onion

2 shallots

3 Tbsp white vinegar

½ head *each* green and red cabbages

Chopped fresh flat-leaf parsley for garnish

Chopped fresh chives for garnish

Put the raisins in a small bowl. Add warm water to cover and soak until plump, about 30 minutes.

To make the dressing, in a bowl, stir together the mayonnaise, buttermilk, and sour cream. Stir in the minced parsley and chives. Season with salt and pepper. Set aside until ready to use.

Using a mandoline or a very sharp knife, cut the carrot into matchsticks. Very thinly slice the red onion and shallots. In a small bowl, combine the carrot, onion, shallots, and vinegar, and toss to coat.

Core and thinly shred the cabbages. In a large serving bowl, toss together the green and red cabbage. Drain the raisins and add them to the cabbage along with the carrot-vinegar mixture and buttermilk dressing, and toss to coat. Taste and adjust the seasoning with salt and pepper. Garnish with the chopped parsley and chives and refrigerate until ready to serve.

6

The Italian antipasto of sweet figs slit and stuffed with thin slivers of salty prosciutto inspired this salad. Grilling the figs caramelizes them and adds a smoky flavor, and serving them with crisped pistachio-studded mortadella and an unctuous pistachio oil dressing reinforces the sweet-salty concept.

GRILLED FIG, ARUGULA & CRISPY MORTADELLA SALAD

serves 4

12 large, soft figs (any variety), stemmed

2 tsp extra-virgin olive oil

6 slices mortadella, cut into ½-inch (12-mm) strips

1½ Tbsp fresh lemon juice

1½ Tbsp pistachio oil

Salt and freshly ground pepper

1½–2 cups (1½ oz/45–60 g) arugula

2 tsp grated lemon zest

1-oz (30-g) piece Parmesan cheese

Prepare a charcoal or gas grill for direct-heat cooking over medium-high heat. Alternatively, preheat a stove-top grill pan over medium-high heat.

Gently rub the figs with the olive oil. Place the figs on the grill rack or in the grill pan and cook, turning them gently once or twice, until plumped and beginning to brown, about 5 minutes. Do not overcook or they will burst. Transfer to a cutting board and let cool for 1–2 minutes. Cut 8 of the figs into quarters. Keep the others whole. Set aside.

In a frying pan, fry the mortadella over medium heat, turning several times, until crispy, 3–4 minutes. Transfer to a plate.

In a small bowl, whisk together the lemon juice, pistachio oil, ⅛ tsp salt, and ⅛ tsp pepper until the vinaigrette is well blended.

In a bowl, combine the arugula with half of the mortadella and drizzle with the vinaigrette. Toss well and divide among individual plates. Tuck 8 fig slices into each salad and scatter the remaining mortadella on top. Garnish each salad with a whole fig and a sprinkling of the lemon zest. Using a vegetable peeler, shave the cheese over the salads and serve.

8

7

Cilantro appears twice in this recipe: the stems season the poaching liquid for the chicken breasts, while the leaves join the greenery of the salad. The mild flavors of the chicken and black beans are sharpened by ripe heirloom tomatoes and tart lime juice, for a bright, tasty summertime dish.

CHICKEN SALAD WITH TOMATOES, BLACK BEANS & CILANTRO

serves 4–6

1 white onion

2 skin-on, bone-in chicken breast halves (about ¾ lb/375 g each)

¼ bunch fresh cilantro, leaves coarsely chopped, stems reserved

2 cloves garlic, crushed, plus 1 clove, minced

Salt and freshly ground pepper

2 Tbsp fresh lime juice

1 jalapeño chile, seeded and minced

⅓ cup (3 fl oz/80 ml) extra-virgin olive oil

2 heirloom tomatoes, preferably 1 red and 1 yellow or green, seeded and cut into ½-inch (12-mm) pieces

½ can (8 oz/250 g) black beans, drained and rinsed

1 head butter lettuce, separated into leaves

Cut the onion in half lengthwise. Cut one half into thin slices and finely chop the other.

Put the chicken breasts in a large saucepan and add the cilantro stems, sliced onion, crushed garlic, and 1 tsp salt. Add water to barely cover the chicken. Bring to a boil over high heat, skimming off any foam on the surface. Reduce the heat to low and simmer, partially covered, for 20 minutes. Remove from the heat, cover, and let stand until a breast shows no sign of pink when pierced with the tip of a sharp knife near the bone, about 15 minutes. Transfer to a plate and let cool, then remove the skin and bones and shred the meat into bite-sized pieces.

Combine the lime juice, half of the minced jalapeño, the minced garlic, ½ tsp salt, and ¼ tsp pepper in a large bowl. Gradually whisk in the olive oil. Add the chicken, tomatoes, chopped onion, chopped cilantro, and black beans. Mix gently to combine. Taste and adjust the seasoning with additional salt, pepper, and chile. Cover and refrigerate to chill, at least 20 minutes or up to 2 hours.

Arrange a couple of lettuce leaves on each salad plate. Spoon some of the salad on top and serve.

8

Available in a wealth of sizes and colors— yellow, orange, zebra striped—heirloom tomatoes are one of the glories of summer. Splash them with a double dose of bright vinegars, and they'll really shine. Other fresh herbs can replace the oregano: try 1 tsp chopped thyme or rosemary, 1 Tbsp chopped flat-leaf parsley, or 2–3 Tbsp chopped basil.

HEIRLOOM TOMATO SALAD WITH TWO VINEGARS

serves 4

6–8 very ripe heirloom tomatoes, in a variety of sizes, shapes, and colors

¼–½ tsp sugar

Salt

2 green onions, including tender green parts, chopped

2 cloves garlic, minced (optional)

2 tsp minced fresh oregano, or to taste

Balsamic vinegar

Sherry vinegar or white wine vinegar

3–5 Tbsp (1½–2½ fl oz/45–75 ml) extra-virgin olive oil

Country-style bread for serving

Slice the tomatoes, capturing their juices. Layer the tomatoes on a platter, sprinkling them with the sugar, salt to taste, green onions, garlic (if using), oregano, and the captured juices as you arrange them.

Drizzle lightly with balsamic vinegar and sherry vinegar and then drizzle generously with olive oil. Let stand at room temperature until ready to serve, up to 2 hours. Serve accompanied with the bread for sopping up the juices.

9

AUGUST

Italian bread salad gets a non-traditional spin with the addition of smoky grilled eggplant and toasty charred corn. The classic flavors shine through in the form of a tomato-basil vinaigrette, full of the herb's sweet anise-like taste.

GRILLED EGGPLANT, CORN & BREAD SALAD WITH TOMATO-BASIL VINAIGRETTE

serves 6–8

2 large, ripe tomatoes (about 1 lb/500 g total weight)

⅓ cup (⅓ oz/10 g) fresh basil leaves, cut into thin ribbons

2 Tbsp balsamic vinegar

8 Tbsp (4 fl oz/125 ml) olive oil, plus more for grill

2 large cloves garlic, minced

Salt and freshly ground pepper

3 ears corn, husks and silk removed

2 large eggplants (about 2½ lb/1.25 kg total weight), cut crosswise into slices ½ inch (12 mm) thick

1 loaf day-old country-style bread, cut into 1-inch (2.5-cm) cubes

To make the vinaigrette, bring a saucepan two-thirds full of water to a boil over high heat. Have ready a bowl of ice water. Using a paring knife, score an X on the bottom of each tomato. Drop the tomatoes into the boiling water and heat until the skins loosen, 15–30 seconds. Using a slotted spoon, transfer the tomatoes to the ice water and let stand until cool. Remove the tomatoes from the ice water and pull off the skins. Core the tomatoes and halve them crosswise. Gently squeeze each half to ease out the seeds, then coarsely chop the tomato flesh.

Transfer the chopped tomatoes to a food processor or blender. Add about one-third of the basil, the vinegar, 1 Tbsp of the olive oil, the garlic, ½ tsp salt, and several grindings of pepper. Process until a chunky vinaigrette forms. Taste and adjust the seasonings. Set aside.

Prepare a charcoal or gas grill for direct-heat cooking over medium-high heat. Brush the corn on all sides with 1 Tbsp of the olive oil and season with salt and pepper. Brush the eggplant slices on both sides with the remaining 6 Tbsp olive oil and season both sides with salt and pepper. ⤳

Grill the eggplant slices, turning once, until softened and grill-marked on both sides, about 12 minutes total. Transfer to a cutting board. Grill the corn, turning frequently, until charred in spots, 10–12 minutes. Transfer to the cutting board. Cut the eggplant slices into ¾-inch (2-cm) pieces. Using a chef's knife, cut the ears of corn in half crosswise. Stand each half flat end down on a cutting board and cut the kernels from the cob.

In a large bowl, combine the eggplant, corn, the remaining basil, and the bread cubes. Pour in the tomato vinaigrette, toss well, and serve.

10

AUGUST

For a salad that includes pasta but is not dominated by it, orzo is a great choice. It is small— the size of a grain of rice—so it blends into the salad easily while adding some substance. A general rule when making pasta salads is to cut the vegetables about the size of the pasta, for the best balance of ingredients with every bite.

ORZO SALAD WITH CHERRY TOMATOES, FETA & OLIVES

serves 6

Salt and freshly ground pepper

1½ cups (9 oz/280 g) orzo pasta

8 cherry tomatoes, quartered

1 cucumber, peeled, seeded, and finely chopped

1 red onion, finely chopped

1 cup (5 oz/155 g) crumbled feta cheese

½ cup (3 oz/90 g) chopped black olives, drained

¼ cup (⅓ oz/10 g) chopped fresh flat-leaf parsley

1 Tbsp fresh lemon juice, or as needed

½ tsp dried oregano

¼ cup (2 fl oz/60 ml) extra-virgin olive oil

Bring a large pot of lightly salted water to a boil. Add the orzo and cook until just tender, according to package directions. Drain well.

In large bowl, combine the orzo, tomatoes, cucumber, onion, cheese, olives, parsley, 1 Tbsp lemon juice, oregano, oil, and ½ tsp pepper. Toss, then cover and refrigerate to chill for at least 20 minutes or up to 2 hours. Taste and adjust the seasoning as needed with salt, pepper, and lemon juice before serving.

11

AUGUST

GRILLED ROMAINE & NOPALES SALAD WITH QUESO FRESCO

serves 4

1½ pink grapefruits

2½ Tbsp avocado oil

Salt and freshly ground pepper

1 large or 2 small pads nopales (cactus paddles) (see note)

1–2 Tbsp extra-virgin olive oil

2 hearts of romaine lettuce, halved lengthwise

2 avocados, pitted, peeled, and diced

4–6 oz (125–185 g) queso fresco, crumbled

Nopales, flat, fleshy, young cactus stems, or pads, are the highlight of this salad. Look for them in Latin American markets, where they are sold already cleaned of the spines except for nubbins at the base of the pad, which need to be removed (see method, at right). Chopped cactus pads can also be used here, but cook them in a hot, dry grill pan or frying pan on the stove top instead of on a grill. Once grilled, the nopales— either whole or chopped—have a denseness and richness comparable to meat, making this salad satisfying for herbivores and omnivores alike. Canned nopales are not recommended for this salad.

Squeeze the grapefruit half to yield ¼ cup (2 fl oz/60 ml) juice and strain into a small bowl. Add the avocado oil, ¼ tsp salt, and ¼ tsp pepper and whisk to mix well. Set aside.

Peel and segment the whole grapefruit. Remove the tough membrane encasing the sections, then cut each section into 3 or 4 pieces. Set aside.

Using a sharp knife, trim about ¼ inch (6 mm) off the edge of the nopales pad. Starting at the base, scrape the knife away from yourself to remove the nubbins of spines. Brush the pad with a little olive oil.

Prepare a charcoal or gas grill for direct-heat cooking over medium-high heat. Place the nopales pad on the grill rack and cook, turning often, until soft, about 5 minutes. Transfer to a cutting board.

Brush the lettuce with some of the olive oil. Place the lettuce, cut side down, on the grill rack and cook, turning once, until lightly charred, about 3 minutes total. Transfer a lettuce half to each individual plate.

Cut the nopales into strips ½ inch (12 mm) wide. Top the lettuce with the nopales, avocados, and grapefruit. Drizzle with the vinaigrette, sprinkle with the cheese, and serve.

12

AUGUST

CREAMY PASTA SALAD WITH LOBSTER

serves 6

Salt and freshly ground black pepper

¾ lb (375 g) pasta shells

2 Tbsp extra-virgin olive oil

¾ lb (375 g) cooked lobster meat or 2–3 frozen lobster tails, thawed and halved lengthwise

½ cup (4 fl oz/125 ml) heavy cream

2 Tbsp tomato paste

3 Tbsp red wine vinegar

Cayenne pepper

8 cherry tomatoes, halved

Chopped fresh flat-leaf parsley for garnish

Luxurious lobster is coated with a rose-colored dressing in this elegant pasta salad fit for an upscale lunch. Pasta shells pool the sauce in their indents (and seem to fit the crustacean theme). Fresh crab can replace the lobster, if desired. Serve with an aromatic white wine, such as a dry riesling.

In a large pot over high heat, bring 5 qt (5 l) salted water to a boil. Add the pasta shells and cook until al dente, according to package directions. Drain the pasta and toss it immediately with 1 Tbsp of the olive oil. Cover and let cool completely in the refrigerator, at least 1 hour or overnight.

If using frozen lobster tails, bring a large pot three-fourths full of salted water to a boil over high heat. Add the lobster tails and boil them until the shells are bright red and the meat is almost opaque throughout, about 8 minutes.

Meanwhile, ready a large bowl full of ice. When the lobster tails are done, transfer them immediately to the bowl and cover with ice. Leave in the ice for 30 minutes. Remove the meat from the tails.

Whether using fresh or frozen, cut the cooked lobster meat into generous bite-sized pieces. Set aside.

In a large bowl, whisk the cream just until it begins to thicken, about 1 minute. Add the remaining 1 Tbsp olive oil, the tomato paste, vinegar, and cayenne to taste. Whisk until mixed thoroughly. Add the pasta shells, lobster, tomatoes, and salt and black pepper to taste. Toss to mix well.

Place in a serving bowl or divide among individual plates, garnish with the parsley, and serve.

13

SCALLOP, MANGO & AVOCADO SALAD

serves 4

FOR THE CHILE-LIME VINAIGRETTE

½ jalapeño chile, seeded and minced

Juice of 2 limes

¼ cup (2 fl oz/60 ml) extra-virgin olive oil

Salt and freshly ground pepper

1 mango, peeled and cut into ½-inch (12-mm) cubes

1 avocado, pitted, peeled, and cut into ½-inch (12-mm) cubes

Juice of ½ lime

2 Tbsp unsalted butter, melted

12 sea scallops, tough muscles removed

6 cups (6 oz/185 g) mixed salad greens

2 green onions, including tender green tops, sliced on the diagonal

Look for uniformly sized sea scallops about 1½ inches (4 cm) in diameter. They should be pale ivory or have the slightest hint of pink, with a mild, sweet scent. The combination of rich scallops and tropical mango and avocado results in a light but satisfying salad.

To make the vinaigrette, in a small bowl, combine the jalapeño and lime juice. Add the olive oil in a thin stream, whisking constantly until the dressing is smooth. Season with ½ tsp salt and pepper to taste. Set aside.

Put the mango and avocado in a bowl, add the lime juice, and toss together. Set aside.

Preheat the broiler and line a rimmed baking sheet with foil. Put the melted butter in a shallow bowl. Add the scallops and turn to coat lightly. Arrange the scallops on the baking sheet, spacing them evenly. Season with salt and pepper to taste. Slide the scallops under the broiler about 6 inches (15 cm) from the heat source and broil until golden on top, about 1½ minutes. Turn the scallops over and broil until the tops are golden and the centers are still slightly translucent, about 1 minute.

In a bowl, toss the salad greens with half of the vinaigrette and divide them among individual plates. Divide the mango and avocado cubes among the plates of greens, scattering them on top. Place 3 scallops on each salad. Add any pan juices from the scallops to the remaining vinaigrette, whisk to recombine, and then drizzle the vinaigrette on and around the scallops. Garnish the salads with the green onions, and serve.

14

SUMMER FRUIT SALAD WITH SAMBUCA

serves 4–6

1 pint (8 oz/250 g) strawberries

1 plum

1 nectarine

1 mango

1 cup (4 oz/125 g) blackberries

1 cup (4 oz/125 g) blueberries

¼ cup (2 oz/60 g) sugar, plus more if needed

Grated zest of 1 lemon

Juice of ½ lemon, plus more if needed

2 Tbsp anise liqueur such as sambuca or anisette, plus more if needed

1 banana

Italians call this marinated fruit salad a macedonia, and it is a favorite way to end a meal. Feel free to vary the ingredients according to what is in the market, adding raspberries, peaches, oranges, or melons, and to adjust the amount of sugar, lemon juice, and/or liqueur to suit your taste. If you prefer, kirsch or another fruit brandy can be used in place of the anise liqueur. The critical step is the long maceration, which forces the fruits to release their juices so their flavors will blend.

Hull the strawberries and halve or quarter if large. Halve, pit, and dice the plum and nectarine.

Peel the mango. Stand the fruit, stem end up, with a narrow side toward you. Position a sharp knife about 1 inch (2.5 cm) from the stem on one side and cut down the length of the fruit, just missing the large pit. Repeat on the other side of the pit. Dice the flesh.

In a large bowl, combine the strawberries, plum, nectarine, mango, blackberries, and blueberries. Add the sugar, lemon zest and juice, and sambuca and stir well. Dice the banana and stir into the salad. Taste and add more sugar, lemon juice, or sambuca, if needed.

Cover and refrigerate the salad for at least 6 hours or up to overnight, stirring occasionally. Taste and adjust the flavorings before serving.

15

Toast pine nuts in a dry nonstick frying pan over medium-low heat, shaking the pan frequently, until fragrant and golden, about 5 minutes. Or, spread them evenly on a baking sheet and place in a preheated 350°F (180°C) oven for about 10 minutes. Remove the nuts just when they are starting to turn golden, and pour them onto a plate to stop the cooking.

ARUGULA & ZUCCHINI SALAD WITH HALIBUT SKEWERS

serves 4

Juice of 1 lemon

2 tsp Dijon mustard

1 tsp minced fresh tarragon

Salt and freshly ground pepper

6 Tbsp (3 fl oz/90 ml) olive oil, plus 1 Tbsp

1¼ lb (625 g) halibut fillet, cut into large cubes

4 small zucchini, halved lengthwise and thinly sliced crosswise

4 small plum tomatoes, cut into thin wedges

¼ red onion, cut into slivers

½ lb (250 g) arugula leaves, stemmed

⅓ cup (2 oz/60 g) pine nuts, toasted *(left)*

Prepare a gas or charcoal grill for direct-heat cooking over high heat or preheat the broiler. Soak 4 bamboo skewers in water for at least 30 minutes.

In a large bowl, whisk together the lemon juice, mustard, tarragon, ½ tsp salt, and a pinch of pepper. Add the 6 Tbsp oil in a thin stream, whisking constantly until the vinaigrette is smooth.

Thread the halibut on the soaked skewers. Season all sides with salt and pepper and brush the skewers with the 1 Tbsp oil. Grill the skewers, turning occasionally, until the halibut is opaque throughout, about 5 minutes. Or, arrange the skewers on a rimmed baking sheet and slide under the broiler 4–6 inches (10–15 cm) from the heat source. Cook, turning occasionally, until lightly golden and opaque throughout, 5–6 minutes total.

Add the zucchini, tomatoes, onion, arugula, and pine nuts to the dressing and toss to coat evenly. Arrange on plates, top with the halibut skewers, and serve.

16

Don't skimp on the chilling time for this pretty green salad: part of its charm comes from the cool, juicy texture of the marinated cucumbers. Let the sweet-tart interplay of the vinegar and sugar really sink in.

SESAME-CUCUMBER SALAD

serves 4–6

4 English cucumbers

Salt

1 Tbsp sugar

½ cup (4 fl oz/125 ml) rice vinegar

3 cloves garlic, minced

Scant 1 tsp red chile flakes

1 Tbsp sesame seeds

6 green onions

Thinly slice the cucumbers crosswise. Combine the cucumbers, ¾ tsp salt, and the sugar in a large bowl and toss to coat the cucumbers evenly with the salt and sugar. Let stand for 30 minutes. Transfer to a colander, rinse, and drain well, then press out the excess moisture with your hands.

In a serving bowl, stir together the vinegar, garlic, chile flakes, and sesame seeds. Add the cucumbers and toss to coat. Thinly slice the green onions, including the tender green parts, and sprinkle them over the top. Cover and refrigerate until well chilled, at least 2 hours or overnight. Serve the salad cold.

17

Serve this well-balanced side dish any time sweet, ripe cherry tomatoes are in the market. It is an ideal companion to grilled chicken and zucchini for a warm-weather supper, and with the filling beans, you won't need to worry about other sides.

WHITE BEAN & CHERRY TOMATO SALAD

serves 6

FOR THE PARSLEY VINAIGRETTE

1 tsp Dijon mustard

2 cloves garlic, pressed

3 Tbsp red wine vinegar

Salt and freshly ground pepper

¼ cup (2 fl oz/60 ml) extra-virgin olive oil, or as needed

1 Tbsp minced fresh flat-leaf parsley

2 cans (15 oz/470 g each) white beans, drained and rinsed

2 cups (¾ lb/375 g) cherry tomatoes, halved or quartered

2 Tbsp chopped fresh flat-leaf parsley

Pecorino romano cheese for shaving

To make the vinaigrette, in a small bowl, whisk together the mustard, garlic, vinegar, ¼ tsp salt, and a few grindings of pepper. Add the oil in a thin stream, whisking constantly until the dressing is smooth. Stir in the minced parsley and set aside.

Put the beans in a serving bowl. Stir in the vinaigrette and tomatoes. Season the beans with salt and pepper to taste. Add a little more oil if needed to moisten the beans. Let stand at room temperature for at least 15 minutes to let the flavors blend.

To serve, sprinkle the beans with the chopped parsley. Using a vegetable peeler, shave cheese over the top, then serve.

18

We tend to take beans for granted in their frozen, canned, and dried forms, but don't underestimate fresh favas and haricots verts in their peak season. Toast the coriander to coax out its flavorful oils, and if you like, add a little minced cilantro as a garnish: the spice and the herb are different parts of the same plant.

MIXED GARDEN BEAN SALAD WITH SHALLOTS

serves 6–8

Salt and freshly ground pepper

½ lb (250 g) fresh shelling beans such as favas or cranberry beans, shelled

1 lb (500 g) wax beans, trimmed and cut into 2-inch (5-cm) lengths

½ lb (250 g) romano beans (optional)

1 lb (500 g) haricots verts, stem ends trimmed

1 tsp ground coriander

¼ cup (2 fl oz/60 ml) fresh lemon juice

2 Tbsp white wine vinegar

2 shallots, minced

¾ cup (6 fl oz/180 ml) grapeseed oil

1 tsp grated lemon zest

Bring a large saucepan of salted water to a boil. Have ready a bowl of ice water. Add the shelling beans and boil until tender, 2–3 minutes. Remove with a slotted spoon, plunge into the bowl of ice water, then drain. (If using favas, pinch the end of each one to pop it out of its skin.) Repeat with the wax beans, romano beans, if using, and haricots verts, cooking the wax beans and romano beans for 7–8 minutes and the haricots verts for 3–4 minutes. Drain and set aside.

In a dry frying pan, toast the coriander over medium-low heat, stirring, until fragrant, 20 seconds. Pour onto a plate and let cool.

In a small bowl, whisk together the lemon juice, vinegar, and shallots. Add the oil in a thin stream, whisking constantly until the dressing is smooth. Stir in the lemon zest and toasted coriander, and season with salt and pepper to taste.

Combine all the beans in a large bowl. Add the vinaigrette and toss. Let stand for at least 1 hour, or refrigerate for up to 3 hours. Serve at room temperature or chilled.

19

Here, grilled shrimp is treated to an imaginative triple-corn base of sweet fresh corn kernels, crunchy cornmeal-fried okra, and whimsical popped corn. Harissa, the spicy North African condiment, is toned down with a little creamy mayonnaise to dress the salad with just the right amount of heat.

CRISPY OKRA, CORN & SHRIMP SALAD WITH HARISSA DRESSING

serves 4

2 Tbsp canola or grapeseed oil, plus more for frying

¼ cup (1½ oz/45 g) popcorn kernels

½ cup (4 fl oz/125 ml) mayonnaise

¼ cup (2 fl oz/60 ml) harissa

2 Tbsp extra-virgin olive oil

Coarse sea salt and freshly ground pepper

12 medium shrimp, peeled and deveined

2 ears corn, husks and silk removed

2 large eggs

1 cup (5 oz/155 g) cornmeal

½ lb (250 g) okra, thinly sliced

Baby spinach for garnish (optional)

In a saucepan, warm the 2 Tbsp canola oil over medium-high heat. When it is hot, add the popcorn kernels, cover, and gently shake the pan over the heat. As the kernels begin to pop, continue shaking until there is only an occasional pop, about 3 minutes. Remove the pan from the heat and uncover it.

In a small bowl, stir together the mayonnaise, harissa, and olive oil until the dressing is well blended. Set aside.

Bring a pot of water to a boil over medium-high heat. Add 2 tsp salt and the shrimp and cook until just opaque and starting to curl, about 2 minutes. Using a slotted spoon, transfer the shrimp to a bowl and set aside.

Hold each ear of corn upright in a large bowl. Using a sharp knife, cut straight down between the kernels and the cob, rotating the ear about a quarter turn after each cut. Set aside.

Pour canola oil into a large frying pan to a depth of ¼ inch (6 mm) and heat over medium-high heat until it registers 375°F (190°C) on a deep-frying thermometer. Line a baking sheet with paper towels. In a shallow bowl, whisk the eggs until blended. In a second shallow bowl, stir together the cornmeal, 1 tsp salt, and 1 tsp pepper. Dip the okra slices into the eggs, allowing the excess to drip off, and then into the cornmeal, shaking off the ↠

excess. Add a few slices at a time to the hot oil. Do not crowd the pan. Fry, turning once, until lightly golden on both sides, about 1 minute per side. Using a slotted spoon, transfer to the paper towel–lined baking sheet. Repeat with the remaining okra.

Divide the popcorn and the corn kernels among individual plates. Top with the okra and place 3 shrimp alongside. Spoon 1 Tbsp of the dressing on each salad. Tuck spinach leaves along the edge of the salads, if desired, and serve with the remaining dressing on the side.

20

Favorite Latin ingredients combine in this protein-packed bean salad. If you plan to eat them right away, choose avocados that yield to gentle pressure. If you're buying them for later in the week, chose slightly underripe avocados; they will ripen at room temperature in a few days.

BLACK BEAN, AVOCADO & SHRIMP SALAD

serves 4–6

½ cup (2 oz/60 g) finely chopped red onion

2 cans (15 oz/470 g each) black beans, drained and rinsed

¼ cup (2 fl oz/60 ml) fresh lime juice

1½ Tbsp olive oil

1 jalapeño chile, seeded and minced

¾ tsp crumbled dried oregano, preferably Mexican

¾ tsp ground cumin

Salt

2 avocados

1 lb (500 g) cooked medium shrimp, peeled and deveined if needed

½ cup (¾ oz/20 g) chopped fresh cilantro leaves

Put the onion in a fine-mesh strainer and rinse under cold running water. Drain well.

In a large bowl, stir together the onion, beans, lime juice, olive oil, jalapeño, oregano, cumin, and ½ tsp salt. Let stand at room temperature for at least 15 minutes to let the flavors blend.

Just before serving, pit the avocados. Scoop the flesh from the peel and cut into 1-inch (2.5-cm) chunks. Gently fold the avocado, shrimp, and cilantro into the beans. Taste and adjust the seasonings and serve.

21

EGGPLANT SALAD WITH CAPERS, CURRANTS & PINE NUTS

serves 4–6

Think of this recipe as a simplified, deconstructed version of caponata, the popular Sicilian cooked eggplant salad. Here, however, the eggplant is cubed and fried instead of braised and the celery is raw. The distinctive sweet-and-sour flavor of the original is captured with currants and lemon.

1 large globe eggplant or 4 Asian eggplants, cut into 1-inch (2.5-cm) cubes

3 Tbsp extra-virgin olive oil

Salt

½ cup (3 oz/90 g) currants

3 celery ribs, finely chopped

3 Tbsp capers

1 tsp fresh lemon juice, plus more if needed

½ cup (½ oz/15 g) fresh flat-leaf parsley leaves

6 to 8 lettuce leaves such as salad bowl or butterhead

3 Tbsp pine nuts

In a bowl, combine the eggplant, 1½ Tbsp of the oil, and ¼ tsp salt and toss to coat. Set aside.

In a large bowl, combine the currants, celery, capers, and 1 tsp lemon juice and toss well. Let stand until the currants soften and the flavors develop, 15–20 minutes.

Heat the remaining 1½ Tbsp olive oil in a large frying pan over high heat. Working in 2 batches if necessary to prevent crowding, add the eggplant cubes and cook, turning them once or twice, until lightly golden on all sides, 5–7 minutes. Transfer to a bowl and let cool slightly.

Add the eggplant to the bowl with the currant mixture and toss well. Taste and add more lemon juice, if desired. Add the parsley and toss again.

Arrange the lettuce leaves on a platter and place the eggplant salad on top. Garnish with the pine nuts and serve.

22

GERMAN POTATO SALAD

serves 4

This is a bacon-lover's potato salad, full of crispy, salty, smoky bits and bites. For a classic German potato salad, look for bacon that has been smoked over applewood, which gives it a sweet flavor. Still-warm potatoes soak up the mustard vinaigrette. Serve with meaty grilled pork chops or bratwursts.

12–14 very small red-skinned potatoes (about 1½ lb/750 g total weight)

Salt and freshly ground pepper

4 slices thick-cut bacon, coarsely chopped

Olive oil as needed

½ yellow onion, halved lengthwise and thinly sliced crosswise

1 large celery rib, thinly sliced

2 Tbsp white wine vinegar

2 tsp minced fresh marjoram

½ tsp dry mustard

½ cup (4 fl oz/125 ml) beef broth

Put the potatoes in a large pot and cover with salted water. Bring to a boil, reduce the heat to medium-high, and cook the potatoes until tender when pierced with a small knife, about 20 minutes. Drain well and return to the pot. Let cool for 10 minutes, then halve.

In a large, heavy frying pan, cook the bacon over medium-high heat until brown and crisp, about 6 minutes. Using a slotted spoon, transfer to paper towels to drain. Pour the drippings from the pan into a small dish.

Return 3 Tbsp of the drippings to the frying pan (if needed, add enough olive oil to yield 3 Tbsp). Add the onion and celery and sauté over medium heat until just beginning to soften, about 3 minutes. Whisk in the vinegar, minced marjoram, ½ tsp salt, ¼ tsp pepper, and the dry mustard. Add the broth, potatoes, and bacon. Cook, tossing gently, until the dressing thickens and coats the potatoes, about 1 minute. Transfer the salad to a serving bowl and serve warm.

23

Shallots and grainy mustard go into the vinaigrette that dresses the greens, tomatoes, and onion that form the bed for thin slices of roasted beef tenderloin and creamy avocado. Don't forget the final sprinkle of sea salt, which will heighten the flavor of the meat.

BEEF TENDERLOIN SALAD WITH TOMATOES & AVOCADO

serves 4

1 cup (8 fl oz/250 ml) red wine

2 cloves garlic, thinly sliced

2 shallots, thinly sliced, plus 2 Tbsp finely chopped shallot

2 bay leaves

2 fresh thyme sprigs

2 fresh rosemary sprigs

1 tsp peppercorns

½ cup (4 fl oz/125 ml) plus 1 Tbsp olive oil

1 lb (500 g) beef tenderloin

Salt and freshly ground pepper

2 Tbsp red wine vinegar

1 tsp whole-grain mustard

6 oz (185 g) mesclun

½ red onion, very thinly sliced

1 cup (6 oz/185 g) grape tomatoes, halved

1 avocado, pitted, peeled, and thinly sliced

Maldon sea salt or coarse sea salt

In a bowl, whisk together the wine, garlic, sliced shallots, bay leaves, thyme, rosemary, peppercorns, and 2 Tbsp of the oil to make a marinade. Place the beef tenderloin in a resealable plastic bag or in a baking dish and pour in the marinade, turning the meat to coat. Seal the bag or cover the dish, and refrigerate for at least 8 hours or up to 24 hours.

Remove the beef from the marinade and season with salt and pepper. Let stand at room temperature for 30 minutes. Preheat the oven to 400°F (200°C).

In a large oven-safe frying pan, warm 1 Tbsp of the oil over medium-high heat. Add the beef and sear until browned on all sides, 3–4 minutes per side. Transfer the pan to the oven and roast, turning the beef occasionally, until an instant-read thermometer inserted into the center of the meat registers 130°F (54°C) for medium-rare, 20–30 minutes. Transfer to a cutting board, cover loosely with aluminum foil, and let rest for 5–10 minutes. »→

In a small bowl, whisk together the vinegar, mustard, and chopped shallot. Add the remaining 6 Tbsp (3 fl oz/90 ml) oil in a thin stream, whisking constantly until the vinaigrette is well blended. Season with salt and pepper.

In a large bowl, combine the mesclun, onion, and tomatoes. Drizzle with the vinaigrette and toss gently. Divide the salad among individual plates and top with the avocado. Cut the beef across the grain and arrange on the salads. Sprinkle with sea salt and serve right away.

24

Cool, refreshing mint brightens this simple salad, in which shaved raw zucchini resembles wide ribbons of pasta. Leaving the zucchini unpeeled adds color and texture. The gentle squash flavor is punctuated by the salty tang of feta cheese. Olive oil infuses the dish with richness, and lemon zest adds bright citrusy notes.

SHAVED ZUCCHINI WITH LEMON, MINT & FETA

serves 4–6

4 zucchini (about 2 lb/1 kg total weight)

¼ cup (2 fl oz/60 ml) extra-virgin olive oil

1 tsp finely grated lemon zest

Salt and freshly ground pepper

¼ cup (⅓ oz/10 g) torn fresh mint leaves

5 oz (155 g) feta cheese, coarsely chopped

Trim the zucchini but do not peel it. Using a sharp vegetable peeler, shave the zucchini lengthwise into long, thin strips, letting the strips fall into a bowl.

In a small bowl, whisk together the olive oil and lemon zest. Drizzle this mixture over the zucchini and season with ¼ tsp each salt and pepper. Add the mint and cheese to the bowl and toss gently. Taste and adjust the seasonings and serve.

25

A trio of green onion, parsley, and mint brings an abundance of verdant flavor to this salad inspired by traditional Middle Eastern tabbouleh. Quinoa makes an earthy backdrop for summery vegetables and a dressing made with fruity olive oil and tangy-sweet pomegranate.

QUINOA SALAD WITH TOMATOES, CUCUMBERS & FRESH HERBS

serves 4–6

1½ cups (9 oz/280 g) quinoa, well rinsed

3 cups (24 fl oz/750 ml) chicken or vegetable broth

Salt and freshly ground pepper

2 large lemons

2 cloves garlic, minced

1 Tbsp pomegranate molasses

1 tsp sugar

½ cup (4 fl oz/125 ml) extra-virgin olive oil

2 large tomatoes

½ large English cucumber

4 green onions, including tender green parts, thinly sliced

¼ cup (⅓ oz/10 g) coarsely chopped fresh flat-leaf parsley

¼ cup (⅓ oz/10 g) coarsely chopped fresh mint

In a saucepan, combine the quinoa, broth, and ¼ tsp salt and bring to a boil over high heat. Cover, reduce the heat to medium-low, and simmer until all of the liquid has been absorbed and the quinoa is tender, about 15 minutes. Immediately transfer the quinoa to a fine-mesh sieve and rinse with cold running water until cooled, 1–2 minutes. Drain well, then transfer to a bowl.

Finely grate the zest from 1 lemon, then halve both lemons and juice the halves to measure 5 Tbsp (2½ fl oz/75 ml) juice. In a small bowl, whisk together the lemon juice and zest, garlic, pomegranate molasses, sugar, ½ tsp salt, and several grindings of pepper until the sugar dissolves. Add the olive oil in a thin stream, whisking constantly until the dressing is well blended. Taste and adjust the seasonings. Add about three-fourths of the dressing to the quinoa and stir well.

Core the tomatoes and halve them crosswise. Gently squeeze each half to ease out the seeds, then cut the tomato flesh into ½-inch (12-mm) pieces. In a small bowl, toss the tomatoes with ¼ tsp salt and let stand until they release their juices, about 5 minutes. Pour into a sieve set over a second bowl. Cut the cucumber into ½-inch (12-mm) ⤜

pieces and add it to the bowl you used to season the tomatoes. Add the green onions and the remaining dressing to the cucumber, toss well, then pour the cucumber mixture over the tomatoes in the sieve to drain. Add the drained tomato-cucumber mixture to the quinoa and stir in the parsley and mint. Taste and adjust the seasonings and serve.

26

As one of the simplest and prettiest salads around, there's good reason why caprese has a devoted following. Slice and plate this any way you like—stuff whole tomatoes with mozzarella and basil leaves; layer big rounds; or toss grape tomatoes with bocconcini.

INSALATA CAPRESE

serves 4

4 large tomatoes, preferably heirlooms

2 balls fresh mozzarella cheese (about 5 oz/155 g total weight)

16 fresh basil leaves

Extra-virgin olive oil for drizzling

Salt and freshly ground pepper

Place the tomatoes on a cutting board, stem sides down. Using a sharp knife, make 4 evenly spaced slits crosswise in each tomato, stopping about ½ inch (12 mm) from the bottom.

Cut the cheese into 16 thin, uniform slices. Working with 1 tomato at a time, insert 1 cheese slice and 1 basil leaf into each slit.

When ready to serve, place the prepared tomatoes on a platter. Drizzle with the olive oil, season generously with salt and pepper, and serve.

27

SHREDDED PORK SALAD WITH TORTILLA CHIPS

serves 4–6

The shredded pork used here is Mexican-style carnitas, available at taquerias and occasionally sold packaged at the meat counter in supermarkets. Do not confuse carnitas with southern-style pulled pork in barbecue sauce. Long, dark, wrinkled negro chiles, also known as pasillas, lend a mildly pungent, smoky flavor to the salad. Fresh tortilla chips are easy to make and are worth the extra step.

4 dried Negro chile peppers

2 cups (16 fl oz/500 ml) boiling water

1 cup (8 oz/250 g) Mexican crema, or 1 cup (8 oz/250 g) light sour cream thinned with 1–2 Tbsp heavy cream

¼ teaspoon salt

1 head iceberg or romaine lettuce, coarsely chopped

½ cup (½ oz/15 g) fresh cilantro leaves, chopped

1 cup (7 oz/220 g) drained canned or home-cooked pinto beans (rinsed if canned)

½ cup (4 oz/125 g) pickled jalapeño chile slices

¾ lb (375 g) carnitas, warmed

2 avocados, pitted, peeled, and diced

½ lb (250 g) queso fresco cheese, crumbled

2 limes, quartered

3 cups good-quality tortilla chips

In a frying pan, toast the chiles over medium-high heat, pressing gently with a spatula and turning several times, until they soften, about 5 minutes. Transfer to a bowl and pour the boiling water over them. Let stand until well hydrated and pliable, about 1 hour. Drain, then remove the stem and seeds and finely chop the chiles. Transfer to a blender, add half of the crema and the salt, and process until almost blended. Add the remaining crema and process until creamy. The crema will be lightly flecked with red. Transfer to a bowl, cover, and refrigerate for at least 1 hour or up to overnight to allow the flavors to develop.

Arrange the lettuce in a layer on a serving platter. Sprinkle with half of the cilantro and top with the beans, half of the jalapeños, ¼ cup (2 oz/60 g) of the crema, the carnitas, the remaining jalapeños, and ¼ cup (2 oz/60 g) of the crema. Finish with the avocados and cheese, and garnish with the remaining cilantro and the limes. Tuck some of the tortilla chips around the edges. Serve the remaining chips and crema on the side.

28

ORZO SALAD WITH GRILLED CORN, TOMATOES & BASIL

serves 4–6

The flavors of summer are captured in this colorful salad. Orzo pasta, which looks like rice kernels, marries well with the simple olive oil dressing and the juicy tomatoes. Grilling the corn caramelizes its sweetness, but in high summer, when fresh corn is at its peak of flavor, it can be added to this salad straight off the cob.

4 ears corn, husks and silks removed

4 Tbsp (2 fl oz/60 ml) extra-virgin olive oil

4 cups (32 fl oz/1 l) low-sodium chicken broth

Salt and freshly ground pepper

1½ cups (10½ oz/330 g) orzo pasta

2 cups (12 oz/375 g) mixed cherry tomatoes, halved

1 cup (1 oz/30 g) fresh purple and green basil leaves, julienned, plus sprigs for garnish

2 tsp red wine vinegar

½ cup (2½ oz/75 g) crumbled queso fresco

Prepare a charcoal or gas grill for direct-heat cooking over medium-high heat. Alternatively, preheat a stove-top grill pan over medium-high heat.

Rub the corn with 1 Tbsp of the oil. Place the corn on the grill rack or in the grill pan and cook, turning frequently, until slightly golden but not charred, about 5 minutes. Remove from the grill.

When the corn is cool enough to handle, hold each ear upright in a large bowl. Using a sharp knife, cut straight down between the kernels and the cob, rotating the ear about a quarter turn after each cut. Set aside.

In a saucepan, bring the broth to a boil over medium-high heat. Add ½ tsp salt and the orzo, and cook according to the package directions. Drain well.

In a bowl, combine the remaining 3 Tbsp oil, the tomatoes, half of the basil, the vinegar, 1 tsp salt, and ¼ tsp pepper and stir well. Add the orzo and the corn, the remaining basil, and half of the cheese. Stir well and transfer to a serving bowl. Top with the remaining cheese, garnish with 1 or 2 basil sprigs, and serve right away.

29

GRILLED CALAMARI & PADRÓN PEPPER SALAD WITH GREEN HARISSA

serves 4

Composing a salad is easy to do with tempting ingredients like the ones used here. Marinated and grilled calamari is the centerpiece, supported by lightly grilled Padrón peppers and lemon slices. The green harissa, made with green chiles and herbs in place of the traditional red chiles used in the North African condiment, is served on the side.

FOR THE GREEN HARISSA

1 serrano chile, seeded and chopped

1 small clove garlic, chopped

½ tsp *each* ground cumin and ground coriander

3 green onions, chopped

1 cup (1½ oz/40 g) tightly packed fresh cilantro sprigs

½ cup (½ oz/15 g) tightly packed fresh flat-leaf parsley sprigs

Salt

2 Tbsp fresh lemon juice

⅓ cup (3 fl oz/80 ml) extra-virgin olive oil, plus more if needed

1 lb (500 g) cleaned squid, cut into bite-sized rings and tentacles

2 Tbsp extra-virgin olive oil

Salt and freshly ground pepper

20 Padrón peppers

3 Meyer lemons, thinly sliced

To make the green harissa, in a blender, combine the chile, garlic, cumin, coriander, green onions, cilantro, parsley, ½ tsp salt, the lemon juice, and oil. Process until smooth, adding more oil if necessary for the desired consistency. Set aside. The sauce can be stored in an airtight container in the refrigerator for up to 3 days, although the flavors will intensify and the color may fade.

In a bowl, combine the squid, oil, ½ tsp salt, and ½ tsp pepper and toss to coat. Let stand at room temperature for 10–15 minutes.

Prepare a charcoal or gas grill for direct-heat cooking over medium-high heat and preheat a grill basket. Alternatively, preheat a stove-top grill pan over medium-high heat.

Place the squid in the grill basket or in the grill pan. Cook, turning several times, just until the squid is opaque and curls, about 1 minute. Transfer to a bowl. Place the peppers and lemon slices on the grill rack or in the pan and cook, turning once or twice, until lightly charred, about 5 minutes.

Arrange the squid, peppers, and lemon slices on a platter. Serve with the green harissa.

30

CELERY, MOZZARELLA & OLIVE SALAD WITH ANCHOVY DRESSING

serves 4–6

This recipe makes the most of celery, an underutilized salad ingredient with a slightly earthy flavor and a toothsome crunch. Layering it with mozzarella, in the style of a caprese salad, and dressing it with an anchovy-rich sauce creates an unusual—and delicious—salad. Serve it with garlic-rubbed grilled bread for mopping up any extra sauce.

1 clove garlic, chopped

8 olive oil–packed anchovy fillets, minced

3 Tbsp extra-virgin olive oil

8 celery ribs, strings removed

½ lb (250 g) fresh mozzarella cheese, cut into thin slices

½ cup (2½ oz/75 g) Niçoise olives, pitted

In a mortar, combine the garlic and anchovies. With a pestle, crush to make a paste. Transfer to a bowl. Gradually add the oil, whisking until well blended. Set aside.

Using a mandoline or a sharp knife, cut the celery on the diagonal into paper-thin slices.

Arrange the celery and cheese on a platter, alternating them. Drizzle with the dressing, scatter the olives on top, and serve.

31

BUTTER LETTUCE SALAD WITH BLUEBERRIES, FETA & ALMONDS

serves 4

Here, a simple savory salad of butter lettuce, feta cheese, chives, and almonds is given a summery spin with fresh blueberries and a tart-sweet raspberry vinaigrette.

3 Tbsp extra-virgin olive oil

4 tsp raspberry vinegar

Salt and freshly ground pepper

2 tsp minced shallot

1½ cups (6 oz/185 g) blueberries

1 Tbsp minced fresh chives

1 head butter lettuce, torn into bite-sized pieces

3 oz (90 g) feta cheese, crumbled

¼ cup (1½ oz/45 g) chopped toasted almonds

In a serving bowl, combine the oil, vinegar, ¼ tsp salt, and ¼ tsp pepper and mix well. Add the shallot, blueberries, and half of the chives. Let stand for 10–15 minutes.

Mix in the lettuce and feta. Garnish with the almonds and remaining chives and serve.

September welcomes fall's first apples and pears, exceptional partners for piquant Stilton cheese and fragrant toasted nuts. Back-to-school season inspires quick and easily packed lunches, such as cold noodles in sesame dressing, couscous with chickpeas, and protein-packed steak and chicken salads. Figs also take center stage—from grilled kebabs with bacon and Parmesan to simple pairings with late-summer produce and nuts.

september

1

The salty-sweet combination of fig and bacon is always popular, and serving the skewers on peppery arugula heightens the flavors. Figs arrive in the market in shades of crimson, green, brown, purple, yellow, and cream. Select those that are fully ripe, indicated by softness and a bent neck, or stem. If a fig is firm to the touch, pass it up, as its sugars have not developed, and it will not ripen off the tree.

GRILLED FIG & BACON KEBABS WITH SHAVED PARMESAN

serves 6–8

2-oz (60-g) piece Parmesan cheese

16 figs (any variety)

5 Tbsp (3 fl oz/80 ml) extra-virgin olive oil

⅓–½ lb (155–250 g) thick bacon slices, cut into pieces 1½ inches (4 cm) long

3 tsp sherry vinegar

Salt and freshly ground pepper

5 cups (5 oz/155 g) baby arugula

Fig leaves for serving (optional)

If using wooden skewers, soak 16 skewers in water for 30 minutes, then drain.

Using a vegetable peeler, shave the cheese into thin pieces. Set aside.

Place the figs in a single layer in a shallow baking dish. Drizzle with 2 Tbsp of the oil and turn gently to coat them.

Thread one piece of bacon onto a skewer, pushing it toward the top, then thread on a fig and push it toward the top. Add another piece of bacon, leaving a long length of skewer empty to use as a handle. Repeat with the remaining skewers, bacon, and figs. Set aside.

In a bowl, whisk together the remaining 3 Tbsp oil, the vinegar, ¼ tsp salt, and ¼ tsp pepper until the vinaigrette is well blended. Set aside.

Prepare a charcoal or gas grill for direct-heat cooking over medium-high heat. Alternatively, preheat a stove-top grill pan over medium-high heat. Place the skewers on the grill rack or in the grill pan and cook, turning once or twice, until the fig skins start to glisten and lightly char and the bacon browns on the outside, 3–5 minutes.

Add the arugula to the bowl with the vinaigrette and toss to coat well.

Line a platter with fig leaves, if desired. Mound the salad on top, scatter with the cheese, and place the kebabs on the platter. Serve hot or warm.

2

Grilling endive caramelizes the leaves and takes away some of its bitter edge. Sweet figs, bold blue cheese, and tart currant-orange dressing complete this salad, which is delicious served with a pinot noir or other earthy red wine.

FIGS & PURPLE ENDIVE SALAD WITH CURRANT DRESSING

serves 4–6

FOR THE CURRANT DRESSING

2 Tbsp dried currants

2 Tbsp fresh orange juice

3 Tbsp extra-virgin olive oil

1 Tbsp balsamic vinegar

1 tsp sugar

1 tsp Dijon mustard

Salt and freshly ground pepper

2 Tbsp pine nuts (optional)

1 fennel bulb, trimmed and thinly sliced lengthwise

6 ripe but firm purple figs, halved

2 large heads purple-tipped Belgian endive, cores intact, halved or quartered lengthwise

1 Tbsp extra-virgin olive oil

1 Tbsp fresh lemon juice

2 Tbsp crumbled blue cheese

Prepare a charcoal or gas grill for direct-heat cooking over medium heat.

Combine the currants and orange juice in a microwave-safe bowl, cover, and microwave on "high" for 1 minute.

In a large bowl, whisk together the 3 Tbsp olive oil, vinegar, sugar, mustard, ½ tsp salt, and a few grindings of pepper. Stir in the currant mixture. Let the dressing stand for 15 minutes.

In a dry small frying pan, toast the pine nuts (if using) over medium-low heat, stirring, until fragrant, 2–3 minutes. Pour onto a plate.

In a bowl, combine the fennel, figs, endive, the 1 Tbsp olive oil, and lemon juice and toss to coat evenly. Put the figs, endive, and fennel in a grill basket and grill, turning often, until the vegetables are wilted and the figs are softened, about 5 minutes. Transfer to the bowl with the dressing and toss gently to mix. Taste and adjust the seasonings, then serve garnished with the crumbled blue cheese and pine nuts.

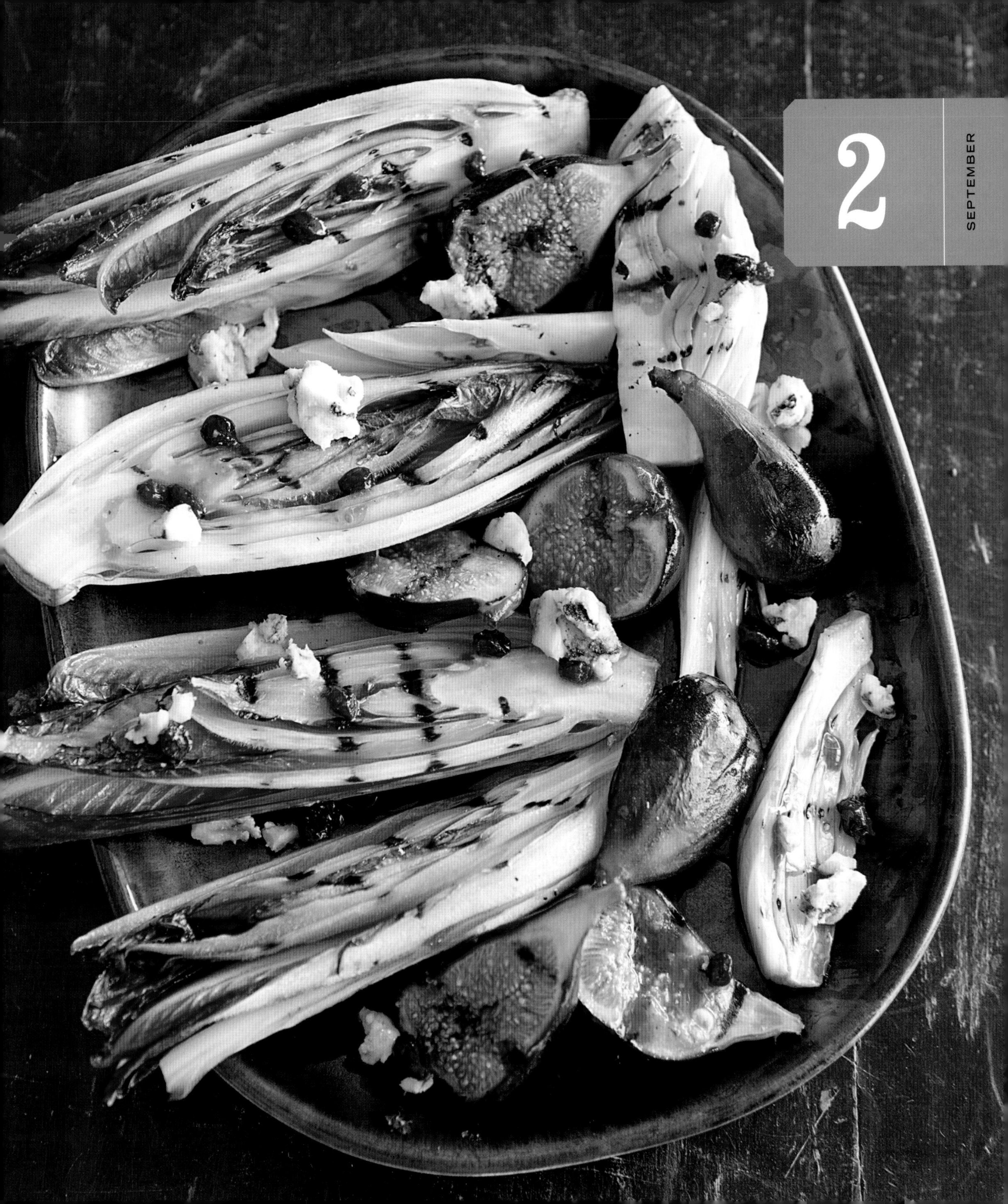

3

COBB SALAD

serves 4–6

3 eggs, hard-cooked (page 70)

8 slices bacon

1 head romaine lettuce, leaves separated and torn into bite-sized pieces

4 cups (1½ lb/750 g) chopped cooked turkey or chicken meat

2 avocados, pitted, peeled, and cubed

2 tomatoes, chopped

4 oz (125 g) Roquefort or other blue cheese, crumbled, plus 1 oz (30 g)

2 cups (4 oz/125 g) chopped stemmed watercress

2 Tbsp minced fresh flat-leaf parsley

2 Tbsp minced fresh chives

¼ cup (2 fl oz/60 ml) red wine vinegar

1 tsp Worcestershire sauce

½ tsp Dijon mustard

1 clove garlic, minced

Salt and freshly ground pepper

⅓ cup (3 fl oz/80 ml) extra-virgin olive oil

Cobb salad is a classic favorite that has stuck around for good reason. With eggs, turkey, bacon, and blue cheese, there's plenty to love. For the poultry in this recipe, use leftover roasted turkey or a purchased rotisserie chicken. Use any blue cheese you prefer, from mild Danish or Maytag to creamy, pungent Gorgonzola.

Cut the hard-cooked eggs into bite-sized pieces and set aside.

In a frying pan, fry the bacon over medium heat until crisp, about 10 minutes. Transfer to paper towels to drain. When cool, crumble and set aside.

On a platter or individual plates, arrange the romaine, eggs, turkey, avocados, tomatoes, and the 4 oz crumbled cheese. Top with the bacon and watercress. Mix together the parsley and chives and sprinkle over the salad.

In a small bowl, whisk together the vinegar, Worcestershire sauce, mustard, garlic, ¼ tsp salt, and ½ tsp pepper. Using a fork, mash in the 1 oz cheese. Add the oil in a thin stream, whisking until smooth.

Pour some of the dressing over the salad and serve, passing the remaining dressing at the table.

4

FALL SALAD OF APPLES & WALNUTS WITH STILTON CHEESE

serves 6

½ cup (2 oz/60 g) coarsely chopped walnuts

6 oz (185 g) Stilton cheese

1 Tbsp extra-virgin olive oil

1 Tbsp red wine vinegar

2 Tbsp heavy cream

Freshly ground pepper

6 sweet eating apples such as Braeburn, Gala, or Red Delicious, cored and cut into ½-inch (12-mm) pieces

4 celery ribs, thinly sliced, plus several whole celery leaves for garnish

2 Tbsp dried currants or raisins

1 Tbsp fresh lemon juice

Apples and blue cheese have a magical affinity, especially when you throw in some toasted nuts. If you prefer, you can toast nuts in the oven: Preheat to 325°F (165°C). Spread the nuts in a single layer on a baking sheet, place in the oven, and toast, stirring occasionally, until the nuts are fragrant and lightly browned, 10–20 minutes.

In a small frying pan, toast the chopped walnuts over medium-low heat, stirring, until fragrant and starting to brown, about 5 minutes. Pour onto a plate to cool and set aside.

Put one-third of the cheese in the bottom of a large bowl. Add the oil and, using a fork, mash together the cheese and oil. Add the vinegar and continue to mash. Add the cream and 1 tsp pepper and mix well to make a thick, chunky dressing.

Add the apples, sliced celery, currants, and lemon juice to the dressing and toss well. Crumble the remaining cheese and sprinkle it over the salad along with half of the walnuts. Mix them into the salad gently and evenly.

Garnish the salad with the remaining walnuts and the celery leaves and serve.

5

ARUGULA, FENNEL & PROSCIUTTO SALAD WITH PEAR VINAIGRETTE

serves 4

Thick, sweet pear nectar, available at most supermarkets, is a boon to salad dressings. It adds a delicious autumnal flavor to this seasonal salad featuring thinly shaved fennel and plump figs.

FOR THE PEAR VINAIGRETTE

⅔ cup (5 fl oz/160 ml) pear nectar

¼ cup (2 fl oz/60 ml) seasoned rice vinegar

Salt and freshly ground pepper

1 fennel bulb, trimmed

5 oz (155 g) mesclun

1 cup (1 oz/30 g) torn arugula leaves

2 oz (60 g) thinly sliced prosciutto, julienned

4 figs, quartered through the stem end

Parmesan cheese for shaving

To make the vinaigrette, in a small bowl, stir together the pear nectar and vinegar. Season with salt and pepper to taste. Set aside.

Using a mandoline or a very sharp knife, cut the fennel bulb crosswise into paper-thin slices and set aside.

In a bowl, combine the mesclun and arugula. Add half of the dressing and toss well. Arrange the greens on individual plates. Top the greens with the fennel, prosciutto, and figs, and drizzle with the remaining dressing. Using a vegetable peeler, shave Parmesan over the salads. Season with pepper and serve.

6

SEPTEMBER

ORZO SALAD WITH TOMATOES, CAPERS & ROASTED GARLIC

serves 4–6

Capers are small in size, but they're mighty in flavor. They dot this salad of rice-like orzo pasta, offering a welcome piquant contrast to sweet grape tomatoes, licorice-like basil, and nutty roasted garlic.

1 head garlic

1½ Tbsp plus ½ cup (4 fl oz/125 ml) extra-virgin olive oil

¼ cup (2 fl oz/60 ml) red wine vinegar

1 tsp sugar

Salt and freshly ground pepper

2 cups (¾ lb/375 g) orzo pasta

4 cups (1½ lb/750 g) grape tomatoes, preferably a mixture of red and yellow, halved lengthwise

¼ cup (2 oz/60 g) capers, rinsed

1 Tbsp finely grated lemon zest

½ cup (½ oz/15 g) fresh basil leaves, torn

Preheat the oven to 400°F (200°C). Slice off the top ½ inch (12 mm) of the garlic head. Set the garlic head cut side up on a square of foil, drizzle it with ½ Tbsp of the olive oil, and wrap tightly in the foil. Bake until soft when gently squeezed, about 1 hour. Unwrap and let cool.

When the garlic is cool enough to handle, squeeze the roasted garlic cloves from the skins; discard the skins. Measure out 2 Tbsp roasted garlic (reserving the remainder for another use) and put it in a small bowl. Add the vinegar, sugar, ½ tsp salt, and several grindings of pepper and whisk until the sugar dissolves. Add the remaining ½ cup plus 1 Tbsp olive oil in a thin stream, whisking constantly until the dressing is well blended. Taste and adjust the seasonings.

Bring a large saucepan two-thirds full of water to a boil over high heat. Add 1 Tbsp salt and the orzo, stir well, and cook until al dente, according to package instructions. Drain in a colander and rinse with cold running water. Drain well again and transfer to a large bowl.

In a bowl, toss the tomatoes with ½ tsp salt and let stand until they release their juices, about 5 minutes, then drain in a sieve. Add the drained tomatoes to the pasta along with about two-thirds of the dressing, ¾ tsp salt, the capers, lemon zest, and basil. Taste and add more dressing, if needed (you may not use it all), and serve.

7

CALAMARI SALAD WITH TOMATO & BLACK OLIVES

serves 4

Salt

1 lb (500 g) cleaned calamari, cut into bite-sized rings and tentacles

1 Tbsp fresh lemon juice

1 tsp red wine vinegar

¼ cup (2 fl oz/60 ml) extra-virgin olive oil

1 large tomato, finely chopped

1 green bell pepper, seeded and minced

½ cup (2½ oz/75 g) oil-cured Mediterranean-style black olives, pitted, or pitted Niçoise olives

¼ cup (1½ oz/45 g) minced red onion

¼ cup (⅓ oz/10 g) minced fresh flat-leaf parsley, plus sprigs for garnish

¼ tsp red pepper flakes

Calamari has tender flesh that cooks in just minutes and readily absorbs the flavors of complementary ingredients. It can be purchased cleaned and ready to cook, sometimes already cut into rings, saving you kitchen time. The tentacles may or may not be included, but if they are, do use them. They add texture and visual appeal to the finished salad.

Bring a saucepan of water to a boil over medium-high heat. Add 1 tsp salt and the squid and cook until just opaque, about 2 minutes. Drain and rinse under cold running water, then drain again and pat dry.

In a bowl, combine the lemon juice, vinegar, oil, tomato, bell pepper, olives, onion, minced parsley, red pepper flakes, and 1 tsp salt and stir to blend. Stir in the squid. Cover and refrigerate for at least 1 hour or up to 6 hours before serving.

Transfer the salad to a serving bowl or individual plates, garnish with parsley sprigs, and serve.

8

GRILLED PORTOBELLO SALAD

serves 4

4 large portobello mushrooms, stems removed

3 Tbsp olive oil, plus ¼ cup (2 fl oz/60 ml)

Salt and freshly ground pepper

2 cloves garlic, minced

2 tsp balsamic vinegar

Juice of 1 lemon

½ tsp minced fresh thyme

3 pears

3 romaine lettuce hearts, torn into bite-sized pieces

Manchego cheese for shaving

Rich and hearty, portobellos have become a mainstay of vegetarian grilling because of their meaty texture and the smoky flavor they take on from the fire. Here they are sliced and arrayed on a bed of romaine, and topped with shavings of sheep's milk cheese.

Prepare a gas or charcoal grill for direct-heat cooking over medium-high heat. Alternatively, preheat the broiler.

Brush both sides of the mushrooms with the 3 Tbsp oil and season generously with salt and pepper. Place the mushrooms, gill side down, on the grill rack and cook without turning for about 8 minutes. Transfer to a plate, rounded sides down, and sprinkle with the garlic and vinegar. Return the mushrooms to the grill, rounded side down, and cook until grill-marked on the outside and softened on the inside, about 10 minutes.

Alternatively, arrange the mushrooms on a rimmed baking sheet and slide under the broiler 4–6 inches (10–15 cm) from the heat source. Cook, using the same timing and seasoning as for grilling.

Meanwhile, in a large bowl, whisk together the lemon juice, thyme, ¼ tsp salt, and a pinch of pepper. Add the ¼ cup oil in a thin stream, whisking constantly until the dressing is smooth.

Cut the warm mushrooms into thin slices. Peel, halve, and core the pears, then cut them into thin wedges. Add the lettuce and pears to the vinaigrette, toss to coat evenly, and arrange on plates. Top with the mushroom slices, use a vegetable peeler to shave the cheese over the salad, and serve.

9

HERRING, BEET & APPLE SALAD

serves 4–6

1¼ lb (625 g) beets, trimmed

1 tsp extra-virgin olive oil

½ yellow onion, cut crosswise into ¼-inch (6-mm) slices

¼ cup (2 fl oz/60 ml) white wine vinegar

1 Tbsp sugar

Salt

2 tart green apples such as Granny Smith, cored and cut into ½-inch (12-mm) dice

1 jar (8 oz/250 g) pickled herring fillets, brine reserved

The juice from the pickled herring is used to make the dressing, which in turn gives the beets a slightly pickled taste. Tart apples add crispness and absorb a hint of the pickled flavor, and they, like the onions, turn a soft pink from color released by the beets. If possible, prepare the salad a day ahead to allow the flavors to blend fully.

Preheat the oven to 350°F (180°C).

Place the beets in a baking dish and rub them with the oil. Roast until the beets are easily pierced with a knife, about 1½ hours. When the beets are cool enough to handle, peel and cut into ¼-inch (6-mm) rounds. Transfer to a large bowl and set aside. The beets can be stored in an airtight container in the refrigerator for up to 1 day.

Meanwhile, in a saucepan, combine the onion, ¾ cup (6 fl oz/180 ml) water, the vinegar, sugar, and ½ tsp salt. Bring to a boil over medium-high heat, cover, reduce the heat to low, and simmer until the onion is very tender, about 45 minutes. Transfer the onion and cooking liquid to a bowl and let cool.

Add the apples along with the onion and cooking liquid to the bowl with the beets.

Cut the herring fillets into bite-sized pieces, add to the bowl, and stir gently to combine. Strain the reserved herring brine and add to the beet mixture to taste, starting with 1 tsp. Cover and refrigerate for at least 4 hours or up to overnight before serving. Serve chilled.

10

FLANK STEAK SALAD WITH WASABI DRESSING

serves 4–6

4 cloves garlic

Coarse sea salt and freshly ground pepper

2 Tbsp red wine vinegar

½ cup (¾ oz/20 g) chopped fresh flat-leaf parsley

2 tsp fresh thyme leaves

¼ cup (2 fl oz/60 ml) extra-virgin olive oil

1¼–1½ lb (500–750 g) flank steak

2 Tbsp wasabi paste

½ cup (4 fl oz/125 ml) mayonnaise

½ cup (4 oz/125 g) sour cream

Heavy cream or half-and-half as needed

2 heads red- or green-leaf lettuce, torn into bite-sized pieces

1 bunch watercress, tough stems removed

1 English cucumber, cut into small dice

1 red onion, minced

The wasabi dressing is an Asian-inspired take on the more traditional horseradish accompaniment to beef. You can use this salad as a template, trading out the cucumbers and onions for tomatoes and radishes, for example, or for oranges and sweet peppers.

In a mortar, combine the garlic and 1 tsp salt. With a pestle, crush the garlic to make a paste. In a bowl, whisk together the vinegar, parsley, thyme, oil, 2 tsp salt, and 1 Tbsp pepper to make a marinade. Pierce the steak on both sides with a fork and rub with the garlic paste. Place in a resealable plastic bag, pour in the marinade, and turn the meat to coat. Seal the bag and refrigerate overnight.

Prepare a charcoal or gas grill for direct-heat cooking over medium-high heat. Remove the steak from the marinade. Place on the grill rack and cook, turning once, until an instant-read thermometer inserted into the thickest part registers 130°F (54°C) for medium-rare, 4–5 minutes per side, or until done to your liking. Transfer to a cutting board, cover loosely with aluminum foil, and let rest for 5 minutes. Cut the steak across the grain into slices ¼ inch (6 mm) thick.

In a small bowl, stir together the wasabi paste, mayonnaise, and sour cream until the dressing is well blended. Add cream, starting with 1–2 tsp, until a medium creamy consistency is reached. Set aside.

In a bowl, toss together the lettuce and watercress. Divide among individual plates. Top with the cucumber, onion, and steak. Drizzle with the dressing and serve right away.

11

GRILLED OCTOPUS SALAD WITH POTATOES & ROASTED GARLIC

serves 4

Charcoal-grilled octopus is popular in Greece and southern Italy, where it is served on its own or as part of a simple salad, as it is here. Octopus is surprisingly easy to prepare. The goal is to cook it until it is tender but still offers a bit of chewy resistance. In this recipe, it is marinated after it is boiled and before it is grilled to enhance its flavor, a step that can be done a day ahead. The garlic and potatoes can be cooked a day in advance, as well.

1 large octopus (about 3 lb/1.5 kg), thawed if frozen

2 carrots, peeled and cut into chunks

1 celery rib, cut into chunks

1 tsp peppercorns

Salt

2 fresh thyme sprigs

1 cup (8 fl oz/250 ml) white wine

3 Tbsp extra-virgin olive oil, plus more for drizzling

½ tsp red pepper flakes

1 head garlic

8 small Yukon gold potatoes (about 1 lb/500 g total weight)

2–3 tsp fresh lemon juice

¼ cup (⅓ oz/10 g) chopped fresh flat-leaf parsley

2 Tbsp chopped fresh mint

Rinse the octopus well under running cold water. If the octopus has not previously been frozen, place it in a large lock-top freezer bag and freeze it overnight, then thaw in the refrigerator to tenderize the flesh. Cut the head off the octopus; discard. Remove the beak at the center of the tentacles; discard.

In a large stockpot, combine the carrots, celery, peppercorns, 1 tsp salt, the thyme, wine, and 6 cups (48 fl oz/1.5 l) water. Bring to a boil over medium-high heat, then reduce the heat to medium-low. Using tongs, lower the octopus into the pot, submerging it fully, and blanch for about 5 seconds. Repeat 3 more times, then leave the octopus in the pot. Increase the heat to medium and simmer until the octopus is tender when pierced with a knife, 40–50 minutes.

Transfer the octopus to a large bowl and let cool, then refrigerate until chilled, about 1 hour. Add 1½ Tbsp of the oil, the red pepper flakes, and ½ tsp salt to the bowl and turn the octopus to coat well. Cover and refrigerate for at least 1 hour or up 24 hours. ➳➳

Preheat the oven to 350°F (180°C). Cut off the top of the garlic head to expose the cloves. Rub with the remaining 1½ Tbsp oil and place in a small baking dish. Roast until the cloves are tender and the skins are crispy and golden, 45–50 minutes. Let cool. Using your fingers, separate the cloves and squeeze the ends to extract the garlic. Set aside.

Put the potatoes in a saucepan, cover with water by 2 inches (5 cm), and add 1 tsp salt. Bring to a boil over high heat, reduce the heat to medium, and cook until tender, about 20 minutes. Drain and let cool briefly, then peel and dice or cut into thin slices.

Prepare a charcoal or gas grill for direct-heat cooking over medium-high heat. Place the octopus on the grill rack and cook, turning once, until slightly charred, about 2 minutes per side.

Transfer the octopus to a cutting board and cut the thickest part of the tentacles into slices ½ inch (12 mm) thick, but leave the thinner ends in pieces about 1 inch (2.5–4 cm) long. Arrange the octopus on a platter and add the potatoes and the garlic. Drizzle with the lemon juice and a little oil. Sprinkle with the parsley and mint. Serve warm or at room temperature.

12

ARUGULA, BLUE CHEESE & GRAPE SALAD

serves 4–6

The purple grapes in this recipe have enough piquancy that no vinegar is needed in the dressing. If you wish, a squeeze of lemon can add a nice vibrancy, but taste your grapes first to gauge the flavor.

6 cups (6 oz/185 g) arugula leaves, stemmed

2 Tbsp extra-virgin olive oil

Salt and freshly ground pepper

1½ cups (9 oz/280 g) seedless purple grapes

5 oz (155 g) blue cheese, crumbled

Put the arugula in a large bowl. In a small bowl, whisk together the oil and salt and pepper to taste to make a dressing. Drizzle the dressing over the arugula and toss well. Add the grapes and cheese and toss again.

Divide the salad among individual plates and serve.

POTATO & RED PEPPER SALAD WITH SAFFRON DRESSING

serves 6

This salad is tinted a warm yellow color from the saffron dressing that coats the tender red potatoes. A handful of slivered peppers and onions lend crisp texture. To reduce the heat from the chile, cut out the membranes, or veins, and discard the seeds, where most of the heat is concentrated.

FOR THE SAFFRON DRESSING

1½ large red jalapeño chiles, seeded and deveined, then minced

1½ Tbsp brine-cured capers, plus ½ Tbsp caper brine

2 Tbsp white wine vinegar

Salt and freshly ground pepper

¼ tsp saffron threads

¼ cup (2 fl oz/60 ml) olive oil

1 large red onion, halved lengthwise and cut crosswise into paper-thin slices

1 large red bell pepper, seeded, deribbed, and cut into matchsticks

12 small red-skinned potatoes (about 2 lb/1 kg total weight)

Salt and freshly ground pepper

To make the dressing, in a large bowl, combine the chiles, capers and caper brine, vinegar, ½ tsp salt, ¼ tsp pepper, and saffron. Add the oil in a slow stream, whisking constantly until the dressing is smooth. Add the red onion and toss to blend well. Let stand for 15 minutes, stirring occasionally, to let the flavors blend. Stir the bell pepper into the dressing.

Meanwhile, put the potatoes in a large pot and cover with salted water. Bring to a boil, reduce the heat to medium-high, and cook the potatoes until tender when pierced with a small knife, about 20 minutes. Drain and let cool to the touch, about 10 minutes.

Cut the potatoes lengthwise into quarters and add to the bowl with the dressing. Toss to coat, season with salt and pepper to taste, and serve.

COUSCOUS SALAD WITH CHICKPEAS, PEPPERS & BLACK OLIVES

serves 4

Couscous, which is sometimes mistakenly called a grain, is actually a pasta, made from wheat dough rolled into tiny pearls. Widely available "instant" couscous has been presteamed and fluffs up in only a few minutes. Fold in hearty chickpeas, meaty olives, and citrus and parsley for this easy but satisfying salad.

2 Tbsp plus ¼ cup (2 fl oz/60 ml) extra-virgin olive oil

1 yellow onion, finely chopped

2 cloves garlic, minced

2¾ cups (22 fl oz/680 ml) chicken broth

Salt and freshly ground pepper

1½ cups (9 oz/280 g) instant couscous

¾ cup (3 oz/90 g) slivered almonds

1 can (15 oz/470 g) chickpeas, drained and rinsed

1 red bell pepper, seeded and chopped

¾ cup (3½ oz/105 g) brine-cured black olives, pitted and chopped

Juice of 1 lemon

¼ cup (⅓ oz/10 g) minced fresh flat-leaf parsley

In a large saucepan over medium-low heat, warm 1 Tbsp of the oil. Add the onion and cook, stirring occasionally, until softened, about 4 minutes. Add the garlic and cook for 1 minute. Add the broth, ½ tsp salt, and several grindings of pepper and bring to a boil. Place the couscous in a large heatproof bowl and pour the hot liquid over it. Blend well with a fork, cover with a plate, and let stand for 5 minutes.

Meanwhile, in a large frying pan over medium heat, warm 1 Tbsp of the oil. Add the almonds and toast, stirring, until crisp and golden, 5–7 minutes. Transfer to a plate and let cool.

Fluff the couscous with a fork. Add the toasted almonds, chickpeas, bell pepper, olives, lemon juice, parsley, and the ¼ cup oil to the couscous. Toss gently to combine. Taste, adjust the seasoning with salt and pepper, and serve.

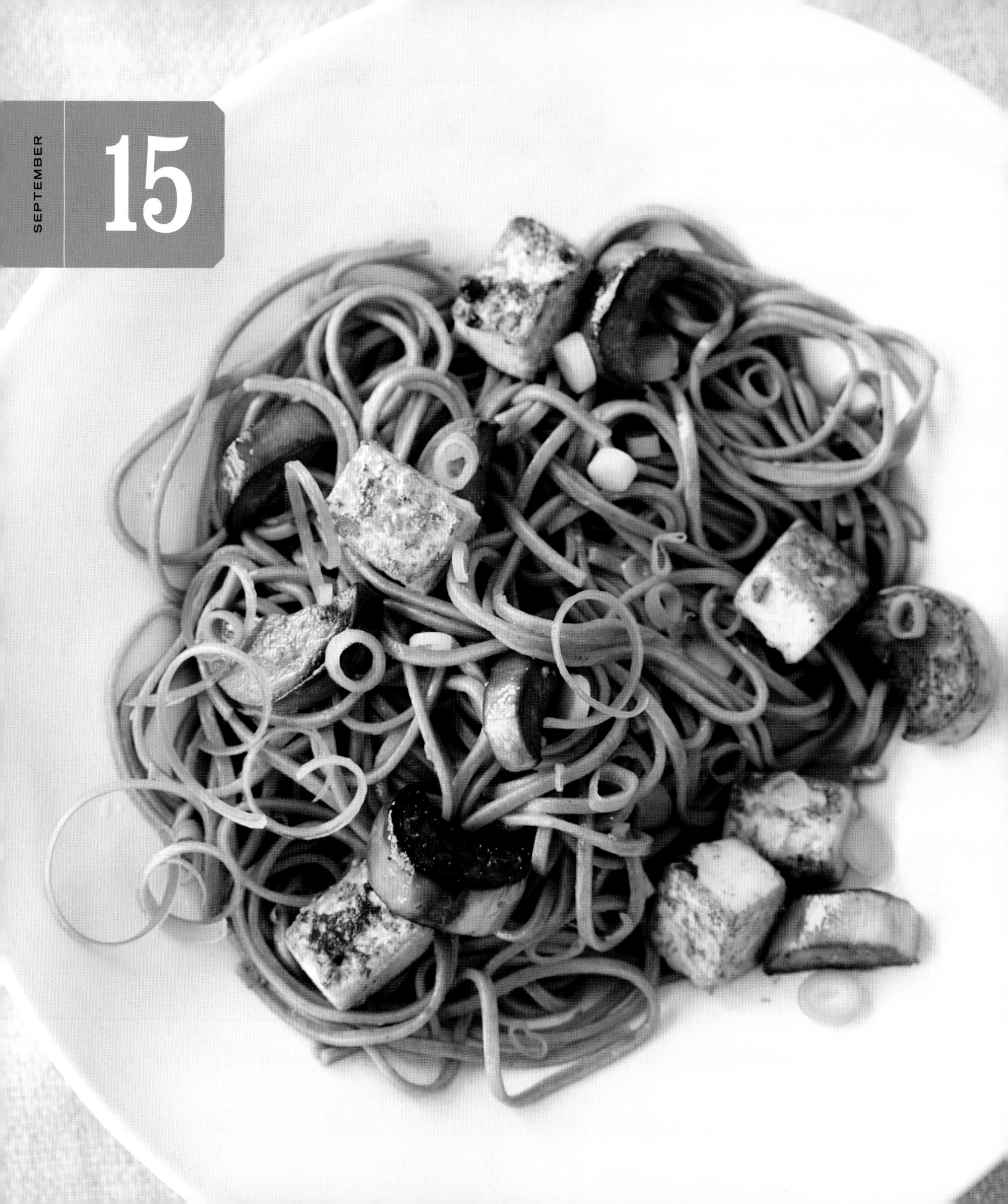
SEPTEMBER
15

15

Soba means "buckwheat" in Japanese, and not surprisingly, soba noodles are made with flour milled from buckwheat groats. Both the noodles and tofu make satisfying background flavors for the slightly caramelized eggplant and ginger-soy dressing.

SOBA NOODLE SALAD WITH TOFU & MARINATED EGGPLANT

serves 4

FOR THE MARINADE

1 Tbsp toasted sesame oil

2 Tbsp sherry vinegar

2 Tbsp soy sauce

½ tsp sugar

1 clove garlic, chopped

FOR THE DRESSING

½ tsp toasted sesame oil

1 Tbsp sherry vinegar

1 tsp soy sauce

2 tsp peanut oil

1 Tbsp grated fresh ginger

3 Japanese eggplants, trimmed

Salt

8 oz (250 g) soba noodles

½ tsp peanut oil, plus 2 Tbsp, or as needed

12 oz (375 g) firm tofu, cut into ½-inch (12-mm) cubes

5 green onions, including tender green parts, thinly sliced

To make the marinade, in a large bowl, combine the 1 Tbsp sesame oil, 2 Tbsp vinegar, 2 Tbsp soy sauce, sugar, and garlic and stir well. Set aside.

To make the dressing, in a large bowl, combine the ½ tsp sesame oil, 1 Tbsp vinegar, 1 tsp soy sauce, 2 tsp peanut oil, and ginger and stir to mix well. Set aside.

Halve the eggplants lengthwise and cut into ½-inch (12-mm) pieces. Add to the bowl with the marinade, toss, and let stand for at least 1 hour.

In a large saucepan over medium-high heat, bring 4 cups (32 fl oz/1 l) water to a boil. Reduce the heat to medium, add 1 tsp salt and the soba noodles and cook until tender but not mushy, about 6 minutes. Drain and rinse with cold water until cool. Drain again, transfer to a bowl, and toss with the ½ tsp peanut oil. Set aside. »»

In a wok over medium-high heat, warm the 2 Tbsp peanut oil, tilting the wok to coat the pan. When the oil is hot, add the eggplant cubes and cook, turning until they are golden and tender, 3–5 minutes. Remove with a slotted spoon and set aside. Put the tofu cubes in the wok, adding more oil if needed, and cook until they are just golden, 3–4 minutes. Remove and set aside along with the eggplant.

Put the soba noodles in the bowl with the dressing and turn to coat. Add the eggplant and tofu and mix and coat. Sprinkle with the green onions and serve.

16

This simple salad incorporates two prized ingredients of Spain. Cabrales cheese, a cave-aged, intensely flavored blue, is produced in specifically designated areas in the Principality of Asturias, in the northwest. Flat, round Marcona almonds, which boast a sweet, delicate taste, are grown along the country's Mediterranean coast.

FIG SALAD WITH CABRALES CHEESE & MARCONA ALMONDS

serves 6

10 cups (10 oz/315 g) torn Bibb or butter lettuce

¼ lb (125 g) Cabrales cheese or other strong blue cheese, crumbled

½ cup (2 oz/60 g) Marcona almonds

1 Tbsp champagne vinegar

½ tsp Dijon mustard (optional)

3 Tbsp olive oil

Salt and freshly ground pepper

6 Black Mission figs, thinly sliced

In a large bowl, combine the lettuce, cheese, and almonds. Set aside.

In a small bowl, whisk together the vinegar and mustard, if using. Add the oil in a thin stream, whisking constantly until the vinaigrette is well blended. Season with salt and pepper.

Drizzle the vinaigrette over the salad and toss to combine. Divide the salad among individual plates, arrange the figs on top, and serve.

17

FRISÉE SALAD WITH BRIOCHE CROUTONS & LARDONS

serves 4

Brioche is distinguished by its high butter and egg content, which accounts for its pale yellow color, light crumb, and rich flavor. It is similar to challah, and both make delicate, airy croutons that create an ideal contrast in this otherwise hearty salad.

4 slices brioche or *pain de mie*

6 oz (185 g) lardons or 6 slices thick-cut bacon, cut into ½-inch (12-mm) pieces

3 Tbsp extra-virgin olive oil

1 Tbsp red wine vinegar

1 tsp Dijon mustard

Salt and freshly ground pepper

2 heads frisée, pale yellow inner leaves only, torn into bite-sized pieces

Preheat the oven to 400°F (200°C).

Trim the crusts from the bread and cut the bread into ½-inch (12-mm) cubes. Spread the bread cubes on a baking sheet. Bake, turning several times, until lightly golden, about 12 minutes total. Let cool.

In a large frying pan, fry the lardons over medium-high heat, stirring occasionally, until crispy, about 7 minutes. Transfer to paper towels to drain.

In a large bowl, whisk together the oil, vinegar, mustard, ¼ tsp salt, and ¼ tsp pepper until the vinaigrette is well blended. Add the frisée and toss to coat well. Add three-fourths each of the lardons and croutons and toss gently. Divide among individual plates, garnish with the remaining lardons and croutons, and serve.

18

ANTIPASTO SALAD WITH PEPERONCINI VINAIGRETTE

serves 6

An array of Italian cured meats and cheese inspired this lively chopped salad, topped with zesty peperoncini. The plate becomes especially pretty if you use a mixture of red and yellow cherry tomatoes. Accompany with toasted slices of garlicky sourdough bread for texture.

FOR THE CROSTINI

¼ cup (2 fl oz/60 ml) extra-virgin olive oil

4 cloves garlic, minced

1 sourdough baguette

Salt

FOR THE PEPERONCINI VINAIGRETTE

¼ cup (2 fl oz/60 ml) red wine vinegar

5 peperoncini, stemmed, seeded, and minced

1 Tbsp minced fresh oregano

2 tsp sugar

6 Tbsp (3 fl oz/90 ml) extra-virgin olive oil

4 cups (1½ lb/750 g) cherry or grape tomatoes, halved lengthwise

3 avocados

8 oz (250 g) provolone cheese, cut into ½-inch (12-mm) cubes

1–2 cups (1–2 oz/30–60 g) arugula leaves, stemmed

10 oz (315 g) thinly sliced prosciutto

To make the crostini, preheat the oven to 350°F (180°C). In a bowl, mix together the ¼ cup oil and the garlic. Cut the baguette into 18 slices, each about ½ inch (12 mm) thick, and arrange in a single layer on a baking sheet. Brush both sides of the baguette slices with the garlic oil and sprinkle lightly with salt. Toast in the oven until crisp and lightly golden, about 10 minutes. Let cool.

In a small bowl, whisk together the vinegar, peperoncini, oregano, sugar, and ¼ tsp salt. Add the 6 Tbsp oil in a thin stream, whisking until the dressing is well blended.

In a bowl, toss the tomatoes with ¼ tsp salt and let stand until they release their juices, about 5 minutes, then drain. Pit and peel the avocados and cut them crosswise into slices about ⅜ inch (1 cm) thick. Sprinkle with a large pinch of salt.

Arrange the tomatoes, avocados, cheese, and arugula on a large platter. Whisk the vinaigrette to recombine, then drizzle it over the arranged salad. Arrange the prosciutto and crostini on the platter and serve.

19

BLACK BEAN, CORN & QUINOA SALAD

serves 6

Quinoa, a South American staple crop, is prized for its earthy yet delicate flavor, as well as its nutritional value: it is the only grain that boasts a complete protein. A medley of corn with glossy black beans, pale gold quinoa, and red tomatoes and bell pepper makes this a colorful, eye-catching salad.

FOR THE LIME DRESSING

2 Tbsp fresh lime juice

3 Tbsp distilled white vinegar

2 Tbsp minced fresh cilantro

1 serrano chile, seeded and minced

¼ tsp dried oregano

Salt and freshly ground pepper

½ cup (4 fl oz/125 ml) olive oil

½ cup (3 oz/90 g) quinoa, well rinsed

½ can (8 oz/250 g) black beans, drained and rinsed

⅔ cup (4 oz/125 g) fresh or thawed frozen corn kernels (from about 1 ear corn)

1 tomato, seeded and finely chopped

1 small red bell pepper, seeded and finely chopped

To make the dressing, in a bowl, whisk together the lime juice, vinegar, cilantro, chile, oregano, ½ tsp salt, and ½ tsp pepper. Add the oil in a thin stream, whisking constantly until the dressing is smooth. Set aside.

In a saucepan over medium-high heat, combine the quinoa and 1½ cups (12 fl oz/375 ml) water. Stir in ¼ tsp salt. Cover and bring to a boil, then reduce the heat to low and simmer until the quinoa is tender and all the water has been absorbed, about 15 minutes. Transfer the quinoa to a colander and rinse under cold running water. Drain thoroughly.

Meanwhile, put the beans in a saucepan and place over medium-low heat. Stir occasionally until warm. Remove from the heat and cover to keep warm.

Combine the quinoa and the black beans in a bowl. Pat the corn dry with paper towels and add to the bowl along with the tomato and bell pepper. Pour in the dressing and toss to coat all the ingredients well. Let stand at room temperature for at least 15 minutes to let the flavors blend before serving.

20

SOUTHWESTERN SALAD

serves 4

Spicy, crunchy, and refreshing, this winter salad includes roasted butternut squash, avocado, jicama, and black beans and is finished with Cotija cheese, a flavorful, crumbly Mexican cow's milk cheese. The salad is hearty enough to be a complete meal, with just crusty bread or rolls on the side.

FOR THE CHIPOTLE VINAIGRETTE

¼ cup (2 fl oz/60 ml) fresh lime juice

1 Tbsp plus 1 tsp agave nectar

2 chipotle chiles in adobo, plus 1 tsp adobo sauce

¼ tsp Dijon mustard

½ cup (4 fl oz/125 ml) extra-virgin olive oil

Salt and freshly ground pepper

½ butternut squash (about 1 lb/500 g), seeded, peeled, and cut into ½-inch (12-mm) dice

Extra-virgin olive oil for drizzling

Salt and freshly ground pepper

2 Tbsp vegetable oil

4 corn tortillas, cut into thin strips

2 heads romaine lettuce, thinly sliced

1 can (15 oz/470 g) black beans, drained and rinsed

12 cherry tomatoes, halved

1 green onion, green part only, thinly sliced

1 avocado, pitted, peeled, and diced

¼ lb (125 g) jicama, peeled and julienned

Thinly sliced red onion for garnish

2 oz (60 g) cotija cheese, crumbled (optional)

To make the vinaigrette, in a blender, combine the lime juice, agave nectar, chiles and adobo sauce, mustard, and olive oil. Purée until smooth. Season with salt and pepper. Set aside.

Preheat the oven to 400°F (200°C). Spread the squash in a single layer on a baking dish, drizzle with olive oil, and season with salt and pepper. Roast, stirring occasionally, until tender, about 15 minutes. Let cool.

In a large sauté pan, warm the vegetable oil over medium-high heat. Add the tortilla strips and stir. Cook, stirring occasionally, until golden brown, 6–8 minutes. Transfer to a paper towel–lined plate and season with salt and pepper. Set aside.

In a large bowl, combine the lettuce, squash, black beans, tomatoes, and green onion. Drizzle with some of the vinaigrette and season with salt and pepper. Toss to coat. Transfer to a platter. Top with the avocado, jicama, red onion, and fried tortilla strips. Sprinkle with the cheese. Drizzle with a little more vinaigrette and serve.

21

SPICY CASHEW CHICKEN SALAD

serves 6

2 Tbsp light sesame oil

½ yellow onion, finely chopped

1½-inch (4-cm) piece fresh ginger, peeled and minced

7 large cloves garlic, minced

1½ lb (750 g) ground chicken

1 cup (5 oz/155 g) cashews

¾ cup (6 fl oz/180 ml) hoisin sauce

6 Tbsp (3 fl oz/90 ml) tamari sauce

1¼ tsp Sriracha chile sauce

2 tsp firmly packed light brown sugar

1 large head butter lettuce, separated into leaves

Salt and freshly ground pepper

3 green onions, including pale green parts, thinly sliced

Salty-sweet hoisin sauce has a deep, spicy, molasses-like flavor. It defines this easy-to-make ground chicken salad, which also includes generous doses of ginger and garlic. Toasted cashews add both a delicious nuttiness and welcome crunch. To serve, mound the salad on a pile of greens, or pass little lettuce cups at a party.

In a large frying pan over medium heat, warm the sesame oil. Add the onion, ginger, and garlic and sauté until aromatic and the onion has softened slightly, about 2 minutes. Add the ground chicken and raise the heat to medium-high. Cook, stirring and breaking up the meat with a wooden spoon, until the chicken is evenly crumbled, cooked through, and no longer pink, about 8 minutes.

Meanwhile, in a dry frying pan, toast the cashews over medium-low heat, stirring, until fragrant, about 5 minutes. Pour onto a plate to cool, then chop and set aside.

In a small bowl, whisk together the hoisin, tamari, Sriracha sauce, and brown sugar. When the chicken is ready, add the hoisin mixture and half of the cashews to the pan and cook, stirring occasionally, until aromatic, about 3 minutes. Remove from the heat and cover to keep warm.

In a large bowl, toss the lettuce with 2 pinches of salt and several grindings of pepper. Divide the lettuce leaves among individual plates or arrange on a platter, and spoon the warm chicken mixture into the lettuce leaves. Garnish with the remaining cashews and the green onions and serve.

22

CELERY, PEAR & TOASTED HAZELNUT SALAD

serves 6–8

8–10 celery ribs, strings removed

½ cup (2½ oz/75 g) hazelnuts

2½ Tbsp hazelnut oil

1 Tbsp white balsamic vinegar or pear vinegar

Salt and ground white pepper

4 ripe pears such as Bosc or Bartlett

Crisp autumn apples and pears are good partners for crunchy celery. Remove the strings from the celery to make slicing easier and ensure a tender bite. Nut oils are more costly than staple varieties, but they are supremely rich and delicious. If you like, walnuts and walnut oil can be substituted for the hazelnuts and hazelnut oil.

Preheat the oven to 350°F (180°C). Using a mandoline or a very sharp knife, cut the celery into slices ⅛ inch (3 mm) thick. Cut the tops into small pieces. Put all the celery in a bowl of ice water and set aside.

Spread the hazelnuts in a single layer on a baking sheet. Place in the oven and toast, stirring once or twice, until the skins start to darken and wrinkle, 12–15 minutes. Remove from the oven and rub in a kitchen towel to remove the skins. Pour onto a plate to cool, then chop coarsely and set aside.

In a large bowl, combine the hazelnut oil, vinegar, and ¼ tsp each salt and pepper and whisk well. Drain the celery and pat dry with a paper towel. Add to the bowl and turn to coat with the vinaigrette.

Peel, halve, and core the pears, then cut them lengthwise into slices ½ inch (12 mm) thick. Set aside.

Using a slotted spoon, remove the celery from the vinaigrette and divide among chilled salad plates. Arrange the pear slices on top and drizzle with the vinaigrette. Sprinkle with the toasted hazelnuts and serve.

SEPTEMBER

23

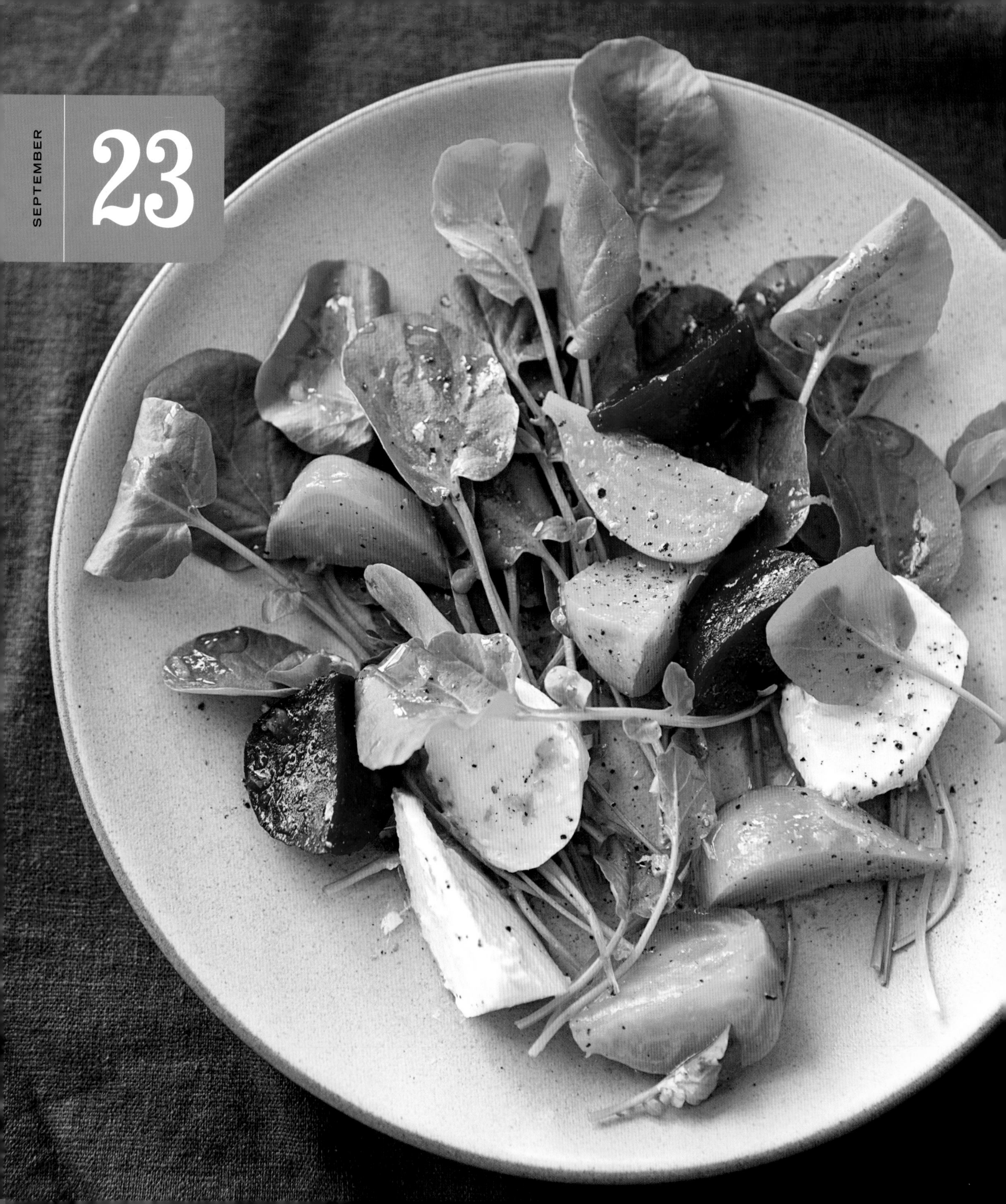

23

BEET & WATERCRESS SALAD WITH FRESH MOZZARELLA

serves 4

1½–1¾ lb (750–875 g) baby red and/or golden beets, or striped Chioggia beets, trimmed

2 Tbsp champagne vinegar

1 tsp grated orange zest

2 Tbsp fresh orange juice

Salt and freshly ground pepper

3 Tbsp extra-virgin olive oil

¼ lb (125 g) watercress, tough stems removed

1 lb (500 g) fresh mozzarella cheese, cut into thin wedges

For a delicious variation on this salad, check your local cheese shop or specialty-foods market for burrata, a fresh mozzarella cheese filled with cream and curds. Its melting texture makes it a delicious counterpoint to the earthiness of beets and the bite of watercress in this salad.

Preheat the oven to 400°F (200°C). Wrap the beets in foil, making a separate packet for each color, and roast until the beets can be pierced easily with a knife, 45 minutes–1 hour. Unwrap and let cool. Gently peel the beets, cut into quarters, and put in a small bowl.

In a large bowl, whisk together the vinegar, orange zest and juice, and ½ tsp salt. Add the oil in a thin stream, whisking constantly until the dressing is smooth. Pour half of the dressing over the beets and stir to coat. Add the watercress to the remaining dressing and toss to coat.

Arrange the watercress on individual plates or on one large platter, and top with beets. Arrange the cheese around the beets and drizzle with any remaining vinaigrette. Season with a few grindings of pepper and serve.

24

SEARED ALBACORE SALAD WITH ROASTED PEACHES & GOAT CHEESE

serves 4

¼ cup (2 fl oz/60 ml) extra-virgin olive oil, plus 2 Tbsp

2 Tbsp champagne vinegar

1 Tbsp minced shallot

1 Tbsp minced fresh flat-leaf parsley

Salt and freshly ground pepper

3 peaches, ripe but not soft, halved, pitted, and cut into ½-inch (12-mm) slices

1 lb (500 g) albacore tuna (about 1 inch/2.5 cm thick)

4 cups (4 oz/125 g) mesclun

6 oz (185 g) fresh goat cheese, cut into four ½-inch (12-mm) rounds

Pairing fish and fruits is common in the tropics, but here the combination takes on a Mediterranean profile with the addition of goat cheese and herb vinaigrette. Searing the albacore but leaving the interior pink creates an appealing contrast of texture and flavor.

Preheat the oven to 400°F (200°C). Line a baking sheet with parchment paper.

In a small bowl, whisk together the ¼ cup (2 fl oz/60 ml) oil, the vinegar, shallot, parsley, and ¼ tsp salt until the vinaigrette is well blended. Set aside.

Brush the peach slices with 1 Tbsp of the oil and place on the prepared baking sheet. Roast until the edges are slightly caramelized but the slices still hold their shape, about 10 minutes. Remove from the oven and keep warm.

Season the tuna on both sides with ¾ salt and ½ tsp pepper. In a large frying pan, warm the remaining 1 Tbsp oil over medium-high heat. When it is almost smoking, add the tuna and sear until the first ¼ inch (6 mm) is golden and opaque, about 1 minute. Turn and sear the other side, about 2 minutes. Transfer to a cutting board, let rest for about 5 minutes, and then cut into thin slices.

Divide the mesclun among individual plates and drizzle each with about 1 tsp of the vinaigrette.

Top the salads with the peaches, tuna, and cheese. Drizzle with the remaining vinaigrette and serve right away.

25

This dish will help you savor those few weeks of the year in late summer when shelling beans are still in abundance, juicy corn is piled high at farm stands, and potatoes are thin-skinned and tender. Roasting the corn makes it slightly chewy and enhances its natural sweetness.

SUCCOTASH SALAD

serves 6–8

Kernels cut from 6 ears of corn

6 Tbsp (3 fl oz/90 ml) olive oil

Salt and freshly ground pepper

2 lb (1 kg) fava beans in the pod, shelled

1 lb (500 g) small potatoes such as fingerling, Yukon Gold, or red-skinned, quartered

FOR THE HONEY VINAIGRETTE

3 Tbsp red wine vinegar

½ tsp Dijon mustard

1 tsp honey

⅓ cup (3 fl oz/80 ml) extra-virgin olive oil

1 can (15 oz/470 g) lima beans, drained and rinsed

¼ red onion, cut into paper-thin slices

2 Tbsp minced fresh flat-leaf parsley

2 tsp chopped fresh thyme

Preheat the oven to 400°F (200°C). Put the corn kernels on a baking sheet. Drizzle with 2 Tbsp of the olive oil and season with salt and pepper. Toss and spread out in an even layer. Roast until the corn is light brown and slightly shriveled, about 15 minutes.

Bring a saucepan three-fourths full of salted water to a boil. Add the fava beans and blanch for 2 minutes. Drain and rinse under cold running water. Pinch each bean to pop it from its skin, and set aside.

In a large frying pan, combine the remaining 4 Tbsp (2 fl oz/60 ml) olive oil and ½ cup (4 fl oz/125 ml) water over medium heat. Add the potatoes, season with salt and pepper, cover, bring to a simmer, and cook until the potatoes are tender and begin to sizzle, 10–20 minutes. Toss the potatoes with the oil remaining in the pan, and sauté until light golden, about 5 minutes.

To make the vinaigrette, in a small bowl, stir together the vinegar, mustard, and honey. Add the olive oil in a thin stream, whisking constantly until the dressing is smooth. Season to taste with salt and pepper.

In a large bowl, combine the roasted corn, fava and lima beans, potatoes, onion, parsley, and thyme. Drizzle with the vinaigrette, toss to coat, and serve.

26

Cucumbers and salmon are a classic combination, but the duo feels fresh when paired with a gingery marinade and some added shoots and greens. If you can find it, try to use wild salmon, as it is leaner than farmed salmon and deeper in flavor. Serve with a dry Japanese beer.

ASIAN SEARED-SALMON SALAD

serves 4

FOR THE GINGER MARINADE

¼ cup (2 fl oz/60 ml) soy sauce

3 Tbsp honey

1 Tbsp peeled and finely grated fresh ginger

Finely grated zest of 2 limes

Juice of 1 lime

1 Tbsp toasted sesame oil

1 cucumber, peeled and finely sliced

Salt

1 Tbsp sugar

1 Tbsp white wine vinegar

2 heads butter lettuce, leaves separated

2 cups (2 oz/60 g) arugula leaves, stemmed

6 green onions, white parts only, thinly sliced

3 Tbsp olive oil

4 salmon fillets, about 6 oz (185 g) each, skin on and pin bones removed

To make the marinade, in a small saucepan, combine the soy sauce, honey, and ginger. Set over low heat and cook, stirring, until the honey is dissolved. Simmer for 1 minute and remove from the heat. Add the lime zest and let stand to cool to room temperature, about 30 minutes. Whisk in the lime juice and sesame oil. Set aside.

In a bowl, combine the cucumber and ¼ tsp salt and let stand for 10 minutes. Stir in the sugar and vinegar. In a large bowl, combine the lettuce leaves, arugula, and green onions. Set aside.

In a nonstick frying pan over high heat, warm the olive oil. Add the salmon fillets, skin side down, and cook until crisp, about 5 minutes. Turn and cook until the flesh is golden, about 5 minutes. Transfer to a dish and generously spoon half of the marinade over the fillets. Let stand until cool.

Before serving, remove and discard the skin from each fillet. Add the remaining marinade and the cucumber and any liquid to the salad and toss to combine. Divide the salad among individual plates. Top each salad with a salmon fillet and serve.

27

SALAD OF GRILLED PORK, PEARS & TOASTED PECANS

serves 6

½ cup (2 oz/60 g) pecans

1 Tbsp peanut oil

Salt and freshly ground pepper

Pinch of sugar

2 pork tenderloins, about ¾ lb (375 g) each, trimmed

1 Tbsp olive oil

FOR THE HAZELNUT VINAIGRETTE

6 Tbsp (3 fl oz/90 ml) olive oil

2½ Tbsp sherry vinegar

1 Tbsp hazelnut oil

2 firm but ripe pears, preferably Bosc

6 handfuls (about 6 oz/185 g) mixed salad greens

Pork matches well to the sweetness of cider, but instead of braising, sear tenderloins for a quick weeknight salad with slices of fresh green pear. If the weather is too chilly to fire up the grill, the broiler works just as well.

Preheat the oven to 350°F (180°C). In a bowl, combine the pecans, peanut oil, salt and pepper to taste, and sugar and toss well to coat the nuts. Spread the pecans evenly on a baking sheet and bake until lightly golden, 5–7 minutes. Let cool.

Prepare a charcoal or gas grill for direct-heat cooking over high heat, or preheat the broiler.

Brush the pork tenderloins with the 1 Tbsp olive oil and season with salt and pepper. Place on the grill rack or on a broiler pan 4 inches (10 cm) from the heat source and cook, turning occasionally to brown evenly, until an instant-read thermometer inserted into the thickest part registers 150°F (66°C) or the pork is pale pink when cut in the thickest portion, about 12 minutes. Transfer to a cutting board, cover loosely with foil, and let rest for 2–3 minutes before carving. Cut crosswise into slices ¼ inch (6 mm) thick.

To make the vinaigrette, in a small bowl, whisk together the 6 Tbsp olive oil, vinegar, and salt and pepper to taste. Add the hazelnut oil in a thin stream, whisking constantly until the dressing is smooth.

Halve, core, and cut the pears lengthwise into very thin slices. In a large bowl, combine the greens, pecans, and vinaigrette and toss to mix well. Arrange the dressed greens on a platter or individual plates, top with the pork and pear slices, and serve.

28

TORTILLA SALAD WITH ROASTED POBLANO DRESSING

serves 4

1 poblano chile

1⅓ cups (10½ oz/330 g) Mexican crema, or 1 cup (8 oz/250 g) sour cream thinned with ⅓ cup (3 fl oz/80 ml) half-and-half

Salt

Juice of 4 lemons

1 small jicama (about ½ lb/250 g), peeled and diced

2 cups (12 oz/375 g) shredded cooked chicken (from about 2 chicken breasts)

1 bunch watercress, tough stems removed

2 Anaheim or other mild green chiles, seeded and minced

1 head red- or green-leaf lettuce, torn into bite-sized pieces

8 red radishes, minced

½ cup (1½ oz/45 g) minced green onion, including tender green parts

8 ounces (250 g) tortilla chips, crushed

1 avocado, pitted, peeled, and diced

In this colorful construction, the seasoned crema dressing binds together jicama, watercress, green chiles, and chicken and mounds them on a bed of greens and crispy tortilla chips to make a main-dish salad.

Over a gas flame or under a broiler, roast the poblano chile until charred, turning once or twice, about 10 minutes. Transfer to a bowl, cover, and let steam for 15 minutes. Remove the skin, stem, and seeds and coarsely chop the flesh. In a food processor or blender, combine the chile and half of the crema and purée until smooth. Transfer to a bowl. Add the remaining crema, ½ tsp salt, and half of the lemon juice and stir until the dressing is well blended.

In a bowl, combine the jicama, chicken, watercress, and green chiles. Pour about half of the dressing on top and stir to coat well. Transfer the remaining dressing to a small serving bowl.

Divide the lettuce, radishes, and green onions among individual plates or bowls. Drizzle the remaining lemon juice over the salads. Top with all but 1 cup (3 oz/90 g) of the tortilla chips and then with the chicken mixture. Garnish with the remaining chips and the avocado. Serve right away, accompanied by the poblano dressing.

29

SMOKED CHICKEN SALAD WITH ROASTED CHERRY TOMATOES

serves 4

This simple chicken and tomato salad gains extra flavor from a basil dressing, but the croutons really steal the show. Savory Parmesan polenta cubes become crispy, panfried delicacies, adding crunch and a hint of sweet cornmeal.

FOR THE POLENTA CROUTONS

2 cups (14 oz/440 g) instant polenta

4 Tbsp (2 oz/60 g) unsalted butter

⅔ cup (3 oz/90 g) grated Parmesan cheese

2 Tbsp olive oil

FOR THE PESTO DRESSING

2 Tbsp extra-virgin olive oil

1 tsp grated lemon zest

2 Tbsp fresh lemon juice

1 Tbsp prepared pesto

2 cups (¾ lb/375 g) cherry tomatoes

3 Tbsp extra-virgin olive oil

Salt and freshly ground pepper

½ tsp fresh thyme, chopped

1 smoked or roasted whole
chicken breast

To make the polenta croutons, in a large, heavy saucepan, cook the polenta according to package instructions. Remove from the heat and vigorously stir in the butter and cheese until evenly distributed. Quickly rinse a 12-by-17-inch (30-by-43-cm) rimmed baking sheet with cold water and shake it dry. Immediately mound the polenta in the pan and, working quickly and using a spatula repeatedly dipped in hot water, spread the polenta in an even layer about ½ inch (12 mm) thick. Cover with a kitchen towel and let stand for at least 1 hour at room temperature, or refrigerate for up to 24 hours. Remove the chilled polenta from the refrigerator about 1 hour before using. Cut the polenta into ½-inch cubes.

In a frying pan over medium-high heat, warm the 2 Tbsp olive oil. When hot, add the polenta cubes, in batches as needed to avoid crowding, and sauté until lightly browned on all sides. Transfer to paper towels to drain.

To make the dressing, in a glass measuring pitcher, whisk together the 2 Tbsp extra-virgin olive oil, lemon zest and juice, and pesto. Set aside. ⟶

Preheat the oven to 400°F (200°C). Put the cherry tomatoes in a bowl and drizzle with the 3 Tbsp olive oil and sprinkle with ¼ tsp each salt and pepper and the thyme. Toss to coat. Place on a baking sheet and roast in the oven until their skins are wrinkled but not yet collapsed, about 15 minutes. Remove from the oven and set aside.

Reset the oven to 350°F (180°C). Wrap the chicken breast in foil and place it in the oven to warm, about 15 minutes. Remove it and slice it very thinly.

Arrange the chicken slices on a serving platter. Top with the cherry tomatoes and drizzle with some of the pesto dressing. Sprinkle with the polenta croutons, add another drizzle of the pesto dressing, and serve.

30

PANZANELLA

serves 6

This hearty Italian salad originated as a way to use up stale bread. Traditionally, it evolved from the bland, salt-free bread of Tuscany, but you can use any day-old country-style bread. The drier the bread, the more absorbent it is, which means it will soak up more of the delicious juices and dressing. As the salad sits, the bread will soften and the flavors will blend together.

2 large tomatoes, cut into bite-sized pieces

1 small English cucumber, peeled, halved lengthwise, and sliced

1 small red onion, halved and very thinly sliced

1 cup (1½ oz/45 g) fresh basil leaves, torn, plus whole small leaves for garnish

½ cup (4 fl oz/125 ml) extra-virgin olive oil, or to taste

3 Tbsp red wine vinegar, or to taste

Salt and freshly ground pepper

6–8 day-old slices country-style bread

In a large mixing bowl, combine the tomatoes, cucumber, onion, and torn basil. Drizzle with the ½ cup olive oil and the 3 Tbsp vinegar and season with salt and pepper. Toss well to coat evenly.

Cut or tear the bread into bite-sized pieces. Place half of the bread in a wide, shallow serving bowl. Spoon half of the tomato mixture over. Layer the remaining bread on top and then the remaining tomato mixture. Cover and let stand for 1 hour.

Toss the salad, then taste and adjust the seasoning with salt, pepper, and vinegar. If the bread seems dry, add a little more olive oil. Garnish with the whole basil leaves and serve.

Fall is the time of year when cool nights and shorter days bring a new crop of produce to market: tender frisée, prickly artichokes, and thick-skinned winter squash, in addition to grapes, pomegranates, and late-season pears. The damp fall weather also bodes well for mushrooms. Seek out wild and local varieties, and enjoy them raw and thinly sliced, or sautéed and tossed with a bold dressing while still warm.

october

1

SMOKED TROUT & APPLE SALAD WITH POLENTA CROUTONS

serves 10–12

Golden polenta croutons flavored with Parmesan add sweet crunch to this elegant salad of delicate flaked trout and crisp sliced apples. You can try other smoked fish in place of the trout, such as sturgeon or whitefish. Serve as a first course at your next dinner party.

FOR THE POLENTA CROUTONS

2 cups (14 oz/440 g) instant polenta

4 Tbsp (2 oz/60 g) unsalted butter

⅔ cup (3 oz/90 g) grated Parmesan cheese

2 Tbsp grapeseed oil

2 small Gala or Fuji apples, cored and thinly sliced

½ lb (250 g) smoked trout, skin and bones removed, flaked with a fork

4 cups (4 oz/125 g) loosely packed mâche

¾ cup (3 oz/90 g) coarsely chopped walnuts

¼ cup (2 fl oz/60 ml) mayonnaise

1 Tbsp fresh lemon juice

Salt and freshly ground pepper

2 Tbsp minced fresh chives

To make the polenta croutons, in a large, heavy saucepan, cook the polenta according to package instructions. Remove from the heat and vigorously stir in the butter and cheese until evenly distributed. Quickly rinse a 12-by-17-inch (30-by-43-cm) rimmed baking sheet with cold water and shake it dry. Immediately mound the polenta in the pan and, working quickly and using a spatula repeatedly dipped in hot water, spread the polenta in an even layer about ½ inch (12 mm) thick. Cover with a kitchen towel and let stand for at least 1 hour at room temperature, or refrigerate for up to 24 hours. Bring the chilled polenta to room temperature for about 1 hour before serving. Cut the polenta into ½-inch cubes.

In a frying pan over medium-high heat, warm the 2 Tbsp oil. When hot, add the polenta cubes, in batches as needed to avoid crowding, and sauté until lightly browned on all sides. Transfer to paper towels to drain.

Arrange the apples on a platter. Scatter with the trout, greens, walnuts, and polenta croutons. In a small bowl, stir together the mayonnaise, lemon juice, ¼ tsp salt, and pepper to taste. Drizzle this dressing over the salad, scatter with chives and a grinding of pepper, and serve.

2

WATERCRESS & ORANGE SALAD WITH TOASTED PUMPKIN SEEDS

serves 6

The peppery bite of watercress pairs well with the bright, sweet taste of oranges in this salad. Pumpkin seeds are known as pepitas in Spanish, and they are a favorite ingredient in Mexican cooking. They are delicious when toasted and sprinkled over salads.

¼ cup (2 oz/60 g) pumpkin seeds

1 tsp extra-virgin olive oil

1 tsp ground cumin

FOR THE SPICY CITRUS DRESSING

¼ cup (2 fl oz/60 ml) fresh lime juice

1 jalapeño chile, thinly sliced and seeded

Salt and freshly ground pepper

⅓ cup (3 fl oz/80 ml) extra-virgin olive oil

3 navel oranges

2 bunches watercress, tough stems removed

In a small bowl, toss the pumpkin seeds with the 1 tsp oil and the cumin. Spread the pumpkin seeds in a dry frying pan over medium heat and cook, stirring constantly, just until they begin to darken, about 5 minutes. Pour onto a plate to cool.

To make the dressing, in a small bowl, whisk together the lime juice, chile, 1 tsp salt, and ¼ tsp pepper. Add the ⅓ cup oil in a thin stream, whisking constantly until the dressing is smooth.

Use a knife to peel the oranges. Cut each in half vertically, then cut each half crosswise into half-moon slices about ¼ inch (6 mm) thick. Put the orange slices in a bowl, add the watercress, and toss to mix.

Just before serving, drizzle the dressing over the watercress and oranges. Taste and adjust the seasoning with salt. Divide the salad among serving plates, sprinkle each serving with the toasted pumpkin seeds, and serve.

THREE-BEAN SALAD WITH CORIANDER VINAIGRETTE

serves 6–8

Salt and freshly ground pepper

½ lb (250 g) fresh flageolet beans or other fresh shelling beans, shelled

1 lb (500 g) yellow wax beans, stem ends trimmed and beans cut into 2-inch (5-cm) lengths

1 lb (500 g) haricots verts, stem ends trimmed

FOR THE CORIANDER VINAIGRETTE

1 tsp ground coriander

¼ cup (2 fl oz/60 ml) fresh lemon juice

2 Tbsp white wine vinegar

2 shallots, minced

¾ cup (6 fl oz/180 ml) safflower oil

1 tsp grated lemon zest

Three-bean salad is a venerable favorite. Here is an updated version that calls for fresh shelling beans, slender French green beans, and pale wax beans. You can substitute other green beans for the haricots verts. The flavor intensifies if the salad is allowed to marinate for at least 1 hour.

Bring a large saucepan three-fourths full of salted water to a boil. Add the shelling beans and boil just until tender, 10–15 minutes. Have ready a bowl of ice water. Scoop out the beans and immediately immerse in ice water to stop the cooking. Scoop the beans out of the ice water and set aside to drain. Repeat with the yellow wax beans and haricots verts, cooking the wax beans for 7–8 minutes and the haricots verts for 3–4 minutes.

To make the vinaigrette, in a small, dry frying pan, toast the coriander over medium heat, shaking the pan occasionally, until aromatic, 2–3 minutes. Pour onto a plate to cool and set aside. In a small bowl, combine the lemon juice, vinegar, and shallots. Add the safflower oil in a thin stream, whisking constantly until the dressing is smooth. Stir in the lemon zest and coriander and season with salt and pepper.

Combine all the beans in a large mixing bowl. Add the vinaigrette and toss to mix well. Let stand for at least 1 hour, or refrigerate for up to 3 hours. Serve at room temperature or chilled.

GREEN GRAPE, PEAR & DUCK SALAD

serves 4

1 duck breast half, about 1 lb (500 g)

Salt and freshly ground pepper

½ tsp ground coriander

2 Tbsp minced shallot

2 Tbsp balsamic vinegar

2 cups (¾ lb/375 g) seedless green grapes, some halved for garnish

2 bunches watercress, tough stems removed

2 green pears, such as Comice or Seckel, cored and thinly sliced

Dark, gamy duck meat classically pairs with fruit flavors—just think of a cherry compote, or an orange glaze. Salads are a fantastic way to feature these same flavors, except with fresh fruit. In this case, rich breast meat joins fall grapes and pears in an elegant dish fit for company.

Remove the skin and fat from the duck by pulling the fatty layer back and cutting it from the meat with a small knife. Set the breast aside. Place the fatty layer, skin side down, in a frying pan over medium heat. Cook, turning occasionally, until about ¼ cup (2 fl oz/60 ml) fat is rendered, 10 minutes. Discard the skin. Measure out 2 Tbsp fat and set aside. (Save the rest for another use.)

Raise the heat to high. Season the duck breast on both sides with 1 tsp salt, ½ tsp pepper, and the coriander. Sear until browned, about 3 minutes. Add the shallot, turn the duck, and cook on the other side for 3 minutes. Reduce the heat to medium and cook until the duck is rosy only in the center, 1–2 minutes. Transfer to a cutting board and let rest.

Add the reserved duck fat to the pan and place over high heat. When the fat is hot and glistening, add ½ cup (4 fl oz/125 ml) water, the vinegar, and the whole grapes to the pan, and stir to scrape up any browned bits on the pan bottom. Simmer until the liquid is reduced by half, about 2 minutes. Slice the duck on the diagonal into thin slices, and pour any collected juices into the pan.

Arrange the watercress on a platter and top with alternating slices of pear and duck. Pour the grape sauce over, scatter with the grape halves, and serve.

5

This contemporary chicken salad forgoes mayo in favor of a lighter, lemony vinaigrette, deliciously drizzled over strips of freshly sautéed breast meat. It also appropriates some of the fresh touches of the famous Waldorf salad—apples, celery, and walnuts.

CHICKEN SALAD WITH APPLES & WALNUTS

serves 4

½ cup (2 oz/60 g) coarsely chopped walnuts

1 large or 2 small bunches watercress, tough stems removed

1 large tart apple such as Granny Smith

½ lemon, plus 1 Tbsp fresh lemon juice

Salt and freshly ground pepper

¼ cup (2 fl oz/60 ml) walnut oil

4 skinless, boneless chicken breast halves (about 2 lb/1 kg total weight)

2 Tbsp unsalted butter

2 Tbsp extra-virgin olive oil

2 or 3 celery ribs with leaves, preferably the tender inner ribs, thinly sliced crosswise

In a dry frying pan over medium-low heat, toast the walnuts, stirring until fragrant and starting to brown, about 5 minutes. Pour onto a plate to cool.

Put the watercress in a serving bowl, cover with a damp kitchen towel, and refrigerate for 20–30 minutes.

Peel, quarter, and core the apple. Cut the quarters in half crosswise and then thinly slice lengthwise. Put them in a bowl. Squeeze the juice from the lemon half over the apple to slow the discoloration. Toss to coat well and set aside.

In a small bowl, stir together the 1 Tbsp lemon juice, ⅛ tsp salt, and pepper to taste until the salt dissolves. Add the walnut oil in a thin stream, whisking constantly until the dressing is well blended. Set aside.

Remove any excess fat from the chicken breasts. Rinse and pat dry with paper towels. Place each breast between 2 sheets of plastic wrap and, using a meat mallet, pound to an even thickness. Season with salt and pepper. In a large frying pan (preferably nonstick), melt the butter with the olive oil over medium-high heat. When hot, add the chicken breasts and sauté, turning once, until lightly browned and opaque throughout, 3½–4 minutes per side. Transfer to a plate and keep warm. ⟩⟩

Add the celery, apple, and half of the walnuts to the watercress. Whisk the dressing to recombine, pour it over the salad, and toss well. Divide among individual plates. Slice the warm chicken breasts crosswise into strips ½ inch (12 mm) thick and arrange them over the salads. Sprinkle with the remaining toasted walnuts and serve.

6

This salad, served throughout the Mediterranean, is best with just-caught octopus. If fresh is not available, frozen octopus is the next best thing. Octopus has a wonderfully meaty texture, and when chilled and thinly sliced, it almost takes on the flavor of lobster.

MEDITERRANEAN OCTOPUS SALAD

serves 4

1½ lb (750 g) octopus, cleaned

Salt and freshly ground pepper

1 clove garlic, crushed

½ cup (4 fl oz/125 ml) extra-virgin olive oil

Juice of 1 lemon

2 green onions, including tender green tops, sliced crosswise

1 red bell pepper, seeded and finely chopped

2 inner celery ribs, thinly sliced

Rinse the octopus well under running cold water. If the octopus has not previously been frozen, place it in a large lock-top freezer bag and freeze it overnight, then thaw in the refrigerator to tenderize the flesh.

In a saucepan, combine the octopus with water to cover and bring to a boil over high heat. Add 2 Tbsp salt and the garlic, cover, reduce the heat to low, and simmer without lifting the lid for about 45 minutes. The octopus should turn white.

Drain the octopus and let cool until it can be handled. Cut into bite-sized pieces and place in a serving bowl. Add the oil and lemon juice, cover, and let marinate for at least 1 hour at room temperature or for up to 4 hours in the refrigerator.

Just before serving, add the green onions, bell pepper, and celery and toss well. Season with salt and pepper and toss again, then serve at room temperature or slightly chilled.

7

7

Scoring the meat before marinating it allows the flavors to penetrate fully, and helps prevent the steak from curling on the grill. Tender rice noodles and a trio of green herbs define this fresh, Asian main. If you can find Thai basil, use it here for authentic flavor.

VIETNAMESE FLANK STEAK SALAD

serves 4

FOR THE SPICY MARINADE

2 Tbsp peeled and grated fresh ginger

½ cup (4 fl oz/125 ml) soy sauce

2 Tbsp Asian fish sauce

2 Tbsp toasted sesame oil

3 cloves garlic, minced

2 green onions, including tender green parts, thinly sliced

1 shallot, minced

1 Thai chile, seeded and thinly sliced

Grated zest and juice of 1 lime

1 flank steak, 1½–1¾ lb (750–875 g), trimmed

Salt and freshly ground pepper

1 head Bibb lettuce, torn into small pieces

1 heart of romaine lettuce, chopped into 1-inch (2.5-cm) chunks

1 carrot, peeled and shredded

1 cucumber, peeled, seeded, and shredded

1 small red onion, thinly sliced

2 Tbsp minced fresh basil, plus small leaves for garnish

2 Tbsp minced fresh mint, plus small leaves for garnish

2 Tbsp minced fresh cilantro, plus small leaves for garnish

1 lb (500 g) Asian cellophane noodles, soaked in water until soft, then drained

To make the marinade, in a bowl, whisk together the ginger, soy sauce, fish sauce, sesame oil, garlic, green onions, shallot, chile, and lime zest and juice. Spoon one-half of the marinade into a small serving bowl and set aside.

Using a sharp knife, score the meat on both sides in a crosshatch pattern, cutting no more than ½ inch (12 mm) deep. Place the steak in a shallow dish, pour the remaining marinade over the top, and turn to coat well. Cover and refrigerate for at least 1 hour or up to overnight.

Prepare a charcoal or gas grill for direct-heat cooking over medium-high heat. ⤳

Remove the steak from the marinade, letting the excess drip back into the pan; discard the marinade. Pat the steak dry with paper towels and season generously with salt and pepper. Grill the steak directly over medium-high heat, turning once and brushing with some of the remaining marinade, until cooked to your liking. Transfer to a carving board, tent with foil, and let rest for 5 minutes.

Assemble the salad in individual bowls by dividing equal portions of the lettuces, carrot, cucumber, red onion, herbs, and noodles among them. Pour 1 Tbsp of the marinade over each bowl.

Slice the steak across the grain into thin strips and place on top of the noodles and salad greens. Garnish with the herb leaves and serve, passing the remaining marinade at the table.

8

The variety of potato salads found across Greece proves the popularity of the dish. In this version, the potatoes soak up a red wine vinaigrette, and are served warm. The addition of capers, coriander, parsley, and lemon zest gives the salad a pleasantly citrusy, salty flavor.

GREEK POTATO SALAD

serves 4–6

1½ lb (750 g) small red potatoes

2 Tbsp red wine vinegar

1 tsp ground coriander

2 Tbsp extra-virgin olive oil

Salt and freshly ground pepper

1 Tbsp capers, preferably salt-packed, rinsed

¼ cup (⅓ oz/10 g) coarsely chopped fresh flat-leaf parsley

1 tsp grated lemon zest

Put the potatoes in a large saucepan with cold water to cover by 2 inches (5 cm) and bring to a boil over medium-high heat. Reduce the heat to medium and cook until tender when pierced with the tip of a knife, 20–25 minutes. Drain the potatoes, let cool until they can be handled, and cut in half. Transfer to a serving bowl, and set aside.

In a small bowl, whisk together the vinegar and coriander. Add the oil in a thin stream, whisking constantly until smooth. Season to taste with salt and pepper. Pour the dressing over the warm potatoes. Scatter the capers, parsley, and lemon zest over the top. Using a fork, toss until the potatoes are evenly coated with the dressing. Set aside for 20 minutes to let the flavors blend, then serve.

TROUT & GREEN PEAR SALAD

serves 4

2 Tbsp sliced almonds

4 skinless steelhead trout or salmon fillets, each about ⅓ lb (155 g) and 1 inch (2.5 cm) thick

Olive oil

Salt and freshly ground pepper

2 Tbsp minced fresh chervil or flat-leaf parsley

2 just-ripe crisp green pears, halved, cored, and cut into thin wedges

2 Tbsp fresh lime juice

1 Tbsp fresh lemon juice

1 bunch watercress, tough stems removed

Fresh pink trout fillets and crisp autumn pears make a good match of delicate flavors. Sprinkle with a mild herb such as chervil, valued for its subtle anise flavor. A member of the classic French fines herbes combination, chervil is far less well known than its sister herbs parsley, tarragon, and chives.

In a dry frying pan, toast the almonds over medium-low heat, stirring, until fragrant, 2–3 minutes. Pour onto a plate to cool.

Prepare a charcoal or gas grill for direct-heat cooking over medium-high heat. Brush the fish with a little oil, season with salt and pepper, and sprinkle with the chervil.

Combine the pears with the lime and lemon juices in a mixing bowl and toss to coat. Set aside. Arrange the fish in a single layer in an oiled grill basket or on oiled heavy-duty foil. Place the basket on or slide the foil onto the grill. Cover the grill and cook, turning once, until the flesh just flakes when prodded with a fork and is barely opaque in the center, about 3 minutes per side. Transfer to a plate, tent with foil, and let rest for 5 minutes.

Add the watercress to the pears and toss gently to combine. Break the trout into bite-sized pieces and toss into the salad. Add the almonds, season to taste with salt and pepper, and toss again gently. Divide among individual plates and serve.

WARM WILD MUSHROOM SALAD WITH BACON VINAIGRETTE

serves 4

1 lb (500 g) mixed wild and cultivated mushrooms

1 Tbsp unsalted butter

3 shallots, minced

2 slices applewood-smoked bacon, cut crosswise into ¼-inch (6-mm) pieces

2 Tbsp extra-virgin olive oil

2 Tbsp sherry vinegar

1 Tbsp whole-grain mustard

Salt and freshly ground pepper

1 head radicchio, cored and separated into leaves

1 cup (1 oz/30 g) arugula leaves, stemmed (optional)

Fry bacon until crisp and brown, and then warm sherry vinegar in the same pan to form a salty-smoky vinaigrette for autumn mushrooms. Bitter radicchio and peppery arugula are layered with the warm mushroom mixture for extra flavor, color, and crunch.

Remove any tough stems from the mushrooms. Trim the bases of the remaining stems. If desired, thickly slice the mushrooms.

In a large frying pan, melt the butter over medium heat. Add about two-thirds of the shallots and sauté until translucent, about 5 minutes. Add the mushrooms and sauté until they are tender and the moisture they release evaporates, 6–8 minutes.

Meanwhile, in another large frying pan over medium-high heat, cook the bacon, stirring occasionally, until browned and crisp, about 6 minutes. Remove from the heat and stir in the remaining shallots, the oil, vinegar, and mustard. Keep warm.

Transfer the mushrooms to a large bowl, add the bacon mixture, and toss to mix. Season to taste with salt and pepper. Add the radicchio and arugula, if using, and toss to coat the leaves well with the dressing. Serve warm.

11

Tahini, or sesame paste, perhaps best known as an ingredient in traditional hummus, is frequently used in Middle Eastern dressings and sauces. Here, its rich sesame flavor and thick, creamy texture is a natural partner with sesame oil for dressing the kale. Chickpeas, which form the base of hummus and are commonly used in Middle Eastern, Indian, and Latin American kitchens, are treated to a sprinkle of mixed spices before roasting.

SHREDDED KALE SALAD WITH TAHINI DRESSING & CRISPY CHICKPEAS

serves 4

FOR THE CRISPY CHICKPEAS

2 cups (12 oz/375 g) drained home-cooked or canned chickpeas (rinsed if canned)

2 tsp extra-virgin olive oil

½ tsp cumin seeds

½ tsp coriander seeds

¼–½ tsp chili powder

Salt and freshly ground pepper

10–12 large leaves cavolo nero or other kale

1 Tbsp fresh lemon juice

Salt

2 tsp tahini paste

2 tsp toasted sesame oil

To make the crispy chickpeas, preheat the oven to 425°F (220°C).

Place the chickpeas between 2 layers of paper towels and pat dry. Some of the skins may come off. You can discard or keep them in; they roast up nicely, too.

In a bowl, combine the chickpeas, oil, cumin seeds, coriander seeds, and chili powder and stir to coat well. Spread in a single layer on a baking sheet. Roast until the chickpeas are becoming golden brown in spots and some begin to split, 20–30 minutes. Taste a chickpea. If you want them crisper, roast for 5–10 minutes longer, but be careful not to burn them. Transfer the chickpeas to a bowl, season with salt and pepper, and toss gently.

Remove the thick stems from the kale leaves. Stack the leaves, several at a time, and roll into a cylinder, then cut crosswise into very thin strips. Transfer to a separate bowl and add the lemon juice and 1 tsp salt. Using your fingers, massage the leaves to soften them, about 5 minutes.

In a small bowl, combine the tahini and sesame oil. Using a fork, mix until the dressing is well blended. Pour over the kale and toss well to coat the leaves. Taste and adjust the seasonings. Spread the kale on a serving platter, scatter the chickpeas on top, and serve.

12

Hearts of romaine, the small, paler yellow leaves in the center of the large heads, are crunchy and tender, with a distinctive flavor that stands up well to assertive ingredients such as blue cheese and garlic croutons. Escarole and frisée, lightly bitter members of the chicory family, can be substituted for the romaine.

HEARTS OF ROMAINE WITH GARLIC CROUTONS

serves 4

FOR THE GARLIC CROUTONS

8 slices baguette, about ½ inch (12 mm) thick, crusts trimmed

2 Tbsp extra-virgin olive oil

3 cloves garlic

¼ cup (2 fl oz/60 ml) extra-virgin olive oil

2 oz (60 g) blue cheese, crumbled

1½ Tbsp red wine vinegar

2 large hearts of romaine lettuce

¼ cup (⅓ oz/10 g) minced fresh flat-leaf parsley

To make the croutons, preheat the oven to 350°F (180°C). Arrange the baguette slices on a baking sheet and brush lightly on both sides with the 2 Tbsp oil. Bake, turning once, until golden, 6–8 minutes total. Remove from the oven and rub on both sides with the garlic. Break each slice into several pieces, making rough croutons. Set aside.

In a bowl, combine the ¼ cup oil and the blue cheese. Using a fork, mash the blue cheese into the oil to make a creamy dressing. Stir in the vinegar.

Cut each romaine heart lengthwise into quarters. Place on a platter or on individual plates. Drizzle generously with the dressing, sprinkle with the parsley, and top with the garlic croutons. Serve.

13

ROASTED PEPPER SALAD WITH GARLIC BREAD

serves 6

4 large red bell peppers

4 large yellow bell peppers

1 Tbsp red wine vinegar

1 Tbsp balsamic vinegar

5 Tbsp (2½ fl oz/75 ml) extra-virgin olive oil

Salt and freshly ground pepper

½ cup (3 oz/90 g) caperberries

⅓ cup (2 oz/60 g) well-drained Kalamata or niçoise olives

½ cup (½ oz/15 g) loosely packed fresh basil leaves

6 slices country-style bread

2 cloves garlic, halved

Caperberries are larger than regular capers—about the size of an olive or a small cherry—and add explosive flavor to this warm salad of sweet roasted peppers. Look for caperberries in Italian delicatessens and specialty foods stores. If unavailable, substitute ¼ cup (2 oz/60 g) regular capers, rinsed and well drained.

Preheat the broiler. Place the peppers on a baking sheet and slide under the broiler about 4–6 inches (10–15 cm) from the heat source. Broil, turning often, until the skins are blackened on all sides, 10–15 minutes. Transfer to a bowl, cover, and let steam until cool, about 10 minutes. Peel and cut the peppers in half lengthwise, remove the seeds and membranes, and cut the peppers lengthwise into strips 1 inch (2.5 cm) wide.

In a small bowl, whisk together the vinegars. Add the oil in a thin stream, whisking constantly until a smooth dressing forms. Season to taste with salt and pepper and set aside.

In a bowl, combine the bell pepper strips, ¼ cup (2 fl oz/60 ml) of the dressing (or as needed), and salt and pepper to taste and toss well. Arrange the bell pepper strips on a serving platter or individual plates and scatter the caperberries, olives, and basil over the top.

Toast the bread until lightly golden on both sides. Lightly rub the garlic halves over one side of each bread slice.

Tuck the garlic bread slices alongside the salad and serve.

14

HARVEST SALAD WITH BLUE CHEESE & ROASTED PEARS

serves 4

2 firm but ripe Bosc pears, halved and cored

½ cup (4 fl oz/125 ml) extra-virgin olive oil, plus 1 tsp

Salt and freshly ground pepper

1 shallot, minced

1 tsp chopped fresh tarragon

¼ cup (2 fl oz/60 ml) champagne vinegar

2 heads assorted lettuce such as Little Gem or red leaf, larger leaves torn and smaller leaves left whole

1 small bunch rainbow carrots, shaved

½ cup (1 oz/30 g) toasted pumpkin seeds (pepitas)

½ cup (2½ oz/75 g) crumbled blue cheese

Roasting pears concentrates their flavor and brings out their sweetness. Here, they are paired with salty blue cheese and tart champagne vinegar to create a bold-tasting salad that highlights the fall fruit. If you're lucky enough to have a vegetable garden, feel free to use whatever baby greens are ready to be picked in place of the lettuce.

Preheat the oven to 375°F (190°C).

Brush the pear halves with the 1 tsp oil and season with salt. Place the pears, cut side down, in a baking pan and roast for 5 minutes. Remove from the oven and, using tongs, gently turn the pears over. Continue roasting until the pears are tender and slightly browned, 3–5 minutes longer. Let cool.

In a small bowl, whisk together the shallot, tarragon, and vinegar. Add the ½ cup (4 fl oz/125 ml) oil in a thin stream, whisking constantly until the vinaigrette is well blended. Season with salt and pepper.

In a large bowl, combine the lettuce and carrots. Drizzle with the vinaigrette to taste and toss to coat well. Place a pear half, cut side up, on each individual plate and divide the lettuce mixture among the plates. Sprinkle the salads with the pumpkin seeds and cheese. Season with salt and pepper and serve.

OCTOBER

16

15

FARRO SALAD WITH ARTICHOKE HEARTS

serves 4–6

1¼ cups (7½ oz/235 g) farro

½ cup (3 oz/90 g) pine nuts

¼ cup (2 oz/60 g) oil-packed sun-dried tomatoes

1 package (14 oz/440 g) frozen artichoke hearts, thawed and brought to room temperature

6 Tbsp (3 fl oz/90 ml) red wine vinegar

3 Tbsp extra-virgin olive oil

½ cup (2½ oz/75 g) finely chopped red onion, rinsed

½ cup (¾ oz/20 g) chopped fresh flat-leaf parsley leaves

Salt and freshly ground pepper

Artichokes thrive in the cool spring, but they have a second, smaller harvest in fall. Their nutty flavor makes them a delicious addition to hearty grain salads. If you can still find good-looking specimens in the market, use fresh hearts in this salad. Quarter the hearts and simmer in salted water until tender, about 8 minutes.

Rinse the farro and put it in a saucepan with 2½ cups (20 fl oz/625 ml) water; bring to a boil. Reduce the heat, cover, and simmer until the grains are tender and the water is absorbed, about 25 minutes.

In a small frying pan, toast the pine nuts over medium-low heat, stirring, until fragrant and starting to brown, 3–4 minutes. Pour onto a plate to cool.

Cut the tomatoes into thin strips, reserving the oil to use in place of some of the olive oil, if you like. Quarter the artichoke hearts.

In a large bowl, whisk together the vinegar and olive oil. Add the cooked farro, sun-dried tomatoes, artichoke hearts, onion, parsley, and toasted pine nuts and mix well. Season generously with salt and pepper and serve.

16

ROASTED BEET & CURLY ENDIVE SALAD WITH BALSAMIC VINAIGRETTE

serves 4

6 small beets, trimmed

¾ cup (3 oz/90 g) coarsely chopped pecans

FOR THE BALSAMIC VINAIGRETTE

¼ cup (2 fl oz/60 ml) balsamic vinegar

Salt and freshly ground pepper

2 Tbsp extra-virgin olive oil

4 cups (4 oz/125 g) torn curly endive leaves, pale inner leaves only

1 cup (1 oz/30 g) arugula leaves

¼ cup (1 oz/30 g) grated orange zest

As the frost sets in, sturdy root vegetables grow even sweeter. Golden beets, or a mixture of golden and red beets, make an especially attractive presentation in this autumnal salad, combined with pleasantly bitter greens and toasted nuts.

Preheat the oven to 350°F (180°C). Wrap the beets in foil, place in a baking pan, and roast, turning occasionally, until tender when pierced with a fork, 40–45 minutes. Remove and let cool until they can be handled, then peel and cut into rounds ¼ inch (6 mm) thick. Place in a bowl, cover to keep warm, and set aside.

In a small frying pan, toast the chopped pecans over medium-low heat, stirring, until fragrant and starting to brown, about 5 minutes. Pour onto a plate to cool, and set aside.

To make the vinaigrette, stir together the vinegar, ¼ tsp salt, and ½ tsp pepper. Add the extra-virgin olive oil in a thin stream, whisking constantly until the dressing is smooth.

Divide the curly endive and arugula among individual plates. Top with the beet rounds and drizzle with the dressing. Garnish with the orange zest and the toasted pecans and serve.

17

A great way to take advantage of leftover roasts, this rice salad has a wide range of textures and flavors, from juicy citrus segments to chewy dried fruit and crunchy nuts. It holds up well, so make it ahead and pack for school and work lunches.

CHICKEN–BROWN RICE SALAD WITH DATES & CASHEWS

serves 4

Salt and freshly ground pepper

2 cups (14 oz/440 g) brown rice

2 skin-on, bone-in chicken breast halves (about 1¼ lb/625 g each)

2 tangerines

3 Tbsp extra-virgin olive oil

2 Tbsp fresh lemon juice

1 tsp red wine vinegar

1 tsp sugar

20 dates, pitted and coarsely chopped

½ cup (3 oz/90 g) chopped cashews

¼ cup (⅓ oz/10 g) torn fresh mint

Preheat the oven to 350°F (180°C).

Combine 4 cups (32 fl oz/1 l) water and 2 tsp salt in a saucepan and bring to a boil over high heat. Add the rice, return to a boil, reduce the heat to low, cover, and simmer until the rice is tender and all the water is absorbed, about 50 minutes. Remove the rice from the heat and let cool to room temperature.

Meanwhile, rub each chicken breast on both sides with ½ tsp salt and ½ tsp pepper. Place in a baking dish and bake until the skin is crisp and the meat is opaque throughout, about 45 minutes. Remove from the oven and let cool, then remove the skin and discard. Pull the meat from the bone and cut it into bite-sized pieces.

Peel and section the tangerines. Cut the sections in half crosswise.

In a serving bowl, combine the rice, oil, lemon juice, vinegar, sugar, 2 tsp salt, and 1 tsp pepper. Stir gently with a wooden spoon. Fold in the chicken, tangerines, most of the chopped dates, half of the chopped cashews, and all but 2 tsp of the mint. Garnish the salad with the remaining dates, cashews, and mint. Serve at room temperature.

18

Mustard, pickles, and pork are a tempting combination in this composed salad. Serve on individual plates for a first course, or arrange the tenderloins on a big platter and serve family style. Sliced baguette and sweet French butter are delicious as accompaniments, and you'll savor any leftovers as sandwiches the next day.

ROASTED PORK TENDERLOIN & CORNICHON SALAD

serves 4–6

2 pork tenderloins, each about ¾ lb (375 g)

Salt and freshly ground pepper

1 Tbsp unsalted butter

3 tsp extra-virgin olive oil

1 head butter lettuce

2 cups (2 oz/60 g) baby arugula leaves

1–2 tsp white wine vinegar

8–12 cornichons

Dijon mustard for serving

Preheat the oven to 400°F (200°C).

Sprinkle the tenderloins with 1 tsp each salt and pepper. In an ovenproof frying pan just large enough to hold the tenderloins, melt the butter with 2 tsp of the olive oil over medium-high heat. When the butter foams, add the tenderloins and sear, turning once, until browned, about 6 minutes total. Transfer the pan to the oven and roast until an instant-read thermometer inserted into the center of a tenderloin registers 150°F (65°C), 12–15 minutes. Transfer the tenderloins to a platter and let rest for 15 minutes.

Separate the head of butter lettuce into leaves; reserve the larger outer leaves for another use. Pat the greens dry. Arrange the smaller, pale yellow inner leaves and the arugula leaves on a platter. Drizzle with the remaining 1 tsp olive oil and vinegar to taste.

Cut the tenderloins into slices ½ inch (12 mm) thick. Arrange the sliced pork and cornichons on top of the greens. Serve, accompanied with Dijon mustard.

19

Try out new flavor combinations with cured meat, tender winter squash, and a zesty Latin dressing. The salsa verde can be made up to 4 hours ahead of time; cover and refrigerate it to preserve the color. You can roast the squash up to 1 hour ahead, tossing with the salsa verde just before serving.

ARUGULA, BUTTERNUT SQUASH & SALAMI SALAD

serves 4

2 Tbsp pine nuts

FOR THE SALSA VERDE

1 clove garlic, sliced

¾ cup (¾ oz/20 g) firmly packed fresh flat-leaf parsley leaves

¼ cup (⅓ oz/10 g) firmly packed fresh mint leaves

2 tsp capers, rinsed

1 tsp Dijon mustard

1 tsp red wine vinegar

¼ cup (2 fl oz/60 ml) extra-virgin olive oil

1 lb (500 g) butternut squash, halved, seeded, peeled, and cut into cubes

2 Tbsp extra-virgin olive oil

Salt and freshly ground pepper

½ lb (250 g) arugula leaves, stemmed

¼ lb (125 g) salami, cut into thin strips

2 tsp red wine vinegar

In a small frying pan, toast the pine nuts over medium-low heat, stirring, until fragrant and starting to brown, 2–3 minutes. Pour onto a plate to cool.

To make the salsa verde, in a blender, combine the garlic, parsley, mint, capers, mustard, the 1 tsp vinegar, and the ¼ cup oil. Purée until the salsa is smooth.

Preheat the oven to 500°F (260°C). On a rimmed baking sheet, toss the squash with 1 Tbsp of the oil, season generously with salt and pepper, and spread in an even layer. Roast, shaking the pan vigorously every 5 minutes, until the squash is tender, about 15 minutes. Let cool in the pan for 5 minutes. Add the salsa verde and toss gently to coat evenly.

In a large bowl, combine the arugula, salami, remaining 1 Tbsp oil, ¼ tsp salt, and a pinch of pepper. Toss to combine, add the 2 tsp vinegar, and toss again. Arrange on plates and top with the squash. Sprinkle with the pine nuts and serve.

20

If you're a garlic afficionado, this flavorful pasta salad is for you. After simmering for almost half an hour, the garlic loses its brash edge and develops a sweet, nutty taste that perfectly complements chicken and pasta.

GARLICKY PENNE & CHICKEN SALAD

serves 6

Salt and freshly ground pepper

¾ lb (375 g) penne or other tube-shaped pasta

7 Tbsp (3½ fl oz/105 ml) extra-virgin olive oil

1 lb (500 g) skinless, boneless chicken breasts (about 2 large half breasts)

24 cloves garlic, peeled

2½ cups (20 fl oz/625 ml) chicken broth

3 Tbsp red wine vinegar

2 tsp minced fresh rosemary

2 tsp minced fresh flat-leaf parsley

Bring a large pot three-fourths full of salted water to a boil. Add the penne and cook until al dente, according to package directions. Drain and toss it immediately with 1 Tbsp of the olive oil. Cover and let cool completely in the refrigerator, 1–24 hours.

In a frying pan over medium heat, warm 1 Tbsp of the olive oil. Add the chicken and cook until golden on one side, about 4 minutes. Turn the chicken, season with salt and pepper to taste, and cook for 3–4 minutes on the second side, or until opaque throughout. Transfer the chicken to a work surface, reserving the frying pan, and cut on the diagonal into thin strips. Let cool.

Place the frying pan back over medium heat, add the garlic, and cook, uncovered, stirring occasionally, until golden brown, 3–4 minutes. Add the chicken broth and continue to cook until the broth has reduced to 2 Tbsp and the garlic is soft, 20–25 minutes. Using a slotted spoon, remove the garlic from the pan and let cool, reserving the reduced cooking liquid.

In a large bowl, whisk together the remaining 5 Tbsp (2½ fl oz/75 ml) olive oil, the reduced cooking liquid, the vinegar, rosemary, and chopped parsley. Add the penne, chicken, and garlic cloves. Toss to mix well and serve at room temperature.

21

Old-fashioned coleslaw is updated here with generous additions of celery, radishes, shrimp, and smoked paprika. A sprinkle of crispy bacon pieces and crumbled blue cheese gives it even more impact. We often think of slaws as side dishes, but this is one that deserves to take center place.

CELERY SLAW WITH SHRIMP & CREAMY CIDER VINAIGRETTE

serves 8

FOR THE CREAMY CIDER VINAIGRETTE

½ cup (4 fl oz/125 ml) mayonnaise

¼ cup (2 oz/60 g) sour cream, or
¼ cup (2 fl oz/60 ml) buttermilk

¼ cup (2 fl oz/60 ml) olive oil

¼ cup (2 fl oz/60 ml) unfiltered cider vinegar

1 tsp dry mustard

1 clove garlic, chopped

2 lb (1 kg) shrimp, peeled and deveined

3 Tbsp extra-virgin olive oil

1 tsp mild Spanish smoked paprika

Salt and freshly ground pepper

¼ lb (125 g) applewood-smoked bacon

½ head green cabbage, cored
and thinly sliced crosswise

5 celery ribs, thinly sliced

6 green onions, including tender
green tops, chopped

1 bunch red radishes, trimmed
and thinly sliced

½ cup (¾ oz/20 g) chopped fresh
flat-leaf parsley

2 oz (60 g) blue cheese, crumbled (optional)

To make the vinaigrette, combine the mayonnaise, sour cream, oil, vinegar, mustard, and garlic in a food processor or blender and process until smooth. Set aside.

In a large bowl, toss together the shrimp, 3 Tbsp olive oil, paprika, and a little salt and pepper. Preheat a large nonstick frying pan over medium-high heat. Add half of the shrimp and sauté until they turn pink and are opaque throughout, about 3 minutes. Transfer to a large bowl and repeat with the remaining shrimp. Set aside to cool.

Rinse and wipe dry the frying pan and return to medium heat. Add the bacon and fry, turning as needed, until crisp, about 6 minutes. Transfer to paper towels to drain. Let cool, then crumble and set aside.

Add the cabbage, celery, green onions, radishes, parsley, and vinaigrette to the shrimp and toss. Season to taste with salt and pepper and toss again. Sprinkle the crumbled bacon and the cheese, if using, over the top, and serve.

22

Chinese black mushrooms, also known as shiitake mushrooms, perfectly balance the lighter components of this salad, all of which serve as a platform for the plump, pink grilled shrimp. English peas, either fresh or frozen, can be added, as well.

JASMINE RICE SALAD WITH GRILLED SHRIMP, MUSHROOMS & SNOW PEAS

serves 6

FOR THE DRESSING

¼ cup (2 fl oz/60 ml) *each* grapeseed oil
and sherry vinegar

3 tsp light soy sauce

2 tsp toasted sesame oil

1-inch (2.5-cm) piece fresh ginger,
peeled and grated

1 tsp honey

1½ cups (10½ oz/300 g) jasmine rice

Salt and freshly ground pepper

1 lb (500 g) snow peas, trimmed and sliced

3 carrots, peeled and shredded or julienned

5 green onions, finely chopped

12 large fresh Chinese black mushrooms
(shiitake), stems removed

24 large shrimp, peeled and deveined

1½ Tbsp grapeseed oil

To make the dressing, in a blender, combine the grapeseed oil, vinegar, soy sauce, sesame oil, ginger, and honey and process until smooth, about 1 minute. Set aside.

In a saucepan, bring 3 cups (24 fl oz/700 ml) water to a boil over medium-high heat. Add the rice and 1 tsp salt. Reduce the heat to low, cover, and simmer until the rice is tender and all of the water has been absorbed, about 20 minutes. Remove from the heat and let cool.

Transfer the rice to a bowl. Add the snow peas, carrots, and green onions. Drizzle with half of the dressing and stir to coat. Set aside.

Prepare a charcoal or gas grill for direct-heat cooking over medium-high heat. In a bowl, mix the mushrooms, shrimp, grapeseed oil, 1 tsp salt, and ½ tsp pepper. Place the mushrooms, cap side down, on the grill rack Cook, turning often, until soft and golden, about 6 minutes. Place the shrimp on the grill rack and cook, turning once or twice, until opaque throughout, 4–5 minutes. Set aside.

Chop the mushrooms and mix them into the rice. Spread the rice mixture on a platter. Drizzle with more dressing. Top with the shrimp and serve with the remaining dressing on the side.

23

Meaty tuna steaks with a cracked peppercorn crust add dimension to this salad. Bitter arugula, crunchy fennel, sweet caramelized onions, and an assertively flavored vinaigrette add to the contrasting tastes and textures.

ARUGULA & FENNEL SALAD WITH BLACK PEPPER–CRUSTED TUNA

serves 6

¼ cup (2 fl oz/60 ml) balsamic vinegar

1 large shallot, minced

2 tsp Dijon mustard

½ tsp sugar

Salt

10 Tbsp (5 fl oz/160 ml) extra-virgin olive oil

2 small sweet onions such as Vidalia, thinly sliced

2 Tbsp black peppercorns

6 tuna steaks (2 lb/1 kg total weight), each about 1 inch (2.5 cm) thick

8 cups (8 oz/250 g) arugula leaves, stemmed

1 large fennel bulb, trimmed and thinly sliced

In a small bowl, whisk together the vinegar, shallot, mustard, sugar, and ¼ tsp salt until the sugar dissolves. Add 7 Tbsp (3½ fl oz/ 105 ml) of the olive oil in a thin stream, whisking constantly until the vinaigrette is smooth and thick. Taste and adjust the seasonings and set aside.

In a large nonstick frying pan over medium heat, warm 2 Tbsp of the olive oil. Add the sliced onions and 1 tsp salt and sauté until the onions are softened and browned, 10–12 minutes. Transfer to a plate and set aside. Wipe the pan clean.

Place the peppercorns in a resealable plastic bag and seal. Using a mallet or the bottom of a small, heavy pan, coarsely crack the peppercorns. Season each tuna steak on both sides with a little salt. Then, dividing them evenly, press the cracked peppercorns into one side of each tuna steak.

Return the frying pan to medium-high heat and add the remaining 1 Tbsp olive oil. When the oil is hot but not smoking, add the tuna steaks, peppered side down. Sear, turning once, until lightly golden on the outside and still dark pink and rare in the center, about 2 minutes per side, or until cooked to your liking. Transfer to a platter, tent with foil, and let rest for 5 minutes. ⟫

In a large bowl, toss together the arugula, fennel, and ¼ tsp salt. Whisk the vinaigrette to recombine, then drizzle about half of it over the arugula mixture and toss well. Taste and adjust the seasonings. Divide the dressed arugula mixture among individual plates. Spoon the sautéed onions over the top. Thinly slice each tuna steak and arrange on top of the onions. Drizzle each salad with some of the remaining vinaigrette and serve.

24

Crispy bacon-wrapped figs are delightful party fare, especially when paired with a decadent Stilton. The figs should be browned just before serving, but you can wrap them with the bacon several hours in advance. Loosely cover them with plastic and refrigerate, letting them return to room temperature before proceeding.

MIXED GREENS WITH BACON-WRAPPED FIGS

serves 8

16 large, plump figs, preferably Black Mission, fresh or dried

8 strips thin-cut smoked bacon, halved crosswise

1 lb plus 2 oz (560 g) mixed baby salad greens

⅓ cup (3 fl oz/80 ml) extra-virgin olive oil

Salt and freshly ground pepper

3½ Tbsp sherry vinegar

8 oz (250 g) Stilton or other blue cheese, crumbled

Wrap each fig in a half-strip of bacon, overlapping it as needed and securing it with a toothpick.

Heat a large nonstick frying pan over medium heat. Add the figs and cook, turning occasionally, until the bacon is browned and crisp on most sides. Remove the toothpicks and turn the figs to finish browning the bacon on all sides. Transfer to a plate and keep warm.

In a very large bowl, toss the greens with the oil. Add ½ tsp salt and toss again. Add the vinegar and toss. Add the cheese, season generously with pepper, and toss again.

Divide the salad among serving plates. Place 2 figs on each plate. Season the figs with pepper and serve.

GRILLED LITTLE GEMS WITH GORGONZOLA & MARCONA ALMONDS

serves 4

¼ cup (3 oz/90 g) honey

1 tsp red pepper flakes

4 heads Little Gem lettuce or 2 hearts of romaine lettuce

1–2 Tbsp extra-virgin olive oil

½ lb (250 g) Gorgonzola dolcelatte cheese, crumbled

¼ cup Marcona almonds

Grilling lettuce, like these Little Gems, brings out its natural sweetness, which here is enhanced by the cheese and honey. Served warm right off the grill, this simple composed salad makes an elegant presentation. The spicy honey is easily whipped up a day in advance, and you can make it in any amount you like, to ensure you have some on hand to use with a cheese plate or other dish.

In a small bowl, stir together the honey and red pepper flakes. Cover and let stand at room temperature for 24 hours.

Halve the Little Gems lengthwise. If using romaine hearts, quarter them lengthwise. Brush the lettuce with the oil. Set aside.

Prepare a charcoal or gas grill for direct-heat cooking over medium-high heat. Alternatively, preheat a stove-top grill pan over medium-high heat. Place the lettuce, cut side down, on the grill rack or in the pan. Cook until lightly charred, about 2 minutes. Turn and grill the other side until lightly charred, about 1 minute.

Transfer 2 Little Gem halves or 2 romaine quarters to each individual plate. Drizzle with the spicy honey and sprinkle with the cheese. Scatter the almonds over the salads and serve right away.

LENTIL, BACON & FRISÉE SALAD

serves 4

FOR THE MUSTARD VINAIGRETTE

2 cloves garlic, sliced

1 shallot, sliced

¼ cup (2 fl oz/60 ml) sherry vinegar

1 Tbsp Dijon mustard

¾ cup (6 fl oz/180 ml) extra-virgin olive oil

Salt and freshly ground pepper

4 slices thick-cut bacon, chopped

2 shallots, minced

1 celery rib, finely chopped

1 carrot, peeled and finely chopped

2 cups (14 oz/440 g) green French (de Puy) lentils

2 cups (16 fl oz/500 ml) chicken broth

1 head frisée, tough stems removed

This classic French preparation of earthy green lentils, curling leaves, and savory bacon relies on a quintessential mustard vinaigrette. Make a big batch of this versatile dressing and use it to drizzle over sliced tomatoes, avocado, or your favorite baby greens. Store the vinaigrette in an airtight container in the refrigerator for up to 1 week.

To make the vinaigrette, in a blender, combine the garlic, sliced shallot, vinegar, mustard, oil, ¾ tsp salt, and ¼ tsp pepper. Process until smooth. Set aside.

In a large, heavy saucepan over low heat, cook the bacon, stirring occasionally, until crisp, about 8 minutes. Using a slotted spoon, transfer to paper towels to drain.

Return the saucepan to low heat, add the minced shallots to the bacon fat, and cook, stirring occasionally, until softened, about 4 minutes. Add the celery and carrot and cook, stirring occasionally, until wilted, 3–4 minutes. Add the lentils, broth, and enough water to just cover the lentils. Bring to a boil, reduce the heat to low, cover, and simmer gently until just tender but not yet mushy, about 20 minutes. Add a little more water if the lentils become too dry. Remove from the heat and let stand, covered, for 5 minutes. Immediately add half of the vinaigrette and toss to combine.

Scatter the frisée on plates and spoon the lentils over the top. Drizzle a little more vinaigrette over the salads. (You will have more vinaigrette than you will need for the lentil salad; store the remainder in the refrigerator for up to 1 week, and whisk to recombine before using.) Sprinkle with the bacon and serve.

27

PORK CHOPS WITH GRILLED RADICCHIO SALAD

serves 4

Olive oil for brushing

4 bone-in pork chops
(about 1 inch/2.5 cm thick)

Salt and freshly ground pepper

2 heads radicchio

¼ cup (2 fl oz/60 ml) walnut oil

1 Tbsp honey

3 Tbsp fresh lemon juice

3 oz (90 g) fresh goat cheese, crumbled

½ cup (2 oz/60 g) chopped toasted walnuts

Grilling radicchio tempers its peppery flavor, and a sweet, nutty vinaigrette further tames its bite in this warm salad served alongside a simple grilled pork chop. Using bone-in chops will give you juicier, more flavorful results. You must still be careful not to overcook them, as lean pork can easily dry out.

Prepare a charcoal or gas grill for direct-heat cooking over medium heat. Alternatively, preheat a stove-top grill pan over medium heat. Lightly brush the grill rack or pan with olive oil.

Season the pork chops with salt and pepper. Place on the grill rack or in the grill pan and cook, turning once, until the chops are golden brown and an instant-read thermometer inserted into the center of the meat registers 150°F (65°C), about 15 minutes. Transfer to a cutting board, cover loosely with aluminum foil, and let rest while you finish the salad.

Meanwhile, quarter the radicchio heads lengthwise, leaving the core intact. Brush the cut sides generously with olive oil and season with salt and pepper. Set aside.

In a small bowl, whisk together the walnut oil, honey, lemon juice, and ¼ tsp pepper until the vinaigrette is well blended. Set aside.

Place the radicchio, cut side down, on the grill rack or in the pan. Cook, turning frequently, until browned and tender when pierced at the core with a knife, about 5 minutes.

Transfer the radicchio to a cutting board and chop into bite-sized pieces. In a large bowl, combine the radicchio, goat cheese, and walnuts. Drizzle with the vinaigrette and toss to coat. Taste and adjust the seasonings.

Divide the pork chops among individual plates and serve the warm salad alongside.

28

APPLE-FENNEL SLAW

serves 4

¼ cup (2 fl oz/60 ml) fresh lime juice

¼ cup (2 oz/60 g) sour cream

¼ cup (2 fl oz/60 ml) mayonnaise

½ tsp paprika

¼ tsp sugar

Salt

¾ cup (1 oz/30 g) fresh cilantro leaves, minced

2 large fennel bulbs, trimmed, quartered, and thinly sliced

2 small tart red or green apples, peeled, cored, and thinly sliced

This is a pretty and modern slaw, full of refreshing sweet-tart flavors. If you prefer a light vinaigrette to a creamy dressing, omit the sour cream and mayonnaise and whisk about ½ cup (4 fl oz/125 ml) olive oil into the lime juice mixture.

In a large bowl, whisk together the lime juice, sour cream, mayonnaise, paprika, sugar, ½ tsp salt, and the cilantro. Add the fennel and apples and toss to mix well. Cover and refrigerate for 1 hour to allow the flavors to blend before serving.

29

CUCUMBER SALAD WITH POMEGRANATE, FETA & MINT

serves 4

2 Tbsp olive oil

¼ cup (2 fl oz/60 ml) fresh lemon juice

2 English cucumbers

1 cup (4 oz/125 g) pomegranate seeds

⅓ cup (⅓ oz/10 g) coarsely torn fresh mint leaves

Salt and freshly ground pepper

1 cup (5 oz/155 g) crumbled feta cheese

Whole pomegranate fruits usually appear in late November, but you may be able to find seeds in the refrigerator case of the produce department. Tart and textured, they give a new direction to this minty cucumber salad.

In a large bowl, add the oil to the lemon juice in a thin stream, whisking constantly until the dressing is smooth.

Slice the cucumbers into rounds ⅛ inch (3 mm) thick. Add the cucumbers, pomegranate seeds, and mint to the bowl with the dressing. Mix gently to coat and season to taste with salt and pepper. Just before serving, gently fold in the cheese and serve.

30

SPICY CRAB SALAD

serves 6

3 cups (18 oz/560 g) cooked crabmeat, picked over for shell fragments

1 or 2 red or green chiles such as Thai or serrano, minced

Finely grated zest of 2 limes

Juice of 1 lime

2 Tbsp coarsely chopped fresh mint

2 Tbsp mayonnaise

Salt and freshly ground pepper

FOR THE LIME DRESSING

6 Tbsp (3 fl oz/90 ml) extra-virgin olive oil

2 Tbsp fresh lime juice

1 small red onion

2 hearts of romaine lettuce, leaves separated and torn into pieces

2 bunches watercress, tough stems removed

3 avocados

This lighter, spicier version of traditional crab salad is dressed in a modest amount of mayonnaise and spiked with fresh lime juice, mint, and chiles. Rather than cook whole crabs, you can purchase freshly cooked lump crabmeat.

Put the crabmeat in a bowl and, using a paper towel, gently pat dry. Add the chiles, lime zest and juice, mint, and mayonnaise to the crabmeat. Stir gently to combine. Season to taste with salt, cover, and refrigerate until serving.

To make the dressing, in a small bowl, add the oil to the lime juice in a thin stream, whisking constantly until the dressing is smooth. Season to taste with salt and pepper.

Slice the onion thinly and soak in hot water for 15 minutes. Reserve one-fourth of the onion to use as a garnish. In a large bowl, combine the remaining onion slices, lettuce, and watercress. Drizzle with the dressing and toss gently to combine.

Halve and pit the avocados. Using a large metal spoon, carefully scoop the flesh of each avocado half from the peel in one piece.

Divide the greens and onion among individual plates. Top each with an avocado half. Spoon some of the crabmeat mixture onto each avocado half. Garnish with the reserved onion slices and serve.

31

TURKEY SALAD WITH TREVISO, APPLE & GRAPES

serves 4

½ cup (2 oz/60 g) finely grated Parmesan cheese

5 Tbsp (3 fl oz/80 ml) extra-virgin olive oil

2 Tbsp red wine vinegar

1 head Treviso or other radicchio, chopped

1 cup (1 oz/30 g) baby arugula

1 Granny Smith apple, cored and cut into ½-inch (12-mm) cubes

½ lb (250 g) large red seedless grapes, halved

½ cup (2 oz/60 g) walnut halves or pieces

1½ lb (750 g) roasted turkey breast, torn into bite-sized pieces

This is an exceptionally colorful salad whose diverse flavors are bound together with an easy-to-make Parmesan dressing. Treviso is the elongated cousin of the more common deep burgundy, sphere-shaped Chioggia radicchio. It is typically lighter colored—almost pink on the inner leaves—and slightly more bitter and is an ideal counterpoint to the sweet grapes and crunchy apples used here.

In a small bowl, whisk together the cheese, oil, and vinegar until the dressing is well blended and creamy.

In a large bowl, combine the radicchio, arugula, apple, grapes, walnuts, and turkey. Drizzle the salad with the dressing and stir gently to coat evenly. Transfer the salad to a platter or serving bowl and serve right away.

Deep autumn promises an abundance of cold-weather vegetables. Shredded kale and Brussels sprouts bring great texture to salads, while roasted beets and squash offer appealing earthy and sweet flavors. Salads can also serve as a vehicle for leftover roasts; try pairing chopped turkey with farro, and roasted chicken with toasted bread. Many of the season's favorite combinations benefit from a last-minute sprinkling of hallmark ingredients, such as pomegranate seeds, dried fruits, and toasted nuts.

1
WARM SPINACH SALAD WITH DELICATA SQUASH & RICOTTA SALATA
page 250

2
ENDIVE SALAD WITH PERSIMMONS & POMEGRANATE
page 250

3
FARRO SALAD WITH TURKEY & ROASTED SQUASH
page 253

8
ROASTED CHICKEN WITH WARM BREAD SALAD
page 255

9
MUSHROOM, RADICCHIO & BULGUR SALAD
page 256

10
KALE SALAD WITH ROASTED FUJI APPLES & POMEGRANATE
page 256

15
MOROCCAN-SPICED CARROT & PARSNIP SALAD
page 261

16
CELERY ROOT RÉMOULADE
page 261

17
SHREDDED KALE SALAD WITH PANCETTA & HARD-COOKED EGG
page 262

22
FRISÉE, ENDIVE & WATERCRESS SALAD WITH ROQUEFORT & PEAR
page 265

23
SPICED APPLE, CRANBERRY & PECAN SALAD
page 267

24
BULGUR WITH PERSIMMONS, PISTACHIOS & POMEGRANATE
page 267

29
CRAB CAKE & BUTTER LETTUCE SALAD
page 270

30
APPLE & CELERY ROOT SALAD WITH STILTON CHEESE
page 270

4

november

1

WARM SPINACH SALAD WITH DELICATA SQUASH & RICOTTA SALATA

serves 4

Delicata squash, which has sweet, pale-orange flesh, is a good source of vitamins A and C, potassium, and iron. When roasted, the pretty scalloped peel of this winter squash becomes tender enough to eat. If you can't find Delicata, use cubes of butternut squash or sweet potato.

1½ lb (750 g) Delicata squash

4 Tbsp (2 fl oz/60 ml) olive oil

Salt and freshly ground pepper

½ cup (2½ oz/75 g) chopped almonds

3 Tbsp sherry or red wine vinegar

8 oz (250 g) baby spinach leaves

4 oz (125 g) ricotta salata or feta cheese, crumbled

Preheat the oven to 400°F (200°C). Rinse and dry the squash. Halve the squash lengthwise and remove the seeds, then cut crosswise into half-moons ½ inch (12 mm) thick. In a 12-by-17-inch (30-by-43-cm) baking pan, toss the squash with 1 Tbsp of the oil, ¼ tsp salt, and a few grindings of pepper. Roast until the squash is tender, about 20 minutes.

In a dry heavy frying pan over medium heat, toast the almonds until browned, about 30 seconds. Transfer to a plate to cool.

In a large bowl, mix the vinegar and ¼ tsp salt. Add the squash, spinach, cheese, and toasted almonds. Heat the remaining 3 Tbsp oil in a small frying pan over medium-high heat. Pour the oil over the salad (carefully, as the oil may spatter), toss to coat and wilt the spinach evenly, and serve.

2

ENDIVE SALAD WITH PERSIMMONS & POMEGRANATE

serves 4

Serve this crisp and refreshing salad when persimmons and pomegranates are in season. Look for the Fuyu variety of persimmons, which are sweet and firm, and easy to cut very thin. Any salty or tangy cheese will do; try using fresh goat cheese or ricotta salata in place of the feta.

¾ cup (3 oz/90 g) pistachios

4 heads red or white Belgian endive

1 large pomegranate

2 Fuyu persimmons

8 oz (250 g) feta cheese, crumbled

Grated zest and juice of 1 lemon

1 tsp champagne vinegar

Salt and freshly ground pepper

½ cup (4 fl oz/125 ml) extra-virgin olive oil

In a small frying pan, toast the pistachios over medium-low heat, stirring, until fragrant and starting to brown, about 5 minutes. Pour onto a plate to cool, then chop coarsely and set aside.

Trim the ends from the endive, separate the leaves, and place in a large bowl. Seed the pomegranate and pat the seeds dry. Using a mandoline or a very sharp knife, slice the persimmons into thin slices.

Add the pomegranate seeds, persimmons, cheese, and pistachios to the endive leaves.

To make the vinaigrette, in a small bowl, whisk together the lemon zest and juice, and vinegar. Season to taste with salt and pepper. Add the oil in a thin stream, whisking constantly until the dressing is smooth.

Drizzle the vinaigrette over the salad and gently toss. Season with additional salt and pepper and serve.

NOVEMBER 3

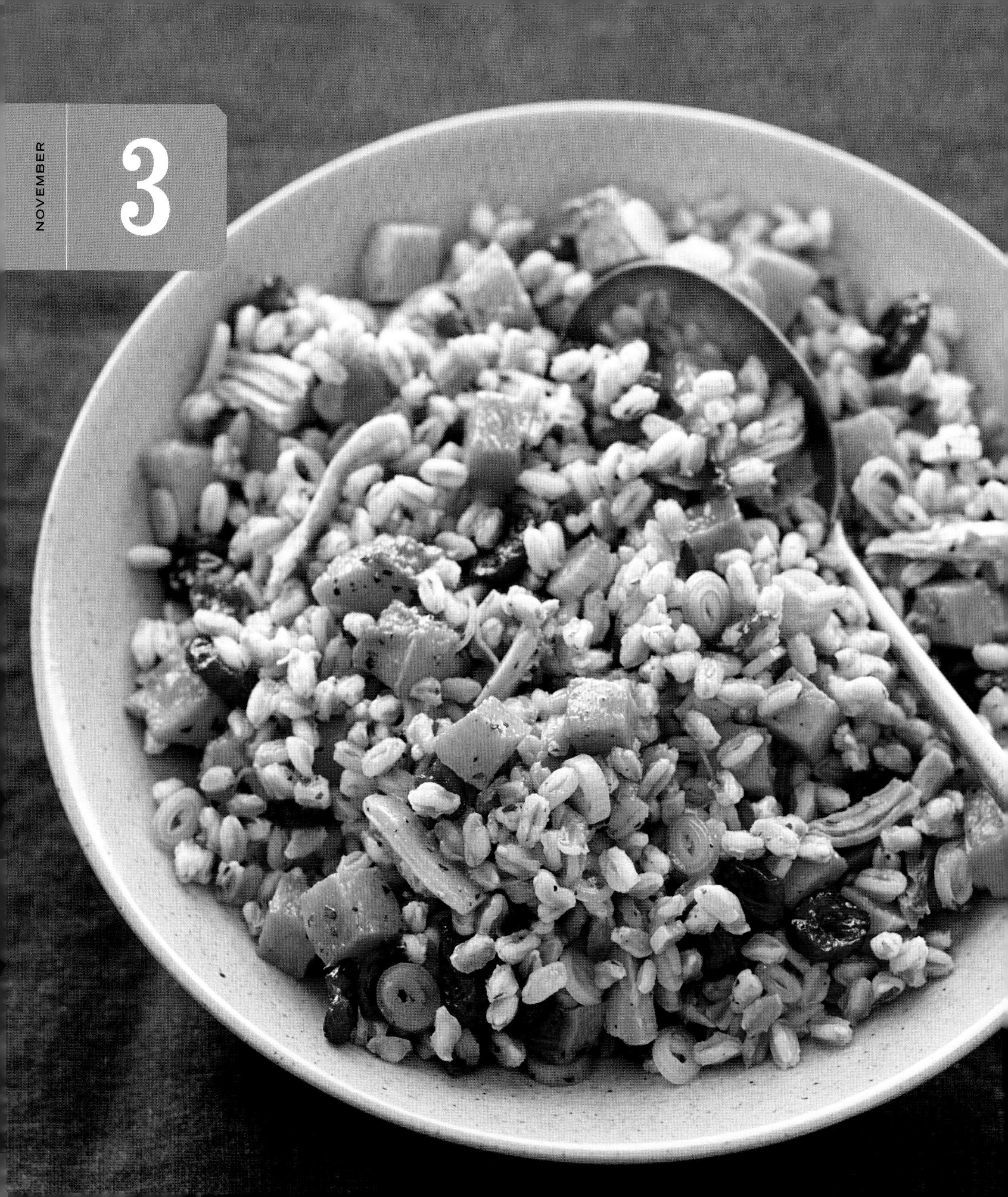

3

FARRO SALAD WITH TURKEY & ROASTED SQUASH

serves 6

1⅓ cups (about 8 oz/250 g) farro

4 cups (32 fl oz/1 l) chicken broth

Salt and freshly ground pepper

1 butternut squash (about 3 lb/1.5 kg), halved, seeded, peeled, and cut into ½-inch (12-mm) cubes

8 Tbsp (4 fl oz/125 ml) extra-virgin olive oil

¼ cup (2 fl oz/60 ml) fresh lemon juice

1 tsp honey

1 Tbsp minced fresh flat-leaf parsley

6 oz (185 g) boneless smoked turkey or chicken, cut into ½-inch (12-mm) cubes

⅔ cup (3 oz/90 g) sweetened dried cranberries

3 green onions, including tender green parts, thinly sliced

In this grain-based salad, sweet-and-sour dried cranberries contrast with smoked turkey and earthy butternut squash. Lemon juice and green onions add freshness, while the nutty taste of farro serves as a neutral flavor backdrop. The result is a dish with an inviting fall spirit and a wonderful layering of tastes and textures.

Put the farro in a saucepan, add the broth and 1 tsp salt, and bring to a boil over high heat. Reduce the heat to medium-low and simmer, uncovered, until the farro is tender and all of the liquid is absorbed, about 30 minutes. Transfer to a large bowl and let cool to room temperature.

Meanwhile, preheat the oven to 400°F (200°C). On a rimmed baking sheet, toss the squash cubes with 2 Tbsp of the oil, 1 tsp salt, and ¼ tsp pepper. Spread the cubes in an even layer on the baking sheet and roast until tender but still slightly firm to the bite, about 12 minutes. Let cool to room temperature.

In a small bowl, whisk together the lemon juice, honey, parsley, ¼ tsp salt, and several grindings of pepper. Add the remaining 6 Tbsp (3 fl oz/90 ml) oil in a thin stream, whisking constantly until the dressing is well blended. Taste and adjust the seasonings.

Add the dressing, squash, turkey, cranberries, and green onions to the cooled farro and toss well. Serve.

4
NOVEMBER

SALT COD SALAD WITH POTATOES & BLACK OLIVES

serves 4

1 lb (500 g) salt cod

1 lb (500 g) Yukon gold or other boiling potatoes

Salt

1 small red onion, halved and thinly sliced crosswise

½ cup (3 oz/90 g) pitted brine-cured black olives, coarsely chopped

¼ cup (2 fl oz/60 ml) extra-virgin olive oil

3 Tbsp fresh lemon juice, plus lemon wedges for serving

1 tsp minced garlic

¼ tsp red pepper flakes, or as needed

¼ cup (⅓ oz/10 g) coarsely chopped fresh flat-leaf parsley leaves

Salt cod is a favorite Mediterranean ingredient. Italians enjoy salt cod in many preparations, including this antipasto salad. Slices of potato and slivers of red onion join the salty, flavorful flakes of fish.

Rinse the salt cod under cool running water, then cut it into 4 pieces. Place in a bowl, add cold water to cover, then cover and refrigerate for 24 hours, changing the water 4 or 5 times.

In a saucepan, combine the potatoes with salted cold water to cover generously and bring to a boil over high heat. Reduce the heat to medium and cook until tender, about 20 minutes. Drain the potatoes, let cool slightly, then peel and slice.

Meanwhile, drain the salt cod. Pour water into a large frying pan to a depth of 2 inches (5 cm) and bring to a boil over high heat. Reduce the heat to low, add the salt cod, and simmer until tender when tested with a fork, 5–7 minutes. Using a slotted spoon, remove the salt cod and blot dry with paper towels.

Remove any bits of skin and bones from the salt cod and arrange the pieces on a serving platter, breaking it up into large chunks. Scatter the potato and onion slices and the olives over the fish.

In a small bowl, whisk together the oil, lemon juice, garlic, and ¼ tsp red pepper flakes, and drizzle the dressing over the salad. Taste and adjust the seasoning with salt and red pepper flakes. Garnish with the parsley, and serve with the lemon wedges.

5

In this updated version of the classic French grated carrot salad, the carrots are shaved lengthwise into long ribbons rather than grated. The toasted pistachios add a welcome crispness. If possible, use a mix of orange, purple, gold, and red carrots for an especially attractive presentation.

CARROT RIBBON SALAD WITH TOASTED PISTACHIOS

serves 4

½ cup (3 oz/90 g) lightly salted pistachios in the shell

4 large carrots (about 1 lb/500 g total weight), peeled

2½ Tbsp extra-virgin olive oil

2 tsp fresh Meyer lemon juice

Salt and freshly ground pepper

Shell the pistachios. In a small frying pan, toast the pistachios over medium-high heat, shaking the pan occasionally, until the nuts are fragrant, 3–4 minutes. Transfer to a cutting board. When the nuts are cool enough to handle, coarsely chop. Set aside.

Using a vegetable peeler and starting at the top, press firmly on a carrot and use a smooth, downward stroke to create a ribbon. Repeat until you can no longer get a ribbon. Reserve the rest of the carrot for another use. Repeat with the remaining carrots. Set aside.

In a large bowl, whisk together the oil, lemon juice, ¼ tsp salt, and ¼ tsp pepper until the vinaigrette is well blended. Taste and adjust the seasonings. Add the carrots and stir to coat well. Sprinkle with the pistachios and serve.

6

Radicchio's brilliant red hues and gentle bitterness are a good foil for sweet pears. Look for Treviso, a variety of radicchio with long, narrow leaves and a mild flavor. Goat cheese and walnuts accompany here, but blue cheese paired with almonds or pistachios could be used in their place.

RADICCHIO SALAD WITH PEARS, WALNUTS & GOAT CHEESE

serves 4

¼ cup (1 oz/30 g) walnuts

2 firm but ripe pears

½ Tbsp fresh lemon juice

1 large head radicchio

½ Tbsp balsamic vinegar, plus more for drizzling

Salt

1½ Tbsp extra-virgin olive oil

3 oz (90 g) soft fresh goat cheese

In a small, dry frying pan, toast the walnuts over medium-low heat, stirring, until fragrant and starting to brown, about 5 minutes. Pour onto a plate and let cool, then chop coarsely.

Halve and core the pears and then cut lengthwise into thin slices. Drizzle with the lemon juice and set aside.

Remove 8 sturdy outer leaves from the radicchio head and set aside. Halve and core the head, then chop it finely.

To make the dressing, in a large bowl, whisk together the ½ Tbsp vinegar and a pinch of salt. Add the oil in a thin stream, whisking constantly to make a smooth dressing. Add the chopped radicchio and toss to coat.

Place the reserved radicchio leaves on individual plates. Spoon the dressed radicchio onto the leaves, partially filling each leaf. Arrange the pear slices on the radicchio. Crumble the cheese on top and sprinkle with the walnuts. Drizzle each plate with a few drops of vinegar and serve.

7

WILTED BEET GREENS WITH ROASTED BEETS & ORANGE VINAIGRETTE

serves 6

This salad celebrates the earthy fall flavor of beets, heightened with sweet citrus. Beet greens are often discarded, but in fact make a delicious salad green when lightly blanched as done here. For convenience, the beets can be cooked up to 3 days ahead and refrigerated still tightly wrapped in foil. Peel the skins from the beets just before serving.

6 bunches beets with leafy green tops, about 3 lb (1.5 kg) total weight

Salt

FOR THE ORANGE VINAIGRETTE

3 Tbsp red wine vinegar

2 tsp finely grated or chopped orange zest

Salt and freshly ground pepper

⅓ cup (3 fl oz/80 ml) extra-virgin olive oil

½ sweet onion such as Vidalia, halved and cut crosswise into thin slices

6 thin navel orange slices, halved

Minced fresh chives for garnish (optional)

Preheat the oven to 400°F (200°C). Trim off and reserve the leafy beet tops and wrap the beets in foil. Roast on a baking sheet until easily pierced with the tip of a knife, about 1 hour. Remove from the oven and let cool in the foil.

Meanwhile, trim the long stems from the beet greens and reserve only the leaves that are free of blemishes, discarding the others. Rinse thoroughly and dry well. Gather the leaves together and cut crosswise into strips 1 inch (2.5 cm) wide.

Half-fill a saucepan with water and bring to a boil over high heat. Add the beet greens and 1 tsp salt and cook, uncovered, until the greens are tender, about 8 minutes. Drain well and set aside.

Unwrap and peel the cooled beets. If there are beet juices in the foil, pour them into a small bowl. Cut the beets into wedges.

To make the vinaigrette, add the vinegar, orange zest, and salt and pepper to taste to any beet juices in the small bowl. Add the oil in a thin stream, whisking constantly until the dressing is smooth.

In a large bowl, combine the beet wedges, onion, cooked beet greens, and dressing. Toss to mix. Divide the salad among individual plates. Garnish each salad with orange slices and minced chives, if using, and serve.

8

ROASTED CHICKEN WITH WARM BREAD SALAD

serves 6

Thyme and bay tucked under the skin of the chicken before roasting give this hearty main-course salad an appealing aromatic finish, while roasted onion slices infused with the chicken juices impart flavor and richness to the bread mixture. If you like, squeeze a little lemon juice over the salad just before carrying it to the table. For a complementary match, pour a full-bodied Chardonnay or similar white.

5 cups (10 oz/315 g) bread cubes (from a country-style loaf)

4 Tbsp (2 fl oz/60 ml) olive oil

1 chicken (4–4½ lb/2–2.25 kg), patted dry

Salt and freshly ground pepper

6 fresh thyme sprigs

2 bay leaves

1 yellow onion, sliced

1 Tbsp currants

2 Tbsp red wine vinegar

½ tsp sugar

2 green onions, white and light green parts, sliced

½ cup (¾ oz/20 g) chopped fresh flat-leaf parsley

Zest of 1 lemon

¼ lb (125 g) arugula

Preheat the oven to 400°F (200°C).

Spread the bread cubes on a baking sheet and drizzle them with 3 Tbsp of the oil. Bake, turning once, until lightly golden, about 15 minutes. Let cool. Leave the oven on.

Generously season the chicken cavity and skin with salt and pepper. Loosen the skin on the breast and slide the thyme sprigs and bay leaves under the skin. Put the yellow onion in a roasting pan and toss with the remaining 1 Tbsp oil. Set a roasting rack on top and place the chicken on the rack. Roast until an instant-read thermometer inserted into the thickest part of the thigh, away from the bone, registers 170°F (77°C), about 1 hour.

Transfer the chicken to a carving board, cover loosely with aluminum foil, and let rest for 10 minutes. Pour the onion and juices into a large bowl and add the bread cubes.

Meanwhile, in a small bowl, combine the currants, vinegar, sugar, and 1 Tbsp water and let stand for 15 minutes. Add to the bowl with the onion and bread, then add the green onions, parsley, and lemon zest. Toss until the bread has absorbed most of the liquid. Season with salt and pepper.

Arrange a bed of arugula on a large platter. Scatter the bread salad on top. Carve the chicken and arrange on the salad. Serve.

9

MUSHROOM, RADICCHIO & BULGUR SALAD

serves 4

2 lb (1 kg) cremini mushrooms, halved

⅓ cup (3 fl oz/80 ml) olive oil, plus 2 Tbsp

3 cloves garlic, coarsely chopped

Salt and freshly ground pepper

3 oz (90 g) thick-cut pancetta or bacon, chopped

1 cup (2½ oz/75 g) bulgur wheat

Boiling water as needed

1 head radicchio, cored and thinly sliced

1 Tbsp sherry vinegar

Parmesan cheese for shaving

Meaty roasted mushrooms are a perfect match for nutty grains and bittersweet radicchio. In place of the cremini, feel free to play with a medley of wild and cultivated mushrooms, such as chanterelle, shiitake, morel, and/or porcini.

Preheat the oven to 475°F (245°C). In a large roasting pan, combine the mushrooms, the ⅓ cup oil, and the garlic. Season generously with salt and pepper and toss to coat evenly. Spread the mushrooms in a single layer. Roast for 5 minutes, turn the mushrooms, and continue roasting until the edges are crisp, 2–3 minutes. Set aside.

In a frying pan over medium heat, cook the pancetta, stirring occasionally, until crisp, about 10 minutes. Using a slotted spoon, transfer to paper towels to drain.

In another frying pan over medium-high heat, toast the bulgur until its nutty aroma is released, 3–4 minutes. Add 2 cups (16 fl oz/500 ml) boiling water and 1 tsp salt to the bulgur, cover, and simmer over low heat until tender, about 20 minutes; or, cook according to the package directions. Transfer to a large bowl. Add the radicchio and the 2 Tbsp oil and toss to combine.

Add the roasted mushrooms, pancetta, vinegar, ½ tsp salt, and a pinch of pepper to the radicchio. Toss to combine and spoon onto individual plates. Using a vegetable peeler, shave the cheese over the salads and serve.

10

KALE SALAD WITH ROASTED FUJI APPLES & POMEGRANATE

serves 8

3 Fuji apples, cored and each cut into 8 wedges

¼ cup (2 fl oz/60 ml) extra-virgin olive oil, plus 1 Tbsp

Salt and freshly ground pepper

2 Tbsp cider vinegar

1 Tbsp finely chopped shallot

1 Tbsp packed light brown sugar

2 tsp Dijon mustard

½ bunch cavolo nero kale (see note), stemmed and leaves torn into bite-sized pieces

½ bunch purple kale, stemmed and leaves torn into bite-sized pieces

¼ lb (125g) mixed baby greens such as chard, arugula, and spinach

¼ cup (1 oz/30 g) pomegranate seeds

Dark green Tuscan (also known as cavolo nero) and curly-leaved purple varieties are used in this kale salad, which gets a colorful makeover for winter with the addition of roasted apples and pomegranate seeds. If you cannot find Fujis at the market, Rome Beauty, Pink Lady, or Gala apples can be used in their place.

Preheat the oven to 450°F (230°C). Line a baking sheet with aluminum foil.

In a bowl, toss the apples with the 1 Tbsp oil and season lightly with salt. Transfer to the prepared baking sheet and roast until softened and browned, 15–20 minutes. Let cool.

In a small bowl, whisk together the vinegar, shallot, brown sugar, and mustard. Add the ¼ cup (2 fl oz/60 ml) oil in a thin stream, whisking constantly until the vinaigrette is well blended. Season with salt and pepper.

In a large bowl, combine the kale, baby greens, and apples. Drizzle with the vinaigrette and toss to coat well. Top with the pomegranate seeds and serve.

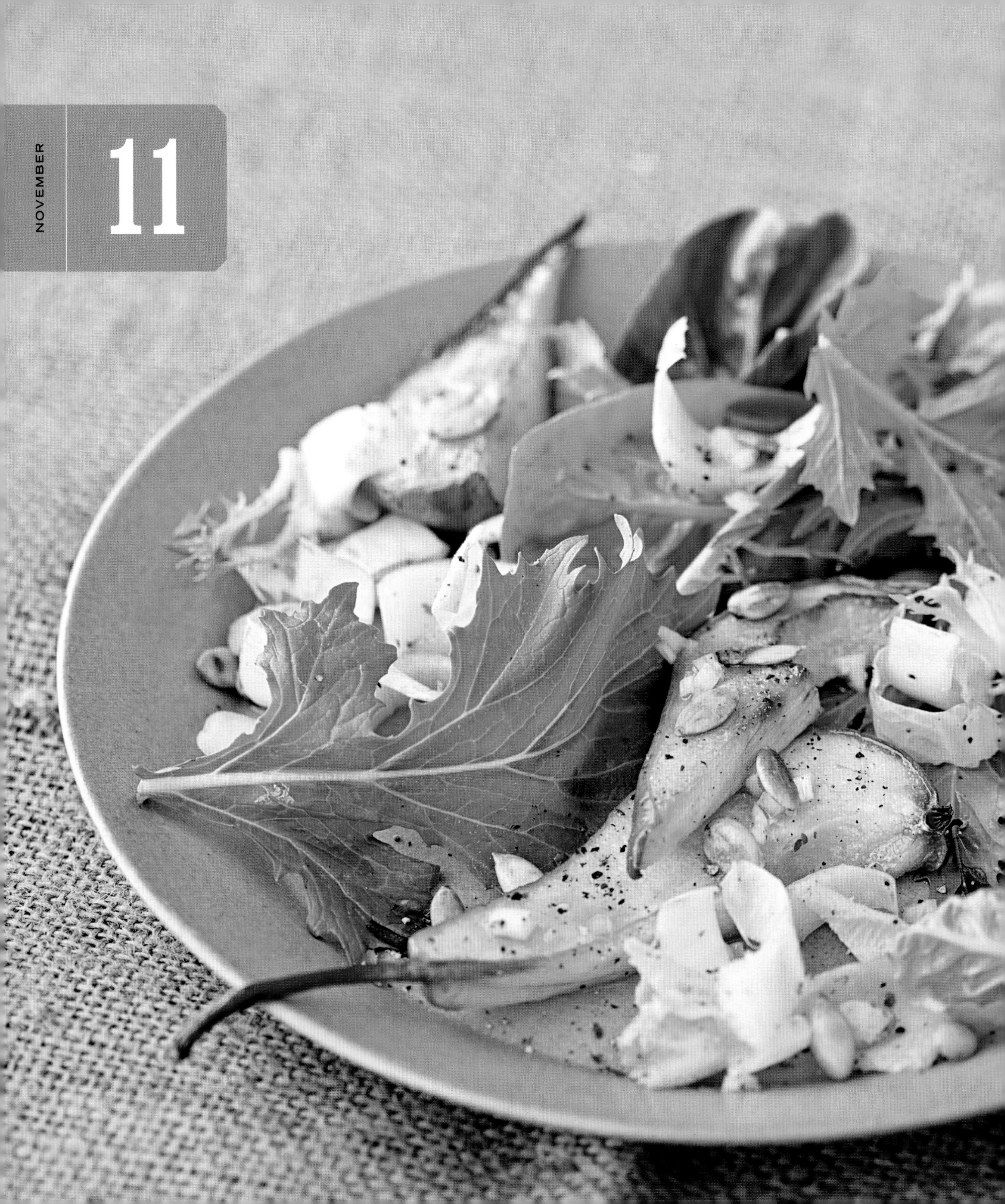

11

MESCLUN & ROASTED PEARS WITH GRAINY MUSTARD VINAIGRETTE

serves 6

Grainy mustard, more robust and less pungent than some other varieties, is delicious mixed with apple juice and cider vinegar in this dressing. The pears turn sweet when roasted, and toasted pumpkin seeds add an appealing crunch. Try this salad with roasted apples or Asian pears as well.

3 firm pears, preferably Anjou or Bosc

2 Tbsp extra-virgin olive oil, plus ¼ cup (2 fl oz/60 ml)

Salt and freshly ground pepper

3 Tbsp pumpkin seeds

¼ cup (2 fl oz/60 ml) cider vinegar

3 Tbsp apple juice

1 large shallot, minced

2 tsp whole-grain mustard

1½ tsp firmly packed light brown sugar

2 large Belgian endives

4 heaping cups (4 oz/125 g) mesclun

Preheat the oven to 400°F (200°C). Halve the pears lengthwise, then core and slice lengthwise about ½ inch (12 mm) thick. Put the slices on a rimmed baking sheet, drizzle with the 2 Tbsp oil, sprinkle with ¼ tsp salt, and toss to coat. Arrange in a single layer and roast for 20 minutes. Carefully turn the slices over and continue to roast until they are golden brown and tender but still hold their shape, about 20 minutes. Let cool.

Meanwhile, in a dry frying pan, toast the pumpkin seeds over medium-low heat, stirring, until starting to brown, 5 minutes. Pour into a bowl and stir in a pinch of salt.

In a small bowl, whisk together the vinegar, apple juice, shallot, mustard, sugar, ¼ tsp salt, and ⅛ tsp pepper. Add the ¼ cup oil in a thin stream, whisking constantly until the dressing is smooth. Taste and adjust the seasonings.

Slice the endives crosswise. In a large bowl, toss together the mesclun, endive, a big pinch of salt, and several grindings of pepper. Whisk the dressing to recombine, then drizzle about half of it over the greens and toss well. Taste and adjust the seasonings. Divide the dressed greens among individual plates. Arrange the roasted pear slices on top of the greens and drizzle with enough of the dressing to coat the greens lightly; you may not need all of it. Sprinkle with the pumpkin seeds and serve.

12

WILD RICE SALAD WITH ROASTED RED PEPPERS & ANCHOVIES

serves 4

Wild rice is not a true rice, but rather the grains of a marsh grass. It is, however, prepared like rice, usually steamed or boiled and then sometimes combined with white or brown rice to create a variety of textures. This anchovy-laced salad makes a delicious starter, accompanied with a crusty baguette and a bowl of olives. You can substitute any rice or grain, varying the cooking time accordingly.

Salt and freshly ground black pepper

1 cup (6 oz/185 g) wild rice

1 Tbsp sherry vinegar

1 tsp red wine vinegar

¼ cup (¾ oz/20 g) chopped green onion, including tender green part

6 olive oil–packed anchovy fillets, minced

2 jarred roasted red bell peppers, chopped

¼ cup (½ oz/15 g) chopped fresh flat-leaf parsley, plus 2 or 3 sprigs

3–4 Tbsp (1½–2 fl oz/45–60 ml) extra-virgin olive oil

In a saucepan over medium-high heat, combine 3 cups (24 fl oz/750 ml) water and 1 tsp salt and bring to a boil. Add the wild rice, return to a boil, then reduce the heat to low, cover, and cook until the rice has absorbed the water and many of the kernels have split, 20–25 minutes. Remove from the heat and let stand, covered, to steam for about 15 minutes.

Transfer the rice to a bowl. Add the sherry and red wine vinegars, green onion, anchovies, all but 1 Tbsp or so of the bell peppers, ½ tsp black pepper, and the parsley. Add 3 Tbsp olive oil and gently mix. If it seems a little dry, add 1 Tbsp olive oil. Cover and let stand for 1 hour to let the flavors blend.

Garnish with the reserved bell pepper and the parsley sprigs and serve.

13

A sprinkle of toasted peanuts and fresh cilantro contributes an intriguing dimension to this Thai-style salad, which is refreshing, pungent, and spicy at the same time. Marinating the cucumber, onion, and chile in the sweetened vinegar mixture mellows their distinctive flavors and softens their textures.

SPICY CUCUMBER SALAD WITH ROASTED PEANUTS

serves 4

⅓ cup (3 fl oz/80 ml) rice vinegar

1½ Tbsp sugar

Salt and freshly ground pepper

1 English cucumber

¼ red onion, thinly sliced

1 jalapeño chile, thinly sliced

Leaves from ¼ bunch fresh cilantro

2 Tbsp roasted peanuts

In a small saucepan, combine the vinegar, sugar, and a pinch each of salt and pepper. Bring to a boil over medium-high heat, then reduce the heat to low. Cook, stirring occasionally, until the sugar dissolves, 2–3 minutes. Remove from the heat and let cool completely.

While the vinegar mixture is cooling, cut the cucumber into slices about ¼ inch (6 mm) thick and put them in a large bowl with the onion and chile. Pour the vinegar mixture over the vegetables and stir well to coat. Let the vegetables stand at room temperature for at least 30 minutes, stirring occasionally, to blend the flavors.

Just before serving, coarsely chop the cilantro and the peanuts. Stir the cilantro into the salad, top with the peanuts, and serve.

14

Hearts of palm and avocado, two popular ingredients in South American cuisine, mingle in this vibrant, fresh salad. You can use other lettuces, such as red or green butter lettuce, endive, arugula, or baby spinach, or a combination of greens. Serve this salad as a starter for a Latin-flavored dinner.

MIXED GREENS WITH HEARTS OF PALM, RED ONION & AVOCADO

serves 6

FOR THE CILANTRO DRESSING

2 Tbsp fresh lime juice

Salt and freshly ground pepper

1 Tbsp minced fresh cilantro

2 tsp extra-virgin olive oil

6–8 cups (6–8 oz/185–250 g) mixed baby salad greens

1 cup (1½ oz/45 g) lightly packed fresh cilantro leaves, plus 2 Tbsp minced

1 can (14 oz/440 g) hearts of palm, drained and rinsed

2 avocados, pitted, peeled, and sliced

½ red onion, thinly sliced

To make the dressing, in a small bowl, whisk together the lime juice, ½ tsp salt, ¼ tsp pepper, and the 1 Tbsp minced cilantro. Add the oil in a thin stream, whisking constantly until the dressing is smooth.

In a large bowl, toss the greens with the 1 cup cilantro leaves. Drizzle the dressing over the greens and toss to coat the greens evenly with the dressing.

Pat the hearts of palm dry with paper towels. Cut each heart of palm crosswise into ½-inch (12-mm) slices.

Divide the dressed greens among individual plates. Top each with some of the hearts of palm, avocados, and onion. Sprinkle with the 2 Tbsp minced cilantro and serve.

15

NOVEMBER

MOROCCAN-SPICED CARROT & PARSNIP SALAD

serves 6

½ cup (2 oz/60 g) pistachios

¼ tsp ground cinnamon

¼ tsp ground cumin

¼ tsp ground coriander

⅛ tsp ground ginger

3 large carrots

3 large parsnips

¼ cup (2 fl oz/60 ml) fresh lemon juice

1 Tbsp honey

¾ tsp harissa

Salt and freshly ground pepper

6 Tbsp (3 fl oz/90 ml) extra-virgin olive oil

⅔ cup (4 oz/125 g) raisins

¼ cup (⅓ oz/10 g) coarsely chopped fresh cilantro or mint

Harissa, a North African chile-and-spice paste, adds a suggestion of heat to this salad, a flavorful medley of earthy and sweet root vegetables. If you can't find harissa, substitute another chile paste such as sambal oelek or a chile sauce such as Tabasco or Sriracha.

In a small, heavy frying pan, toast the pistachios over medium-low heat, stirring, until fragrant and starting to brown, about 5 minutes. Pour onto a plate to cool, then chop coarsely, and set aside.

In the same dry frying pan, toast the cinnamon, cumin, coriander, and ginger over medium-low heat, stirring constantly, until fragrant, about 2 minutes. Pour onto a plate to cool, and set aside.

Peel the carrots and parsnips and shred them on the large holes of a box grater. Set aside.

In a small bowl, whisk together the toasted spices, lemon juice, honey, harissa, and a scant ½ tsp salt. Add the oil in a thin stream, whisking constantly until the dressing is well blended. Taste and adjust the seasonings.

In a serving bowl, stir together the pistachios and a pinch of salt. Add the carrots and parsnips, raisins, ½ tsp salt, several grindings of pepper, and the dressing and toss well. Taste and adjust the seasonings. Sprinkle with the cilantro and serve.

16

NOVEMBER

CELERY ROOT RÉMOULADE

serves 4

1 large or 2 medium celery roots, peeled and cut into slices ¼ inch (6 mm) thick

Salt

2 Tbsp fresh lemon juice

1 cup (8 fl oz/250 ml) mayonnaise

2–3 Tbsp Dijon mustard

In traditional French bistros, celery root rémoulade is typically served as part of an assortment of vegetable salads, which might include diced beets, shredded carrots, sliced tomatoes, or a tangle of greens, all dressed with vinaigrette.

In a saucepan, combine the celery root, 1 tsp salt, lemon juice, and water to cover by about 2 inches (5 cm). Bring to a boil over medium-high heat and cook for 3–4 minutes. The celery root should be just tender to the bite, not mushy. Drain well and, using a sharp knife, cut into thin slices, then stack the slices and cut them into julienne. Alternatively, use the julienne attachment on a mandoline to julienne the celery root. Place in a bowl.

In a small bowl, stir together the mayonnaise and 2 Tbsp of the mustard. Taste the mixture. It should be well seasoned with the mustard but still taste of both ingredients. Add more mustard or mayonnaise as desired. Pour the sauce over the celery root and mix well. Cover and chill for at least 1 hour or up to 12 hours before serving.

SHREDDED KALE SALAD WITH PANCETTA & HARD-COOKED EGG

serves 4–5

Shredding and briefly blanching kale for a salad softens its sturdy texture, but keeps it crunchy enough to support hearty, heavier ingredients like hard-cooked eggs and pancetta. The kale can be left raw, too, for a crunchier effect.

5 large eggs

2 bunches kale

Salt and freshly ground black pepper

¼ lb (125 g) thick-cut pancetta or bacon, coarsely chopped

3 Tbsp extra-virgin olive oil

1 clove garlic, minced

4 Tbsp (2 fl oz/60 ml) balsamic vinegar

2 Tbsp red wine vinegar

4 Tbsp (⅓ oz/10 g) fresh flat-leaf parsley

½ tsp cayenne pepper

To hard-cook the eggs, place them in a saucepan just large enough to hold them. Add cold water to cover by 1 inch (2.5 cm) and bring just to a boil over high heat. Remove the pan from the heat and cover. Let stand for 15 minutes. Have ready a bowl of ice water. Drain the eggs, then transfer to the ice water and let cool before peeling. Mince the eggs and set aside.

With a knife, strip the ribs from the kale, then roll the leaves up and slice them thinly crosswise. Bring a large saucepan three-fourths full of water to a boil over medium-high heat. Add 1 tsp salt and the kale and cook until the greens are just tender, about 5 minutes. Using a slotted spoon, lift out the kale and drain it well. Rinse under cold running water until cool. Drain again and gently squeeze out the excess liquid from the kale with your hands, then coarsely chop it. Gently squeeze out the liquid with your hands again. Set aside.

In a frying pan, cook the pancetta or bacon over medium heat, turning occasionally, until nearly golden, about 5 minutes. (If using bacon, pour off the rendered fat at this point.) Add 1 Tbsp of the oil and the garlic and cook just until the garlic is golden, about 1 minute. Using a slotted spoon, transfer the pancetta or bacon and garlic to paper towels to drain. ⟫

Add 2 Tbsp of the balsamic vinegar to the frying pan and cook over medium heat, stirring to scrape up any browned bits on the pan bottom. Pour into a bowl and whisk in the remaining 2 Tbsp balsamic vinegar, the red wine vinegar, and the remaining 2 Tbsp oil. Add the kale, the pancetta and garlic, 3 Tbsp of the parsley, and ½ tsp black pepper. Mix well. Add the minced eggs and gently fold them in.

Garnish the mixture with the remaining 1 Tbsp parsley and the cayenne and serve.

BROCCOLI & BLACK OLIVE SALAD WITH SUN-DRIED TOMATOES

serves 4–6

Various varieties of broccoli are popular in both Western and Eastern cuisines, and all of them readily take on different flavor profiles depending on the ingredients with which they are prepared. This recipe emphasizes Mediterranean flavors.

4 cups (8 oz/250 g) broccoli florets (from about 4 heads)

1½ cups (7½ oz/235 g) sliced oil-cured black olives

1 cup (4 oz/125 g) walnuts, toasted and coarsely chopped

½ cup (4 oz/125 g) oil-packed sun-dried tomatoes, drained and chopped

3 Tbsp extra-virgin olive oil

2–3 tsp red wine vinegar

Salt and freshly ground pepper

⅓ cup (1¾ oz/50 g) crumbled feta or fresh goat cheese (optional)

Cut the broccoli florets in half or, if large, into quarters. Transfer to a large bowl and add the olives, walnuts, and sun-dried tomatoes.

In a small bowl, whisk together the oil and vinegar until the vinaigrette is well blended. Pour over the broccoli mixture and stir to coat well. Season with salt and pepper and stir again. Transfer to a serving bowl or platter, garnish with the cheese, if desired, and serve.

19

A fried egg is a good topping for just about anything, and this healthy kale and Brussels sprouts salad is no exception. The Parmesan crisps, although simple to make, add a fancy note. If you don't love anchovies, they can be omitted or a bit of bacon or sausage can be substituted for them. This salad works especially well as a brunch dish.

CRISPY KALE & BRUSSELS SPROUTS SALAD WITH FRIED EGG

serves 4

½ cup (2 oz/60 g) grated Parmesan cheese

½ lb (250 g) Brussels sprouts

14 leaves cavolo nero kale

2½ Tbsp extra-virgin olive oil, plus more if needed

Salt and freshly ground black pepper

⅛ tsp red pepper flakes

4 large eggs

8–12 olive oil–packed anchovy fillets

Preheat the oven to 400°F (200°C). Line a baking sheet with parchment paper.

Place 8 mounds of cheese, each about 1 Tbsp, on the prepared baking sheet, spacing them well apart. Press lightly with the back of a spoon to slightly flatten. Bake until the cheese has melted and formed a lacy pattern and the edges are golden, 3–5 minutes. Let cool. Leave the oven on.

Trim the Brussels sprouts and remove any tough outer leaves. Halve them lengthwise, then cut each half into slices ¼ inch (6 mm) thick. Transfer to a bowl.

Remove the thick stems from the kale leaves. Stack the leaves, several at a time, and roll into a cylinder, then cut crosswise into very thin strips. Add to the bowl with the Brussels sprouts along with 1½ Tbsp of the oil, ¼ tsp salt, ½ tsp black pepper, and the red pepper flakes. Toss well.

Spread the vegetable mixture on a baking sheet. Roast until the Brussels sprouts are tender and the edges of the kale and sprouts are beginning to crisp, 6–7 minutes. Remove from the oven and set aside.

In a frying pan, warm the remaining 1 Tbsp oil over medium heat, adding more oil if needed. Crack the eggs into the pan and fry until the whites are firm and the yolks are still runny, about 4 minutes.

Divide the vegetables among individual plates, mounding them slightly. Top each with a fried egg and garnish with 2 or 3 anchovies. Using a spatula, gently remove the Parmesan crisps, garnish each plate with 2 crisps, and serve right away.

20

This salad brings together Southeast Asian ingredients, with fresh herbs, sharp ginger, delicate oils, and tender bites of shellfish. The rice noodles cook in seconds, making this a quick, fresh weeknight meal.

VIETNAMESE SHRIMP & NOODLE SALAD

serves 4

½ lb (250 g) rice stick noodles

FOR THE LEMONGRASS DRESSING

2 lemongrass stalks, pale inner core only, minced

2 Tbsp peeled and finely grated fresh ginger

Juice of 1 lime

3 Tbsp Asian fish sauce

2 tsp toasted sesame oil

1 tsp sugar

1 Tbsp peanut oil

1 lb (500 g) small shrimp, peeled and deveined

12 green onions, including tender green parts, thinly sliced

¼ cup (⅓ oz/10 g) coarsely chopped fresh mint

1 romaine lettuce heart, torn into bite-sized pieces

½ cup (2½ oz/75 g) dry-roasted peanuts, chopped

In a large bowl, soak the rice stick noodles in hot water to cover for 15 minutes. Drain.

Meanwhile, to make the dressing, in a bowl, whisk together the lemongrass, ginger, lime juice, fish sauce, sesame oil, and sugar. Set aside.

Bring a large pot of water to a boil. Plunge the soaked noodles into the water for 5 seconds and drain immediately. Rinse well under running cold water and drain again. Add to the dressing and toss to coat evenly.

In a frying pan over medium-high heat, warm the peanut oil. Add the shrimp and cook, stirring frequently, until evenly pink, 2–3 minutes. Add the shrimp, green onions, and mint to the noodles and toss to combine. Arrange the lettuce on plates and top with the noodle mixture. Sprinkle with the peanuts and serve.

21

WATERCRESS & ENDIVE SALAD WITH WARM BACON VINAIGRETTE

serves 8–10

A member of the chicory family with a faintly bitter taste, Belgian endive is at its best during the coldest months. The leaves can be stuffed with fillings as an hors d'oeuvre, or chopped or cut into shreds to add crispness to winter salads. Here, fragrant toasted pecans and crumbled bacon top off its bold flavor.

½ cup (2 oz/60 g) pecan halves

3 heads Belgian endive, preferably red

3 bunches watercress, tough stems removed

¼ sweet red or white onion, thinly sliced

1 bunch radishes, thinly sliced

FOR THE WARM BACON VINAIGRETTE

3 Tbsp extra-virgin olive oil

2 slices bacon, finely chopped

1½ Tbsp distilled white or red wine vinegar

1 tsp sugar

Salt and freshly ground pepper

In a dry frying pan, toast the pecan halves over medium-low heat, stirring, until fragrant and starting to brown, about 5 minutes. Pour onto a plate to cool, and set aside.

Core the endive heads, then halve crosswise and slice very thinly. In a large bowl, combine the watercress, endive, onion, and radishes. Set aside.

To make the vinaigrette, in a frying pan, heat 1 Tbsp of the oil over medium heat. Add the bacon and cook until crisp, about 5 minutes. Using a slotted spoon, transfer the bacon to paper towels to drain. Reserve the frying pan and the bacon fat.

Just before serving the salad, place the reserved pan over medium heat and add the remaining 2 Tbsp oil. Heat until fragrant, 1–2 minutes. Remove the pan from the heat. Add the vinegar and sugar and stir to combine. Pour the vinaigrette over the salad and toss immediately to coat well and partially wilt the leaves. Taste and season with salt and pepper, then toss again.

Divide among individual plates, sprinkle with the bacon and the pecans, and serve.

22

FRISÉE, ENDIVE & WATERCRESS SALAD WITH ROQUEFORT & PEAR

serves 6

For vibrant greens, wash and spin dry the frisée, endive, and watercress, then combine in a bowl an hour before serving, cover with a damp paper towel, and refrigerate until ready to dress and serve. Other blue-veined cheeses can be substituted for the Roquefort here: try Gorgonzola, Cabrales, or Stilton.

FOR THE CHAMPAGNE VINAIGRETTE

2 Tbsp champagne vinegar

½ tsp honey

6 Tbsp (3 fl oz/90 ml) walnut oil

1 firm but ripe pear, such as Anjou or Bartlett

Salt and freshly ground pepper

1 head frisée, cored and torn into bite-sized pieces

2 heads Belgian endive, cored and cut lengthwise into narrow strips

1 bunch watercress, tough stems removed

6 oz (185 g) Roquefort cheese

To make the vinaigrette, in a small bowl, whisk together the vinegar and honey. Add the oil in a thin stream, whisking constantly until the dressing is smooth.

Peel, core, and cut the pear into ¼-inch (6-mm) pieces. Stir the pear into the vinaigrette and season to taste with salt and pepper. Let stand at room temperature for at least 30 minutes or up to 4 hours.

In a large bowl, combine the frisée, endive, and watercress. Whisk the vinaigrette, drizzle it over the greens, and toss to coat the leaves well. Cut the cheese into 6 slices. Divide the greens among individual plates, top each with a slice of cheese, and serve.

23

SPICED APPLE, CRANBERRY & PECAN SALAD

serves 4

¾ tsp ground cumin

⅛ tsp cayenne pepper

½ Tbsp olive oil

½ cup (2 oz/60 g) pecan halves

1½ Tbsp sugar

¼ cup (2 oz/60 g) plain yogurt

¼ cup (2 fl oz/60 ml) mayonnaise

1 Tbsp honey

½ tsp sherry vinegar or balsamic vinegar

2–3 large sweet apples such as Gala, Golden Delicious, or Fuji

2 large celery ribs, thinly sliced

¼ cup (1 oz/30 g) dried cranberries

4 red-leaf lettuce leaves

Apples and celery are a tried-and-true combination, but this salad spices it up for the holiday season with a crunch of candied pecans. The dressing is cut with a little yogurt, so it's not too rich.

In a bowl, combine half of the cumin and half of the cayenne. In a small saucepan, warm the oil over medium heat. Add the pecans and stir until the nuts are lightly browned, about 5 minutes. Sprinkle with the sugar and cook, stirring constantly, until the sugar melts and begins to brown, 2–3 minutes. Add the hot nut mixture to the bowl containing the spices and stir to coat. Let cool completely. Chop the nuts coarsely. Set aside.

In a small bowl, stir together the yogurt, mayonnaise, honey, and vinegar. Add the remaining cumin and cayenne.

Quarter and core each apple. Cut each quarter in half crosswise, then slice lengthwise. In a large bowl, combine the apples, celery, and dried cranberries. Add the yogurt dressing and toss to coat.

Line individual plates with lettuce leaves. Mound an equal amount of the salad in the center of each plate. Sprinkle with the spiced nuts and serve.

24

BULGUR WITH PERSIMMONS, PISTACHIOS & POMEGRANATE

serves 4

1 cup (6 oz/185 g) bulgur wheat

1 cup (8 fl oz/250 ml) boiling water

Salt

¼ cup (2 fl oz/60 ml) fresh lemon juice

¼ cup (2 fl oz/60 ml) extra-virgin olive oil

1 cup (1½ oz/45 g) chopped fresh flat-leaf parsley, plus extra for garnish

⅓ cup (½ oz/15 g) minced fresh mint, plus extra for garnish

½ cup (1½ oz/45 g) chopped green onion, including tender green parts

½ cup (2 oz/60 g) shelled pistachios

3 Fuyu persimmons, finely chopped

¼ cup (1 oz/30 g) pomegranate seeds

Whole grains, like nutty-tasting bulgur, take well to a wide range of seasonings, fruits, and nuts. This recipe showcases the Middle Eastern flavors of pistachio and pomegranate. For a heartier version, top the finished salad with grilled thinly sliced lamb.

In a heatproof bowl, combine the bulgur, boiling water, and 1½ tsp salt and stir to blend. Cover and let stand until the bulgur is soft and all of the water has been absorbed, 15–20 minutes. Add the lemon juice, oil, parsley, mint, and green onion and stir to combine. Let stand at room temperature for at least 15 minutes or up to 2 hours to let the flavors develop.

In a small frying pan, toast the pistachios over medium-high heat, shaking the pan occasionally, until the nuts are fragrant, 3–4 minutes. Roughly chop the pistachios. Transfer to a small bowl.

Just before serving, add the persimmon and all but 1 Tbsp each of the pistachios and pomegranate seeds to the bulgur and stir gently to mix well. Transfer the salad to a serving bowl. Sprinkle with the remaining pistachios and pomegranate seeds and serve.

25

Snap up Fuyu persimmons when they make their brief appearance in late autumn. The jewel-like orange fruits are delicious eaten out of hand. Sliced and tossed with apples and a light vinaigrette, they become the basis for this distinctive seasonal salad.

PERSIMMON & YELLOW APPLE SALAD

serves 4

2 Fuyu persimmons

2 yellow apples, such as Golden Delicious

2 tsp fresh lemon juice

2 Tbsp finely ground walnuts

1½ Tbsp sherry vinegar

Salt and freshly ground pepper

¼ tsp sugar

2 Tbsp walnut oil or extra-virgin olive oil

Cut the persimmons in half lengthwise, scoop out any seeds with a spoon, and cut the halves into ½-inch (12-mm) cubes. Core the apples and cut into slices ¼ inch (6 mm) thick.

Combine the persimmon cubes and apple slices in a large bowl and drizzle with the lemon juice. Toss well, then set aside.

In another bowl, combine the ground walnuts, vinegar, ½ tsp salt, ¼ tsp pepper, and the sugar. Add the oil in a thin stream, whisking constantly until the dressing is well blended. Pour the dressing over the persimmons and apples, toss, and serve.

26

Green French lentils have a nutty, peppery flavor and a firm texture that holds up well to cooking and marinating. This flavorful legume salad makes a wonderful accompaniment to a broiled salmon fillet or steak.

GREEN LENTIL SALAD WITH RED PEPPERS & SHALLOTS

serves 4

1 cup (7 oz/220 g) small green French (du Puy) lentils, picked over and rinsed

3 Tbsp extra-virgin olive oil

1½ cups (6 oz/185 g) thinly sliced shallots

½ cup (2½ oz/75 g) jarred roasted red peppers, cut into strips

3½ Tbsp sherry vinegar

3 Tbsp coarsely chopped fresh flat-leaf parsley leaves

Salt

Bring a pot of water to a boil. Add the lentils, reduce the heat, and simmer until they are tender to the bite, 18–25 minutes.

While the lentils cook, heat 2 Tbsp of the oil in a large nonstick frying pan over medium-high heat. Add the shallots and cook until softened, 2–3 minutes. Reduce the heat and cook, stirring frequently, until the shallots are browned, 5–8 minutes. Set aside.

Drain the lentils and put them in a large bowl. Stir in the peppers, vinegar, parsley, ½ tsp salt, the shallots, and the remaining 1 Tbsp oil.

Serve warm or at room temperature, stirring well before serving.

27

NOVEMBER

The warm flavors of spices, honey, and brown sugar dominate this salad. Curry powder, a blend that includes cumin and chile, among other spices, flavors the pecans. The dressing is seasoned with cumin and chile as well and calls for honey, which turns the sweet potato cubes a lush golden brown. The pecans can be addictive, so you may want to double or triple the recipe to have extra on hand.

HONEY-GLAZED SWEET POTATO & CURRIED PECAN SALAD

serves 4

FOR THE DRESSING

¼ cup (2 fl oz/60 ml) extra-virgin olive oil

2 Tbsp sherry vinegar

2 tsp honey

¼ tsp chili powder

¼ tsp ground cumin

Salt

FOR THE CURRIED PECANS

1 tsp curry powder

½ tsp light brown sugar

Salt

½ cup (3 oz/90 g) pecan halves

1 Tbsp unsalted butter, melted

FOR THE SWEET POTATO

1 large sweet potato, cut into ½-inch (12-mm) cubes, peeled

2 tsp extra-virgin olive oil

Salt and freshly ground pepper

1 Tbsp honey

2 cups (2 oz/60 g) baby spinach

2 cups (2 oz/60 g) baby arugula

6 oz (185 g) fresh goat cheese, crumbled

Preheat the oven to 350°F (180°C). Line a baking sheet with aluminum foil or parchment paper.

To make the dressing, in a large bowl, whisk together the oil, vinegar, honey, chili powder, cumin, and ¼ tsp salt until the dressing is well blended. Set aside.

To make the curried pecans, in a small bowl, stir together the curry powder, brown sugar, and ⅛ tsp salt. Put the pecans in a separate small bowl and pour the melted butter over them. Add the curry mixture and stir to coat well. Place the pecans in a single layer on the prepared baking sheet. Roast, stirring once or twice, until the pecans are fragrant and a slight crust has formed on them, about 15 minutes. Let cool. Leave the oven on. The pecans can be stored in an airtight container at room temperature for up to 7 days.

To make the sweet potato, put the sweet potato cubes in a single layer in an oven-safe frying pan. Drizzle with the oil, sprinkle ⟩⟩→

with ½ tsp salt and ¼ tsp pepper, and stir to coat well. Roast in the oven, turning them once or twice, until tender when pierced with a knife, about 15 minutes. Using an oven mitt, transfer the pan to the stove top and place over medium-high heat. Drizzle the potato cubes with the honey and cook until golden brown underneath, about 4 minutes. Turn them and brown the other side, about 2 minutes. Remove from the heat and keep warm.

Add the spinach and arugula to the bowl with the dressing and toss to coat. Divide the greens among individual plates. Top with the sweet potato cubes and the pecans. Dot with the goat cheese and serve.

28

NOVEMBER

This salad presents an ideal opportunity to use up leftover roasted turkey. Dried cranberries could easily replace the cherries, if you'd like to savor the holiday flavors a little longer. This is an excellent choice for packed lunches, and equally appealing mounded on lettuce greens or tucked between toasted slices of wheat bread.

TURKEY & CELERY SALAD WITH DRIED CHERRIES

serves 4

1 small celery root, about ¾ lb (375 g)

4 celery ribs, finely chopped

2 cups (¾ lb/375 g) chopped cooked turkey or chicken, chilled

¼ cup (1½ oz/45 g) pine nuts

¼ cup (1½ oz/45 g) dried tart cherries, halved, or other dried fruits

2 Tbsp light sour cream

2 Tbsp mayonnaise

1 tsp Dijon mustard

1½ Tbsp champagne vinegar

Salt and freshly ground pepper

8–10 lettuce leaves

Peel the celery root and shred it on the large holes of a box grater. Place in a large bowl.

Add the celery, turkey, pine nuts, dried cherries, sour cream, mayonnaise, mustard, vinegar, and ½ tsp each salt and pepper to the celery root and mix well. Cover and refrigerate for at least 1 hour or up to 24 hours before serving.

Line a platter or individual plates with the lettuce leaves, mound the turkey mixture on top, and serve.

269

29

CRAB CAKE & BUTTER LETTUCE SALAD

serves 4

2 large eggs

1 Tbsp mayonnaise, plus ⅓ cup (3 fl oz/80 ml)

1 lb (500 g) cooked crabmeat, picked over for shell fragments and squeezed to remove excess water

½ cup (1 oz/30 g) fresh fine white bread crumbs

Salt and freshly ground pepper

4 green onions, including tender green parts, finely chopped

2 tsp Dijon mustard

Juice of 1 lemon

2 Tbsp unsalted butter

2 heads butter lettuce, torn into bite-sized pieces

In many areas, crab season kicks off in late November. The milky-sweet meat is a treat when formed into little cakes and panfried. If you can resist eating them immediately on their own, a bed of tender butter lettuce and a drizzle of creamy lemon dressing are a match made in heaven.

In a bowl, whisk the eggs lightly. Add the 1 Tbsp mayonnaise, the crab, bread crumbs, 2 tsp salt, ½ tsp pepper, and green onions. Stir with a fork until well mixed. Divide the mixture into 8 equal portions and gently form each portion into a small patty.

In a small bowl, whisk together the ⅓ cup mayonnaise, the mustard, lemon juice, and ¼ tsp pepper until smooth.

In a large frying pan, melt the butter over medium-low heat. Working in batches if needed, add the crab cakes and cook without moving them until golden brown on the first side, about 4 minutes. Turn and cook until golden brown on the second side, 3–4 minutes. Arrange the lettuce on plates and place the crab cakes on top. Drizzle with the dressing and serve.

30

APPLE & CELERY ROOT SALAD WITH STILTON CHEESE

serves 6

⅓ cup (1¾ oz/50 g) hazelnuts

5 apples (about 2 lb/1 kg) total weight), cored and cut into small cubes

6 Tbsp (3 fl oz/90 ml) fresh lemon juice

2 medium celery roots (about ¾ lb/375 g each), peeled

8 celery ribs, cut into ¼-inch (6-mm) pieces

⅓ lb (155 g) Stilton cheese

½ cup (4 fl oz/125 ml) mayonnaise

2 Tbsp extra-virgin olive oil

Freshly ground pepper

18 large Belgian endive leaves

This salad is a mix of crunchy textures balanced by soft, creamy Stilton cheese. For a more visually appealing presentation and a more complex flavor, use an array of apple varieties, such as Gala, Pink Lady, Golden Delicious, Winesap, and Northern Spy. Because the apples aren't peeled, the different colors of their skins will add to the visual appeal.

In a small frying pan, toast the hazelnuts over medium-high heat, shaking the pan occasionally, until the nuts are fragrant, 3–4 minutes. Transfer to a cutting board. When the nuts are cool enough to handle, rub off the skins, and coarsely chop the nuts. Set aside.

Put the apples in a large bowl, sprinkle with 3 Tbsp of the lemon juice, and stir to coat. Grate the celery root on the large holes of a box grater. Add to the bowl along with the celery and stir to combine. Crumble in half of the cheese and stir again.

In a small bowl, stir together the mayonnaise, oil, ¼ tsp pepper, the remaining 3 Tbsp lemon juice, and 2–3 Tbsp of the cheese. Using a fork, mash the cheese and then whisk until the dressing is smooth and well blended. Add the dressing to the apple mixture and stir to coat well.

Arrange the endive leaves on a platter and top with the salad. Crumble the remaining cheese over the salad, sprinkle with the hazelnuts, and serve.

Fresh salads are a welcome addition to the holiday table, balancing out rich roasts and creamy gratins. Brisk winter days call for crisp greens, from unassuming iceberg and pleasantly bitter arugula to refreshing endive and vibrant radicchio. Add a touch of decadence here and there with special-occasion ingredients like fragrant chestnuts, potent Stilton cheese, or elegant seafood, such as smoked trout, crab, oysters, or lobster.

4
LYONNAISE SALAD WITH SAUSAGES & POTATOES
page 276

5
CRISPY CHICKEN & CABBAGE SALAD WITH PEANUT DRESSING
page 277

6
INSALATA VERDE
page 277

7
NAPA CABBAGE & KUMQUAT SALAD WITH SEARED SCALLOPS
page 279

11
RED CABBAGE SALAD WITH APPLES & DRIED FRUIT
page 282

12
WARM BORLOTTI BEAN & RADICCHIO SALAD
page 282

13
WARM BRUSSELS SPROUT SALAD WITH CHESTNUTS & PROSCIUTTO
page 283

14
RED OAKLEAF LETTUCE & FRISÉE SALAD WITH PERSIMMON
page 283

18
WARM BRUSSELS SPROUT AND APPLE SALAD
page 286

19
DUCK BREAST SALAD WITH WALNUTS & ORANGES
page 287

20
GRAPEFRUIT, AVOCADO & FENNEL SALAD
page 287

21
ASIAN NOODLE SALAD WITH SALMON & SNOW PEAS
page 288

25
BEET & STILTON SALAD WITH ORANGE VINAIGRETTE
page 292

26
GRAPEFRUIT, ENDIVE & POMEGRANATE SALAD
page 292

27
TACO SALAD IN TORTILLA BOWLS
page 293

28
SMOKED RAINBOW TROUT SALAD WITH CRANBERRY SALSA
page 293

december

1

WARM SPINACH & BACON SALAD

serves 6–8

8 Tbsp (4 fl oz/125 ml) extra-virgin olive oil

1 lb (500 g) button mushrooms, halved

1½ Tbsp fresh lemon juice

2 cloves garlic, thinly sliced

1 tsp minced fresh thyme

¼ tsp red pepper flakes

Salt and freshly ground black pepper

3 large eggs

10 oz (315 g) baby spinach

8 slices thick-cut applewood-smoked bacon, chopped

3 Tbsp balsamic vinegar

1 Tbsp whole-grain mustard

1 small red onion, thinly sliced

1½ cups (9 oz/280 g) cherry tomatoes, halved

Smoky, salty bacon makes almost everything taste better, and this hearty salad is no exception. It may even make kids happily eat their greens. Bacon has lots of presence here, so look for good-quality, thick-cut bacon for the tastiest results. And try not to eat all the crisp bits while you assemble the salads. Chopped hard-cooked egg is the classic topping, but you can top each serving with a poached egg if you prefer.

In a frying pan over medium-high heat, warm 2 Tbsp of the oil. Add the mushrooms and sauté until they release their juices and brown lightly, 5–6 minutes. Transfer to a bowl. Add 4 Tbsp (2 fl oz/60 ml) of the oil, the lemon juice, garlic, thyme, red pepper flakes, and salt and pepper to taste, and toss to coat. Let marinate for at least 1 hour.

To hard-cook the eggs, place them in a saucepan just large enough to hold them. Add cold water to cover by 1 inch (2.5 cm) and bring just to a boil over high heat. Remove the pan from the heat and cover. Let stand for 15 minutes. Have ready a bowl of ice water. Drain the eggs, then transfer to the ice water and let cool. Peel and coarsely chop the eggs.

Put the spinach in a large bowl. In a large frying pan over medium heat, fry the bacon, stirring occasionally, until crisp and browned, about 7 minutes. Transfer to paper towels to drain. Pour off all but 2 Tbsp of the fat in the pan. Off the heat, whisk the vinegar and mustard into the fat in the pan, then whisk in the remaining 2 Tbsp oil. Season with salt and pepper, drizzle over the spinach, and toss to coat well.

Divide among individual plates, top with the onion, tomatoes, marinated mushrooms, chopped eggs, and bacon and serve.

2

WINTER PEAR SALAD WITH BLUE CHEESE, WALNUTS & POMEGRANATE

serves 4

⅓ cup (1½ oz/45 g) walnut pieces

FOR THE CIDER DRESSING

3 Tbsp cider vinegar

1 Tbsp honey

1 tsp Dijon mustard

Salt and freshly ground pepper

2 Tbsp extra-virgin olive oil

8 oz (250 g) mixed baby greens

2 pears such as Bartlett, cored and sliced

½ cup (2 oz/60 g) pomegranate seeds

1 oz (30 g) blue cheese, crumbled

Combining mixed baby greens with some favorite elements of a winter cheese plate, this succulent salad makes a stunning starter. The juicy pomegranate seeds and slightly tart cider dressing brighten toasted walnuts, thin slices of grainy pear, and a potent blue cheese. Any variety of blue works here, from mild Gorgonzola to more powerful Stilton and Roquefort, all perfect matches for pear.

In a dry frying pan, toast the walnut pieces over medium-low heat, stirring, until fragrant and starting to brown, about 5 minutes. Pour onto a plate to cool, then coarsely chop and set aside.

To make the dressing, in a large bowl, whisk together the vinegar, honey, mustard, ¼ tsp salt, and ⅛ tsp pepper. Add the oil in a thin stream, whisking constantly until the dressing is smooth.

Add the greens, pears, pomegranate seeds, and walnuts to the bowl of dressing and mix gently to coat. Divide the salad among individual plates, garnish each with some cheese crumbles, and serve.

3

SMOKED CHICKEN SALAD WITH TARRAGON DRESSING

serves 4

This classy little salad of smoked chicken and fresh herbs is perfect to make ahead for brunch, lunch, or a first course dinner—even as a topping for crostini. Serve with a crisp Sauvignon Blanc or an Austrian white such as Grüner Veltliner.

FOR THE TARRAGON DRESSING

2 tsp Dijon mustard

2 tsp champagne vinegar

1 Tbsp chopped fresh tarragon

¼ tsp sugar

Salt and freshly ground pepper

3 Tbsp extra-virgin olive oil

1 Tbsp walnut oil

4 heads Belgian endive, 2 red and 2 white, about 2½ oz (75 g) each

¼ lb (125 g) boneless smoked chicken

2 Tbsp chopped fresh tarragon

To make the dressing, in a small bowl, whisk together the mustard, vinegar, 1 Tbsp tarragon, the sugar, ¼ tsp salt, and pepper to taste. Add the olive and walnut oils in a thin stream, whisking constantly until the dressing is smooth. Cover and refrigerate until ready to serve, up to 4 hours.

Trim off the base of each endive and separate the leaves. Cut the leaves crosswise into 1–2 inch (2.5–5 cm) pieces and put in a bowl. Cut the chicken into bite-sized pieces and add to the bowl.

Just before serving, whisk the dressing to recombine. Toss the salad with enough of the dressing to coat the chicken and endive lightly; you may not need all of it. Divide the salad among individual plates, garnish with the tarragon, and serve.

4

LYONNAISE SALAD WITH SAUSAGES & POTATOES

serves 4

Lyon is considered the gastronomic capital of France, and this humble salad, made with good-quality ingredients, is similar to salads found in bistros throughout the city and surrounding area. Sturdy, leafy escarole stands up to the big flavors that compose the salad, and a grainy mustard vinaigrette adds the perfect bright flavor note. The potatoes can be cooked a day ahead.

½ lb (250 g) small Yukon gold potatoes, peeled or unpeeled

Salt and freshly ground pepper

1 Tbsp unsalted butter

4 Tbsp (2 fl oz/60 ml) extra-virgin olive oil, plus more if needed

1 clove garlic, chopped

4 baguette slices, cut into small dice

4 sausages such as bratwurst or Toulouse

1 tsp *each* red wine vinegar and balsamic vinegar

2 tsp whole-grain mustard

1 large head escarole, pale yellow and green inner leaves only

4 ounces Gruyère cheese, cut into ½-inch (12-mm) cubes

Put the potatoes in a saucepan and cover with salted water by 2 inches (5 cm). Bring to a boil over high heat, reduce the heat to medium, and cook until tender, about 20 minutes. Drain. When cool enough to handle, cut into ½-inch (12-mm) cubes.

In a large frying pan, melt the butter with 1 Tbsp of the oil over medium-high heat. When hot, add the potatoes and sprinkle with ¼ tsp salt and ¼ tsp pepper. Cook, turning once, until golden brown, about 5 minutes per side. Transfer to a bowl. Reduce the heat to medium. Add the garlic and bread cubes. Fry, turning occasionally, until golden, about 3 minutes, adding more oil if necessary. Transfer to a separate bowl.

In the same pan, fry the sausages over medium heat, turning several times, until cooked through, about 10 minutes. Transfer to a cutting board. When cool enough to handle, cut into ½-inch (12-mm) slices.

In a large bowl, whisk together the remaining 3 Tbsp oil, the vinegars, mustard, ¼ teaspoon salt, and ¼ teaspoon pepper until the vinaigrette is well blended. Add the escarole and toss to coat well. Add the potatoes, the cubed cheese, and most of the croutons and sausage slices. Toss gently.

Transfer the salad to a platter or individual plates. Garnish with the remaining croutons and sausage. Serve warm.

5

CRISPY CHICKEN & CABBAGE SALAD WITH PEANUT DRESSING

serves 6

In this Asian-inspired recipe, the roasted taste of natural peanut butter provides the backbone of the salty-sweet dressing. Sesame seeds are a nutty complement to the crispy chicken. The crunchy texture in this main course salad makes for a crowd-pleasing dish.

½ cup (2½ oz/75 g) all-purpose flour

2 large eggs

1 cup (4 oz/125 g) panko bread crumbs

Salt and freshly ground pepper

3 skinless, boneless chicken breast halves (about 1½ lb/750 g total weight)

1 head napa cabbage

⅓ cup (3 fl oz/80 ml) peanut oil

2 Tbsp sesame seeds

FOR THE PEANUT DRESSING

¼ cup (2½ oz/75 g) natural peanut butter

¼ cup (2 fl oz/60 ml) rice vinegar

¼ cup (2 fl oz/60 ml) peanut oil

1 Tbsp toasted sesame oil

2 Tbsp brown sugar

1 tsp tamari sauce

3 large carrots, peeled and shredded

12 leaves green-leaf lettuce

Put the flour in a shallow bowl. In a second shallow bowl, whisk the eggs until blended. In a third shallow bowl, stir together the panko, ½ tsp salt, and several grindings of pepper. Season the chicken breasts on both sides with salt and pepper. One at a time, dip the breasts first in the flour, coating evenly and shaking off the excess, then in the egg, allowing the excess to drip off, and finally in the seasoned panko, coating evenly and shaking off the excess. Place on a large plate and refrigerate for 30 minutes.

Halve the cabbage lengthwise and core. Cut each half crosswise into thin slices. Set aside.

Preheat the oven to 350°F (180°C). In a large nonstick frying pan, warm the peanut oil over medium-high heat until hot but not smoking. Add the breaded chicken breasts and cook on the first side until golden brown, about 4 minutes. Turn and cook on the second side until golden brown, about 2 minutes. Transfer to a rimmed baking sheet and bake until an instant-read thermometer inserted into the thickest part of a breast registers 160°F (71°C), 15–20 minutes. ⟶

Meanwhile, in a dry frying pan, toast the sesame seeds over medium-low heat, stirring, until fragrant and starting to brown, about 2 minutes. Pour onto a plate and let cool.

To make the dressing, in a food processor or blender, combine the peanut butter, vinegar, peanut oil, sesame oil, brown sugar, tamari, ¾ tsp salt, and 2 Tbsp water and process until smooth. Taste and adjust the seasonings.

Remove the chicken from the oven, sprinkle lightly with salt, and tent with foil. Let rest, then cut crosswise into thin slices.

In a large bowl, toss the cabbage and carrots with 2 big pinches of salt and several grindings of pepper. Drizzle with about one-third of the dressing and toss well.

Line individual salad plates with 2 lettuce leaves. Top with the cabbage-carrot mixture and chicken slices. Drizzle with the remaining dressing, sprinkle with the sesame seeds, and serve.

6

INSALATA VERDE

serves 4

This take on a simple staple showcases the edible wild greens found in the Italian countryside. Choose your favorite mixture of local greens and the best extra-virgin olive oil and red wine vinegar you can find.

3 green onions, white parts only, thinly sliced

Salt and freshly ground pepper

2 tsp red wine vinegar

2 Tbsp extra-virgin olive oil, plus more as needed

4 cups (4 oz/125 g) tender and sturdy bitter greens such as arugula, radicchio, escarole, and/or watercress leaves, in any combination

1 cup (1 oz/30 g) mâche or field greens

Put the green onions in a large serving bowl. Sprinkle with salt and pepper, and add the vinegar and then the oil. Mix vigorously with a fork.

Add the bitter greens and mâche to the bowl, and toss to coat well. Taste and add a little more salt and oil if needed, and serve.

DECEMBER 7

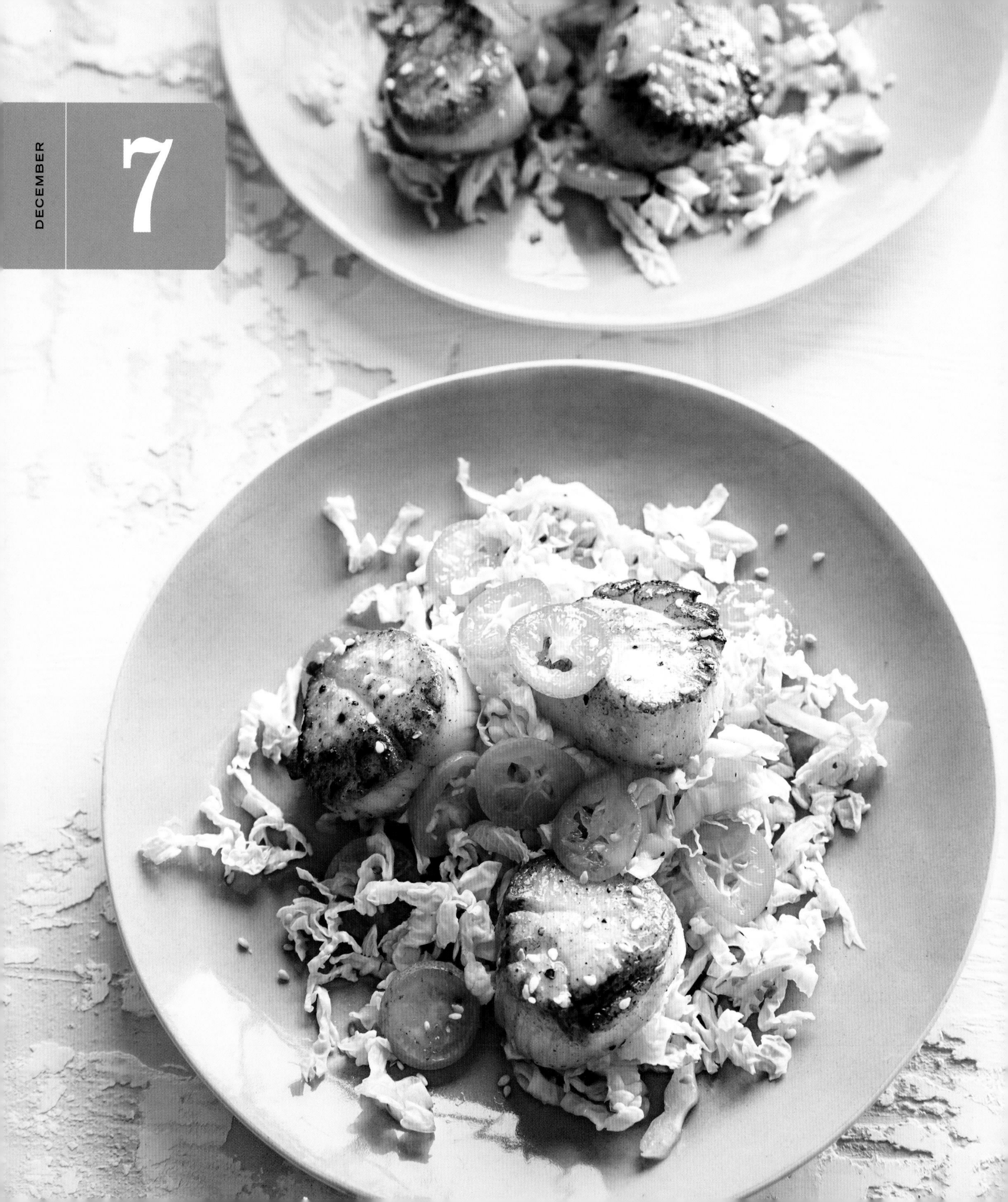

7

NAPA CABBAGE & KUMQUAT SALAD WITH SEARED SCALLOPS

serves 4

Pale green, mild Chinese cabbage marries well with the sweet-sharp tang of kumquats and the saltiness of fermented black beans. Look for the beans in Asian markets, where they are typically sold in plastic bags.

12 large sea scallops, tough muscles removed

1 tsp sesame seeds

2 tsp light soy sauce

1 Tbsp fresh lemon juice

½ tsp sugar

1 head napa cabbage, shredded

12–15 kumquats, cut crosswise into paper-thin slices and seeded

Salt and freshly ground pepper

2 tsp unsalted butter

2 tsp extra-virgin olive oil

Rinse the scallops and pat dry.

In a small frying pan, toast the sesame seeds over medium heat, stirring every 2–3 minutes, until lightly golden, about 2 minutes total. Transfer to a small bowl and set aside.

In a large bowl, whisk together the soy sauce, lemon juice, and sugar until the dressing is well blended. Add the cabbage and half of the kumquats and stir well.

Season the scallops with 1 tsp salt and ½ tsp pepper. In a large frying pan, melt the butter with the oil over medium-high heat and sear, turning once, until a golden crust has formed and the scallops are still translucent in the center, 1–2 minutes per side. Do not overcook.

Divide the cabbage mixture among individual plates and top each with 3 scallops. Garnish with the remaining kumquats and the sesame seeds and serve.

8

ARUGULA WITH ORANGES, MARCONA ALMONDS & PECORINO

serves 4–6

Delectable Spanish Marcona almonds are lighter in color and richer in taste than other types of almonds. They add elegance and depth to this exquisite salad of sweet oranges and salty-tangy cheese. Grassy extra-virgin olive oil contributes a lusciousness that rounds out the contrasting tastes.

4 oranges, peeled and segmented with a knife, juices caught and reserved

½ tsp honey

Salt and freshly ground pepper

2 Tbsp extra-virgin olive oil

¾ cup (3 oz/90 g) Marcona almonds, coarsely chopped

6 cups (6 oz/185 g) baby arugula leaves

Pecorino romano cheese for shaving

After segmenting the oranges, measure out 3 Tbsp of the juice. In a small bowl, whisk the orange juice with the honey, ⅛ tsp salt, and a few grindings of pepper. Add the oil in a thin stream, whisking constantly until the dressing is smooth. Taste and adjust the seasonings.

In a small bowl, stir together the almonds and ¼ tsp salt. Put the arugula in a large bowl. Whisk the dressing to recombine, then drizzle it over the arugula and toss well. Taste and adjust the seasonings. Divide the dressed arugula among individual plates, mounding it in the center. Top each mound with the orange segments, and sprinkle the oranges very lightly with salt. Scatter the almonds over the salads. Using a vegetable peeler, shave the cheese over the salads and serve.

9

SALAD OF WINTER GREENS & FRIED OYSTERS

serves 6

1 cup (5 oz/155 g) all-purpose flour

2 large eggs

1½ cups (7½ oz/235 g) yellow cornmeal

¼ tsp cayenne pepper

Salt and freshly ground black pepper

24 shucked oysters, drained and picked over for shell pieces

FOR THE SOUR CREAM–CHIVE DRESSING

½ cup (4 oz/125 g) sour cream

¼ cup (2 fl oz/60 ml) buttermilk

¼ cup (⅓ oz/10 g) minced fresh chives

1½ tsp fresh lemon juice

½ tsp Dijon mustard

½ tsp sugar

¼ cup (2 fl oz/60 ml) grapeseed oil

1 small head romaine lettuce, thinly sliced

1 small head radicchio, thinly sliced

Here, snipped chives suffuse a tangy sour cream dressing with their subtle, onionlike essence. The dressing's creamy coolness is the perfect balance to the spicy cornmeal that coats the briny fried oysters. A bed of romaine and radicchio offers crunch and color.

Put the flour in a shallow bowl. In a second shallow bowl, whisk the eggs until blended. In a third shallow bowl, stir together the cornmeal, cayenne, ½ tsp salt, and ¼ tsp pepper. One at a time, dip the oysters first in the flour, coating evenly and shaking off the excess, then in the eggs, allowing the excess to drip off, and finally in the seasoned cornmeal, coating evenly and shaking off the excess. Place the coated oysters on a large plate and refrigerate for 30 minutes.

Meanwhile, to make the dressing, in a food processor or blender, combine the sour cream, buttermilk, chives, lemon juice, mustard, sugar, a scant ½ tsp salt, and several grindings of pepper. Process until well blended. Taste and adjust the seasonings, and set aside.

Remove the coated oysters from the refrigerator and let stand at room temperature for 20 minutes. In a large frying pan, preferably nonstick, warm the oil over medium-high heat until hot but not smoking. Working in batches to avoid crowding, add the oysters to the pan and cook, turning once, until golden brown and slightly crisp, about 2 minutes on each side. Using a slotted spoon, transfer ⟩⟩

to paper towels to drain. When all of the oysters are cooked, sprinkle them lightly with salt and tent loosely with foil to keep warm.

In a large bowl, toss together the romaine, radicchio, ¼ tsp salt, and several grindings of pepper. Divide the greens among individual plates. Divide the fried oysters among the salads, drizzle each serving with about 2 Tbsp dressing, and serve.

10

CURRIED CELERY ROOT & APPLE SALAD WITH GOLDEN RAISINS

serves 6

6 Tbsp (2 oz/60 g) slivered blanched almonds

1 celery root (about ¾ lb/375 g)

2 Granny Smith apples

2 tsp fresh lemon juice

Salt and freshly ground pepper

½ cup (4 fl oz/125 ml) plus 1½ Tbsp mayonnaise

1½ tsp honey

1⅛ tsp curry powder

6 Tbsp (2 oz/60 g) golden raisins

2 Tbsp coarsely chopped fresh flat-leaf parsley

The spiciness and golden hue of curry powder enlivens this simple slaw-like salad while adding depth of flavor. Curry both accentuates the earthy taste of the celery root and complements the sweetness of the apples and raisins.

In a dry frying pan, toast the almonds over medium-low heat, stirring, until fragrant and lightly golden, 3–4 minutes. Pour onto a plate and let cool.

Peel the celery root and shred on the large holes of a box grater.

Halve and core the apples, then cut them into thin strips. Sprinkle with ½ tsp of the lemon juice to prevent them from discoloring.

Sprinkle the almonds with a pinch of salt and stir. In a large bowl, whisk together the mayonnaise, the remaining 1½ tsp lemon juice, the honey, the curry powder, a scant ½ tsp salt, and ¼ tsp pepper. Stir in the almonds, celery root, apples, raisins, and parsley until combined. Taste and adjust the seasonings and serve.

11

RED CABBAGE SALAD WITH APPLES & DRIED FRUIT

serves 4

½ head red cabbage, about 1 lb (500 g), cored and thinly sliced crosswise

Salt and freshly ground pepper

Red wine vinegar or cider vinegar

5 dried apricots, chopped

5 dried golden figs such as Calimyrna, chopped

5 dried pears, chopped

5 prunes, pitted and chopped

1 tart apple such as Granny Smith, cored and julienned

1–2 Tbsp grapeseed oil

Several pinches of ground cumin

½ tsp sugar, or as needed

2–3 heaping Tbsp walnut pieces

Combining cabbage with vinegar and seasonings, then letting it sit awhile, will mellow the assertive flavor. In addition, the vinegar turns the natural blue tinge of red cabbage a bright shade of scarlet. If you like, substitute 2 Tbsp golden raisins for the prunes. Other winter fruits, such as pears, Fuyu persimmons, or pomegranate seeds, may be used in place of the apple.

In a bowl, combine the cabbage with salt, pepper, and vinegar to taste, and toss well. Cover and let stand for at least 2 hours at room temperature or overnight in the refrigerator. Drain off all but 1 Tbsp of the liquid.

Add the apricots, figs, pears, prunes, and apple to the cabbage and toss well. Drizzle with 1 Tbsp of the oil and add the cumin and sugar. Season with salt and pepper. Toss well, then taste and adjust the seasonings, adding more oil if needed to coat. Top with the walnuts and serve.

12

WARM BORLOTTI BEAN & RADICCHIO SALAD

serves 4

2 oz (60 g) sliced pancetta, chopped

3 Tbsp extra-virgin olive oil

1 clove garlic, lightly crushed

2-inch (5-cm) sprig fresh rosemary

1 can (15 oz/470 g) borlotti or cranberry beans, drained and rinsed

Salt and freshly ground pepper

1 small head radicchio, trimmed and cut crosswise into narrow strips

1 Tbsp fresh lemon juice

2 Tbsp chopped fresh flat-leaf parsley

This salad, which hails from Italy's Veneto region, is a study in contrasts: warm, creamy beans against lightly bitter radicchio and salty, crisp pancetta. Cannellini or other white beans can be substituted for the borlotti beans. Serve this salad as a light meal on its own or as an accompaniment to grilled tuna or steak or roasted chicken.

In a saucepan large enough to hold the beans, cook the pancetta over medium heat, stirring often, until crisp, about 5 minutes. Using a slotted spoon, transfer the pancetta to paper towels to drain.

Add 1 Tbsp of the oil to the fat in the pan and warm over medium heat. Add the garlic and rosemary and sauté until the garlic is lightly golden, about 2 minutes. Stir in the beans and season with salt and pepper. Reduce the heat to medium-low, cover, and cook, stirring occasionally, for 5 minutes to blend the flavors.

Remove the beans from the heat and remove and discard the rosemary and garlic. In a serving bowl, toss together the beans, radicchio, and reserved pancetta. Add the remaining 2 Tbsp oil and the lemon juice and toss again.

Taste and adjust the seasoning with salt and pepper, sprinkle with the parsley, and serve.

13

Chestnuts have
a short season,
so the fresh nuts
can be difficult to
find. But vacuum-
packed, ready-to-use
chestnuts are sold
in specialty stores
and in some
well-stocked
markets. Here,
the sweet, earthy
flavor of chestnuts
combines with
the slightly nutty
flavor of roasted
Brussels sprouts
and the richness of
prosciutto to make
a warm salad
that's perfect for
the cool days of
fall and winter.

WARM BRUSSELS SPROUT SALAD WITH CHESTNUTS & PROSCIUTTO

serves 4

1 Tbsp walnut oil

2 tsp red wine vinegar

Salt and freshly ground pepper

1 lb (500 g) Brussels sprouts, trimmed, outer leaves removed, and sprouts quartered lengthwise

2 Tbsp extra-virgin olive oil

6–8 oz (185–250 g) jarred peeled chestnuts

2 oz (60 g) thinly sliced prosciutto, cut into ½-inch (12-mm) strips

Preheat the oven to 400°F (200°C).

In a large bowl, whisk together the walnut oil, vinegar, ¼ tsp salt, and ¼ tsp pepper until the vinaigrette is well blended. Set aside.

Put the Brussels sprouts in a shallow baking dish and drizzle with the olive oil, turning them to coat. Sprinkle with ½ tsp salt and ½ tsp pepper. Roast for 20 minutes, stirring every 5–10 minutes to ensure even browning. During the last 5–7 minutes of cooking, add the chestnuts, turning them once or twice, until warmed through.

Remove the dish from the oven. Cut the chestnuts into quarters. Add the Brussels sprouts to the bowl with the vinaigrette and stir gently to coat. Add the chestnuts and half of the prosciutto and stir gently again.

Mound the salad on a platter or divide among individual plates. Garnish with the remaining prosciutto and serve right away.

14

This vibrant salad
gets its rich colors
from persimmon,
red lettuce, and
pomegranate seeds.
After toasting the
hazelnuts, rub them
vigorously in a clean
kitchen towel to
loosen and remove
the bitter skins.

RED OAKLEAF LETTUCE & FRISÉE SALAD WITH PERSIMMON

serves 4

FOR THE HONEY-MINT VINAIGRETTE

3 Tbsp extra-virgin olive oil

1 Tbsp fresh mint leaves

1 Tbsp white wine vinegar or pear vinegar

½ tsp honey

Salt and ground white pepper

¼ cup (1 oz/30 g) hazelnuts

Leaves from 1½–2 heads red oakleaf lettuce

Leaves from ½ head frisée

1 Fuyu persimmon, peeled, seeded if needed, and cut into thin wedges

Seeds from ½ pomegranate, or 3 Tbsp (1 oz/30 g) dried cranberries

To make the vinaigrette, in a food processor or blender, combine the oil and mint and process until well blended. Add the vinegar and honey and process until incorporated. Pour the dressing into a small bowl and season with salt and white pepper to taste.

In a dry frying pan, toast the hazelnuts over medium-low heat, stirring, until fragrant and starting to brown, about 5 minutes. Pour onto a plate to cool. Rub in a clean kitchen towel to remove the skins, chop coarsely, and set aside.

Tear the oakleaf and frisée leaves into bite-sized pieces and put them in a large bowl. Add the persimmon. Whisk the vinaigrette to recombine, add most of it to the salad, and toss well to coat. Taste and adjust the amount of vinaigrette and the seasonings. Sprinkle with the pomegranate seeds and hazelnuts and serve.

15

*Members of the
chicory family,
radicchio and frisée
are prized for their
pleasantly bitter
taste. Radicchio,
which is native
to Italy, boasts
striking variegated
purplish red leaves,
which hold up
particularly well
in salads. Frisée, a
longtime favorite of
French cooks, is a
slightly immature
curly endive, with
a smaller head and
more delicate,
tender leaves.*

SALAD OF WINTER GREENS, BEETS & GRILLED SALMON

serves 4

2 large beets

4 Tbsp (2 fl oz/60 ml) olive oil, plus more for brushing

Salt and freshly ground pepper

1 fennel bulb, trimmed

1 tsp orange zest

2 Tbsp fresh orange juice

1 Tbsp fresh lemon juice

1 Tbsp Dijon mustard

3 Tbsp chopped mixed fresh herbs such as parsley, tarragon, and chives

1 lb (500 g) salmon fillet, pin bones removed, cut into 8 strips ½ inch (12 mm) wide

6 cups (6 oz/185 g) mixed winter greens such as radicchio and frisée

1 bunch fresh chives, cut into 2-inch (5-cm) lengths

Leaves from ½ bunch fresh tarragon

Preheat the oven to 350°F (180°C).

Place the beets on a baking sheet. Coat the beets with 1 Tbsp of the oil and season with salt and pepper. Cover the baking sheet with aluminum foil and roast until the beets are easily pierced with a knife, about 1 hour. When the beets are cool enough to handle, peel them. Using a mandoline or a sharp knife, cut the beets into julienne. Set aside.

Halve the fennel. Using a mandoline or a sharp knife, cut the fennel into paper-thin slices. Place in a bowl of ice water and soak for 15 minutes, then drain. Set aside.

In a small bowl, whisk together the orange zest and juice, lemon juice, and mustard. Add the remaining 3 Tbsp oil in a thin stream, whisking constantly until the dressing is well blended, then whisk in the mixed herbs. Season with salt and pepper. Set aside.

Prepare a charcoal or gas grill for direct-heat cooking over medium-high heat. Alternatively, preheat a stove-top grill pan over medium-high heat.

Brush the salmon on both sides with oil and season with salt and pepper. Place the salmon on the grill rack or in the grill pan and cook, turning once, until opaque throughout, 1–2 minutes per side. Transfer to a plate. ⟶

In a large bowl, toss together the greens, chives, tarragon, beets, and fennel. Drizzle with two-thirds of the dressing and toss to coat. Season with salt and pepper. Divide the salad among individual plates. Top each with 2 salmon strips and drizzle with the remaining dressing. Serve right away.

16

*Groceries stock celery
year-round, but its
natural peak season
is in fact winter.
The humble vegetable
stars in this salad,
which takes advantage
of both the stalks and
tender green leaves.
Salty prosciutto and
pecorino add protein
and punch, but you
can substitute any
ham or hard grating
cheese you like.*

CHOPPED CELERY, PARSLEY & PROSCIUTTO SALAD

serves 6

1 fennel bulb, trimmed and halved lengthwise

6 celery ribs, thinly sliced on the diagonal

4 green onions, including tender green parts, thinly sliced on the diagonal

1 cup (1 oz/30 g) fresh flat-leaf parsley leaves

¼ cup (⅓ oz/10 g) small fresh mint leaves

Salt and freshly ground pepper

3 Tbsp extra-virgin olive oil

2 Tbsp fresh lemon juice, or as needed

6 thin slices prosciutto

Pecorino romano cheese for shaving

Using a mandoline or a very sharp knife, cut the fennel bulb halves crosswise into thin slices.

Put the celery, fennel, green onions, parsley, and mint in a bowl and season with salt and pepper. Drizzle with the oil and the 2 Tbsp lemon juice and toss gently. Taste and season with salt and more lemon juice, if desired. Arrange the prosciutto on a serving platter and top with the fennel mixture. Using a vegetable peeler, shave the cheese over the salad and serve.

17

ICEBERG WEDGES WITH BLUE CHEESE DRESSING

serves 6

½ cup (4 fl oz/125 ml) mayonnaise

½ cup (4 oz/125 g) sour cream

Juice of 1 lemon

Dash of Tabasco sauce

Salt and freshly ground pepper

6 oz (185 g) blue cheese, crumbled (about 1½ cups)

3 Tbsp minced fresh chives, plus slivers of chive for garnish

1 head iceberg lettuce, chilled

A wedge of iceberg lettuce topped with a thick, luscious blue cheese dressing is an all-time classic. If available, add a sprinkling of halved cherry or grape tomatoes. This favorite makes a fitting first course for a New York–style steak dinner.

In a small bowl, whisk together the mayonnaise, sour cream, lemon juice, Tabasco, ¼ tsp salt, and ¼ tsp pepper. Stir in the cheese and 3 Tbsp chives. Taste and adjust the seasonings.

Using a small, sharp knife, core the iceberg lettuce. Remove and discard the outer leaves if they are limp or blemished. Cut the head into 6 uniform wedges.

Place each wedge on an individual plate. Spoon a generous amount of the dressing over each wedge. (You may not need all of the dressing.) Garnish with the chive slivers and serve.

18

WARM BRUSSELS SPROUT & APPLE SALAD

serves 4–6

¼ lb (125 g) bacon, diced

¾ lb (375 g) Brussels sprouts, trimmed and halved

2 apples, peeled, cored, and diced

1 shallot, minced

2 Tbsp sherry vinegar

1 Tbsp honey

Salt and freshly ground pepper

¼ cup (1 oz/30 g) chopped toasted walnuts

Both Brussels sprouts and apples reach their peak in autumn, making them a natural pairing in a warm salad that gets an extra kick of salty, savory flavor from sautéed bacon. Look for flavorful fall apples that hold their shape when cooked, such as Honeycrisp, Fuji, or Pink Lady.

In a large sauté pan, cook the bacon over medium heat, stirring occasionally, until crispy, 5–7 minutes. Using a slotted spoon, transfer to paper towels to drain. Pour the fat into a heatproof bowl and reserve.

Add the Brussels sprouts to the pan and cook over medium heat, stirring occasionally, until browned and slightly soft, about 15 minutes. Add the apples and cook until slightly soft, about 5 minutes. Transfer to a serving bowl.

In a small bowl, whisk together 2 Tbsp of the reserved bacon fat, the shallot, vinegar, and honey until the vinaigrette is well blended. Season with salt and pepper.

Drizzle the vinaigrette over the Brussels sprouts mixture and fold in the walnuts and bacon. Taste and adjust the seasonings and serve right away.

DUCK BREAST SALAD WITH WALNUTS & ORANGES

serves 4

2 boneless duck breast halves
(4–6 oz/125–185 g each)

Salt and freshly ground pepper

3 Tbsp sherry vinegar

7 Tbsp (3½ fl oz/110 ml) extra-virgin
olive oil

1 head radicchio, torn into
1-inch (2.5-cm) strips

2 heads frisée, pale yellow inner leaves only

½ cup (2 oz/60 g) walnuts, toasted and
coarsely chopped

2 oranges, peeled and segmented with
a knife

You can serve this elegant salad as a first course or a light main course. The fruit can vary with the season, such as cherries in spring, thinly sliced nectarines in summer, or pomegranate seeds in late fall. Parmigiano-Reggiano or fresh goat cheese is a nice addition.

Season the duck breasts with salt and pepper. Using a sharp knife, score the skin by making a crisscross pattern, being careful not to cut into the meat.

Warm a large sauté pan over medium-low heat. Place the duck, skin side down, in the pan and cook until the skin is very crisp and golden, 12–15 minutes. Turn the duck over and sear the other side, then continue cooking until the meat is just springy when pressed with a finger for rare to medium-rare, 3–5 minutes longer, or until cooked to your liking. Transfer to a cutting board, cover loosely with aluminum foil, and let rest for 3–5 minutes before slicing.

Pour the vinegar into a small bowl. Add the oil in a thin stream, whisking constantly until the vinaigrette is well blended. Season with salt and pepper.

In a large bowl, toss together the radicchio and frisée. Drizzle with half of the vinaigrette and toss to coat well. Divide the salad among individual plates and scatter the walnuts and orange segments on top.

Cut the duck across the grain into very thin slices and divide among the salads. Drizzle with the remaining vinaigrette and serve right away.

GRAPEFRUIT, AVOCADO & FENNEL SALAD

serves 4

2 Tbsp champagne vinegar

1½ tsp finely grated grapefruit zest

2 Tbsp fresh grapefruit juice

1 Tbsp finely chopped shallot

2 tsp sugar

1 tsp Dijon mustard

¼ cup (2 fl oz/60 ml) walnut or grapeseed oil

Salt and freshly ground pepper

10 oz (315 g) mâche

1 small fennel bulb, trimmed, cored, and
very thinly sliced

2 ruby red grapefruits, peeled and
segmented with a knife

1 avocado, pitted, peeled, and sliced

Brighten winter days with this refreshing salad, which makes a wonderful first course to precede simply cooked salmon fillets or whole trout. Walnut oil lends a subtle nutty taste to the vinaigrette, though a more neutral oil, such as grapeseed, can be substituted.

In a small bowl, whisk together the vinegar, grapefruit zest and juice, shallot, sugar, and mustard. Add the oil in a thin stream, whisking constantly until the vinaigrette is well blended. Season with salt and pepper.

In a large bowl, combine the mâche, fennel, and grapefruit segments. Drizzle with the vinaigrette to taste and toss to coat evenly. Divide the salad among individual bowls, top with the avocado, and serve.

21

ASIAN NOODLE SALAD WITH SALMON & SNOW PEAS

serves 4–6

Here, the cooling mint and citrus enhance the noodles and salmon. If Chinese egg noodles are unavailable, you can substitute linguine. This salad can be made a day ahead, covered, and refrigerated until ready to serve.

2 carrots, peeled and julienned

1/2 lb (250 g) snow peas, trimmed and julienned

3/4 lb (375 g) salmon fillet, pin bones removed

1 lb (500 g) Chinese egg noodles

1 Tbsp peanut oil

FOR THE DRESSING

1/4 cup (2 fl oz/60 ml) rice vinegar

1 Tbsp fresh lime juice

1 Tbsp honey

2 cloves garlic, minced

1 1/2 tsp peeled and grated fresh ginger

2 Tbsp minced fresh basil, plus sprigs for garnish

2 Tbsp minced fresh mint, plus sprigs for garnish

Salt and freshly ground pepper

1/4 cup (2 fl oz/60 ml) peanut oil

2 tsp toasted sesame oil

Preheat the oven to 400°F (200°C). Bring a saucepan two-thirds full of water to a boil and have ready a bowl of ice water. Add the carrots and cook for 30 seconds. Scoop out and immerse them in the ice water. Repeat with the snow peas, cooking them for 1 minute. Set aside.

Put the salmon in a small roasting pan and bake until opaque throughout, 12 minutes. Let cool, then flake into bite-sized pieces.

Bring a large pot of water to a boil. Add the noodles, stir, and cook until barely tender and still firm, about 7 minutes or according to package directions. Drain and rinse under cold running water until cooled. Drain well, put in a large bowl, and toss with the 1 Tbsp peanut oil.

To make the dressing, in a small bowl, whisk together the vinegar, lime juice, honey, garlic, ginger, minced basil and mint, and salt and pepper to taste. Add the 1/4 cup peanut oil and the sesame oil in a thin stream, whisking constantly until the dressing is smooth. ⟫

Pour the dressing over the noodles and toss to coat. Add the carrots and snow peas and toss again. Carefully fold in the salmon, keeping the pieces intact. Taste and adjust the seasonings. Garnish with the herb sprigs. Cover and refrigerate until ready to serve.

22

SKIRT STEAK SALAD WITH CITRUS & ARUGULA

serves 4

Marinated skirt steak is a delicious partner for winter citrus. If it's too cold to grill outside, cook the steak in a grill pan over high heat for 3–4 minutes per side, or in a frying pan for the same amount of time. For a spicier dressing, add some minced jalapeño chile to the lime juice and oil mixture before tossing with the arugula, orange, and radishes.

1/4 cup (2 fl oz/60 ml) soy sauce

1/4 cup (2 fl oz/60 ml) fresh orange juice

4 Tbsp (2 fl oz/60 ml) fresh lime juice

1 Tbsp peeled and minced fresh ginger

2 cloves garlic, minced

1/2 tsp Asian red chile paste

1 1/2 lb (750 g) skirt steak, about 1/2 inch (12 mm) thick, cut into 2 or 3 pieces for ease of handling

1 1/2 Tbsp extra-virgin olive oil

8 oz (250 g) wild or baby arugula leaves

1 navel orange, peeled with a knife and sliced crosswise

5 radishes, trimmed and sliced if desired

5 kumquats, sliced

Combine the soy sauce, orange juice, 1 Tbsp of the lime juice, the ginger, garlic, and chile paste in a zippered plastic bag. Add the steak, shake to mix the marinade, and refrigerate for 8–24 hours.

Prepare a charcoal or gas grill for direct-heat cooking over high heat. Oil the grill rack. Remove the steak from the bag and discard the marinade. Grill the steak, turning once, for 4–6 minutes total for medium-rare. Transfer to a platter and let stand for 10 minutes.

In a large bowl, whisk together the remaining 3 Tbsp lime juice and the oil. Add the arugula, orange, radishes, and kumquats and mix well. Mound on a platter. Cut the steak across the grain into slices 1/4 inch (6 mm) thick, arrange over the salad, and serve.

DECEMBER 23

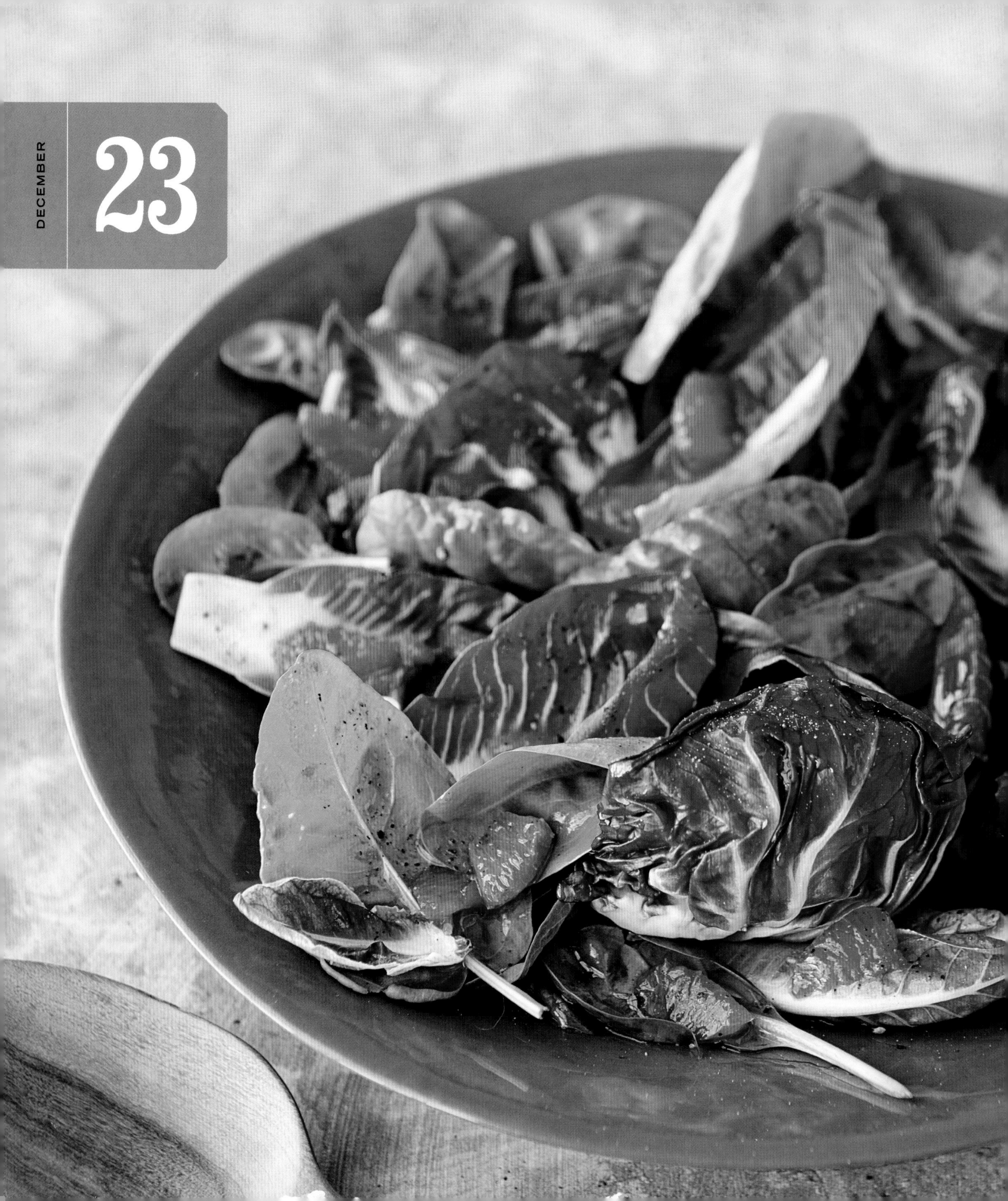

RADICCHIO, SPINACH & RED SORREL SALAD

serves 4–6

This red-and-green medley is a feast for the eyes as well as the palate. Blood oranges impart their deep color to the vinaigrette, and small bites of the orange segments tucked among the leaves are both gorgeous and delicious.

FOR THE BLOOD-ORANGE VINAIGRETTE

1 blood orange, peeled and segmented with a knife

¼ cup (2 fl oz/60 ml) red wine vinegar

½ cup (4 fl oz/125 ml) extra-virgin olive oil

Salt and freshly ground pepper

1 head radicchio, leaves torn

4 cups (4 oz/125 g) baby spinach leaves

1 cup (1 oz/30 g) red sorrel leaves or additional baby spinach leaves

To make the vinaigrette, using a fork, break up the blood orange segments into bite-sized pieces. Add the vinegar and then the oil in a thin stream, whisking constantly until the vinaigrette is smooth. Season to taste with salt and pepper and set aside.

Combine the radicchio, spinach, and sorrel in a serving bowl and toss with the vinaigrette. Season to taste with salt and pepper and serve.

CRAB, FENNEL & RADICCHIO SALAD WITH TRUFFLE OIL

serves 10–12

This show-stopping salad is worthy of a celebratory eve. Fresh Dungeness crab needs no embellishment, but decadent truffle oil sends it over the top. Mound the crab salad on individual radicchio leaves, which are perfect to pass with cocktails.

1 fennel bulb, trimmed and coarsely chopped

1 lb (500 g) cooked Dungeness or other crabmeat, picked over for shell fragments

2 shallots, minced

2 celery ribs, finely chopped

2 Tbsp minced fresh chives

2 Tbsp minced fresh flat-leaf parsley

3 Tbsp white or black truffle oil

1½ Tbsp fresh lemon juice

1 Tbsp mayonnaise

Salt and freshly ground pepper

3 large or 4 medium heads radicchio

In a bowl, combine the fennel, crabmeat, shallots, celery, chives, and parsley. Add the truffle oil, lemon juice, mayonnaise, ½ tsp salt, and a few grindings of pepper. Gently mix with a fork until evenly blended; do not break up the lumps of crabmeat. Taste and adjust the seasonings.

Remove and discard any blemished leaves from each head of radicchio. Separate the largest outer leaves, keeping them as intact as possible. You should have about 40 cupped leaves (reserve the inner leaves for another use). Arrange on serving platters.

Mound about 2 Tbsp of the crab salad in each radicchio cup. Serve at once, or refrigerate for up to 1 hour and then let stand at room temperature for 10 minutes before serving.

25

DECEMBER

Roasted beets have a deep, rich, and comforting taste. Select a mix of red, orange and golden beets for a festive, jewel-toned salad. You can cook them a day or two ahead and refrigerate, still wrapped in foil, until you are ready to peel and slice them for this salad. Stilton, a sharply flavored English blue cheese, balances the natural sweetness of the beets, but other blue-veined cheeses, such as Gorgonzola, Roquefort, or Danish blue, can be substituted.

BEET & STILTON SALAD WITH ORANGE VINAIGRETTE

serves 4

4 beets (about 1¼ lb/625 g total weight), trimmed

FOR THE ORANGE VINAIGRETTE

3 Tbsp fresh orange juice

1 Tbsp red wine vinegar

1 Tbsp minced fresh dill

1 tsp grated orange zest

¼ tsp minced garlic

Salt and freshly ground pepper

2 Tbsp extra-virgin olive oil

3 green onions, including tender green parts, thinly sliced on the diagonal

1 Tbsp finely slivered orange zest

10 oz (315 g) mixed salad greens

½ cup (2½ oz/75 g) thinly sliced English cucumber

3 oz (90 g) Stilton cheese, crumbled

Fresh dill sprigs for garnish

Preheat the oven to 400°F (200°C). Wrap the beets in foil and roast on a baking sheet until easily pierced with the tip of a knife, about 1 hour. Remove from the oven and let cool in the foil. Unwrap and peel. Cut each beet crosswise into 4 or 5 slices and put in a bowl.

To make the orange vinaigrette, in a small bowl, whisk together the orange juice, vinegar, minced dill, grated orange zest, garlic, ½ tsp salt, and a grinding of pepper. Add the oil in a thin stream, whisking constantly until the dressing is smooth.

Pour all but 2 Tbsp of the vinaigrette over the beets. Add half of the green onions and half of the slivered orange zest; stir gently just to blend. In a separate bowl, combine the salad greens and the reserved 2 Tbsp vinaigrette and toss to coat the greens.

Divide the salad greens among individual plates. Top with the beets and tuck the cucumber slices in among the beets. Drizzle any vinaigrette remaining in the bowl over the beets. Sprinkle the salad with the remaining green onions and slivered orange zest. Top with the cheese, garnish with the dill sprigs, and serve.

26

DECEMBER

Grapefruit and pomegranate rise to the occasion for festive winter gatherings. This recipe aims to serve a crowd, and your guests may be grateful for a light starter, free of cheese or nuts, to balance out the often decadently rich holiday table.

GRAPEFRUIT, ENDIVE & POMEGRANATE SALAD

serves 10–12

3 heads butter or Bibb lettuce, leaves separated and torn into large pieces

2 bunches watercress, tough stems removed

3 heads Belgian endive, cored and separated into leaves

3 pink grapefruits, peeled and segmented with a knife, juices caught and reserved

1 Tbsp fresh orange juice

⅛ tsp lemon or orange oil

2 Tbsp balsamic vinegar

3 Tbsp minced shallots

6 Tbsp (3 fl oz/90 ml) extra-virgin olive oil

Salt and freshly ground pepper

½ cup (2 oz/60 g) pomegranate seeds

In a large serving bowl, toss together the lettuce, watercress, and endive. Add the grapefruit segments to the bowl, scattering them over the greens.

To make the dressing, in a food processor or blender, combine 2 Tbsp of the reserved grapefruit juice, the orange juice, citrus oil, vinegar, shallots, olive oil, and ¼ tsp each salt and pepper. Process until smooth, then taste and adjust the seasonings.

Pour the dressing over the salad. Add the pomegranate seeds, toss, and serve.

292

27

TACO SALAD IN TORTILLA BOWLS

serves 4

There's nothing too mysterious about taco seasoning mix—make some at home, store it in an airtight container, and you can make this fun and pleasing salad anytime. Blend 2 Tbsp chili powder, 1½ tsp ground cumin, 1 tsp salt, 1 tsp black pepper, ½ tsp paprika, and ¼ tsp each onion powder, garlic powder, dried oregano, and red pepper flakes. Adjust the quantities to taste and desired spiciness.

FOR THE TORTILLA BOWLS

Four 8-inch (20-cm) flour tortillas

Corn oil

Salt

FOR THE DRESSING

1 Tbsp mild tomato salsa

1 Tbsp red wine vinegar

2 tsp fresh lime juice

4–6 Tbsp (2–3 fl oz/60–90 ml) extra-virgin olive oil

1 lb (500 g) ground beef

¼ cup (1 oz/30 g) taco seasoning mix (about ½ package; see note)

1 cup (7 oz/220 g) canned black or pinto beans, drained and rinsed

½ head iceberg lettuce

3 plum tomatoes, chopped

1 avocado, pitted, peeled, and chopped

1½ cups (6 oz/185 g) shredded Cheddar cheese

Tortilla chips for serving (optional)

To make the tortilla bowls, preheat the oven to 350°F (180°C). Choose 4 shallow ovenproof bowls 4–6 inches (10–15 cm) in diameter. Brush corn oil over both sides of each tortilla and sprinkle with salt. Line the bowls with the tortillas to make bowl shapes. Bake the tortillas in the bowls until browned and crisp, about 12 minutes. Remove the tortillas from the oven, let cool, then remove them from the bowls and place each on a plate.

To make the dressing, in a small jar with a tight-fitting lid, mix the salsa, vinegar, and lime juice. Add 4 Tbsp (2 fl oz/60 ml) of the oil, cover, and shake until mixed. Taste and add more oil if needed. Set the dressing aside.

Place a large frying pan over medium heat. Add the ground beef and cook, using a wooden spoon to break it up, until cooked, 8–10 minutes. Add the seasoning mix and ⅔ cup (5 fl oz/160 ml) water to the pan. Bring to a boil over high heat. Reduce the heat to low and simmer, stirring often, until the liquid is absorbed, about 12 minutes.

Meanwhile, put the beans in a saucepan and place over medium-low heat. ⤗

Stir occasionally until warm. Remove from the heat and cover to keep warm.

Cut the lettuce into slices and separate the pieces. Divide the lettuce among the tortilla bowls, then top each with equal portions of the tomatoes, beans, and avocado.

Using a slotted spoon, divide the meat among the salads. Sprinkle the cheese on top. Spoon some of the dressing over each salad and serve with tortilla chips, if desired.

28

SMOKED RAINBOW TROUT SALAD WITH CRANBERRY SALSA

serves 4

Tart cranberries are tempered with sugar and complemented by a little heat from jalapeño chile and fresh ginger to create a condiment that nicely balances the rich taste of the smoked fish. The salsa goes equally well with such rich meats as game and pork.

1 cup (4 oz/125 g) fresh cranberries, coarsely chopped

¼ cup (2 oz/60 g) sugar

Juice of 1 lime

½ jalapeño chile, seeded and minced

1-inch (2.5-cm) piece fresh ginger, peeled and grated

2 Tbsp minced yellow onion

Salt

1 Tbsp chopped fresh cilantro

2 heads red or green Belgian endive

3 Tbsp extra-virgin olive oil

1 Tbsp red wine vinegar

1 bunch watercress, tough stems removed

½ lb (250 g) smoked trout, broken into pieces

In a bowl, mix the cranberries, sugar, lime juice, jalapeño, ginger, onion, and ½ tsp salt. Let stand at room temperature for at least 15 minutes or up to 4 hours. Just before serving, stir in the cilantro.

Cut the endive in half lengthwise and remove the core. Cut 2 of the halves lengthwise and julienne them. Coarsely chop the remaining halves.

In a bowl, whisk together the oil, vinegar, and ¼ tsp salt until blended. Add the endive and watercress and toss to coat.

Divide the salad among individual plates. Top with some salsa and the smoked trout. Serve with more salsa to spoon alongside.

29

LOBSTER SALAD WITH GRAPEFRUIT & AVOCADO

serves 6–8

1 grapefruit, peeled and segmented with a knife, juices caught and reserved

2½ Tbsp champagne vinegar

Salt and freshly ground pepper

2 tsp minced shallot

5 tsp minced fresh chives

3½ Tbsp extra-virgin olive oil

1½ lb (750 g) cooked lobster meat, picked over for shell fragments

2–2½ cups (2–3 oz/60–90 g) mixed baby salad greens

1 avocado, pitted, peeled, and sliced

The grapefruit juice in this vinaigrette, along with the grapefruit sections in the salad, accentuates the sweetness of succulent lobster. Smooth, creamy avocado adds a hint of richness. If using frozen lobster tails, allow enough time to thaw them overnight in the refrigerator.

In a large bowl, whisk together 2 tsp of the reserved grapefruit juice, 2 Tbsp of the vinegar, ½ tsp each salt and pepper, the shallot, and 3 tsp of the chives. Add 2 Tbsp of the oil in a thin stream, whisking constantly until the dressing is smooth. Add the lobster meat and turn gently until well coated.

Divide the greens among individual plates or shallow bowls. Arrange the grapefruit segments on the greens. Top with the lobster mixture and then with the avocado. Add the remaining 1½ Tbsp oil and remaining ½ Tbsp vinegar to the bowl, mix well, and drizzle over the salads. Garnish with the remaining 2 tsp chives and serve.

30

WARM PURPLE POTATO SALAD

serves 4

2½ lb (1.25 kg) small purple potatoes

Salt and freshly ground pepper

3 Tbsp extra-virgin olive oil

2 tsp red wine vinegar

¼ cup (1 oz/30 g) finely chopped celery

¼ cup (1 oz/30 g) finely chopped red onion

¼ cup (⅓ oz/10 g) minced fresh flat-leaf parsley

Freshly boiled potatoes, still warm and steaming, soak up vinaigrettes. It's an easy method for imparting flavor to this favorite comfort salad. Purple potatoes are eye-catching, but you could just as easily use other types of small potatoes.

Put the potatoes in a large pot and add cold water to cover by 3 inches (7.5 cm) and 1 tsp salt. Bring to a boil, then reduce the heat to medium-low and cover. Simmer until tender, about 15 minutes. Drain and let cool to the touch. Peel and carefully cut into slices ¼ inch (6 mm) thick.

Combine the potato slices, oil, and vinegar in a shallow bowl and turn gently to coat. Add the celery, red onion, parsley, ½ tsp salt, and ½ tsp pepper. Gently stir until well mixed. Cover and let stand at room temperature for 20 minutes before serving.

31

ARUGULA SALAD WITH QUINCE PASTE & SERRANO HAM

serves 6

1 cup (8 oz/250 g) quince paste

1 tsp fresh lemon juice

Salt and freshly ground pepper

1½ Tbsp extra-virgin olive oil

5 oz (155 g) arugula leaves, stemmed

9 oz (280 g) thinly sliced serrano ham or prosciutto

Often called by its Spanish name, membrillo, quince paste is a delicious accompaniment for nuts and cheeses. In this salad, it balances the salty ham and peppery arugula.

Dip a sharp knife into very hot water and cut the quince paste into slices ¼ inch (6 mm) thick. Trim the slices into triangles or diamonds, if desired. Set the slices aside.

In a large bowl, whisk together the lemon juice and salt and pepper to taste. Add the oil in a thin stream, whisking constantly until the dressing is smooth. Add the arugula and toss thoroughly. Arrange the prosciutto on 6 individual plates. Divide the arugula salad among the plates, scatter with the quince paste slices, and serve.

INDEX

weldon**owen**

1045 Sansome Street, San Francisco, CA 94111
www.weldonowen.com

SALAD OF THE DAY

Conceived and produced by Weldon Owen, Inc.
In collaboration with Williams-Sonoma, Inc.
3250 Van Ness Avenue, San Francisco, CA 94109

A WELDON OWEN PRODUCTION

Printed and bound in China

First printed in 2016
10 9 8 7 6 5 4 3 2 1

Library of Congress Cataloging-in-Publication
data is available.

ISBN 13: 978-1-68188-066-2
ISBN 10: 1-68188-066-0

Weldon Owen is a division of
Bonnier Publishing.

WELDON OWEN, INC.

President and Publisher Roger Shaw
SVP, Sales and Marketing Amy Kaneko
Finance and Operations Director Philip Paulick

Associate Publisher Amy Marr
Senior Editor Lisa Atwood
Associate Editor Emma Rudolph

Creative Director Kelly Booth
Associate Art Director Lisa Berman
Senior Production Designer Rachel Lopez Metzger

Production Director Chris Hemesath
Associate Production Director Michelle Duggan

Director of Enterprise Systems Shawn Macey
Imaging Manager Don Hill

Photographer Erin Kunkel
Food Stylist Robyn Valarik
Prop Stylists Leigh Noe, Glenn Jenkins

ACKNOWLEDGMENTS

Weldon Owen wishes to thank the following people for their generous support in producing this book:
Amanda Anselmino, Kris Balloun, David Bornfriend, Emma Boys, Lauren Charles, Pranavi Chopra, Kara Church,
Sarah Putman Clegg, Ken DellaPenta, Becky Duffet, Gloria Geller, Taylor Louie, Carolyn Miller, Julie Nelson,
Elizabeth Parson, Hannah Rahill, Sharon Silva, and Jason Wheeler.